The Spirituality of Following Jesus in John's Gospel

The Spirituality of Following Jesus in John's Gospel

An Investigation of *Akolouthein* and Correlated Motifs

Sean Seongik Kim

FOREWORD BY
D. G. van der Merwe

⌒PICKWICK *Publications* · Eugene, Oregon

THE SPIRITUALITY OF FOLLOWING JESUS IN JOHN'S GOSPEL
An Investigation of *Akolouthein* and Correlated Motifs

Copyright © 2017 Sean Seongik Kim. All rights reserved. Except for brief quotations in critical publications or reviews, no part of this book may be reproduced in any manner without prior written permission from the publisher. Write: Permissions, Wipf and Stock Publishers, 199 W. 8th Ave., Suite 3, Eugene, OR 97401.

Pickwick Publications
An Imprint of Wipf and Stock Publishers
199 W. 8th Ave., Suite 3
Eugene, OR 97401

www.wipfandstock.com

PAPERBACK ISBN: 978-1-5326-1294-7
HARDCOVER ISBN: 978-1-5326-1296-1
EBOOK ISBN: 978-1-5326-1295-4

Cataloguing-in-Publication data:

Names: Kim, Sean Seongik. | Foreword by van der Merwe, D. G.

Title: The Spirituality of Following Jesus in John's Gospel : An Investigation of *Akolouthein* and Correlated Motifs / Sean Seongik Kim.

Description: Eugene, OR: Pickwick Publications, 2017 | Includes bibliographical references and index.

Identifiers: ISBN 978-1-5326-1294-7 (paperback) | ISBN 978-1-5326-1296-1 (hardcover) | ISBN 978-1-5326-1295-4 (ebook)

Subjects: LCSH: Bible. John—Criticism, interpretation, etc. | Jesus Christ—Friends and associates. | Christian life—Biblical teaching. | Spiritual life—Biblical teaching.

Classification: LCC BS2601 K4 2017 (print) | LCC BS2601 (ebook)

Manufactured in the U.S.A.   06/04/19

Unless otherwise noted, Scripture quotations in English are from the New Revised Standard Version (NRSV), copyright, 1989, by the Division of Christian Education of the National Council of the Churches of Christ in the U.S.A. Used by permission. All rights reserved.

Also used: the Complete Jewish Bible (CJB), copyright, 1998, by David H. Stern. Published by Jewish New Testament Publications, Inc. Distributed by Messianic Jewish Resources International. Used by permission. All rights reserved. The English Standard Version (ESV), copyright, 2001, 2007, by Crossway Bibles, a division of Good News Publishers. It includes the January 2008 update. Used by permission. All rights reserved. The NET Bible (NET), Version 1.0, copyright, 1996–2006, by Biblical Studies Press, L.L.C. Used by permission. All rights reserved. The New American Standard Bible (NASB). Copyright © The Lockman Foundation 1960, 1962, 1963, 1968, 1971, 1972, 1973, 1975, 1977, 1988, 1995. All rights reserved. Quotations designated (NIV) are from THE HOLY BIBLE: NEW INTERNATIONAL VERSION®. NIV®. Copyright © 1973, 1978, 1984, 2011 by International Bible Society, www.ibs.org. All rights reserved worldwide. The Revised Standard Version (RSV), copyright, 1952 [2nd edition, 1971], by the Division of Christian Education of the National Council of the Churches of Christ in the U.S.A. Used by permission. All rights reserved.

The abbreviations used in this book are those set out in *The SBL Handbook of Style: For Ancient Near Eastern, Biblical, and Early Christian Studies* (Peabody, MA: Hendrickson, 1999).

*To Mary, Samuel, and Daniel
with enduring love and gratitude*

Contents

Foreword by D. G. van der Merwe | xiii

PART I
Preliminaries

Chapter 1: Introduction | 3
   I. Literature Review | 5
      A. Previous Scholarship on ἀκολουθεῖν in the Fourth Gospel as Biblical Studies | 6
      B. Previous Scholarship on ἀκολουθεῖν in the Studies of Spirituality | 15
   II. The Problem Statement | 18
      A. Importance of ἀκολουθεῖν in the Fourth Gospel | 18
      B. The Scholarly Gap to be Filled | 20
   III. Limitations of the Study and Points to Be Studied Further | 20
   IV. Methodology: A Literary-Theological Approach | 22

Chapter 2: Spirituality: A Brief Reasoning, Understanding, and Application in this Research | 24
   I. Understanding the Term Spirituality | 25
      A. Prominent Authors on the Term Spirituality | 25
      B. More Working Definitions | 33
      C. Summary | 34

II. Spirituality: Its Relation to Theology | 36
   III. Spirituality Communicated in the Text | 37
   IV. Closing | 39

Chapter 3: Socio-Historical Background of the Fourth Gospel | 41
   I. Various Theories of the Johannine Community | 41
   II. Suffering as the Historical Life Setting of the Johannine Community | 44
      A. 5:15–18 | 47
      B. 7:1, 7, 19, 25 | 50
      C. 8:37–47 | 50
      D. 9:22, 34 | 51
      E. 15:18—16:4 (17:14) | 53
   III. Summary | 57

Chapter 4: The Occurrences of ἀκολουθεῖν Outside the Fourth Gospel | 59
   I. Ἀκολουθεῖν in Greco-Roman and Judaism Literature | 60
      A. Greco-Roman Literature | 60
      B. Judaic Literature | 64
      C. Conclusion | 68
   II. Ἀκολουθεῖν in the Other Books of the New Testament | 69
      A. In the Synoptic Gospels | 69
      B. In the Book of Revelation (14:1–5) | 84
      C. Conclusion | 87

PART II

Ἀκολουθεῖν in the Fourth Gospel

Introduction | 89

The Texts to Investigate | 91

Chapter 5: Following Jesus to Where He Is and to
  See Heaven (1:35–51) | 93
  I. Literary Structure and Key Motifs | 94
  II. Following Jesus of the Two Disciples (1:35–42) | 95
    A. Following Jesus and the Lamb of God | 95
    B. Following Jesus and Where He Is | 101
    C. Following Jesus and Witnessing | 104
  III. Following Jesus and Philip's Journey of Discipleship | 106
    A. The First Disciple to Whom "ἀκολούθει μοι" was Given | 106
    B. Philip's Evangelism | 106
    C. Philip as a Follower of Jesus in 1:43–46; 6:5–7; 12:20–22; 14:7–10 | 107
  IV. Following Jesus and Seeing Heaven Opened (1:51) | 111
  V. Conclusion | 113

Chapter 6: Following the Guiding Light to the Father (8:12) | 115
  I. The Text 8:12 within the Unity of the Two Chapters | 116
  II. The Backgrounds Considered | 117
  III. Following the Light in Association with the "Where" Motif | 122
    A. Key Motifs in Chapters 7 and 8 as the Context of 8:12 | 122
    B. The Darkness and the "Where" Problem | 125
    C. To Have the Light of Life | 130
    D. Following the Light | 132
  IV. Conclusion | 134

Chapter 7: Following the Good Shepherd who Acts for
  His Sheep (10:1–42) | 136
  I. The Context: Literary and Socio-Historical | 138
  II. Following Jesus Implied in 10:1–42 | 139
    A. Following Jesus Who Owns and Knows the Followers from Before | 140

B. Following the Shepherd Who Acts Many Works for
      His Sheep | 145
   C. The Shepherd's Drawing Other Sheep | 150
   D. Co-Ministry of the Father and the Son for
      the Followers | 150
 III. Conclusion | 152

Chapter 8: Following Jesus on the Path of Death to
         Glory (12:26) | 154
   I. Death Motif as Literary-Theological Context of ἀκολουθεῖν | 155
   II. To Serve/Servant and Following Jesus | 161
   III. Following Jesus and the Promised Reward | 163
      A. Where I Am, My Servant Also Will Be | 163
      B. The Father will Honor | 166
   IV. Conclusion | 170

Chapter 9: Human Inability; Divine Ability (13:21—14:3) | 172
   I. An Unparalleled Association of ἀκολουθεῖν with
      the Denial Prediction | 174
   II. Literary Context and Semantic Relations | 175
   III. Following Jesus Communicated in 13:21—14:3 | 180
      A. The "Where" (ὅπου/ποῦ) Motif | 181
      B. Human Inability and ἀκολουθεῖν | 183
      C. What Makes Them Able to Follow (ἀκολουθεῖν) | 188
   IV. Conclusion | 194

Chapter 10: Shepherd as the One Shepherded in Love (21:1–19) | 196
   I. Linguistic Constituents and Their Relations | 198
   II. Spirituality of Following Jesus Implied in 21:1–19 | 202
      A. Following Jesus and His Presence and Provision | 202
      B. Following Jesus and the Centrality of Love | 208

C. Following Jesus and Feeding His Sheep | 214

D. Following Jesus and the "Where" Motif | 218

E. Following Jesus and the Guaranteed Victory | 222

III. Conclusion | 222

PART III

Conclusion

Chapter 11: Summary and Reflections | 227

I. Summary by Chapter | 227

II. Following Jesus Arranged in the (Redemptive) Historical Framework | 232

A. *From* Eternity | 232

B. *To* the Father | 234

C. *With* Jesus | 236

D. *By* the Works of the Father, the Son, and the Holy Spirit | 238

E. *Into* Eternity | 240

Bibliography | 243

Scripture Index | 265

Foreword

JOHANNINE SCHOLARSHIP HAS COME a long way. It was especially since the mid nineteenth century that the following issues have been explored in depth: (1) the Fourth Gospel and the Synoptics; (2) the historicity of the Fourth Gospel; (3) the Johannine community and its historical situation; (4) the Fourth Gospel and other Christian traditions; (5) the Johannine language and symbolism; (6) the Fourth Gospel and "the Jews"; (7) the Fourth Gospel and the Dead Sea Scrolls; and (8) the historical Jesus. Discipleship (following Jesus) featured nowhere. Even during the second half of the twentieth century literature about this theme was vague. Until 1972 a thematic-theological approach highlighted some characteristics of discipleship as they appeared in all four Gospels. The study of R. M. Jiménez (*El discípulo de Jesucristo, según el evangelio de S. Juan*, 1972) was the first substantial approach to research about discipleship in the Fourth Gospel where he focused on the disciple's relationship with the triune God. This caused a paradigm shift because he was the first to restrict the study of discipleship to only the Fourth Gospel.

During the 1980s, interest about Johannine discipleship increased. This was probably due to Rudolf Bultmann's appropriation of an existentialist perspective of the Fourth Gospel and Louis Martyn's publication *History and Theology in the Fourth Gospel* (1979) which influenced Johannine scholarship for about one and a half decades. For Martyn the historical setting and origins of the gospel in the Johannine community was not the ministry of Jesus, but Judaism. After Bultmann and Martyn more attention was paid to the situation and circumstances of the readers. This contributed to a greater interest in discipleship and ecclesiology in the Fourth Gospel. Since 1980 a number of publications on Johannine discipleship, from various perspectives, were published.

During the middle of the twentieth century, a new paradigm, Christian spirituality, emerged and gained momentum during the last decades of the twentieth century. The massive interest in Christian spirituality does not mean that Christian spirituality did not exist prior to this interest at all. It did but was limited to certain Christian denominations such as the Roman Catholic Church, Orthodox Churches, and later the Pentecostals. In the twenty-first century (postmodern era), spirituality has now become a buzz word that defines our era. Kees Waaijman (*Spirituality: Forms, Foundations, Methods*) points out that spirituality occupies an important place within churches, between churches, and in interreligious dialogue. This interest in Christian spirituality started a revival in the academic study of spirituality and really gained momentum as time went on. It also promoted academic research in Johannine literature from an early Christian spirituality perspective.

This monograph by Dr. Kim, *The Spirituality of Following Jesus in John's Gospel: An Investigation of ἀκολουθεῖν and Correlated Motifs*, an adaptation of his doctoral thesis, verifies this interest. This work is a welcome and timely contribution of the interpretation of a Johannine theme from the perspective of early Christian spirituality. The Johannine theme "to follow Jesus" (ἀκολουθεῖν Ἰησοῦν) is one of the major subjects or themes in the Fourth Gospel and constitutes the essence of Johannine discipleship. Jesus' invitation "follow me" (ἀκολούθει μοι) in the Synoptic Gospels occurs at the point where Jesus called individuals to "follow him" in discipleship. In the Fourth Gospel, the verb ἀκολουθεῖν occurs at the beginning (1:37, 38, 40, 43) where Jesus recruited his first disciples and also in the final narrative of discipleship before Jesus' departure (21:19, 22). It also occurs several more times (8:12; 10:1–42; 12:26; 13:36—14:3) in close connection with the major Johannine understandings of Jesus as the lamb of God, the light of the world, the good shepherd, and in the parable of a grain of wheat.

In this study, Kim profoundly explores the Spirituality embedded in the act of following Jesus according to the Fourth Gospel. He investigates the implications imparted in the pericopes where ἀκολουθεῖν is employed in spiritual nuances. Kim remarkably points out how the Evangelist leads the readers through the text into the Spirituality of following Jesus, by communicating the implications of ἀκολουθεῖν: in 1:35–51, "to be with Jesus where he is" takes central importance, and in following him, Jesus leads them to heaven opened, i.e., ultimately to the Father. In 8:12, John reveals the nature of human darkness as the ignorance of the "where" aspect of life, i.e., from where one comes and to where one goes. The Evangelist invites the readers to the Spirituality of "being led by Jesus the light" for he is the only one who knows from where he came and to where he goes. In 10:1–42, John draws the readers into the unique Spirituality of following Jesus by stressing the gravity of what Jesus does (with the Father) for his followers. This factor is greater than any human deed begun for Jesus, and determines the journey to be followed. In 12:26, John communicates the Spirituality of following Jesus through the path of death. The Father will honor such a follower with the reward of being with Jesus where he is in honor and glory. In 13:36—14:3, John indicates that following Jesus is impossible for humankind, including the disciples on their own, but only possible through the works of Jesus and God. In 21:1–19, John leads readers to the rich Spirituality of following Jesus by telling them: Jesus' presence and provision is that which restores and upholds them to continue the journey; love functions as its central driving force; while the journey is comprised of shepherding other followers of Jesus. This journey is ultimately the passage, through death, to triumph and glory in the risen Jesus. In the social milieu, where Jesus' followers are persecuted and even killed by the world (both the Jews and Roman power), the Evangelist encourages them with the reminder that the journey of following Jesus will ultimately culminate in the participation of the glory and honor in that communion between Jesus and the Father, even though on earth the followers walk through the passage of suffering and death, just as Jesus did.

In his research, Kim has pointed out that in the field of biblical studies, no substantial research has been devoted to further develop the biblical theology of following Jesus according to the Fourth Gospel by examining the whole profile of ἀκολουθεῖν. In the field of Spirituality, there is no literature to date which has studied the Johannine spirituality of "following Jesus." In his study, Kim attempts to fill the lacuna in the fields of both biblical studies and Johannine spirituality with regard to the verb ἀκολουθεῖν.

Dr. Kim's reasoning, discourse analysis, and literary and theological interpretation as applied to a spirituality paradigm, are remarkable. The unique contribution of this study is thus his focus on Johannine reasoning and the analysis of this reasoning by way of discourse analysis applied to early Christian spirituality. Kim is concerned with the entire Gospel throughout this work. He kept the literary and theological fabric as a whole in sight. His research is most informative throughout. He continuously addresses the relevance of following Jesus, both for the early Christian community at the end of the first century CE and for the church today.

Dirk G. van der Merwe
University of South Africa
Pretoria

PART I
Preliminaries

CHAPTER 1

Introduction

The present study will investigate the entire profile of ἀκολουθεῖν (to follow) in relation to correlated motifs in those texts of the Fourth Gospel where it is used with the connotation of discipleship. To do so, the methodology of literary-theological exegesis under the discipline of biblical studies will be employed. From the outcomes of the exegesis, the Spirituality[1] of following Jesus communicated in John's Gospel will be reflected and developed. The primary texts to be investigated are 1:35–51; 8:12; 10:1–42; 12:26; 13:21—14:3; 21:1–19.

A couple of questions have contributed towards the launching of the present study on the theological significance and Spirituality of "following Jesus" according to the Fourth Gospel. First, is there any uniqueness in the theological implications communicated by ἀκολουθεῖν in the Fourth Gospel? If the name *John: the Maverick Gospel*[2] is intended for the whole book, there could be a maverick-ish quality and characteristic, even in this common term of ἀκολουθεῖν that John shares with the other Gospel books, as much as it is found in some particularly Johannine vocabularies such as light, life, glory, and to remain. I presuppose that even though John uses the common verb ἀκολουθεῖν, there is a unique property in the Johannine use of the term. If it is true that John uses the common term ἀκολουθεῖν in his own way to deliver his own distinctive implications, what are they? What distinguishing messages and connotations does the fourth evangelist impart by the use of recurring ἀκολουθεῖν? How is it communicated in association with other correlated motifs in the texts? It is my intent to excavate the distinguishing implications of the term in the Johannine usage.

The second question is related to the search for the characteristics of the Johannine Spirituality portrayed by the motif of "following Jesus."

---

1. As explained in chapter 2, the term "spirituality" is capitalized when it refers to the biblical (Johannine) Spirituality. If it is used as a generic term, it is lower-cased.

2. Kysar, *Maverick*.

The Fourth Gospel is typically known as the "spiritual Gospel."[3] It is the nest of Christian mysticism, from which concepts such as *perichoresis*,[4] immanence,[5] and deification[6] have been developed. Certainly, it is a profoundly mystical and spiritual Gospel. Therefore, a question springs up: How do the spiritual characteristics of this "spiritual Gospel" enhance the meaning of "following Jesus"? What distinctive respects of the Spirituality of following Jesus are communicated by the association of ἀκολουθεῖν with correlated motifs in the texts of the Gospel?

I have noticed in my reading of the Gospel that it is both an earthy and spiritual Gospel. In the Fourth Gospel, heaven and earth kiss each other. It is the Gospel where heaven and earth are intertwined. Jesus is at the center of this interwoven-ness. It happens uniquely in and through Jesus, who came from heaven with full divinity and assumed full humanity, in whom divinity and humanity are perfectly combined and harmonized. When Jesus calls men and women to "follow" (ἀκολουθεῖν) him, this involves not only the earthly dimension, but the spiritual and heavenly dimension as well. Different from the Synoptic use of the term that mainly focuses on following Jesus in earthly activities (such as, being a fisher of men, preaching the good news, and making disciples), "following Jesus" in the Fourth Gospel involves not only the earthly aspect, but also the heavenly aspect (to be where Jesus is as participation in his intimate communion with the Father; to see his glory in the place where Jesus will be with the Father; and to be with him in the glory of the Father). As Jesus is at the center of the interwoven-ness of heaven and earth, the act of "following Jesus" leads his followers into the experiences of the heavenly dimensions (which will be explored in this study) beyond emulating Jesus or doing his mission in the earthly life.

In the present investigation of the term ἀκολουθεῖν in the Fourth Gospel, I expect to test whether my reading is plausible, that is, whether John conveys the above understanding by the employment of the term in association with correlated motifs in the above listed pertinent pericopes.

---

3. Grech, *New Testament Spirituality*, 103.

4. It refers to "mutual indwelling of the Father and the Son" and mutual existence in dynamic fellowship of life as revealed in 14:10, 11. Torrance, *The Christian Doctrine*, 102–3, 168–73.

5. Ridderbos, *John*, 559–60.

6. The idea of deification is well developed in the Greek Patristic tradition from 1:14; 10:34; chapters 14–17 together with 2 Pet 1:4. Among them is St. Athanasius the Archbishop of Alexandria. In section 54 of *On the Incarnation*, St. Athanasius articulates the idea: "He, indeed, assumed humanity that we might become God." According to Russell, "Reference to deification occurs eight times in the third discourse, on the first occasion in the course of an exegesis of John 17." Russell, *The Doctrine of Deification*, 173–75. See also Ware, *The Orthodox Church*, 231–38; Clement, *The Roots*, 263–69.

Some derivable questions are added: What characteristics and dimensions of Spirituality does John communicate by employing ἀκολουθεῖν in combination with other motifs in the texts? If "spirituality"[7] is about "the lived experience of God" or "experiencing God," how does the journey of "following Jesus" lead his followers to experience God and divine realities?

Like the Synoptic Gospels, the Fourth Gospel is a narrative that calls for a radical life for the followers of Jesus in the earthly dimension. Yet, more importantly, it is the Gospel that invites readers into a profound spiritual experience of God and divine realities in and through Jesus. In Christ Jesus, flesh sees, touches, and experiences the mystery of the Father. Jesus is the ladder by which men and women reach heaven. Heaven and earth, the above and the below, are linked by the ladder. Jesus, who came down from heaven, connects the realities of the above and the below. Jesus, who is from the bosom of the Father (1:18), draws men and women to the Father and into the circle of the Divine Trinity. Therefore, the life of "following Jesus" is a life seriously engaged in the heavenly realities. The journey of "following Jesus" is a journey of experiencing God not only in the dimensions of doing some Christian actions, that is, in obeying him, keeping his words, washing each other's feet, and proclaiming his gospel, but also in the dimension of participating in the Son's communion with the Father and being incorporated into the glory of the Father in and through the Son.

First, in this chapter, a literature review will be offered, followed by a statement of the problem, limitations, and methodology of the present study.

I. Literature Review

The literature review is divided into two subsections: First, a review of previous scholarship in biblical studies on the term ἀκολουθεῖν in the Fourth Gospel; second, a review of previous literature on the Johannine Spirituality of following Jesus, particularly as it relates to ἀκολουθεῖν. The literature review will be guided by two questions: (1) To what extent has ἀκολουθεῖν in the Fourth Gospel been investigated? (2) To what degree has previous research been done on ἀκολουθεῖν in connection with ὅπου/ποῦ (where Jesus is/goes) or correlated motifs to present the Johannine Spirituality of following Jesus?

---

7. For more discussion on the term "spirituality" and its definition, see chapter two of the present study. Some outstanding writers one might want to refer to are: Waaijman, *Spirituality*, 307–9; Schneiders, "Biblical Spirituality," 134–35; Schneiders, "Biblical Spirituality: Text and Transformation," 128–29; McGrath, *Christian Spirituality*, 1–4.

From the outcome of the literature review, a problem statement will be constituted.

A. Previous Scholarship on ἀκολουθεῖν in the Fourth Gospel as Biblical Studies

1. Rudolf Bultmann

In his commentary on the Gospel of John, Bultmann states in a footnote that the repetition of ἀκολουθεῖν "is meant to depict their 'discipleship'"[8] in 1:37, 38, 40, 43 together with the occurrences in 8:12; 10:4, 5, 27; 12:26; 13:36, 37; 21:19, 20, 22. He also discusses the text 13:36—14:4 under the subtitle "the promise of discipleship."[9] Certainly, discipleship was, to some degree, the theme that caught this influential theologian's attention. Yet, he very briefly comments on this important term ἀκολουθεῖν, and does not develop, any further, the theological implications communicated by the term and its association with ὅπου εἰμὶ ἐγώ/ὅπου ὑπάγω (where Jesus is/goes) or correlated motifs. For Bultmann, ἀκολουθεῖν is a motif that is meant to be explored by someone else in the future.

2. C. H. Dodd

In his earlier work, *The Interpretation of the Fourth Gospel* (1953), Dodd neglects the motif of "following" in his list of the "leading themes" of the Fourth Gospel.[10] In his monograph, *Historical Tradition in the Fourth Gospel* (1965), Dodd recognizes in the texts 1:43; 21:22; 12:26 that "[t]he call to 'follow' Christ is so fundamental to the whole gospel picture of his Ministry."[11] It is impressive that he spares a subsection for Jesus' saying, ἀκολούθει μοι (follow me). In the brief subsection (just over one page), he makes insightful observations, noting that the verb ἀκολουθεῖν recurs "in a saying conceived as a rule for the Christian life." Furthermore, he explores the following of Christ in relation to "his death."[12] Yet, Dodd's development of the verb is too brief to cover the whole profile of the term

---

8. Bultmann, *John*, 99.
9. Ibid., 595–603.
10. Dodd, *Interpretation*.
11. Dodd, *Tradition*, 352.
12. Ibid.

in depth. He does not pay attention to ἀκολουθεῖν in relation to ὅπου/ποῦ (where Jesus is/goes).

3. Raymond E. Brown

Brown comments that to "'follow' is the term par excellence for the dedication of discipleship."[13] He also remarks that "[w]e hear of following as a disciple in viii 12, x 4, 27, xii 26, xiii 36, xxi 19, 22."[14] For Brown, "[d]iscipleship is the primary Christian category for John."[15] Yet, his attention to ἀκολουθεῖν is not extended any further. He does not investigate the term in any article or monograph, and he excludes ἀκολουθεῖν from the list of significant Johannine vocabularies in the appendix of his commentary. Any theological connotation derived from the association of ἀκολουθεῖν with ὅπου εἰμὶ ἐγώ/ ὅπου ὑπάγω or related motifs appears outside of his concern.

4. Barnabas Lindars

In his commentary on John's Gospel, Lindars points out that ἀκολουθεῖν is the "vocabulary of discipleship."[16] Yet, he does not devote any further attention to investigating the term or its implications imparted by its association with correlated motifs.

5. Rudolf Schnackenburg

In an excursus in his commentary, Schnackenburg discusses the theme of "The Disciples, the Community and the Church in the Gospel of John."[17] He makes a clear point in regard to the identity of the disciples, and to "the gospel's understanding of the group of the disciples."[18] Schnackenburg identifies the disciples in the gospel as three groups: (a) the disciples that are "made believers by Jesus through his word and signs"; (b) "the later community in contrast to the unbelieving Jews"; (c) the later believers that "are challenged and tempted and their faith is inadequate."[19] He first examines the disciples'

---

13. Brown, *John*, 1:78.
14. Ibid.
15. Brown, *The Community*, 191.
16. Lindars, *John*, 315.
17. Schnackenburg, *John*, 3:203–17.
18. Ibid., 3:205.
19. Ibid., 3:206–7.

self understanding in the Johannine images of the church (i.e., the flock, the branches, his own, children of God, the bride). Then, he characterizes the Johannine community as the missionary and "constantly expanding"[20] church beyond the idea of "the elect and chosen."[21] Yet, in this excursus, although he focuses on μαθητής (disciple), Schnackenburg does not pay any attention to the motif of following Jesus and ἀκολουθεῖν terminology.

In dealing with individual passages that include ἀκολουθεῖν, Schnackenburg gives closer and more intriguing attention than other scholars do. He observes the connection among 12:26, 13:36ff, 14:3, and 21:18f by ἀκολουθεῖν or ὅπου εἰμὶ ἐγώ/ὅπου ὑπάγω.[22] Further he indicates that "[t]he typically Johannine formulation 'where I am' means the goal the disciples will reach through their death."[23] For Schnackenburg "where I am (there where Jesus is)" is "the goal towards which Jesus' way is leading."[24] In commenting on 21:19, he states that "[t]he notion that to follow in such a way leads through death into glory (there where Jesus is)"[25] is latently imparted by the text. Although these observations and comments are fascinating and provide insights, they are unfortunately very brief. Schnackenburg does not try to integrate them to expound the ways in which ἀκολουθεῖν conveys the unique concept of "following Jesus" in the Fourth Gospel.

6. Marinus de Jonge

In the first chapter of his book, *Jesus: Stranger from Heaven and Son of God*, de Jonge expounds the mission of the disciples, the role of the Spirit that operates in and through the community of disciples, the true nature of discipleship, and divine initiative in discipleship.[26] It is noteworthy that he develops in a separate section the divine initiative behind the deeds of disciples and God's operation through them, imbedded in the terms "to choose," "to draw," "to give," and "to know." As for the term "to follow," de Jonge lists the occurrences of the term where it denotes discipleship, and points out that it is one of the dimensions of the true nature of discipleship together with "to remain" and "to come and see." While he makes a strong argument for the role of the Spirit and divine initiative in Christian disciple-

20. Ibid., 3:216.
21. Ibid., 3:213–14.
22. Ibid., 3:55–56.
23. Ibid., 2:385.
24. Ibid., 3:55.
25. Ibid., 3:367.
26. De Jonge, *Jesus: Stranger*.

ship, de Jonge does not pay detailed attention to excavating the theological depth of ἀκολουθεῖν in the Gospel.

7. Matthew Vellanickal

In the article, "Discipleship according to the Gospel of John,"[27] Vellanickal argues that the meaning of "following Jesus" in the Fourth Gospel is unique. He points out that in the Fourth Gospel, "Jesus presents himself as 'Teacher' or 'Master' . . . in the sense of the Son of Man, who is the Revealer of the Father,"[28] and a disciple is "one who follows Jesus as the Light (8:12), and the Shepherd (10:4, 27) or Teacher (12:26; 13:36, 37; 21:19, 22)."[29] As for ἀκολουθεῖν, Vellanickal remarks that in the Gospels it is used to denote "following Jesus," which in turn "implies that the following means a self-commitment in a sense which breaks all other ties"[30] (Matt 8:22; Luke 9:60). Emphasizing "being united with Jesus"[31] and "deepening of experience of Christ,"[32] Vellanickal concludes that "[u]nlike the Synoptics, John presents the discipleship in terms of a life of faith and union with Christ,"[33] and the mission of the disciples is "no longer a 'fishing of men,' but a testimony to the unique experience of Jesus."[34]

8. Fernando F. Segovia

In his article, "'Peace I Leave with You; My Peace I Give to You': Discipleship in the Fourth Gospel,"[35] Segovia explores the characterization of discipleship in the context of narrative applying the approach of redaction or composition criticism. He sees the "characterization as taking place in four basic stages" according to the progress of the belief of "the elect" in Jesus and the rejection of "the world" to Jesus and his claims. For Segovia, the Johannine conception of discipleship reveals three fundamental components: (a) the narrative presents a deliberate and sustained contrast between Jesus'

27. Vellanickal, "Discipleship," 131–47.
28. Ibid., 132.
29. Ibid., 136.
30. Ibid.
31. Ibid.
32. Ibid., 140–41.
33. Ibid., 147.
34. Ibid.
35. Segovia, "'Peace I Leave with You,'" 76–102.

disciples and the world, where the latter term refers primarily to the Jews; (b) exclusive to this contrast lies belief in, or acceptance of, Jesus' claims regarding his origin, ministry, and goal; (c) such belief is portrayed as necessitating and undergoing a process of gradual understanding and perception, above all with respect to the events comprising Jesus' hour and the necessity for missionary activity. He then concludes that "the community's relentless antagonism toward the 'world' and exclusivistic self conception as the 'children of God' evidenced through such a portrayal of the disciples reveal a highly sectarian group and self-understanding."[36] By detecting the progress of the narrative, Segovia makes a contribution to the Johannine concept of discipleship by focusing on the centrality of belief in Jesus within the historical *Sitz im Leben* of the contrast between the elect and the world. However, for Segovia the significance of "following Jesus" conveyed in the repetition of ἀκολουθεῖν was outside of his scholarly attention in his exploring of the characterization of discipleship.

9. Andreas J. Köstenberger

Köstenberger, in a comprehensive manner, contributed to the understanding of mission theology of the Fourth Gospel in his doctoral dissertation and in the subsequent book, a revision of the dissertation.[37] He examines not only the explicit use of the word "send," but also other words with missional connotation in a broad sense. These include "come, go, become," "descend, ascend, leave," "follow," "bring, lead, gather," "work, do," "sign," and "harvest, bear fruit."[38] According to Köstenberger, some terms are exclusively used for Jesus' mission (descend, ascend, come into the world, and return), and for the disciples (follow). For Köstenberger, Jesus' mission is threefold:[39] (1) Jesus was sent from the Father to do the Father's will, and is seen as a model of the dependent servant who has an intimate relationship with the Father through obedience to his will. (2) Jesus is the one who has come from the Father and is returning to him. That return to the Father is through the supreme act of obedience via his death on the cross. (3) Jesus' mission is seen in his eschatological role of shepherd/teacher who calls his followers to the same kind of fruit-bearing that he has demonstrated. The mission of the disciples is to follow Jesus by first coming to him, and then bearing fruit in

---

36. Segovia, "Introduction: Call and Discipleship," 9.

37. Köstenberger, "The Missions of Jesus and the Disciples"; and Köstenberger, *The Missions of Jesus and the Disciples*, respectively.

38. Ibid., 28–31.

39. Curtis, review of Köstenberger, *The Missions of Jesus and the Disciples*, 142–43.

their lives and within their witnessing. The disciples are those who are called to expand Jesus' mission in "harvesting," "fruit bearing," and "witnessing."

As to the study of "following Jesus," Köstenberger first lists the occurrences of ἀκολουθεῖν used for the disciples and traces some of them in the section, *Identification of Semantic Clusters*.[40] Afterward, in three pages, Köstenberger summarizes the meaning of "following Jesus" as one of the two movements in the disciples' mission. He outlines the meaning of "following" from literal to figurative, from that of Jesus' original disciples to that of the wider circle of disciples, its involvement with "death" and the two different ways of "following" depicted by the two different disciples. Although Köstenberger tries to cover quickly the various references of "following" in the Gospel, one cannot expect from his work, due to the limits of the study, a detailed investigation in a comprehensive manner of the term ἀκολουθεῖν and its correlated motifs.

10. *Melvyn R. Hillmer*

Hillmer understands discipleship in two dimensions: discipleship "as relational" and "as action."[41] To elucidate "discipleship as relational," he focuses on the term "know" in the image of the good shepherd, the term "remain" in the image of the vine and branch, the term "friends," and "the Beloved Disciple" as the ideal figure of intimate relationship with Jesus. To explain "discipleship as action," (before dealing with other terms such as "obey," "love," and "keep"), he first remarks on ἀκολουθεῖν briefly and concludes that "To follow Jesus . . . is to follow his teachings and his example."[42] By noting that the vocabularies for discipleship are "tremendously varied with considerable interweaving themes,"[43] he hints at the need to study discipleship terms in connection to other motifs. However, although he recognizes the import of ἀκολουθεῖν for the understanding of discipleship in John, his dealing with ἀκολουθεῖν is too cursory, and he does not allow any room to scrutinize the whole profile of the recurrence of the motif.

---

40. Köstenberger, *The Missions of Jesus and the Disciples*, 30–37.
41. Hillmer, "They Believed in Him: Discipleship," 77–97.
42. Ibid., 90.
43. Ibid., 92.

11. D. G. van der Merwe

In his doctoral thesis, "Discipleship in the Fourth Gospel," van der Merwe investigates the term μαθητὴς and develops the concept of Johannine discipleship in the structure of "agency motif" with the descent-ascent schema.[44] As the Father sent the Son, Jesus sent his disciples to the world. Van der Merwe contends that discipleship is the continuation and expansion of Jesus' mission through the disciples after his departure. Yet, the term ἀκολουθεῖν does not get a sufficient amount of attention in the thesis. In his article, "*Imitatio Christi* in the Fourth Gospel," he makes brief mention of the term only once.[45]

12. Rekha M. Chennattu

In her doctoral dissertation,[46] Chennattu makes an endeavor to spell out Johannine discipleship in the context of the Old Testament covenant,[47] focusing on the Jewish background of the Fourth Gospel. The three sections of the Gospel (1:35–51; chapters 13–17; chapters 20–21) are investigated to establish her thesis. In the exegesis of 1:35–51, she tries to find some similarities between the call of the Old Testament Israel and the call account of the New Testament disciples, and then suggests that "the evangelist uses the occasion of the call stories to present a paradigm of covenant relationship."[48] In dealing with chapters 13–17, Chennattu contends that the chapters "reflect a covenant renewal ceremony very similar to that of Joshua 24," and points out several Old Testament covenant themes. In the study of chapters 20–21, she states that what is promised in chapters 13–17 is realized in the community of the disciples.[49] Chennattu closes the study with an attempt

---

44. Van der Merwe, "Discipleship in the Fourth Gospel."

45. Van der Merwe, "*Imitatio Christi*," 131–48.

46. Chennattu, "Johannine Discipleship as a Covenant Relationship." The dissertation was published afterward: Chennattu, *Johannine Discipleship*.

47. For many decades, scholars have suggested that there are links between the Old Testament covenant motif and the Johannine writings. Malatesta, *Interiority and Covenant*; Simoens, *La Gloire d'aimer*; Schneiders, *Written That You May Believe*. Scholarly interest in interpreting the Gospel books in light of the Old Testament covenant has begun to increase as some recent publications reflect: Chennattu, *Johannine Discipleship*; Brown, "Gift upon Gift"; Lunde, *Following Jesus, The Servant King*.

48. Chennattu, *Johannine Discipleship*, 72.

49. It is unfortunate that Chennattu does not pay any attention to the Covenant of Redemption between the Father and the Son, imbedded in 8:29; 10:18; 12:49; 15:10; and especially in 17:4, 5, 6. The Covenant of Redemption is the foundation of the covenant relationship (Covenant of Grace) between God and man in the Old Testament

to explain the socio-historical situation that led the Johannine community to understand Christian discipleship in the paradigm of the Old Testament covenant. This work has a certain value in terms of the attempt to grasp Johannine discipleship in the covenant perspective. However, Chennattu does not give enough attention to the significance of ἀκολουθεῖν in the selected texts, and fails to consider the import of ἀκολουθεῖν in connection to covenant motif in the Johannine discipleship.

13. Craig S. Keener

In his recent commentary, Keener situates the Fourth Gospel in the historical milieu of rabbinic and Mediterranean worlds by consulting an enormous amount of ancient literature. However, he pays little attention to the motif of "following Jesus," stating only that ἀκολουθεῖν "represents standard Jewish language for discipleship."[50] There is no further comment on the term or on Jesus' significant call of ἀκολούθει μοι (follow me) in 1:43 and 21:19, 22.

14. Jerome H. Neyrey

Neyrey's commentary on the Fourth Gospel employs the methodology of socio-rhetorical interpretation, which mainly examines literary-rhetorical, cultural-historical, and ideological textures within the text.[51] As for the theme of "following," Neyrey is silent. He does not pay attention to the motif in dealing with Jesus' call to Philip ("Follow me") in 1:43, and other passages in which the term ἀκολουθεῖν appears. In the entire commentary, the only remark he makes on the theme is found in his comment on 21:19: "'Follow' strongly suggests complete imitation of Jesus, especially by a death that will give God glory, just as Jesus did."[52]

---

and New Testament. The discipleship in John as a covenant relationship is possible on the grounds of the eternal Covenant between the Father and the Son because it gives efficacy to the covenant relationship between God and humanity. For discussions on the Covenant of Redemption between the Father and the Son, refer to Witsius, *The Economy of the Covenants*, 1:165–92; Berkhof, *Systematic Theology*, 265–71; Turretin, *Institutes of Elenctic Theology*, 2:177–78.

50. Keener, *John*, 1:468.
51. Neyrey, *John*.
52. Ibid., 340.

15. Craig R. Koester

In his study of the theology of John's Gospel, Koester thinks through and addresses major themes of the Book by approaching "the Gospel narrative in its present form" rather than attempting to identify backgrounds of the themes from ancient sources.[53] His work is notable for his close attention to the biblical text and for his scrupulous treatment of the themes, which include: God, the problem of sin and death and evil of the world, Jesus and his crucifixion and resurrection, the Spirit, the present and future of faith, discipleship and Christian community in the pluralistic world. However, Koester pays no attention to the overarching motif of "following Jesus" in dealing with discipleship.

16. J. G. van der Watt

In his article on Johannine style, van der Watt scrutinizes the appearance of some words, such as "eternal life," "love," and "follow" to present how "John uses the stylistic feature of repetition."[54] After investigating the repetition of the first two words, he examines the stylistic function of ἀκολουθέω as the linguistic and thematic link with other terminologies.[55] Then, he concludes that "[t]he repetition of the word ἀκολουθέω is again used to link related contexts (a cohesive strategy) and thus developing a particular theme in the latter part of the Gospel."[56] Although he pays attention to ἀκολουθέω in the full scope of the Gospel, the focus of the study is not on developing the meaning or theological implications of "following Jesus" through the exegesis of the passages that contain ἀκολουθέω, but rather on examining the Johannine style of repetitions of vocabularies to see how "they are combined and interrelated to form a wider semantic network."[57]

---

53. Koester, *The Word of Life*.

54. Van der Watt, "Johannine style," 75–99.

55. He briefly gives attention to the combination of the motifs ἀκολουθέω, ὅπου εἰμὶ ἐγώ, and ψυχὴν in chapters 12–14 as an example of the feature of repetition, though not in all the texts that have both ἀκολουθεῖν and ὅπου/ποῦ (where Jesus is/where Jesus is going to). He does not reflect further on the theological implications of "following Jesus." However, the article can be a starting point for exploring the motif of "following" (ἀκολουθεῖν) since it lists all appearances of the term ἀκολουθεῖν, and pays attention to the association of ἀκολουθεῖν with the "where" motif in the Fourth Gospel.

56. Ibid., 94.

57. Ibid.

17. Conclusion

As presented in the literature review above, in the academic field of biblical studies, there is no substantial research that explores the theological implications of "following Jesus" by investigating the whole profile of ἀκολουθεῖν in the Fourth Gospel. Research on the implications of "following Jesus" which are communicated by the term ἀκολουθεῖν and its connection with ὅπου/ποῦ (where Jesus is/where Jesus goes to) or correlated motifs in the Fourth Gospel remains unexplored territory.

B. Previous Scholarship on ἀκολουθεῖν in the Studies of Spirituality

1. Sandra M. Schneiders

In her lengthy doctoral dissertation, Schneiders writes a biblical theology on Johannine Spirituality based on detailed exegesis of the resurrection narrative in John 20.[58] To my knowledge, it is the first research in this area among doctoral theses and scholarly publications and is unique in at least two aspects: one, the study uses the term of "Johannine Spirituality" in the title of the literature; and two, the study develops Johannine Spirituality as an academic discipline through thorough exegesis of a text in the Fourth Gospel. For Schneiders, the center of the Johannine resurrection narrative (John 20) is the fact that "Jesus came and stood in(to) the midst of them" as the fulfillment of the new covenant promise in Ezekiel 36–37. Johannine Spirituality experienced by the disciples in the Easter event is "Jesus' 'coming to them'" (20:19), and as the result, they "see" him, which is "essentially to experience him as indwelling."[59] The result of this indwelling (cf. 14:18–20) of the glorified Jesus is "an experienced sharing in the filial relationship of Jesus to the Father."[60]

In the article on Johannine Spirituality in *The New Westminster Dictionary of Christian Spirituality*, Schneiders says that to have *life* in Jesus' name (or, to participate in his own divine life) is "the capsule expression of Johannine Spirituality."[61] "The life of God which Jesus shares with his disciples is *love*." By believing in Jesus the Word of God, who is God's self revelation, the believers share in "Jesus' divine life" and experience "the very

---

58. Schneiders, "The Johannine Resurrection Narrative."
59. Ibid., 635.
60. Ibid., 636.
61. Schneiders, "Johannine Spirituality," 385–87.

life of God." For Schneiders, both the role of Jesus as the Word of revelation and the role of humanity's response to the Word by believing *into* Jesus are crucial in Spirituality. Six characteristics of Johannine Spirituality are pointed out: mystical spirituality, personal spirituality, egalitarianism in the community, love as the criterion of holiness, the Spirit as the source of life, and eternal life as shared in the present life. As the article closes, Schneiders summarizes that Christian spirituality is living of love "modeled" by Jesus in washing his disciples' feet.

Research on the Spirituality of "following Jesus" through an investigation of the term ἀκολουθεῖν and its correlation with the "where" motif has been outside the scope of Schneiders' interest in developing Johannine Spirituality.

2. Stephen S. Smalley

Under the entry "Johannine Spirituality" in *The Westminster Dictionary of Christian Spirituality*, Smalley delineates Johannine Spirituality in the context of eternal life which is "mediated to believers" through Jesus, the Word made flesh, who is "one being with God" and also "flesh, and thus one with man."[62] For Smalley, Johannine Spirituality is characteristically a mutual "abiding" relationship, which begins from within the indwelling relationship between the Father and the Son, and expands to the relationship between believers and Jesus, and to the relationship among believers themselves. He states that believers "experience God" in three ways: Worship in the Spirit, service for others, and mission for the world. For Smalley, the incarnated Son makes the spiritual life of believers possible; the power of the Spirit sustains it. Overall, he rightly points out the significant role of the incarnated Son and the empowerment of the Spirit in the spiritual life of believers. However, Smalley does not pay attention to the significance of ἀκολουθεῖν in Johannine Spirituality.

3. Mary L. Coloe

In her first monograph, *God Dwells with Us: Temple Symbolism in the Fourth Gospel*, Coloe explores Johannine Christology—Jesus as God's dwelling place among his people—as it is portrayed in the imagery of the temple in the Fourth Gospel.[63] In a second book, *Dwelling in the Household*

---

62. Smalley, "Johannine Spirituality," 230–32.
63. Coloe, *God Dwells with Us.*

of God: Johannine Ecclesiology and Spirituality, in order to develop the Spirituality of Johannine community, Coloe investigates the symbolism of "my Father's household" (οἶκον/οἰκίᾳ τοῦ πατρός μου, 2:16; 14:2), which runs throughout the Gospel (though not overtly, except for a couple of places).[64] By employing a narrative-critical approach, she formulates a suggestive work of Johannine Spirituality from the intimated traces of the betrothal and formation of God's household, gathering of the household, birthing of the household, death and eternal life of the household, welcoming into the household, indwelling in the household, and resurrecting of the household. She explicates "the religious, indeed mystical, experience of mutual indwelling of believers and Jesus, which grounds their experience of community life as life in the household of God."[65] However, Coloe misses the important fact that in the Gospel, the journey of "following Jesus" leads the followers into the mutual "indwelling" with Jesus in the household of God, which is conveyed by the combination of the motif of ἀκολουθεῖν (following Jesus) and the ὅπου/ποῦ motif.

4. Prosper Grech

In the chapter, "Response to the Light: John," in his book on New Testament Spirituality, Grech outlines Johannine Spirituality in a thematic reading of the Gospel and the First Epistle of John.[66] After acknowledging the Gospel as a "spiritual Gospel," Grech argues that, in reading John, one needs both "prayerful meditation" and "strict exegesis" because John uses symbolic language and dualism in his writings. Grech limits his study to the typical themes: the Word of life, reading the signs, the bread of life, "I and the Father are one" in the "I Am" sayings, self-revelation to the disciples and the role of *Parakletos*, eternal life, and lastly, Christ's intercessory prayer. He concludes that "the substance of Johannine Spirituality" is "the response, by the help of the Spirit, to the Father's love in sending the Logos-Son into the world, in real flesh, to bring the light of revelation to all so that all may know God's true nature in the person, words, and deeds of Jesus Christ."[67] The response of humanity is "remaining in the light" and "walking in the only way to God, in Christ."[68] However, in dealing with Johannine Spirituality, Grech misses

---

64. Coloe, *Dwelling in the Household of God*.
65. Ibid., vii.
66. Grech, *New Testament Spirituality*, 103–24.
67. Ibid., 123.
68. Ibid., 123–24.

the significance of the theme of "following Jesus" and the Spirituality that is particularly conveyed by ἀκολουθεῖν and correlated vocabularies.

5. Conclusion

As presented in this literature review, in the academic discipline of spirituality, there has been no literature that explores the Johannine Spirituality of "following Jesus" by investigating the whole profile of the term ἀκολουθεῖν and its association with correlated motifs in the Fourth Gospel.

II. The Problem Statement

This section has two subsections. First, the importance of the term ἀκολουθεῖν in the Fourth Gospel will be explained. Second, the scholarly gap identified from the above literature review of previous scholarship on ἀκολουθεῖν in the field of the New Testament studies and in the academic discipline of spirituality will be underlined.

A. Importance of ἀκολουθεῖν in the Fourth Gospel

The motif of "following Jesus" is one of the major subjects or themes in the Fourth Gospel. Unlike the preconception that the term ἀκολουθεῖν might appear rarely in the Fourth Gospel, it appears both in the opening (1:37, 38, 40, 43) and closing (21:19, 22) chapter. Jesus' call "follow me" (ἀκολούθει μοι), which is typically given at the starting point of discipleship for individuals in the Synoptic Gospels, here in the Fourth Gospel is given at the beginning and also in the final narrative of discipleship before Jesus' departure. It also occurs several more times in close connection to the major Johannine understandings of Jesus as the lamb of God, the light of the world, and the good shepherd, and in the parable of a grain of wheat. The texts where ἀκολουθεῖν appears in the Fourth Gospel are as follows. The occurrences in figurative meaning are highlighted.

Chapters	1	6	8	10	11	12	13	18	20	21
Verses	37	2	12	4	31	26	36	15	6	19
	38			5		37				20
	40			27						22
	43									

As presented in the above figure and also as Hillmer remarks, the motif of "following Jesus" is pervasive in nearly the entire scope of the Gospel.[69] Thus, without a proper understanding of the concept and theological implications of "following Jesus" by investigating the term ἀκολουθεῖν, one can hardly grasp the distinct picture of the Johannine relationship between the Lord Jesus and his followers, Jesus' expectations for his followers, the goal to which Jesus intends to lead them, the shape of the life of Jesus' followers on earth and in the future, and how his followers will experience God.

The frequency of appearance of ἀκολουθεῖν in the Fourth Gospel is second only to Matthew,[70] and is more than that of Mark and Luke. Thus, the motif of following Jesus imparted by ἀκολουθεῖν is no insignificant subject in John compared to its appearances in the other books of the New Testament. However, limited attention has been devoted to the term in the Fourth Gospel whereas a substantial amount of scholarly attention has been given to the term in the Synoptics.[71] The insufficient attention to ἀκολουθεῖν in the Fourth Gospel probably stems from the general notion that the motif of "following Jesus" is a "characteristically synoptic expression."[72] There is a tacit presumption that there would be no special or distinctive implications of "following Jesus" that are communicated by ἀκολουθεῖν in the Fourth Gospel. (In other words, there is a presupposition that the implications imparted by ἀκολουθεῖν in John will not be different from the implications imparted in the Synoptics.) The issue of whether ἀκολουθεῖν is a particular Synoptic expression and whether there is no distinguishing implication and significance in the Johannine employment of ἀκολουθεῖν will become clear once the investigation of ἀκολουθεῖν in the Fourth Gospel is done in this research.

---

69. Hillmer notes that the motif of following Jesus occurs repetitively in the Fourth: "For at the beginning of his Gospel (1:35–51) and in the epilogue (21:19–23) it is made clear that to be a disciple of Jesus is to follow him, and throughout the Gospel this theme of following Jesus constantly reappears." Hillmer, "They Believed in Him: Discipleship," 89.

70. The word ἀκολουθεῖν appears in the New Testament in the following order according to its number of occurrences: Matthew, 25 times; John, 19; Mark, 18; Luke, 17; Revelation, 6; Acts, 4; 1 Corinthians, 1.

71. Franzmann, *Follow Me: Discipleship*; Kingsbury, "The Verb *Akolouthein* ('To Follow')," 56–73; Best, *Following Jesus: Discipleship*; Stock, *Call to Discipleship*; Trakatellis, "'Ακολούθει μοι/Follow me' (Mark 2:14)," 271–85; Sweetland, *Our Journey with Jesus*; Kingsbury, "On Following Jesus," 45–59; Green, *The Way of the Cross*; Taylor, "Following Jesus Through Mark," 87–106; Wegener, *Cruciformed*; Shiner, *Follow Me! Disciples*; Meyer, "Taking Up the Cross," 230–38; Skinner, "Denying Self," 321–31; Mukasa, "The Blind Man of Jericho," 38–45.

72. Schnackenburg, *John*, 2:190.

B. The Scholarly Gap to be Filled

As presented in the Literature Review section, in the field of biblical studies, no substantial research has been devoted to develop the biblical theology of following Jesus in the Fourth Gospel by examining the entire profile of ἀκολουθεῖν. The research on the theological implications conveyed by ἀκολουθεῖν in connection with the ὅπου/ποῦ (where Jesus is/goes to) motif and other correlated motifs in the Gospel still remains unexplored territory. In the academic discipline of spirituality, there has been no literature that has studied the Spirituality of "following Jesus" by investigating the whole profile of the term ἀκολουθεῖν in the Fourth Gospel. The present research attempts to fill the gap in the fields of both biblical studies and Johannine Spirituality in relation to ἀκολουθεῖν.

III. Limitations of the Study and Points to Be Studied Further

The present study does not attempt to cover the whole scope of the theme of following Jesus in the Fourth Gospel. This study is devoted to exploring the distinctive Spirituality of following Jesus which is particularly communicated by the association of the term ἀκολουθεῖν with correlated motifs in the near context of pertaining texts of the Gospel. Therefore, the extent of its investigation is limited to the pericopes where ἀκολουθεῖν appears. The present research does not include the implications of following Jesus communicated by ὑπόδειγμα (example) and καθώς (just as) in 13:15 because ἀκολουθεῖν is not associated with them, and moreover, ἀκολουθεῖν appears only in the negative sense at the ending part of the chapter to indicate the inability of the disciples in following Jesus (13:36, 37). Although the role of the Holy Spirit is indispensable for the life of following Jesus (14:26; 16:13; 20:22; cf. Mark 13:11) just as it is crucial for Jesus' ministry (1:32; 3:34; cf. Matt 12:28; Luke 4:1, 14, 18), the discussion on the role of the Spirit in the life of following Jesus will be limited in this research because ἀκολουθεῖν is not directly associated with the Holy Spirit in the Fourth Gospel.

The pursuit of the Spirituality of "following Jesus" in this study will be limited in terms of providing a "how to" guide for the practice of Spirituality. As a study under academic discipline, my research will focus on explicating a biblical theology and the connotations of the Spirituality of "following Jesus" communicated by ἀκολουθεῖν in the texts of the Fourth Gospel. In engaging in theological synthesis and development of the Spirituality of "following Jesus," attention will be limited to the scope of Johannine Spirituality.

Spirituality from a psychological perspective, a historical point of view, and other religious views will not be incorporated.

In probing the texts pertaining to my aim, I am not concerned with the establishment of the texts from the viewpoint of textual criticism. Instead, the text of NA28 will be accepted as the loci of my exegesis and my development of the Spirituality of "following Jesus" according to the Fourth Gospel. I am not interested in source critical concerns either. Instead of wrestling with the various probabilities of composition and source-redaction theories, my research will be performed in the present canonical form of the Gospel as it is and as a "narrative unity."[73]

Further study in the Spirituality of following Jesus according to the Fourth Gospel, beyond the investigation of ἀκολουθεῖν in the current study, needs to investigate the following terms and motifs, or focus on the following approaches. First, καθώς (just as) is an important motif to be considered not only because it appears more frequently (31 times) in the Gospel than any other books in Scripture, but also because it conveys profound theological implications tied to following Jesus in the schema of Father-Son-disciples (5:23, 30; 6:57; 8:28; 10:15; 12:50; 13:15, 34; 14:31; 15:9 10, 12; 17:11, 14, 16, 18, 21, 22, 23; 20:21). Second, ἀποστέλλω (to send, 17:18; 20:21),[74] πέμπω (to send, 20:21),[75] and μαθητής (disciple, 8:31; 15:8)[76] are other terms to be examined. Third, the Spirituality of following Jesus ought to be studied in the context of each of the main figures of the Gospel. For instance, the Beloved Disciple, Nicodemus, the Samaritan woman, the blind man, and others, as Culpepper[77] lists in *Anatomy of the Fourth Gospel*, are each deserving of attention. Fourth, an investigation into the perspective of the role of the Holy Spirit (3:6, 8; 4:24; 6:63; 7:39; 14:17, 26; 15:26; 16:13; 20:22) will excavate other important dimensions of the Spirituality of following Jesus.

---

73. This is the approach that Culpepper employs in a fresh and technical way, applying the literary approach of Seymour Chatman to probe the literary elements of the Fourth Gospel as a narrative whole. This is found in Culpepper, *Anatomy*.

74. Among the New Testament books, ἀποστέλλω appears most in the Fourth Gospel (27 times). 1:16, 19, 24; 3:17, 28, 34; 4:38; 5:33, 36, 38; 6:29, 57; 7:29, 32; 8:42; 9:7; 10:36; 11:3, 42; 17:3, 8, 18, 21, 23, 25; 18:24; 20:21.

75. The Fourth Gospel is the book where πέμπω is employed most (31 times). 1:22, 33; 4:34; 5:23, 24, 30, 37; 6:38, 39, 44; 7:16, 18, 28, 33; 8:16, 18, 26, 29; 9:4, 12, 44, 45, 49; 13:16, 20; 14:24, 26; 15:21, 26; 16:5, 7; 20:21.

76. The word μαθητής occurs most frequently in the Fourth Gospel among the Gospel books (74 times in John; 71 in Matthew; 42 in Mark; 37 in Luke).

77. Culpepper, *Anatomy*, 115–25, 132–44.

IV. Methodology: A Literary-Theological Approach

An exegesis of a biblical text and a subsequent theological study of a specific motif require multi-dimensional tasks. One approach alone is not capable of expounding the full meaning of a text and its theological implications. To expound the meaning of a text and its theological connotations to the fullest extent, one has to perform studies in the combination of various approaches and criticisms, such as both the diachronic and synchronic approaches,[78] as well as both the historical-critical and literary-narrative approaches.[79] Yet, because it is nearly impossible to employ these diverse criticisms and methodologies in one study, I cannot but limit the methodology of the present study. I limit the method to the approaches that are concerned with the present text as it stands now in its final canonical form. I aim to "treat texts as finished wholes rather than as patchwork collections,"[80] as literary criticism does. Approaches that pay attention to the historical process of the composition and development of the text will not be employed.[81] Rather, assuming that "the text is sufficient in and of itself for the process of interpretation,"[82] I will investigate the text as a narrative whole by an exegetical approach[83] with the help of narrative analysis which is sensitive to settings, structure, ordering of events, point of view, causal links, characters, characterization, symbolism, progress and development of plot, and intertextuality including the Old Testament quotations

---

78. Nielsen, "Johannine Research," 11–30.

79. Powell notes four features of literary criticism: (i) it focuses on the finished form of the text; (ii) it emphasizes the unity of the text as a whole; (iii) it views the text as an end in itself; (iv) it is based on communication models of speech theory (in particular, a speech-act model proposed by Roman Jakobson). Powell, *What Is Narrative Criticism?*, 7–8.

From a different perspective, Bartlett divides the various approaches, in the history of biblical studies since Bultmann, into three ways: the world behind the text, the world in front of the text, and the world we bring to the text. Bartlett, "Interpreting and Preaching," 48–63.

80. Weima, "Literary Criticism," 151.

81. For a discussion on the theories of the composition and source-redaction of the text of the Fourth Gospel, refer to Smith, *The Composition and Order*; Fortna, *The Gospel of Signs*; Carson, "Current Source Criticism," 411–29; Brown, *The Community*; Smith, *Johannine Christianity*; Fortna, *Predecessor*; Brodie, *The Quest for the Origin*; Von Wahlde, *The Earliest Version of John's Gospel*; Von Wahlde, *The Gospel and Letters of John*.

82. Weima, "Literary Criticism," 153.

83. The exegetical method is drawn from two exegesis guide books: Fee, *New Testament Exegesis*; Stuart, *Old Testament Exegesis*.

and allusions.[84] This work will be engaged in structural analysis to outline sentence structure and syntactical relations. It will also engage in literary-discourse analysis to recognize literary features and rhetorical devices in order to identify the author's effective way of communication, and it will engage in lexical and semantic analysis to examine words, phrases, allusions, images, and concepts. I will also endeavor to interpret the text not only in the scope of a small unit, but also in the larger context of the Fourth Gospel where necessary, and even beyond that, in the canonical context because the Gospel is a part of the canonical Scripture. The interpretation of the text in the wider canonical context will help to explicate how the references or allusions employed in the text are interconnected to the usage of other Books of Scripture and how the other usages of the words, concepts, or allusions shed light on their meaning in the research texts. In this course of literary-theological engagement, I expect to discover what distinctive implications of following Jesus are communicated by ἀκολουθεῖν in its association with correlating motifs, and the Spirituality of following Jesus into which the fourth evangelist invites the readers by the text.

---

84. Powell, "Narrative Criticism," 239–55. For succinct descriptions of narrative criticism as compared to structuralism, rhetorical criticism, and reader-response criticism, see Powell, *What Is Narrative Criticism?*, 11–21.

CHAPTER 2

Spirituality

A Brief Reasoning, Understanding,
and Application in this Research

INTEREST IN "SPIRITUALITY" HAS been rapidly growing both in academia as one of academic disciplines and in the field of the devotional practice of religions. As evidence of the growing trend, Schneiders points out that in "the original edition of *The Catholic Encyclopedia* (1913–22)[1] there was no article under the heading 'spirituality,'" but in "the current edition of *The New Catholic Encyclopedia*[2] there are eight articles with the 'spirituality' in their titles and thirteen references to spirituality in the index."[3] Since 1977 Paulist Press has published over 130 volumes of monographs under the project entitled "Classics of Western Spirituality." In 1983 *The Westminster Dictionary of Christian Spirituality*[4] was published and updated dictionaries on spirituality followed as reference tools for spirituality.[5] In 1987 The Crossroad Publishing Company launched to publish monographs under the series titled "World Spirituality: An Encyclopedic History of the Religious Quest" which, in addition to Christian spirituality, cover various sects such as Buddhist, Confucian, Hindu, Islamic, Jewish, and modern esoteric spiritualities. Today, a countless number of scholarly journal articles and monographs are being published with increasing speed. Interest in and searching for "spirituality" is a popular phenomenon everywhere—the religious field,

---

1. Herbermann et al., eds., *Catholic Encyclopedia*.
2. Catholic University of America staff, ed., *New Catholic Encyclopedia*.
3. Schneiders, "Theology and Spirituality," 256.
4. Wakefield, ed., *Westminster Dictionary of Christian Spirituality*.
5. Sheldrake, ed., *New Westminster Dictionary of Christian Spirituality*; Downey, ed., *New Dictionary of Catholic Spirituality*; Scorgie et al., *Dictionary of Christian Spirituality*.

academia, and even in the secular world. It is no longer novel to hear people say that they are "spiritual, though not religious."

Although "spirituality" receives such ever-increasing attention, there is no consensus on the definition of spirituality. This is due to its character of unavoidable ambiguity and inclusiveness. It is necessary, therefore, to look into the definition of spirituality by surveying some already-known popular definitions, and then to propose a working definition for the present study. The relation of spirituality with theology and text will be considered as a foundation for the current study.

I. Understanding the Term Spirituality

The term "spirituality" has its origin in Christian usage and its root reference is to the presence and influence of the Holy Spirit.[6] The essential focus of the objective and content of spirituality in Christianity falls on entering, achieving, and enriching the relationship with God and the lived experience (experience of living out) of that relationship.

A. Prominent Authors on the Term Spirituality

1. Alister E. McGrath

Finding the etymology of "spiritual" from the Hebrew word *ruach* (a term translated as "spirit," "breath," or "wind"), McGrath remarks that "[t]o talk about 'the spirit' is to discuss what gives life and animation to someone."[7] Considering the significance of the role and influence of the Holy Spirit (*ruach*) as that which generates, develops, and sustains the life of faith, it is not too great a leap to say that "spirituality" is about the life of faith; namely, that which drives and motivates the life of faith and which people find helpful in developing and sustaining it.[8] McGrath goes further in defining the term. He first ventures to articulate a basic definition of spirituality: "Spirituality concerns the quest for a fulfilled and authentic religious life, involving the bringing together of the ideas distinctive of that religion and the whole experience of living on the basis of and within the scope of that

---

6. Schneiders, "Theology and Spirituality," 258.
7. McGrath, *Christian Spirituality*, 1–2.
8. Ibid., 2.

religion."⁹ In this basic definition, that which takes its center is "a fulfilled and authentic religious life" and "the whole experience of living."

In defining "Christian spirituality," McGrath states that it "concerns the living out of the encounter with Jesus Christ." "The term 'Christian spirituality' refers to the way in which the Christian life is understood and the explicitly devotional practices which have been developed to foster and sustain that relationship with Christ."[10] Therefore, "Christian spirituality may be thus understood as the way in which Christian individuals or groups aim to deepen their experience of God, or to practice the presence of God."[11] McGrath submits a conclusive summary that "Christian spirituality is reflection on the whole Christian enterprise of achieving and sustaining a relationship with God."[12]

From what has been said by McGrath, it appears apparent that spirituality is the quest for a fulfilled and authentic life. Furthermore, the central ideas that comprise spirituality in Christianity include developing and sustaining a relationship with Jesus and God and the experience of living out of that relationship.

2. Sandra M. Schneiders

According to Schneiders, the adjective "spiritual" (*pneuma* in Greek), from which the substantive "spirituality" is derived, is a Christian neologism that the Apostle Paul coined in his Epistles. It was used to denote that which is associated with the manifestation of or influenced by the Holy Spirit of God. For instance, "spiritual persons" (1 Cor 2:13, 15), "spiritual blessings" (Eph 1:3; Rom 15:27), "spiritual things" (1 Cor 9:11), "spiritual truths" (1 Cor 2:13), "the law is spiritual" (Rom 7:14), "spiritual gifts" (1 Cor 12:1), "spiritual songs" (Eph 5:19), and "spiritual wisdom and understanding" (Col 1:9). Among these examples, the most outstanding use appears in contrast between the "spiritual person" (ὁ πνευματικὸς) and the "natural person" (ψυχικὸς ἄνθρωπος) in 1 Cor 2:14–15. Here, the contrast is not between a living person (a person with a human spirit in the sense of soul) and a dead person (a person who lacks a soul). Both the "spiritual" person and the "unspiritual" person are alive, possessed of body and soul. That which determines whether a person is spiritual or unspiritual is the fact of whether a person is influenced, controlled, and led by the Spirit of

---

9. Ibid.
10. Ibid., 2–3
11. Ibid.
12. Ibid.

God. In other words, the "spiritual" person is the one who "is indwelt by the Holy Spirit of God."[13]

Although in its original use, when it was coined by Paul, the term "spiritual" was tightly associated with the influence of the Holy Spirit of God, it "has become a generic term for the living of the human capacity for self-transcendence, regardless of whether that experience is religious or not."[14] To put it another way, "spirituality has lost its explicit reference to the influence of the Holy Spirit and come to refer primarily to the activity of human spirit."[15] Therefore, "spirituality refers to the experience of consciously striving to integrate one's life in terms not of isolation and self-absorption but of self-transcendence toward the ultimate value one perceives."[16] Elsewhere she elaborates the definition to be more specific: "spirituality is the actualization of the basic human capacity for transcendence in and through the experience of conscious involvement in the project of life-integration through self-transcendence toward the horizon of ultimate value one perceives."[17] Spirituality is "available to every human being who is seeking to live an authentically human life."[18]

Schneiders admits that there is no standard or generally accepted definition for "Christian spirituality," just as there is no universally accepted definition for "spirituality." Her multi-layered proposal, however, is a helpful one: "Christian spirituality," she argues, is "primarily 'the *lived experience* of Christian faith,'"[19] and secondly "the *academic discipline* which studies this existential phenomenon *as* religious and *as* experience."[20] The primary definition of Christian spirituality as an activity of human life is an "engagement with the Absolute (in which case the spirituality would be religious) in

---

13. Schneiders, "Theology and Spirituality," 257–60; Schneiders, "Spirituality in the Academy," 680–81.

14. Schneiders, "Religion and Spirituality," 4.

15. Ibid.

16. Ibid., "Theology and Spirituality," 266.

17. Ibid., "Biblical Spirituality: Text and Transformation," 129.

18. Ibid., "Spirituality in the Academy," 682.

19. That is, "the subjective appropriation of faith and resultant living of discipleship in its individual and corporate actualization(s)." Schneiders, "Biblical Spirituality: Text and Transformation," 128–29.

20. Ibid., 129. It is to be noted that "spirituality as an academic discipline" is *not* a lived experience of God, a divine reality, or the Christian faith itself, but a *study* of spirituality as an intellectual enterprise. However, it needs to be kept in mind that "the study of spirituality impacts lived spirituality" (Waaijman, *Spirituality*, 311). On this point, Schneiders ("Spirituality in the Academy," 695) writes, "[R]esearch in the area of spirituality is self-implicating, often at a very deep level, and the transformation experienced through study reverberates in the ongoing research."

the person of Jesus Christ through the gift of the Holy Spirit (in which case the spirituality would be Christian)."[21] "The ultimate horizon" of Christian faith is "the triune God revealed in Jesus Christ into whose divine life we are incorporated by the gift (grace) of the Spirit."[22]

In addition to the definitions of "spirituality" and "Christian spirituality," it is worthwhile to note what "biblical Spirituality" means. Though there could be additional meanings, Schneiders proposes three.[23] The first meaning she offers is perhaps the most fundamental: "Biblical Spirituality refers to the *spiritualities that come to expression in the Bible* and witness to patterns of relationship with God that instruct and encourage our own religious experience."[24] Secondly, the term biblical Spirituality "designates a *pattern of Christian life* deeply imbued with the spirituality(ies) of the Bible."[25] It can refer to "an integrated contemporary spirituality that is markedly biblical in character"[26] although not all Christian spiritualities are equally biblical. Thirdly, biblical Spirituality is "*a transformative process of personal and communal engagement with the biblical text.*"[27] The transformative process transpires when the biblical text is approached and meditated on as the Word of God in a serious pursuit of "entering into relationship with God,"[28] not as a collection of historical events or religious literature.

3. Philip Sheldrake

As for the etymological root of the term "spirituality," Sheldrake, in the article, "What is Spirituality?," states that the Latin root of the word *spiritualitas* "attempts to translate the Greek noun for spirit, *pneuma*, and its adjective

---

21. Ibid., 682.

22. Schneiders, "Biblical Spirituality," 134.

23. Ibid., 134–36.

24. There are a variety of biblical spiritualities imbedded in the Scriptures. These include "the dialogical spirituality of the deuteronomistic tradition" in which Yahweh the God of covenant "intervenes directly and participates in" the history of the covenant people Israel, "the spirituality expressed in the prayer and poetry of the Psalms that have been practiced by Christians in the light of the mystery of Christ," "the profoundly Christocentric spirituality of Paul," "the contemplative Jesus-centered spirituality of John," "the ecclesiastical spirituality of the pastorals," and "the apocalyptic spirituality of the Revelation." Ibid., 135.

25. Ibid.

26. Ibid.

27. Ibid., 135–36.

28. Ibid., 136.

pneumatikos as they appear in the New Testament Pauline letters."[29] As he argues, "to be united to Christ is to enter into the sphere of the Spirit" (1 Cor 6:17) and "faith in the Lord is from and in the Spirit" (1 Cor 2:10f.). Upon the basis of the etymological origin, Sheldrake remarks that "the 'spiritual' is what is under the influence of, or is a manifestation of, the Spirit of God."[30] This is quite similar to those understandings offered by Schneiders.

After mentioning the original usages of the Pauline Epistles, Sheldrake briefly surveys the history[31] of how the term[32] "spirituality" has been perceived and used. First, he notes that "the Latin noun *spiritualitas* (spirituality), as opposed to the adjective *spiritualis* (spiritual)," did not appear until the fifth century when St. Jerome, in a letter ascribed to him, "exhorts the reader so to act as to advance in 'spirituality' (*ut in spiritualitate proficias*)."[33] The original meaning of the term, as closely associated with living by the influence of the Spirit of God just as described in the Pauline Epistles, was maintained until the twelfth century.[34]

In the twelfth century, under the influence of scholasticism, as a new philosophical trend in theology, in which a sharp distinction between spirit and matter became apparent, the term "'spiritual' began to be applied to intelligent creatures as opposed to non-rational creation" and "corporeality" disdaining the body. The original understanding of the Pauline concept faded away gradually over the next few centuries.[35]

In the seventeenth century, the term appeared in France "in reference to the spiritual life," which expressed "a personal, affective relationship with God."[36] Yet, it did not receive positive attention, but the term was used "pejoratively of enthusiastic or quietistic movements."[37] In the eighteenth and nineteenth centuries, various terms were used to describe the spiritual life in relationship to God and devoted religious life. Terms such as "devotion,"[38]

29. Sheldrake, "What is Spirituality?," 23.

30. Ibid.

31. If one is interested in the historical survey of the characteristics of spirituality in each era, refer to the six articles in Part III of *The Blackwell Companion to Christian Spirituality*. Holder, ed., *Blackwell Companion to Christian Spirituality*, 71–174.

32. For another survey on the history of the use of the term, refer to Principe, "Toward Defining Spirituality," 44–47.

33. Sheldrake, "What is Spirituality?," 24.

34. Ibid.

35. Ibid.

36. Ibid.

37. Ibid.

38. Cf. Waaijman, *Spirituality*, 345–48. "The basic word 'devotion' (devotio, bhakti, islam) situates the reality of spirituality in the field of tension between an inward attitude

"piety,"[39] "godliness," and "perfection" were employed. However, the term "spirituality" did not appear in the mainstream religious or theological realm, except for in the groups outside the mainline churches.

In the early twentieth century, the term "spirituality" emerged among "Roman Catholics in France and then passed into English through translations of French writings."[40] It was used to distinguish "between dogma and the study of the spiritual life" with an "increasing emphasis on religious consciousness and the experiential."[41] As noted above, over the past few decades, the term "spirituality" has been used more intensely than in any other century.

After surveying the history of "spirituality" according to eras and traditions, Sheldrake conclusively remarks, "Spirituality is understood to include . . . a conscious relationship with God, in Jesus Christ, through the indwelling of the Spirit and in the context of the community of believers."[42] In another place, he submits a definition of spirituality: "It describes the ways that individuals and groups seek to enter into a conscious relationship with God, to worship, to formulate their deepest values and to create appropriate lifestyles in dialogue with their beliefs about God, the human person and creation."[43]

(dedication, surrender) with vivid affective colors (inwardness, fervency) on the one hand, and external practices (rituals, prayers, times, places, objects) on the other."

39. Cf. Ibid., 348–50. "The basic word 'piety' interprets the reality of spirituality as a sensitive but strong attachment to God and his creatures. This attitude is inwardly aimed at permeating all sectors of life: the relation to God, the life of society, and one's personal lifestyle. Moreover, it encompasses all the layers of human conduct: the inner affections, a heartfelt reverence, the shaping of one's personal life, an authentic life praxis, and trustworthy religiousness." When one refers to J. I. Packer's summary statement on the definition of "true piety" according to Jonathan Edwards, the Puritan theologian and philosopher, one will notice that there is considerable similarity between "true piety" and spirituality. "True piety was to him a supernatural gift, dynamic in character and intensely experimental in its outworking. It was, in fact, a realized communion with God through Christ, brought into being by the Holy Spirit and expressed in responsive affections and activities." Packer, *A Quest for Godliness*, 311. By the term "true piety," Edwards imparts what spirituality points to.

40. Sheldrake, "What is Spirituality?," 25.

41. Ibid.

42. Ibid., 40.

43. Sheldrake, "The Study of Spirituality," 162.

4. Kees Waaijman

In Part 2[44] of his massive monograph, *Spirituality: Forms, Foundations, Methods*, Waaijman deals with the term "spirituality"[45] with the question, "What is spirituality?". He starts with noting that the basic word "'spirituality' has a comprehensive semantic range: it embraces the divine and human spirit; overarches asceticism and mysticism; integrates biblical tradition (*ruach*) with Hellenistic intuitions (*nous*); exceeds the boundaries of religions and philosophies of life."[46] While the semantic range of the term is widely inclusive, the "core process evoked by the term 'spirituality'" is one of relationship: it is, in short, "the dynamic relation between the divine Spirit and the human spirit."[47] The dynamic relation between the Spirit of God and the human spirit is a "relational whole in which the divine and human realities shape each other reciprocally"[48] through an intense personal and intimate relationship. This is possible only because God is not an impersonal deity but a God (the name is *Yahweh*) who is "intimately connected with the genesis of personhood"[49] and "companionately present in every person's life journey,"[50] and a human being is not only a soul (*nephesh*) that has an inner space which is "empty and seeks to be filled"[51] but also one who is "created after God's image and unto his likeness (Gen 1:26)"[52] as found in the *Imago-Dei*[53] motif.

The dynamic relational process between the Spirit of God and the human spirit produces "total transformation."[54] It is because the Spirit of God is the One who creates transformation, as Waaijman presents that the Spirit (*ruach*) of God is "creatively at work in all his creatures (Gen 1:2; Ps 104:30; Eccl 11:5), recreates them when they are injured or exhausted (Ps

---

44. In Part 2 of the monograph, Waaijman discusses on the fundamental characteristics of the area of spirituality and the object of research and the methodology of the discipline of spirituality. Waaijman, *Spirituality*, 307–589.

45. Similar to Schneiders's understanding, Waaijmann also views "spirituality" in two perspectives: the first is "lived spirituality" (spirituality understood in the light of its praxis) and the second is "the science of spirituality" (which is the discipline of spirituality that studies spiritual praxis with critical detachment).

46. Ibid., 360–61.
47. Ibid., 361.
48. Ibid., 425.
49. Ibid., 431.
50. Ibid.
51. Ibid., 438.
52. Ibid., 446.
53. Ibid., 446–54, 510–12.
54. Ibid., 362.

51:8–12; Ezek 37:2–10), liberates them from oppression (Judg 6:34; 3:10; 14:6, 9; 15:4), endows them with a spirit of wisdom (Isa 11:2) and justice, and redeems them in the end (Rom 8:21–27)."[55] The same Spirit (*pneuma*) of God, as stated in a Pauline Epistle, is the One who "moves people toward 'love, joy, peace, patience, friendliness, generosity, faithfulness, gentleness, and self-control' (Gal 5:22)" from the state of *sarx* that "denotes a spiritual attitude which is the same as that of the unclean spirit of the gospels: 'fornication, impurity, licentiousness, idolatry, sorcery, feuds, strife, jealousy, explosions of anger, self-seeking, dissension, factions, envy, drunkenness, carousing, and the like' (Gal 5:19; cf. 5:15–26; 6:3, etc.)."[56]

Waaijman goes further and expands the discussion on the divine-human transformation to five levels:[57] from transformation in creation (the transformation of God's creation of human beings from non-being to being) to transformation in re-creation (the transformation from malformation to reformation) to transformation in conformity (the transformation of form-appropriation which is being transformed by the Deity)[58] to transformation in love (the highest state attainable in this life)[59] and to transformation in glory[60] (a process people situate on the other side of death). For Waaijman, "transformation"[61] occupies an essential part in the definition of spirituality: as he writes, "contemporary authors frequently use the word 'transformation' precisely in the places where they seek to conceptualize spirituality in terms of its essence."[62]

In a nutshell, "spirituality," according to Waaijman, is the divine-human relational process which is also a layered process of transformation.[63]

---

55. Ibid., 361.

56. Ibid., 362.

57. Ibid., 455–81.

58. Which can be understood in relation to "conformity to Christ" as is expressed, "that Christ is formed in you" (Gal 4:19).

59. "In the transformation in love three distinct perspectives stand out: (a) the soul's outgoing movement toward God who draws it into himself; (b) the movement of God toward the soul to take up residence in it; (c) the intimacy of the Spirit who holds sway between the two, a reality which is called 'spiritual marriage.'" Waaijman, *Spirituality*, 469.

60. Ibid. "Transformation in glory 'will be effected perfectly in heaven, in life with God, in all those who merit seeing themselves in God.'"

61. Refer to Schneiders, Coleman, McGinn, Frohlich, and other scholarly works as Waaijman (ibid., 455–56) references them in footnotes 85–89.

62. Ibid., 455.

63. Ibid., 305, 425.

B. More Working Definitions

For a fuller understanding of the term "spirituality," it is worthwhile to make reference to some of the many working definitions offered by notable writers.[64]

George Ganss

Spirituality is a lived experience, the effort to apply relevant elements in the deposit of Christian faith to the guidance of men and women towards their spiritual growth, the progressive development of their persons which flowers into a proportionately increased insight and joy.[65]

Richard P. McBrien

Spirituality has to do with our experiencing of God and with the transformation of our consciousness and our lives as outcomes of that experience.[66]

Don A. Saliers

Spirituality refers to a *lived* experience and a disciplined life of prayer and action, but it cannot be conceived apart from the specific theological beliefs that are ingredients in the forms of life that manifest authentic Christian faith.[67]

William Stringfellow

Whatever else may be affirmed about a spirituality which has a biblical precedent and style, spiritual maturity or spiritual fulfillment necessarily involves the whole person—body, mind and soul, place, relationships—in connection with the whole of creation throughout the era of time. Biblical spirituality encompasses the whole person in the totality of existence in the world, not some fragment or scrap or incident of a person.[68]

---

64. A couple of authors are added to the list found in McGrath, *Christian Spirituality*, 3–4.
65. Ganss, Introduction to *Ignatius of Loyola*, 61.
66. McBrien, *Catholicism*, 1058.
67. Saliers, "Spirituality," 460.
68. Stringfellow, *Politics of Spirituality*, 22.

Richard Woods

[Spirituality] is the self-transcending character of all human persons, and everything that pertains to it, including, most importantly, the ways in which that perhaps infinitely malleable character is realized concretely in everyday life situations.[69]

Walter Principe

Spirituality, in this author's opinion, points to those aspects of a person's living a faith or commitment that concerns his or her striving to attain the highest ideal or goal. For a Christian this would mean his or her striving for an ever more intense union with the Father through Jesus Christ by living in the Spirit.[70]

Arthur Holder

[Spirituality is] the lived experience of Christian faith and discipleship.[71]

C. Summary

On the basis of the discussion above, I will provide a summary of the aspects of spirituality. At least three aspects of spirituality appear commonly in the definitions given by the scholars: (1) spirituality as an essential nature of human beings *(anthropological)*; (2) spirituality as a lived experience *(experiential)*; (3) spirituality as an engagement and relationship with God *(theological)*.

The first and most fundamental aspect, which applies to all human beings whether or not one is religious/Christian, is *spirituality as the essential nature of human beings*. This aspect reveals the *anthropological* dimension of spirituality as it is a universal pursuit of all human beings. It is expressed in the phrases made by scholars:

> "Seeking to live an authentically human life" (Schneiders)
>
> "The quest for a fulfilled and authentic religious life" (McGrath)
>
> "The self-transcending character of all human persons" (Woods)

---

69. Woods, *Christian Spirituality: God's Presence*, 9.
70. Principe, "Toward Defining Spirituality," 51.
71. Holder, Introduction to *Blackwell Companion to Christian Spirituality*, 1.

In these remarks, it is indicated that spirituality is "a quest for authentic life as a human being." Every human being longs to achieve self-transcendence beyond one's human limitations, and reach the state one is created to become.

The second aspect is *spirituality as the lived experience*. Most scholars include the wording, "lived experience," "living," "transformation," or "experiencing":

> "The lived experience" (Schneiders, Ganss, Saliers, Holder)
>
> "The living of the human capacity for self-transcendence" (Schneiders)
>
> "The experience of living out of the relationship" (McGrath)
>
> "To create appropriate lifestyles" (Sheldrake)
>
> "A person's living" (Principe)
>
> "To do with our experiencing" (McBrien)
>
> "A layered process of transformation" (Waaijman)
>
> "The transformation of our consciousness and our lives as outcomes of that experience" (McBrien)

These phrases convey the *experiential* dimension of spirituality as the existential life experience,[72] which brings in transformation and enhancement in actual daily life realities, as opposed to theoretic knowledge or dogma that remains in the capacity of the mind.

The third aspect is *spirituality as an engagement and relationship with God*. This dimension reveals that spirituality is essentially *theological* because it is necessarily in relation *with God*. Most of the above authors include "God" or "the Absolute" in defining the term spirituality:

> "Our relation to the Absolute" (Waaijman)
>
> "Engagement with the Absolute" (Schneiders)
>
> "Achieving and sustaining a relationship with God" (McGrath)
>
> "Entering into relationship with God" (Schneiders)
>
> "The divine-human relational process" (Waaijman)

---

72. For more discussions on spirituality and experience, refer to Hay, "Experience," 419–41.

"To seek to enter into a conscious relationship with God" (Sheldrake)

These phrases indicate that spirituality is indispensably associated with God (*theological*) and is possible by encountering and developing a relationship with God, who created human beings to become fully human through the dynamic conversation, interconnectedness, and relationship with him.

Spirituality is fundamentally *anthropological*, particularly *experiential*, and indispensably *theological*.

II. Spirituality: Its Relation to Theology

In this section, the relation of spirituality with theology will be considered. The term theology is coined by the combination of the two Greek words *theos* (god) and *logos* (word or discourse). Therefore, theology could be said to be "discourse about God."[73] According to the *Oxford Advanced Learner's Dictionary*, the definition of "theology" is "the study of the nature of God and religious belief." It is an intellectual enterprise and science that pursues a systematic understanding of God and reflection on the content of Christian faith.

Prior to the eighteenth century, there was no separation between the pursuit of an intellectual understanding of God and the pursuit of knowing God in intimate relationship with him and in Christian practices. McGrath states (quoting Edward Farley), "theology, in this classic sense of the term, is a 'heartfelt knowledge of divine things,' something which affects the heart and the mind."[74] According to John Calvin, "to know God is to be changed by God; true knowledge of God leads to worship, as the believer is caught up in a transforming and renewing encounter with the living God."[75] Similar to Calvin's view, for Thomas Aquinas, "theology had its origins in God, spoke of God, and led to God."[76] To be led to God indicates that one is led into a personal relationship with God in order to experience him in loving mutual relationship. However, after the eighteenth century, due to the character of objectivity and "detachment as essential to academic integrity"[77] in Western academia, theology has lost the "sight of the relational aspects of the

---

73. McGrath, *Christian Spirituality*, 26.
74. Ibid., 28.
75. Ibid.
76. Ibid., 31.
77. Ibid., 32.

Christian faith"[78] and the connection between doing theology and prayer, and theology as doxology or an act of worship.

Acknowledging the current trend of doing theology in Western academia (although the original purpose of theology is not to obtain the abstract and theoretical understanding of God in detachment), the relation between theology and spirituality can be said that the former is about the theory of Christian faith and God, and the latter the practice of the Christian life, as McGrath remarks.[79] Spirituality may be distinguished from theology in that the former is about the relational and experiential way of knowing God, whereas the latter is about the intellectual and theoretical way of knowing about God.

However, the two are mutually dependent, just as someone says, "theology gives substance to spirituality, and spirituality gives life to theology." In other words, "properly understood, theology embraces, informs, and sustains spirituality."[80] Theology is "the intellectual articulation of spirituality,"[81] while spirituality is the existential and experiential fruition of theology. There is no spirituality without theology, and no theology without spirituality. Theology and spirituality support and complete each other. As for the inter-dependent relationship between theology and spirituality, Schneiders writes, "[U]nless theology is grounded in the taste of mystery and in [the] search of God through conversion, it is empty and sterile. But unless spiritual experience is involved in the search for understanding and thus in the movement of reflection, it remains inarticulate for itself and for others."[82] Thus, it is no surprise to say, "only a theology that is rooted in the spiritual commitment of the theologian and oriented toward praxis will be meaningful in the church of the future."[83]

III. Spirituality Communicated in the Text

The intent of this study is to study the Spirituality of following Jesus implied and communicated by the term ἀκολουθεῖν in theological and literary association with correlated motifs in the texts of the Fourth Gospel. Because its task is to write the Spirituality of the biblical text, it is necessary to identify

---

78. Ibid., 31.
79. Ibid., 25.
80. Ibid., 27.
81. Schneiders, "Biblical Spirituality," 135.
82. Schneiders, "Spirituality in the Academy," 677–78n9.
83. Ibid., 677.

the possible relations between the biblical text and Spirituality, and present the dimension of Spirituality which will be investigated in this study.

According to Schneiders, there are at least three Spiritualities in relation to the text: (1) the Spirituality that produced the text (discerned by exegesis and criticism); (2) the Spirituality in the text (the subject of biblical theology/Spirituality); (3) the Spirituality the text produces (hermeneutical engagement).[84]

First, the Spirituality that produced the text: It is the Spirituality *behind* the text. It reflects the religious experience of the faith group or community that functioned as the matrix of the birth of the text and influenced the process of the composition of the text. This type of Spirituality is, for instance, the Exodus Spirituality that was experienced by the people in the historical event of passing through and at the shore of the Red Sea, the Spirituality of the community led by Nehemiah and Ezra that the people might experience it in the process of rebuilding the Temple and the walls of the city, or the Spirituality of the Matthean community, which influenced the process of the composition of the Matthean text. These kinds of Spirituality can be traced and reconstructed by the method of historical criticism. Yet, behind the text and rarely stated explicitly, these are unavoidably hypothetical in their nature.

Second, the Spirituality *in* the text: It is the Spirituality that is expressed or implied in the text. In its nature, Spirituality is not hypothetical because it is communicated in the Scripture text as it presently stands. As for this Spirituality, Schneiders elaborates:

> In the text as it now stands there are certain relatively coherent and integrated patterns of religious experience, which seem to have certain characteristic features. These may be associated with a particular author (real or attributed), book, tradition (e.g., Pauline, Deuteronomistic, prophetic, or apocalyptic spirituality), or with themes or motifs that seem to represent a characteristic way of relating to God, such as wisdom, covenant, creation, atonement, or kenotic spirituality.[85]

All these Spiritualities are found and imparted *in* the biblical text. They are close to and in many ways indistinguishable from the task and subject of biblical theology.

Third, the Spirituality *before* the text: It is the Spirituality that the text produces in the life of the readers. It is the Spirituality experienced by the

---

84. In formulating the three categories of Spirituality presented here, I relied heavily on Schneiders, "Biblical Spirituality: Text and Transformation," 130–34.

85. Ibid., 130–31.

readers in the process of the appropriation of the implications or messages of a Scripture text through their continuing engagement and interaction with it. This kind of Spirituality may not be greatly different from the Spirituality communicated in the text because it is essentially produced by the text. Yet, it is more like applied Spirituality because it is the product of the hermeneutical engagement with the text.[86] In the process of the hermeneutical interaction with the text, the life situations, issues, prior knowledge, or experiences of the readers get in, affecting their reading of the text. In essence the Spirituality before the text can be said to be homogeneous with the Spirituality in the text; yet, in its final appearance it is different and even unique because it emerges clothed with the garment of the life setting of the time. Its distinction depends on the dialogue between the text and the readers, the attitude of the readers on how to engage with the text, and the approach, that is, whether the readers are pulled into the text or they pull the text to the dynamics and concerns of their life by stretching the implications of the text.

IV. Closing

On the basis of the discussions of the term "spirituality," I submit a working definition for the present study. In short, Spirituality is the lived experience of God and divine reality. To expand on this statement, Spirituality is the lived experience of an authentic human life by a lively relationship with God who revealed himself in Christ Jesus, preserved this revelation of himself in Scripture, and continues revealing himself through Scripture by the illumination of the Holy Spirit.

The term "Spirituality" is capitalized in this study for the purpose of distinction. "Spirituality" as it is employed in the present study refers to that distinct Spirituality which is particularly rooted in the revelation of God through Jesus and the Holy Spirit as preserved in Scripture. Yet, it lacks the modifier, "biblical," because "Spirituality" includes the anthropological aspect of the general term "spirituality" as that quest whereby human beings seek to experience authentic human life.

The current study is neither concerned with the Spirituality *behind* the text,[87] nor with the Spirituality *before* the text. The task of this study is

---

86. In regard to a spiritual hermeneutic in the engagement with the text ("the praxis of spiritual reading"), refer to Waaijman, *Spirituality*, 690–771.

87. Only as a preliminary step will the socio-historical data be surveyed in chapter 3 of the present study in order to provide a historical environment in which the fourth evangelist communicates the Spirituality of following Jesus by ἀκολουθεῖν.

similar to that of writing a biblical theology because the present study seeks to investigate (biblical) Spirituality *in* the text, which is expressed and communicated in the Johannine text and into which the fourth evangelist pulls his readers by the employment of the term ἀκολουθεῖν in literary-theological association with correlated motifs.

CHAPTER 3

Socio-Historical Background of the Fourth Gospel

THE PURPOSE OF THIS chapter is to delineate the social and historical life setting of the Fourth Gospel as far as the text testifies and alludes to it. It is to set the socio-historical context for the development of the Spirituality of "following Jesus" according to the Gospel. Scholars have suggested various theories for the history and nature of the Johannine community since the significant work of Martyn.[1] Yet, none of the suggestions are exempt from critique for their undeniably hypothetical nature. My task in this chapter is not to deal with the detailed history of the ongoing discussions of the Johannine community. Rather, it is to briefly introduce the past theories, and delineate, from textual evidence, the socio-historical background of the Fourth Gospel. This background, I will argue, focuses on suffering as the life setting for the first-century followers of Jesus. Acknowledging the limitation of information to reconstruct the details of the *Sitz im Leben* of the Johannine community, I will endeavor to collect textual data in the Gospel and define suffering and persecution as one of the critical social setting of the first-century Christian disciples in the Gospel. The finding of social circumstances will be used in the following chapters as the historical backdrop to the Spirituality of following Jesus.

I. Various Theories of the Johannine Community

Through his influential work, *History and Theology in the Fourth Gospel*, Martyn triggered significant impetus for research into the Johannine community. In the monograph he argues that the Gospel is a "two-level drama"[2] that presents the historical milieu of both the time of Jesus and

1. Martyn, *History and Theology*.
2. For recent criticism of the theory of a "two-level drama," see the article: Hägerland,

that of the Johannine community. The Gospel "no longer simply dealt with the narrative of Jesus in Galilee or Jerusalem alone, but also reflected the situation of the Johannine Christians decades later in other places. By telling the story of Jesus in this particular way, the Jesus-events are integrated with the history of these Christians dating from decades later—truly a *two-level drama*."[3] As the blind man in John 9 was put out of the synagogue because he refused to deny his faith in Jesus, the Johannine Church also was expelled from the synagogue under the Jewish practice of *birkat-ha-minim* (the cursing of heretics) in the synagogue.

Culpepper's concept of the "Johannine school"[4] attempts to define the nature of the Johannine community by comparing the characteristics of the Johannine writings with those of ancient Greek philosophical schools and Jewish religious schools. After considering these shared characteristics, Culpepper concludes that the Johannine community was a school.

Cullmann's concept of the "Johannine circle"[5] traces the origin of the Johannine community to the early Christianity of Jesus' ministry and to "the conversion of members of a heterodox, marginal Judaism."[6] The community, according to Cullmann, was related to Hellenistic Christians that were from marginalized Judaism and shared some contacts with Qumran Judaism, the Baptist sect, and the Samaritans.

Having been influenced by Martyn's hypothesis, Brown proposes a four stage history for the "Johannine community" in his monograph,[7] wherein he contends that the Johannine community experienced persecution and expulsion from the synagogue. This was followed by a schism within the community as the Johannine Epistles reflect. According to Brown, the historical factors of the Johannine community in the process of its development influenced the composition of the Fourth Gospel.

Meeks, in his important article, "The Man from Heaven in Johannine Sectarianism,"[8] characterizes the Johannine community as an isolated sectarian social group. According to Meeks, the Gospel "describes the progressive alienation of Jesus from the Jews" and "defines and vindicates the existence of the community that evidently sees itself as unique, alien from

---

"John's Gospel: A Two-Level Drama?," 309–22.
    3. Van der Watt, *An Introduction to the Johannine*, 114.
    4. Culpepper, *The Johannine School*.
    5. Cullmann, *The Johannine Circle*.
    6. Kysar, "Community and Gospel," 356.
    7. Brown, *The Community of the Beloved Disciple*.
    8. Meeks, "The Man from Heaven," 44–72.

its world, under attack, misunderstood, but living in unity with Christ and through him with God."[9]

Cassidy in his monograph[10] suggests that the Johannine community was facing persecution from Roman power[11] for its Christian faith without reference to any unacceptable social behaviors. To prove his argument Cassidy presents the correspondence between Pliny and Trajan the emperor and John's intentional choice of Jesus' titles ("Savior of the world," "Lord," and "Lord and God") which were used of Roman emperors and the deliberate construction of the narrative of the Roman trial of Jesus.

Recent scholarship on the Johannine community is noteworthy, particularly the arguments of Reinhartz, Bauckham, and Fuglseth. Against Martyn's expulsion theory, Reinhartz argues[12] that the Fourth Gospel "implies at least three different models of the historical relationship between the Johannine community and the Jewish community."[13] As the basis of other possible models of the relationship between these two communities, Reinhartz refers to the narrative of 11:1–44 where members of the Johannine community were comforted by some Jews, and the fact that the believers chose to separate themselves from the Jews deserting the synagogue as in 12:11.

Bauckham argues that the Gospels were written to be circulated; that is, they were not composed for any one specific community, but rather they were meant to be circulated among the churches for general readership.[14] If Bauckham's argument is correct, the socio-historical circumstances described in the Gospel pertain not only to the Johannine community, but also to that of the general churches in the socio-historical milieu of the late first century. As he states, "The Gospels have a historical context, but that context is not the evangelist's community. It is the early Christian movement in the late first century."[15]

Another fresh yet contentious view on the Johannine community is that proposed by Fuglseth over against the widely assumed "sectarian"

---

9. Ibid., 68–70.

10. Cassidy, *John's Gospel in New Perspective*.

11. Cf. Brown and Moloney acknowledge in the notes of 16:2 that there is a possibility of reference to Roman persecution. Yet, both of them give more weight to the killing of Christians, as serving God is mostly related to the Jews and therefore "the writer is thinking of Jewish persecution of Christians rather than of Roman persecution." Brown, *John*, 2:691. See also Moloney, *John*, 435.

12. Reinhartz, "The Johannine Community, 111–38.

13. Ibid., 121.

14. Bauckham, "For Whom Were the Gospels Written?," 9–48.

15. Ibid., 46.

view. In his monograph, *Johannine Sectarianism in Perspective*,[16] Fuglseth employs sociological criticism and presents three models (rejection, acceptance, and conjunction),[17] each of which correlates to the response of one of three groups (the communities of Qumran, Philo, and John) to the outsiders and to the Jerusalem temple. He concludes that whereas the Qumran community is sectarian and the Philo community is more accepting, the Johannine community is "neither exclusive 'sect' nor a mere inclusive group."[18] It is rather a "cult" community which represents the beginning of a new and innovative religion based on new insight and revelation proffered by the Johannine Jesus.[19]

In summary, the nature and historical context of the Johannine community has multi-dimensional aspects and characteristics. Yet, among the various aspects of its life setting, there are three important dimensions that draw my attention in relation to the present study: One, that the Christian community experienced traumatic conflict in Jewish society, including their expulsion from the synagogue, severe persecution, and life threatening suffering delivered by their own countrymen; two, that the community suffered persecution from Roman power; and three, that the community, as a unique religious group misunderstood and attacked by outsiders, was struggling to continue its life "in unity with Christ and through him with God."[20] In the midst of the challenging life setting of this particular religious, social, and political milieu, the first-century Christian believers in John needed an ongoing support for corroborating their Christian identity; they also needed theological confirmation for rejuvenating their existence as the followers of Jesus.

II. Suffering as the Historical Life Setting of the Johannine Community

In this section, I will observe the textual data of the Fourth Gospel to examine how the texts reflect suffering and persecution as one of the critical life settings for Jesus' followers in the Gospel. The focus will be on the suffering of Jesus and the first-century disciples. The main passages to be examined are (1) 5:15–18; 7:1, 7, 19, 25; 8:37–47; (2) 9:22, 34; and (3) 15:18–16:4a.

---

16. Fuglseth, *Johannine Sectarianism in Perspective*.
17. Ibid., 175.
18. Ibid., 372.
19. Ibid., 55, 372.
20. Meeks, "The Man from Heaven," 70.

The first three texts (1) concern the intention of the Jews[21] to kill Jesus; the fourth text (2) concerns the persecution of Jesus' followers during the life-time of Jesus; and the last text (3) highlights the coming persecution of Jesus' followers.

Why is it necessary to begin with the texts that depict the persecution of Jesus? It is necessary because the followers share the life and destiny of the one followed. The life of Jesus' followers is the continuation of the life of Jesus whom they follow. They will be experiencing the same persecution and suffering that their Lord faced (15:18–21). Therefore, in order to understand this persecution as a historical situation in the lives of Jesus' followers, it is necessary to begin with the historical reality of the persecution that Jesus experienced.

My investigation of these pericopes is not to implement a detailed exegesis of each text. It will be limited to an examination of the nature and characteristics of the suffering and persecution of Jesus and his followers which will be driven by the following questions: (1) In what way and to what degree did Jesus and his followers suffer persecution?; (2) why were Jesus and his followers persecuted?; and (3) how did Jesus react to the suffering? And how did Jesus encourage his followers to respond to this suffering?

Before examining the texts, it is worthwhile to organize, in a table, the verses and the key terms according to the objects of suffering and persecution. The key terms that demonstrate the suffering of Jesus and his followers are διώκω (to persecute), ἀποκτείνω (to kill), μισέω (to hate), and ἀποσυνάγωγος (expelled from the synagogue).[22]

---

21. As for the referent of "the Jews" (οἱ Ἰουδαῖοι), Kysar (*Maverick*, 82) succinctly states, "'The Jews' often refers to the religious authorities, to be sure, but the term also includes a wider class of opponents. 'The Jews' are stylized types of those who reject Christ, and that usage illuminates this strange category. The specific ethnic characteristic is lost in the Fourth Gospel." For further discussions of οἱ Ἰουδαῖοι, see von Wahlde, "The Johannine 'Jews,'" 33–60; Culpepper, *Anatomy*, 125–32; Brown, *An Introduction to the Gospel of John*, 157–72; von Wahlde, "'The Jews' in the Gospel of John," 30–55; Bennema, "The Identity and Composition," 239–63; Reinhartz, "Judaism in the Gospel of John," 382–93.

22. Other terms that indicate the same theme are (1) θλῖψις which is used for the disciples' life in this world in 16:33 "In the world you will have *tribulation*" (ESV); "In the world you have *trouble and suffering*" (NET); "In the world you face persecution" (NRSV); and (2) φόβος in 7:13, "Yet no one would speak openly about him *for fear of the Jews*"; 19:38, "After these things, Joseph of Arimathea, who was a disciple of Jesus, though a secret one because of *his fear of the Jews*, asked Pilate to let him take away the body of Jesus"; 20:19, "When it was evening on that day, the first day of the week, and the doors of the house where the disciples had met were locked *for fear of the Jews*, Jesus came and stood among them and said, 'Peace be with you.'"

Terms	Related to Jesus
διώκω	5:16 Therefore the Jews <u>started persecuting Jesus</u>, because he was doing such things on the sabbath.
	15:20 If they <u>persecuted me</u>, . . .
ἀποκτείνω	5:18 For this reason the Jews <u>were seeking all the more to kill him</u>, . . .
	7:1 He did not wish to go about in Judea because the Jews <u>were looking for an opportunity to kill him</u>.
	7:19 Why are you <u>looking for an opportunity to kill me</u>?
	7:25 Now some of the people of Jerusalem were saying, 'Is not this the man whom they are <u>trying to kill</u>?'
	8:37 I know that you are descendants of Abraham; yet you <u>look for an opportunity to kill me</u>, because there is no place in you for my word.
	8:40 but now you <u>are trying to kill me</u>, a man who has told you the truth that I heard from God.
	11:53 So from that day on they <u>planned to put him to death</u>.
μισέω	7:7 The world cannot hate you, but it <u>hates me</u> because I testify against it that its works are evil.
	15:18 If the world hates you, be aware that it <u>hated me</u> before it hated you.
	15:23–25 Whoever <u>hates me</u> <u>hates my Father</u> also. . . . But now they have seen and <u>hated both me and my Father</u>. It was to fulfill the word that is written in their law, 'They <u>hated me</u> without a cause.'

Terms	Related to disciples
διώκω	15:20 . . . they <u>will persecute you</u>.
ἀποκτείνω	12:10 So the chief priests <u>planned to put Lazarus to death as well</u>.
	16:2 Indeed, an hour is coming when those who <u>kill you</u> will think that by doing so they are offering worship to God.

Terms	Related to disciples
μισέω	15:18,19 If the world <u>hates you</u>, be aware that it hated me before it hated you. . . . Because you do not belong to the world, but I have chosen you out of the world—therefore the world <u>hates you</u>. 17:14 the world <u>has hated them</u> because they do not belong to the world, just as I do not belong to the world.
ἀποσυνάγωγος	9:22 . . . for the Jews had already agreed that anyone who confessed Jesus to be the Messiah would be <u>put out of the synagogue</u>. 9:34 And they <u>drove him out</u>. 12:42 But because of the Pharisees they did not confess it, for fear that they would be <u>put out of the synagogue</u>; 16:2 They will <u>put you out of the synagogues.</u>

A closer look will be given to the pericopes that contain the listed terms in order to examine the nature and characteristics of the suffering, the reasons and mode of the persecution, how Jesus faced it, and how Jesus' followers are expected to face it.

A. 5:15–18

On a Sabbath during a festival of the Jews, Jesus healed a man who had been ill for thirty-eight years. When it was reported to the Jews that it was Jesus who healed the man, they started persecuting (διώκω) him. The persecution came from religious leaders of Jesus' own nation for whom he was sent from the Father, to whom he was preaching the truth and revealing the Father (1:10–11, 18; 8:40). Although the tension between Jesus and the world was alluded in 1:5, 10–11 by the world's ignorance and refusal of Jesus, the conflict between Jesus and the Jews started with Jesus' cleansing of the temple (2:18–19) and began to impose distress on his activities (4:1–3). Yet, in the present text the fourth evangelist for the first time mentions that from this point the Jews[23] "began[24] persecuting Jesus" (5:16).

23. According to the employment of the term οἱ Ἰουδαῖοι in the Fourth Gospel (and following most translations: NRSV, RSV, ESV, NAU, NKJ, NJB, and NAB), the present study uses the term "the Jews" to refer to those who persecuted Jesus and sought to kill him.

24. NAB, NET, NIV, NJB, and NRSV make the meaning apparent by rendering

In 5:15–18 the two important terms διώκω (to persecute) and ἀποκτείνω (to kill) appear together. The verb διώκω[25] is employed in two verses in the Fourth Gospel: twice with Jesus as the object of persecution (5:16; 15:20) and once with the disciples (15:20). In its first use in 5:16 for the persecution of Jesus, the verb is used in imperfect tense indicating the action of the persecution was not temporal, but "ongoing and repeated."[26] Even though the verb does not appear often in the Gospel afterward, from that point on, "the persecution of Jesus is a constant theme reverberating through the Gospel until the climax is reached in the Cross."[27] The persecution doesn't stay at the level of mere hostility, but it escalates to a hideous desire to kill Jesus (5:18).[28] This is the first appearance of the word ἀποκτείνω[29] in relation to Jesus, and afterward it occurs frequently (7:1, 19, 25; 8:37, 40; 11:53). That the tense of the verb ζητέω (to seek) in μᾶλλον ἐζήτουν αὐτὸν οἱ Ἰουδαῖοι ἀποκτεῖναι ("the Jews were seeking all the more to kill him," 5:18) is also the imperfect tense shows that the Jews were continually seeking to kill him during the life-time of Jesus.

The evangelist is diligent in identifying the reason[30] for the Jew's persecution of Jesus and their seeking to kill him. It is identified by ὅτι ταῦτα

---

that the Jews "started/began persecuting" Jesus.

25. In both the Old Testament (the LXX) and New Testament, the word διώκω has two meanings: (1) "persecution" and (2) "exhortations to strive for a goal" or "pursuit of Christian objectives." In the entry article for διώκω, Ebel summarizes how the word is used to depict persecution of God's messengers and Jesus and his disciples. That persecution may be a sign that one is on God's side. It is especially in the midst of persecution that Christians experience the help, strength, and saving power of Christ. Ebel, "διώκω," *NIDNTT* 2:805–7.

26. Moloney, *John*, 174.

27. Lindars, "The Persecution of Christians," 48–49.

28. Keener, *John*, 1:645.

29. In the New Testament, ἀποκτείνω "occurs 74 times especially often in the four gospels and Revelation (15 times); only 5 instances are found in the (Pauline) Epistles. In these passages the verb nearly always refers to the violent killing of God's messengers, whether in direct narrative (Matt 14:5, of Herod's intention with regard to John; cf. Mark 6:19), in parables (Mark 12:5ff. and parallels of the laborers in the vineyard; cf. Matt 23:37), or prophetically with reference to the disciples in the synoptic apocalypse (Matt 24:9). Its use in the three synoptic passion predictions (Mark 8:31; 9:31; 10:34; and parallels) is of central significance. The witness who is to be killed and upon whom the attacks are concentrated is the Son (cf. 1 Thess 2:15). In John it is noteworthy that ἀποκτείνω is almost always combined with ζητέω (to seek), or βουλεύω (to plan) (e.g., John 7:1, 19ff.; 11:53). The disciples also come within the scope of this threat (Acts 21:31; 23:12–14)." Coenen, "ἀποκτείνω," *NIDNTT* 1:430.

30. Emphasis is given to the reasons in both verses 16 and 18 by the twice-repeated structure of διὰ τοῦτο ... ὅτι ...

ἐποίει ἐν σαββάτῳ ("because he was doing such things on the sabbath," 5:16). That is, Jesus made a man whole on the Sabbath and called God his Father, thus enraging the establishment. The evangelist does not pay much attention to Sabbath controversy, but even omits the Jews' question, which is most likely about the basis on which Jesus was healing the man on the Sabbath. In answering to the Jews, unlike the Synoptic Gospels (Matt 12:1–14; Mark 2:23–28; Luke 6:1–5) with the focus on the theology of Sabbath that the Son of Man is the lord of the Sabbath and the Sabbath is for humankind, John uniquely emphasizes Jesus' relationship with the Father by calling God "my Father" (ὁ πατήρ μου 5:17).[31] Jesus proclaims that he is working because the Father is still working, by which the Jews understand Jesus is making himself equal to God.[32] Under the attack of the opponents, even knowing that his answer would increase the level of persecution, Jesus is not reluctant to reveal who the Father is and his relationship with the Father because that is his mission entrusted from the Father.

From the above observation, three points are noteworthy as to the nature of the suffering of Jesus. First, as indicated in the tense of the two key verbs, the persecution and threat of death were not one time experience of temporal suffering, but a repeated and continuing reality during the life of Jesus until the persecutors finally see the death of Jesus. Second, the reason for the persecution is none other than that Jesus was doing the works of the Father as his Father was working (5:17). The reason for the Jews' increased hostility and pursuit of him was centered on Jesus' revealing his own identity as the Son of the Father and God as his own Father. From the Jews' perspective, the reason for persecuting Jesus stemmed from their ignorance of who Jesus is and who the Father is and of the relationship between the Father and the Son. Three, Jesus' reaction to the persecution is worthy of mention. Amid the persecution and suffering, Jesus continued his mission, which is to reveal who the Father is and his relationship with the Father, not because the environment of his mission was friendly, but because the Father who sent him was still working in and with him.

---

31. The Father-Son relationship expressed in Jesus' intimate calling God "my Father" functions as the essential motivation of Jesus' life and mission, and it appears intensively throughout the Gospel (2:16; 5:17, 43; 6:32, 40; 8:19, 49, 54; 10:18, 25, 29, 37; 14:2, 7, 20–21, 23; 15:1, 8, 10, 15, 23–24; 20:17).

32. About "thereby making himself equal to God," Barrett comments, "This inference John of course admits, but rightly presents it as extremely provocative to the Jews." Barrett, *John*, 256.

For others opinions, refer to Bultmann, *John*, 245; Meeks, "Equal to God," 309–21; Moloney, *John*, 174, "Only 'the Jews' say that Jesus makes himself 'equal with God' (*isos to theo*). Jesus does not claim an equality that makes of him 'another God,' but [a] oneness that flows from his relationship with God."

B. 7:1, 7, 19, 25

In 7:1, 7, 19, and 25, the word ἀποκτείνω (to kill) occurs three times to indicate that the Jews were continually seeking to kill Jesus, and the word μισέω (to hate) is used in reference to Jesus as the explicit object of hatred (7:7) after its first use in relation to the light as the object of hatred (3:20).[33] Aware of the escalating desire of the Jews to kill him since the healing of the man in Jerusalem, Jesus stayed in Galilee rather than go about in Judea. Although it seemed that Jesus was hiding from the Jews, this quickly proved not to be the case. Jesus went up to Judea (7:10),[34] and began to teach at the temple (7:14). Regardless of whether his decision to go up to Judea afterward was because "the Father signaled Jesus in some way,"[35] or because of "Jesus' unconditional response to the greater design of his Father,"[36] it is obvious that the persecution and increasing threat of death never deterred Jesus from doing his mission of teaching the truth of the Father. In his teaching, Jesus confronts the Jews saying, "Did not Moses give you the law? Yet none of you keeps the law" (7:19), and subsequently challenges them in regard to their abuse of the law by their misinterpretation of the law (7:21–24). In the midst of the threat of killing and verbal abuse (7:20, "You have a demon"), Jesus, as the Word of the Father and the true embodiment of the law, urges the Jews to "judge with right judgment" (7:24).[37] Yet, the threat of killing is becoming widely known even among the crowds in Jerusalem (7:25).

C. 8:37–47

In 8:37–47, the word ἀποκτείνω (to kill) appears twice; this time from Jesus' own lips in disputing with the Jews (8:37, 40) over their evil pursuit to kill him.[38] The text goes deeper to the root of persecution. It clarifies the

---

33. The study of the theme of "hatred" will be dealt with in the pericope 15:18—16:4a later.

34. It is not surprising that Jesus reverses what he said before (7:8) like other cases in 2:4–7; 4:48–50. Jesus moves according to higher motivation and call, not by the logic of human behavior.

35. Carson, *John*, 309.

36. Moloney, *John*, 240.

37. See Keener, *John*, 1:717–18 for the understanding of this phrase in the context of early Jewish context.

38. The Jews' pursuit to kill Jesus becomes more intense. The Jews have been trying to arrest him (7:30, 32, 44; 10:39) and gave public orders for that purpose, "Now the chief priests and the Pharisees had given orders that anyone who knew where Jesus was should let them know, so that they might arrest him" (11:57).

nature of persecution itself by conveying Jesus' own insight into, and interpretation of, their desire to kill. The Jews' desire to kill Jesus springs from their attitude toward Jesus' word (8:37, 43, 47) and truth (8:40, 45–46). The evil desire is boiling in their hearts because there is no room in them to accept Jesus' word (8:37). One's rejection of Jesus' word and truth does not end in a neutral state. The one who refuses the truth of God is exposed to the danger of brewing a further evil intention to destroy the one who says the truth of God.

Jesus goes deeper to the root of their refusing his words and consequent search to kill him. This relates to the issue of who their father is, that is, the origin of their beings (8:38, 41, 44). The fundamental reason for refusing Jesus' words and seeking to kill him is that God is not their father (8:42) and they are not from God (8:47, "Whoever is from God hears the words of God. The reason you do not hear them is that you are not from God"). The Jews, who seek to kill Jesus, claim that they are the children of Abraham (8:39), but in fact they are the offspring of the devil (8:44, "You are from your father the devil, and you choose to do your father's desires"). According to the nature of the devil and following him, they seek to destroy the one who brings the truth of God.

The conflict between those who are from God the Father and those who are from the devil is inevitable. It is the continuation of the spiritual war that started in the Garden of Eden between the seed of the Father and the seed of the devil (Gen 3:15). The persecution and suffering that Jesus and his followers encounter in this world is not a novel and strange phenomenon, but part of an inevitable struggle to claim the children of the Father.

D. 9:22, 34

Now the focus moves from the persecution of Jesus to that of his followers. 9:22 and 9:34 function uniquely in the Fourth Gospel in two ways. Firstly, these texts depict how the believers, during the life-time of Jesus, experienced suffering in their daily life. Secondly, by presenting a man as a model, the text demonstrates how Jesus' followers are expected to face persecution and suffering fearlessly.

The hostility toward Jesus from the Jews permeated the Jewish community. Even the crowd in Jerusalem was not free to speak openly about Jesus for the fear of the Jews (7:13). In these hostile circumstances, on a Sabbath day, Jesus again healed and opened the eyes of the man born blind. The blind man was under interrogation by the Jews because he was healed by Jesus, and forced to deny the fact that Jesus opened his eyes. The religious authorities of the community and his neighbors, who were supposed to share with him in the joy of recovering his eyesight, were busy hurling doubting questions at him. The parents of the blind man, the individuals expected to stand close beside in support of him, lost their courage to support their own son for the fear of the Jews (9:21-22a). The fear was not a merely emotional one, but very pragmatic, affecting their daily life. As it is stated in the official decision of the Jewish authority, "anyone who confessed Jesus to be the Messiah would be put out of the synagogue" (9:22b). Many people lost their courage to confess their faith in Jesus for the fear of being expelled from the synagogue (12:42).

The synagogue was not a mere religious gathering place, but functioned as the center of everyday life. For the Israelites every dimension of life, whether it was religious, educational, legal, or social net-working, revolved around the synagogue.[39] The word ἀποσυνάγωγος (expelled from the synagogue) is particular to John (9:22; 12:42; 16:2). There were various levels of excommunication in the Jewish society, yet ἀποσυνάγωγος here does not mean any partial or temporal excommunication. It is, rather, as most scholars agree, complete excommunication, which is "exclusion from the national and religious fellowship of the Jews, συναγωγή denoting here the entire community."[40] It is absolute banishment[41] for the condemned and cursed whether it is initiated under the practice of *birkat ha-minim* or not.[42]

It was in this atmosphere that the formerly blind man fearlessly confessed the name, Jesus. He faced the antagonistic reality of being expelled from his own community, the nest and root of his life (9:28, 34). It is noteworthy that by the progressive advancement of the use of Jesus' titles from the man's own lips, the fourth evangelist traces how the man's knowledge and faith in Jesus grows in the course of courageous reaction to the persecution.

---

39. For the significance and function of the synagogue in the lives of the Israelites, see Schrage, "συναγωγή, ἀποσυνάγωγος," *TDNT* 7:798-852; Chilton and Yamauchi, "Synagogue," 1145-53.

40. Schrage, "συναγωγή, ἀποσυνάγωγος," *TDNT* 7:798-852.

41. For various degrees of punishment and temporal excommunication implemented in the synagogue, see Barrett, *John*, 361-62; Keener, *John*, 1:787-88. Considering the fact that even "the person thus temporarily excommunicated was forbidden all dealings with the Israelites except his wife and children" (Barrett, *John*, 361), the complete excommunication indicate absolute exclusion from the community in every aspect of communal life, losing all financial, educational, and social rights, including one's own foundation. In a word ἀποσυνάγωγος in the text meant social death for those put out of the synagogue.

42. For discussion of the relation between the ἀποσυνάγωγος and *birkat ha-minim*, see Carson, *John*, 369-72.

His confession of faith and knowledge in Jesus grows from knowing Jesus as "the man called Jesus" (9:11). He goes on to see Jess as "a prophet" (9:17) and "a man from God" (9:33), and then as a figure worthy of confession: "Lord, I believe" (9:38a). Finally, he "worshipped"[43] Jesus (9:38b). While facing the enmity of the Jews fearlessly, the man's faith was growing. What is not to be ignored is that Jesus revealed himself as the Son of Man (9:35) to the individual who fearlessly faced persecution for the name of Jesus.

When this man's community casts him out (9:34) and his own parents are unable to be his comfort and encouragement (9:20–23; cf. Ps 27:10[44]), Jesus visits, cares for, and shows his close presence to the man, revealing his glory to this suffering follower (9:35–37). In the farewell discourse, Jesus comforts and encourages his disciples who will face suffering and persecution (16:1–4, 33; cf. 14:27). Before that, in this text of chapter 9, a model of the fearless life of a Jesus' follower, who courageously faces persecution, is shown, and Jesus' presence with a persecuted follower is demonstrated for the encouragement of the Christian followers. This text also forewarns Jesus' followers that they are expected to face persecution and suffering fearlessly.

E. 15:18—16:4 (17:14)

Now we come to 15:18–16:4,[45] which contains the most information about the suffering and persecution of Jesus' followers in the Fourth Gospel. The major terms that portray Christian disciples' social hardship (to persecute, to hate, expelled from the synagogue, and to kill) are all mentioned here in 15:18–16:4. Also, all three Persons of the Divine Trinity, Father, Son, and Holy Spirit appear together in this text. The text is located in the "innermost" part of Jesus' farewell discourse as one of the important components of the address.[46] Though it is recorded over the two chapters, it is to be viewed "as a

---

43. Barrett (*John*, 365) grasps the man's action of worship (καὶ προσεκύνησεν αὐτῷ) as "that of Christian faith and worship," which he compares with the "actions of men to theophanies in the Old Testament (e.g., Exod 3:6)."

44. Ps 27:10 "Even though my father and mother have left me, *ADONAI* will care for me" (CJB).

45. Scholars have noted a close similarity (Bruner, *John*, 907–09) between this Johannine text about the hatred and persecution from the world to Jesus' disciples and the teachings of Jesus about the suffering and persecution of the disciples in the Synoptic Gospels—Jesus' mission charge for the disciples (Matt 10:16–42; Mark 13:9–13; Luke 21:12–19), sermon about the end time (Matt 24:9–14), and two Beatitudes (Matt 5:10–12; Luke 6:22–23,26). It demonstrates that the hatred and persecution from the world toward Christian disciples was universal during the late first century.

46. While proposing a chiastic structural analysis on the farewell discourse (chaps. 13–17), Segovia locates the text (15:18–16:3) as one of the innermost components. He

unified and coherent strategic whole that interacts with its literary structure and development."[47]

The purpose of Jesus' telling of the coming persecution is intimated by the two imperatives/indicatives, γινώσκετε (to come to know, 15:18) and μνημονεύετε (to remember, 15:20), at the beginning section, and explicitly expressed by the two clauses, Ταῦτα λελάληκα ὑμῖν ἵνα μὴ σκανδαλισθῆτε[48] ("I have said these things to you to keep you from stumbling," 16:1) and ταῦτα λελάληκα ὑμῖν ἵνα ὅταν ἔλθῃ ἡ ὥρα αὐτῶν μνημονεύητε αὐτῶν ("I have said these things to you so that when their hour comes you may remember," 16:4), at the closing section. It is to warn and equip his followers to be ready for the coming sufferings. In order to be ready for the coming tribulation, the disciples need to know and remember the nature of, and reason for, the sufferings. Therefore, in this text, Jesus focuses on the nature of, and fundamental reason for, the persecution as well as the disciples' mission during the persecution.

The persecutors are called "the world" in the text whereas in the previous chapters (except for 7:7) they are mostly called "the Jews" (οἱ Ἰουδαῖοι). The world (ὁ κόσμος)[49] in the text refers to those who belong to the "moral

---

states, "The innermost components (C: 15:1-11; 15:18—16:3) focus on two contrasting pairs of themes, joy/hatred and abiding/persecution-exclusion, again with a difference in the order of presentation . . . At the very centre (D) lies 15:12-17, with its presentation of the command to love one another." Segovia, *The Farewell*, 38-39.

47. Ibid., 208. The text can be divided into either four sections (15:18-21; 21-25; 26-27; 16:1-4a) or three sections combining the first two sections (15:18-25; 26-27; 16:1-4a) or three sections combining the last two sections (15:18-21; 22-25; 15:26-16:4a). Refer to Segovia, *The Farewell*, 169-70; Keener, *John*, 2:1019-28. For further discussions on minority options for the division of the text, see Segovia, *The Farewell*, 174-78. Yet, there is no universal agreement on the literary division of the text. It is possible to divide the unit according to the appearance of the three Persons of the Divine Trinity: 15:18-21, hatred of the world in relation to Jesus; 15:21-25, hatred of the world in relation to the Father; 15:26-27, witnessing with the Holy Spirit under the hatred of the world; 16:1-4a, summary exhortation for the coming persecution. Lindars ("The Persecution of Christians," 48-69) also presents a fine analysis of 15:18—16:4a viewing the pericope as part of the process of the composition of chapters 15-16 from source and redaction approach.

48. The verb σκανδαλίζω (cf. Matt 26:31; 1 John 2:10) appears only twice in the Fourth Gospel (16:1; 6:61). In 16:1 it is employed to warn and protect the disciples from "giving up the true Christian faith" under the pressure of persecution. Brown, *John*, 2:690; Barrett, *John*, 484.

49. Though there are various references to "the world" in the Fourth Gospel, Brown (*John*, 1:508-10) accurately points out that "in the second half of the Gospel, 'the world' is rather consistently identified with those who have turned against Jesus under the leadership of Satan."

order in active rebellion against God,"⁵⁰ and thus refuse Jesus, the Word of God. By identifying the persecutors as "the world," Jesus indicates that the persecutors of Jesus and his followers are not only the Jews, but those who are against Jesus and his word, beyond the boundary of nation and time, regardless of whether they are Jews or those who represent Roman power.⁵¹

The mode of persecution is multidimensional. It starts with "hatred,"⁵² which is the inner impetus of persecution (stated by the verb διώκω in 15:20 and 5:16). In its final form, hatred brings in "killing"⁵³ of Jesus and his followers. Particularly, for the followers of Jesus within the Jewish social boundary, hatred and persecution appear first in the form of expulsion from the synagogue (16:2a).⁵⁴ And a future time is coming when the persecutors will think that they offer a service to God by killing the followers of Jesus (16:2b).⁵⁵

The essential nature of the suffering of Jesus' followers is communicated by the two εἰ ("if") phrases of 15:18, 20, and further supported by the quotation in 15:20, which is from 13:16 that the hatred and persecution that the followers will suffer is precisely the same thing that Jesus has

---

50. Carson, *John*, 525.

51. Keener includes those who represent a worldly kingdom in the category of the term, "the world": "Whereas 'the Jews' form a prism for 'the world,' they are not, however, its only representatives in this Gospel; they collaborate with Pilate, who defends a worldly kingdom (18:36)." Keener, *John*, 2:1018.

52. The word μισέω is repeated seven times in the text (15:18*2, 19, 23*2, 24, 25). The hatred in the pericope is "real hatred, and not, as in the Semitic idiom (cf. 12:25), a matter of liking less" as Barrett (*John*, 480) remarks similarly to Brown's (*John*, 2:686) comment. See also Segovia, *The Farewell*, 179; Malina and Rohrbaugh, *Social-Science Commentary*, 87.

53. 5:18; 7:1, 19, 25; 8:37, 40; 11:53; 12:10; 16:2; 21:18–19; cf. Acts 2:23; 3:15; 12:2; 1 Thess 2:15.

54. For more explanation on excommunication from the synagogue, see the above study on 9:22, 34.

55. On whether it is persecution (killing) by the Jews or by the Roman power, see the above footnote 11 and Moloney, *John*, 434–35.

It is likely that the evangelist thought he did not need to identify who πᾶς ὁ ἀποκτείνας ὑμᾶς would be because of the following two reasons. One, the πᾶς is both the Jews and those who work under the Roman power as in the Gospel it was clearly identified that those who killed Jesus were both the Jews and the Roman power (19:6–7, 13–16). Two, the readers of the Gospel most likely already knew that both the Jews and those who belong to the Romans have killed Jesus' followers—Stephen was killed by the Jews (Acts 7:57—8:3) and James by Herod (Acts 8:1–2). Therefore, the word πᾶς is the most appropriate one to refer to the persecutors who would kill the followers of Jesus.

experienced.⁵⁶ If Jesus has been hated⁵⁷ by the world, his followers will be hated by the same world (15:18, 19; 17:14).

Considerable material is devoted to identifying the fundamental reasons for this hatred. The world hates Jesus' followers: (1) because the disciples do not belong⁵⁸ to the world (15:19; 17:14), but belong to Jesus; (2) because the disciples are chosen out of the world by Jesus (15:19; cf. 6:70; 13:18; 15:16); (3) because they bear Jesus' name (15:21); and (4) because the world does not know God, the one who sent Jesus (15:21; 16:3). The reason for the hatred is both christological (related to Christ) and theological (related to God). The world hates the disciples because they are one with Christ and belong to him (christological). Yet, the deeper reason for the hatred lies in the world's ignorance of God (theological). The reasons are interconnected. Due to a lack of ability to know God revealed in Jesus and the consequential lack of the knowledge of God, the world hates Jesus and his followers. And because the world refuses to know, and therefore does not know, Jesus, who is the authentic revelation of God, there is no way the world can truly know God. Underneath the hatred of the world, there is a deficiency of the true knowledge of God and Jesus, which is the opposite of eternal life (17:3).⁵⁹

Furthermore, the hatred of the world is towards the Father (15:23, 24). The world hated the Father when the Word of God came and spoke the truth to it (15:22), because the Word exposed the world's wrong and testified that its deeds were evil (7:7). The world hated God more and more when Jesus came and performed God's works (15:24) because it lacked the ability to recognize God in Jesus' works. Likewise, the hatred from the world to Jesus' followers is related to their ministry of God's truth in preaching and works (15:20).

---

56. Jesus not only was persecuted, but also is being persecuted still with his church, his followers (cf. Acts 9:4, 5).

57. As the tense of the verb μεμίσηκεν is perfect, "the world's hatred of Christ was no passing phenomenon," but "a permanent attitude." Morris, *John*, 678.

58. The preposition ἐκ in the phrase ἐκ τοῦ κόσμου conveys the connotation of one' origin (ibid., 679) that defines one's identity and essence of existence beyond the denotation of where one physically belongs to. The similar use of the preposition may be seen in the clause ὁ ὢν ἐκ τοῦ θεοῦ τὰ ῥήματα τοῦ θεοῦ ἀκούει· διὰ τοῦτο ὑμεῖς οὐκ ἀκούετε, ὅτι ἐκ τοῦ θεοῦ οὐκ ἐστέ (8:47). Cf. ἐκ θεοῦ ἐγεννήθησαν (1:13); ἐκ τοῦ πνεύματος (3:8).

59. The importance of true knowledge of God is a recurrent theme in the Gospel, often in the contrast between Jesus' and the disciples' knowledge of the Father and the world's ignorance of the Father (7:29; 8:19, 55; 10:15; 14:17; 17:25).

With a quotation (15:25) from a Psalm,[60] the text leads Jesus followers to understand the world's hatred within the historical backdrop. The hatred of the world started long before Jesus came. Since the day when Satan initiated a war against God and his people in the Garden of Eden (Gen 3), the seed of the devil has persecuted the seed of God. The righteous Abel was persecuted by the evil Cain (Gen 4). As quoted in 15:25, David was also persecuted without cause (Ps 35:19; 69:4; 109:3). The same persecution came upon Jesus. By hating Jesus and God, they fulfill what was written in their law (15:25). The hatred Jesus' followers will face is the same ancient hatred of the world that has been throughout the history of humanity.

At the closing two verses of chapter 15, Jesus draws the disciples' attention to the mission of his followers in the midst of hatred and persecution. Carson comments, "The focus shifts from the cause of persecution to the response of Jesus' disciples to persecution."[61] While the hatred and persecution of the world is actively at work, the Holy Spirit testifies about Jesus (15:26). Therefore, the followers of Jesus must[62] testify about Jesus (15:27). The Holy Spirit is the power of Christian witness.[63] In fact, it is the three Persons of the Divine Trinity who testify together with the Christian followers through their witness about Jesus. Jesus himself sends the Holy Spirit from the Father to strengthen the followers when they do the work of witnessing. Therefore, the followers of Jesus are expected not only to endure the hatred and persecution of the world, but they are to be actively involved in and devoted to the ministry of testifying about Jesus together with Father, Son, and Holy Spirit.

III. Summary

From the above mentioned scholarly theories and understandings of the Johannine community, suffering and persecution came up as one of the main characteristics of the socio-historical setting of the life of the late first-century Christian followers. In order to figure out the nature and characteristics of the suffering and persecution, we have observed relevant texts in the Fourth Gospel with the questions: In what ways and to what degree

---

60. 15:25 "It was to fulfill the word that is written in their law, 'They hated me without a cause.'"

61. Carson, *John*, 528.

62. In both possibilities (indicative and imperative) of the tense of the verb μαρτυρεῖτε, NIV renders it as imperative, "And you also must testify"; NRSV as an official order that should be done, "You also are to testify."

63. Bultmann, *John*, 553.

did Jesus and his disciples suffer persecution? What were the reasons for the persecution? And how did Jesus face suffering and how did he charge the disciples to respond to it?

First, suffering and persecution are *practical and deadly*. The first-century followers of Jesus were expelled from their own community, losing the foundation of their social life and facing fatal privation of all opportunities in the areas of finance, education, and law. Furthermore, they lived under the ongoing threat of being killed. Some of them were actually murdered just like the Lord Jesus was murdered by the persecutors.

Second, the reason for persecution is *spiritual*. The followers of Jesus are hated for being followers of Jesus, that is, for their spiritual identity. They are persecuted because they do not belong to the world, but to Jesus and to the Father. Out of its own spiritual ignorance, its inability to recognize and know God in Jesus, the world is seeking to destroy the lives of Jesus' followers. It is an inevitable spiritual war between the children of God and the offspring of the devil.

Third, Jesus' followers are expected to fearlessly face hatred and persecution and *continue* the task of testifying about Jesus. The world's hatred and persecution is closely related to the testifying to the truth of Jesus. Jesus spoke the truth of God and his word condemned the world's evil deeds, so the world hated him. When Jesus' followers testify to the truth of Jesus, the world will hate them and seek to get rid of them. In the midst of an environment of hostility and antagonism, they are to continue the mission of testifying about Jesus. The disciples who locked the door for fear of the persecutors (20:19), who needed to touch the Lord's hands and side to believe in him (20:27), and who needed to feed on the Lord's loaf at the Sea of Tiberias to overcome the wound of their past failures (13:38; 16:32; 18:17, 25–27; 21:1–14), will be able to continue testifying about Jesus in and together with the Holy Spirit (15:26; 16:8–11) as the Lord Jesus himself is continuing his ministry of testifying about the Father by sending the Spirit from the Father (15:16; 16:7).

CHAPTER 4

The Occurrences of ἀκολουθεῖν Outside the Fourth Gospel

THE POINT OF DEPARTURE for the investigation of the Spirituality of "following Jesus" implied by the association of ἀκολουθεῖν with correlated motifs is that the ordinary verb ἀκολουθεῖν, which means "to come after" in its literal meaning, does not convey a fixed meaning on its own, but communicates various meanings and overtones by its association[1] with other factors that control the logic of the context. The implications communicated by ἀκολουθεῖν are formulated by its association with other words and motifs in the sentence and the immediate and larger literary context. Therefore, in order to discover the implications and the Spirituality of following Jesus created by ἀκολουθεῖν in a specific passage, both the subject and object of the verb and the flow of the theme of the discourse are to be investigated in relation to the associated terms and ideas.

The current chapter is comprised of two separate sections. First, the usages of the term ἀκολουθεῖν in Greco-Roman literature and Judaism documents will be delineated by focusing on some exemplary cases. Second, the occurrences of the term in the other books of the New Testament, outside of the Fourth Gospel, will be surveyed by observing what words and ideas are linked to the term.

Different degrees of the methodology will be employed according to the texts. For the usages of ἀκολουθεῖν in Greco-Roman and Hebrew documents, a simple survey will be made. For other biblical texts outside of the Fourth Gospel, a minimal amount of exegetical work will be exercised. A fuller exegetical and theological probe will be applied to the texts of the

---

1. Many scholars believe the term ἀκολουθεῖν is employed to create diverse connotations by its association with other words and terms in particular literary environments. Barclay, *New Testament Words*, 41–46; Kingsbury, "The Verb *Akolouthein* ('to Follow')," 58–60.

Fourth Gospel in addition to the discourse analysis and the investigation of the correlated words and themes.

I. Ἀκολουθεῖν in Greco-Roman and Judaic Literature

Before the Fourth Gospel used the term ἀκολουθεῖν, Greco-Roman and Judaic literature had used it with various meanings in diverse literary contexts. The purpose of this section is to briefly see how ἀκολουθεῖν was used in Greco-Roman and Judaic literature. Some exemplary cases of the usages according to the object and context will be traced to survey how the term has been used in various literary contexts for communicating different meanings and implications. The survey will prove that this common verb can be employed to communicate various connotations according to its object and context. The survey is not intended to give a comparison with the use of the term in the Fourth Gospel. Rather, it will focus on the fact that the ancient writers used the verb in various literary contexts for conveying various meanings and connotations. This will demonstrate the possibility and legitimacy for the fourth evangelist to employ the term ἀκολουθεῖν to impart his own unique messages and implications within the framework of his own literary context.

A. Greco-Roman Literature

The verb ἀκολουθεῖν has been used in Greco-Roman literature to convey diverse meanings in various connotations. As summarized in the table,[2] the uses of the verb are presented in four categories in BAGD (2nd ed.) and

2. The categories of the uses of ἀκολουθέω in BAGD (2nd ed.) and BDAG (3rd ed.) and in Barclay's work are:

ἀκολουθέω	BAGD	BDAG	Barclay
1. To move behind someone in the same direction (*come after*)	✓	✓	
2. To accompany someone who takes the lead (*accompany, go along with*)	✓	✓	✓
3. To follow someone as disciple (*be a disciple, follow*)	✓	✓	
4. To comply with (*follow, obey*); *obeying* the laws; *following or obeying* someone else's advice or opinion	✓	✓	✓✓

five categories in BDAG (3rd ed.) adding the fifth one.³ William Barclay determines that the uses of the verb appear in Classical Greek literature in six categories.⁴ One, "for soldiers *following their leader and commander*"; two, "a slave *following or attending* his master"; three, "*following or obeying* someone else's advice or opinion"; four, "*obeying* the laws"; five, "*following the thread or argument of a discourse*"; and six, "*attaching oneself to someone* in order to extract some favor which is desired." All these usages can be summarized into eight categories. The categories of the usages of the verb will be presented with details of the linked object and literary context.

First, in its literal sense the verb ἀκολουθεῖν means "to move behind someone in the same direction (*come after*)."⁵ Diodorus Siculus, the first-century BCE Greek historian, who wrote the universal history *Bibliotheca historica*, used the verb in this sense. When his friends sent for him, Hermocrates the Syracusan set out leading three thousand soldiers and arrived at an agreed place at night. Yet, not all of his soldiers were able *to follow* him.⁶ The verb also appears in the fourth-century BCE Greek historian Xenophon's *Hellenica* in the context that Leontiades says to Phoebidas, "Phoebidas, it is within your power this day to render the greatest service to your fatherland; for if you will *follow* me with your hoplites, I will lead you into the Acropolis. And this once accomplished, be sure that Thebes will be completely under the control of the Lacedaemonians and of us who are your friends; . . ." (emphasis added; Xen. Hell. 5, 2, 26).⁷

ἀκολουθέω	BAGD	BDAG	Barclay
5. A slave *following or attending* his master			✓
6. *Following* the thread or argument of a discourse			✓
7. *Attaching oneself to someone* in order to extract some favor which is desired			✓
8. To come after something else in sequence (*follow*)		✓	

3. "To come after something else in sequence, *follow*, of things."

4. Barclay, *Words*, 41–46.

5. BDAG, s.v. ἀκολουθέω.

6. "Although not all his soldiers had been able to accompany him, Hermocrates with a small number of them came to the gate on Achradinê, and when he found that some of his friends had already occupied the region, he waited to pick up the late-comers" (Diod. S. 13, 75, 7). Cited 30 June 2012. http://penelope.uchicago.edu/Thayer/E/Roman/Texts/Diodorus_Siculus/13D*.html.

7. Cited 5 June 2012. http://perseus.uchicago.edu/perseus-cgi/citequery3.pl?dbname=GreekTexts&query=Xen.Hell. 5.2.26&getid=0.

Second, the verb ἀκολουθεῖν means "to accompany someone who takes the lead (*accompany, go along with*)."⁸ Thucydides (7, 57, 9), the fifth-century BCE classic historian of the Greeks who wrote a history of the Peloponnesian War, used the verb to communicate this meaning in the context of persuasion: "the Dorian Argives *to join* the Ionian Athenians in a war against Dorians."⁹

Third, in its figurative sense, the verb ἀκολουθεῖν implies "to follow someone as disciple (*be a disciple, follow*)."¹⁰ Diogenes Laertius, the third-century CE biographer of the Greek philosophers, used the term in his writing on the life of Parmenides: "Parmenides, a native of Elea, son of Pyres, was a pupil of Xenophanes (Theophrastus in his *Epitome* makes him a pupil of Anaximander). Parmenides, however, though he was instructed by Xenophanes, was no *follower* of his" (Diog. L. 9, 21 of Parmenides).¹¹

Fourth, the verb ἀκολουθεῖν means "to comply with (*follow, obey*)"¹² or "*following or obeying* someone else's advice or opinion." Thucydides (3, 8, 6) used the verb in this way to refer to the one who "follows an orator in thought (γνώμῃ)."¹³ In a similar sense, the Greek philosopher Plato (Phaedrus, 232a) used the verb to indicate the one who follows "the lover." Aristotle (Eth. M., II, 6, p. 1203b, 19 f.) used it to point out those who follow "the wise man."¹⁴ During the first and second century CE, Epictetus (Diss., I, 6, 15), the Stoic and preacher of ethics, used the verb together with φύσει in religious and philosophical connotations. Marcus Aurelius Antonius, the emperor-philosopher, also used the verb together with θεῷ in the similar sense. For the Stoics, to "follow" *nature* or *God* is the "basic direction of the philosophical life."¹⁵ In these usages, the verb ἀκολουθεῖν "virtually means identification of one's being through incorporation. Behind this lies the

---

8. BDAG.

9. ". . . τῶν δὲ ἄλλων ἑκούσιος μᾶλλον ἡ στρατεία ἐγίγνετο ἤδη. Ἀργεῖοι μὲν γὰρ οὐ τῆς ξυμμαχίας ἕνεκα μᾶλλον ἢ τῆς Λακεδαιμονίων τε ἔχθρας καὶ τῆς παραυτίκα ἕκαστοι ἰδίας ὠφελίας Δωριῆς ἐπὶ Δωριᾶς μετὰ Ἀθηναίων Ἰώνων ἠκολούθουν, Μαντινῆς δὲ καὶ ἄλλοι Ἀρκάδων μισθοφόροι ἐπὶ τοὺς αἰεὶ πολεμίους σφίσιν ἀποδεικνυμένους ἰέναι εἰωθότες καὶ τότε τοὺς μετὰ Κορινθίων ἐλθόντας Ἀρκάδας οὐδὲν ἧσσον διὰ κέρδος ἡγούμενοι πολεμίους, . . ." Thucydides, *The Peloponnesian War* 7, 57, 9. Cited 5 June 2012. http://www.perseus.tufts.edu/hopper/text?doc=Perseus%3Atext%3A1999.01.0199%3Abook%3D7%3Achapter%3D57%3Asection%3D9.

10. BDAG.

11. Cited 30 June 2012. http://www.perseus.tufts.edu/hopper/text?doc=Perseus%3Atext%3A1999.01.0258%3Abook%3D9%3Achapter%3D3.

12. BDAG.

13. Kittel, "ἀκολουθέω," *TDNT* 1:210–16.

14. Ibid.

15. Blendinger, "ἀκολουθέω," *NIDNTT* 1:480–83.

Greek view of the innate relationship of rational man with God"[16] in the philosophical connotation.

Fifth, the verb ἀκολουθεῖν is very commonly used for "a slave *following or attending* his master."[17] In his work, *Characters*,[18] which is the collection of the descriptions of undesirable personality traits, Theophrastus (the successor to Aristotle in the Peripatetic school) sketches a man who "compels his slave to walk before him instead of following behind him, as a slave would normally do, so that he can be sure the slave will not dodge away (Theophrastus, *Characters* 18.8)."[19]

Sixth, the verb ἀκολουθεῖν is very commonly used for "*following* the thread or argument of a discourse."[20] During his argument, the Greek philosopher Socrates tries to explain his point by saying, "Come, then, follow me on this line, if we may in some fashion or other explain our meaning"[21] (Plato, *Republic* 474c).

Seventh, the verb ἀκολουθεῖν commonly appears in the papyri for "*attaching oneself to someone* in order to extract some favor which is desired."[22] "One writes in advice to another: '*stick to* Ptollarion all the time. . . . *Stick to* him so that you may become his friend.'"[23] Here the verb is employed to convey the meaning of staying close to a person to be his friend ("stick to").

Eighth, the verb ἀκολουθεῖν means "to come after something else in sequence (*follow*)." The Shepherd of Hermas used the term in this sense in the Fifth *Similitude*. The Shepherd gave a series of similitude to Hermas (the similitude of the field, and of the master of the vineyard, and of the slave who staked the vineyard, and of the stakes, and of the weeds that were plucked out of the vineyard, and of the son, and of the friends) in Hs 5,2,1–11. He could not comprehend their meanings, so he persistently requested that they be explained to him (Hs 5,3,1–5,4,5). Finally, the Shepherd began to expound their meanings to him: ". . . I shall unfold to you the meaning of the similitudes of the field, and of all the others that follow (καὶ τῶν λοιπῶν τῶν ἀκολουθούντων πάντων), that you may make them known to every one.

---

16. Ibid.

17. Barclay, *Words*, 42.

18. Cited 2 July 2012. http://perseus.uchicago.edu/perseus-cgi/citequery3.pl?dbname=GreekTexts&getid=0&query=Theophr.%20Char.%2018.8.

19. Barclay, *Words*, 42.

20. Ibid.

21. Cited 2 July 2012. http://perseus.uchicago.edu/perseus-cgi/citequery3.pl?dbname=GreekTexts&getid=0&query=Pl. Resp. 474c.

22. Barclay, *Words*, 42.

23. Ibid.

Hear now, he said, and understand them" (Hs 5,5,1).[24] Here the phrase, καὶ τῶν λοιπῶν τῶν ἀκολουθούντων πάντων, refers to the other sequent parables that come after the similitudes of the field.

B. Judaic Literature

The term ἀκολουθεῖν is employed also in Judaic literature. First, we will survey the usages of the Hebrew corresponding expression to ἀκολουθεῖν and additionally pay brief attention to the rabbinic understanding of the idea of following God. Then, we will examine how the Greek word ἀκολουθεῖν is used in the LXX including the Old Testament apocrypha.

1. הָלַךְ אַחֲרֵי

The Hebrew expression that corresponds to the Greek term ἀκολουθεῖν is הָלַךְ אַחֲרֵי. The phrase הָלַךְ אַחֲרֵי is mostly used "as a technical term for apostasy into heathenism," especially in Hosea, Jeremiah, and the Deuteronomic writings in the context of Israelite idolatry (Judg 2:12; Deut 4:3; 6:14; 1 Kgs 21:26; Jer 11:10; Hos 1:2; 2:7, 13).[25] The expression occasionally occurs in the context of stern warnings against idolatry, that is, not to follow pagan gods. For example, it is used in Deut 13:5, "The LORD your God you shall follow (אַחֲרֵי יְהוָה אֱלֹהֵיכֶם תֵּלֵכוּ), him alone you shall fear, his commandments you shall keep, his voice you shall obey, him you shall serve, and to him you shall hold fast." Kittel argues that the expression הָלַךְ אַחֲרֵי appears much less predominantly with the idea of following the LORD God in the Old Testament.[26] It is true that the main calling of the LORD God for the Israelites is that they should "walk in his ways."[27] The repeating expression, "to walk in his ways" (Deut 26:17, וְלָלֶכֶת בִּדְרָכָיו, πορεύεσθαι ἐν ταῖς ὁδοῖς αὐτοῦ), is the most noticeable and repeating call in the Deuteronomic writings and the Prophets (Deut 10:12; 28:9; Josh 22:5; 1 Kgs 8:58; Isa 2:3; Mic 4:2). Although הָלַךְ אַחֲרֵי is not employed as the main expression to command the Israelites to follow God, there is one reference which says that they followed the leading of the Lord God in their journey through the wilderness (Jer 2:2, "you followed me in the wilderness," לֶכְתֵּךְ אַחֲרַי בַּמִּדְבָּר) as he went in front

---

24. Shepherd of Hermas. *Similitude* 5 5:1.
25. Kittel, "ἀκολουθέω," *TDNT* 1:211.
26. Ibid.
27. Ibid.

of them in the pillar of cloud by day and in the pillar of fire by night (Exod 13:21, 22) to lead them to the promised land.

2. The Idea of Following God in Rabbinic Literature

As for the idea of following God, it rarely occurs in the rabbinic literature because it seems contrary to the concept of the transcendence of God. In the *Babylonian Talmud*, it is questioned whether a human being really is able to follow God, "Is it then possible for a man to go behind the Shekinah? We read: 'For the Lord thy God is a consuming fire' (Deut 4:24), b.Sot., 14a."[28] And also, in the *Midrash on Leviticus*, similar doubts are raised: "Is it then possible for flesh and blood to go behind the Holy One, blessed be He? It is written of Him: 'Thy way is in the sea . . .' (Ps 77:19) . . . And is it then possible for flesh and blood to mount up to heaven and to cling to the Shekinah? Of this it is written: 'For the Lord thy God is a consuming fire' (Deut 4:24), Lv. r. 25 on 19:23."[29] The rabbinic understanding in Judaism is that human beings are not able to follow the transcendent God because of the ontological difference between God and human beings. Instead, rabbinic literature grasps the concept of following God in the limited way of imitating the "qualities of God" in ethical terms only.[30]

3. Ἀκολουθεῖν in the LXX

The term ἀκολουθεῖν occurs in the LXX only on a few occasions: seven times in the canonical books and six times in Apocrypha. Predominantly, it is used in reference to *going somewhere with or after someone*. Balaam's going with the messengers of Balak (Num 22:20); Abigail's going after the messengers of David (1 Sam 25:42); Ruth's following (in its literal meaning in Hebrew, *clinging tightly to*) Naomi on her return to Bethlehem (Ruth 1:14); the foreign captives' walking in chains behind Israel in triumph (Isa 45:14); the walking of all men of Israel behind the triumphal procession of Judith (Jdt 15:13). All these occurrences indicate going after or with someone to somewhere. However, some movements of the followings do not end with a simple geographical move. Abigail's following the servants of David leads her to be a wife of King David, which ushers her life into a family of God that functions in the mainstream of Messianic Kingdom. Especially, Ruth's

---

28. Kittel, "ἀκολουθέω," *TDNT* 1:212.
29. Ibid.
30. Ibid.

following Naomi doesn't simply convey the meaning of physical following. The Hebrew corresponding verb דָּבַק, which is translated as ἀκολουθεῖν, means *to cleave* or *to cling tightly to* (Ruth 1:14, Ρουθ δὲ ἠκολούθησεν αὐτῇ, וְרוּת דָּבְקָה בָּהּ). Therefore, the verb ἀκολουθεῖν indicates that Ruth's resolute action (of staying together permanently with Naomi) goes beyond the simple description of an outward action. It reflects the decisive turning point that draws her whole life journey toward the people of God: She becomes the great grandmother of King David (Ruth 4:13–22) and eventually one of the important female figures in the genealogy of the Messiah (Matt 1:5). Ruth's action of "following" Naomi, the action of clinging tightly to one of the significant figures of the people of God, is well contrasted with Orpah's turning back to her own people, that is, outside of the Kingdom of God. In this case, the verb ἀκολουθεῖν implies spiritual connotation.

Second, on two occasions, the verb ἀκολουθεῖν is used in the context of following pagan gods. One is in Hos 2:7, where the sinful act of Israel's going after heathen gods is depicted in the analogy of a whore who, leaving her husband behind, is "going after her lover" (ἀκολουθήσω ὀπίσω τῶν ἐραστῶν μου).[31] Here, going after does not simply mean going with someone to somewhere, but it includes the action of following someone in love, that is, giving one's heart to the other in a negative context. The other usage occurs in Judith 5:6–8 and describes the life of "following" other gods in Mesopotamia in the legacy of the forefathers. Here the verb ἀκολουθεῖν includes the denotation of "serving and worshipping" other gods as it is contrasted with the action of worshipping the God of heaven.[32]

Third, as the verb ἀκολουθεῖν is used in the meaning of "to comply with or obey" in ancient Greek documents, for example, to refer to the one who "follows an orator in thought (γνώμη)" as presented above, in Judaic literature also it is used in the same meaning of "obey." Two occasions of the usage are found in the Old Testament apocrypha. Characteristically, the verb is used here in relation to "command" (λόγος) and "laws" (νόμος): One, in the context of "keeping the command" (ἠκολούθησαν τῷ λόγῳ) of Nebuchadnezzar king of the Assyrians (Jdt 2:4); the other is in relation to obeying the laws of God, namely, the Jews became invulnerable because they

---

31. Hos 2:5 "For their mother has played the whore; she who conceived them has acted shamefully. For she said, 'I will go after my lovers (ἀκολουθήσω ὀπίσω τῶν ἐραστῶν μου); they give me my bread and my water, my wool and my flax, my oil and my drink.'"

32. Jdt 5:6–8 "These people are descended from the Chaldeans. At one time they lived in Mesopotamia, because they did not wish to follow the gods (ἀκολουθῆσαι τοῖς θεοῖς) of their ancestors who were in Chaldea. Since they had abandoned the ways of their ancestors, and worshiped the God of heaven, the God they had come to know, their ancestors drove them out from the presence of their gods. So they fled to Mesopotamia, and lived there for a long time."

followed the laws ordained (διὰ τὸ ἀκολουθεῖν τοῖς ὑπ' αὐτοῦ προτεταγμένοις νόμοις) by their great Defender in heaven (2 Macc 8:36).

Fourth, the verb ἀκολουθεῖν is employed to convey the meaning of "turning to someone to get help." As the only occurrence in the Old Testament, the verb is used in Ezek 29:16[33] to portray Israel's sinful deed of turning to the military power, Egypt, to get help from them instead of trusting the divine help of God.

Fifth, the verb ἀκολουθεῖν appears to refer to "all other things that follow." When the delicacies of the Assyrians were prepared on the table, Judith said, "I will have enough with the things I brought with me" (ἐκ τῶν ἠκολουθηκότων μοι χορηγηθήσεται, Jdt 12:2). Here τῶν ἠκολουθηκότων is employed to simply refer to "the things" that she brought with her.

Lastly, the verb ἀκολουθεῖν appears with spiritual significance, that is, with a connotation of discipleship (1 Kgs 19:19-20). It is the scene where the Prophet Elijah called Elisha to be his successor. It is to be regarded as a divine call from God through Elijah because it was the LORD God who commanded Elijah to call him as his replacement for the ministry of divine judgment (19:16-17). Though Elisha was not informed about God's calling for him to be the successor of Elijah's prophetic office, Elisha instantly recognized it by the symbolic action of Elijah's throwing the mantle over him. It is a symbol of the call to the prophetic office. Also, the mantle is depicted as the instrument of spiritual power (2 Kgs 2:8). After Elijah's departure, it was given to Elisha and he performed the same miracle that Elijah did (2:13-14). Therefore, Elisha's action of "following" (ἀκολουθεῖν) as the response to the call is not a mere action of going after a respected teacher. It obviously has a religious and spiritual connotation. Kittel's opinion that in the Old Testament, "following" has no religious significance, and that this act of "following" expresses little more than a relationship of respect is unconvincing. Furthermore, the spiritual implication and gravity of the term "follow" in καὶ ἀκολουθήσω ὀπίσω σου ("and I will follow you," 1 Kgs 19:20) from Elisha's own lips are well intimated in the subsequent decisive actions that he slaughtered the oxen he has used for plowing in his past life and burned his plowing equipment to cook the meat and had a farewell feast with his parents and friends and then followed the Prophet. By noting that, "Behind Luke 9:57-62 par. Matt 8:19-22 (and Mark 1:16-18) stands the call of Elisha to be a disciple of Elijah (1 Kgs 19:19-21)," G. Schneider

---

33. Ezek 29:16 "The Egyptians shall never again be the reliance of the house of Israel; they will recall their iniquity, when they turned to them for aid . . . ," (καὶ οὐκέτι ἔσονται τῷ οἴκῳ Ισραηλ εἰς ἐλπίδα ἀναμιμνήσκουσαν ἀνομίαν ἐν τῷ αὐτοὺς ἀκολουθῆσαι ὀπίσω αὐτῶν . . .).

rightly shows that the term ἀκολουθεῖν is used with a spiritual and religious connotation in the text.[34]

C. Conclusion

As shown by the above appearances of ἀκολουθεῖν in classical Greek literature and the LXX, what determines the meaning of the term ἀκολουθεῖν is not the verb itself, but the associating words and motifs that surround the term as a semantic network. The implication communicated by ἀκολουθεῖν is determined by the literary context. In both Greco-Roman and Judaic literature, the term is employed to communicate diverse implications according to the object that comes after and the literary context in which it occurs. It is used both in the context of warning against backsliding of apostasy and in the context of calling someone into the prophetic office. It is employed to express literal, philosophical, religious, and spiritual meanings—from a simple action of going after or together with someone to a geographical location to a profound and decisive action of following that leads one into a whole new dimension of life in relation to God's economy and his ministry. All those diverse meanings and imports are created by the juxtaposed or associated words and motifs within the literary contexts. It indicates that the meanings and theological implications communicated by the employment of ἀκολουθεῖν in the Fourth Gospel, which will be investigated in PART II of the study, are certainly dependent upon its associated words and motifs and the intended logic of the literary context. In the hands of John, the skillful craftsman of language with a profound theology, the plain term ἀκολουθεῖν is open to impart distinct meanings and even abstruse implications according to how vocabularies and motifs surrounding it are combined.

As for the idea of following a divine being, while the term ἀκολουθεῖν is hardly used to convey the idea of following God in Judaic literature, in Greek literature it is used to communicate the idea of following the gods of rational man in philosophical life. Before the Fourth Gospel used the verb ἀκολουθεῖν in religious and spiritual connotation, "[a]lready in secular Greek the ordinary sense of 'following' or 'going behind' someone has given rise to that of following in an intellectual, moral or religious sense."[35] Yet, in what distinct religious and spiritual connotation the fourth evangelist employs the term is the problem to be investigated in the present study.

---

34. Schneider, " ἀκολουθέω," *EDNT* 1:49–52.
35. Kittel, " ἀκολουθέω," *TDNT* 1:210.

II. Ἀκολουθεῖν in the Other Books of the New Testament

Among the total 90 occurrences of the term ἀκολουθεῖν in the New Testament, 19 appearances are seen in the Fourth Gospel, and the other 60 occurrences are found in the Synoptics (25 in Matthew; 18 in Mark; 17 in Luke). Only 11 cases are seen in the other books in the New Testament (4 in Acts; 1 in 1 Cor 10:4; 6 in Revelation). Although there are compounds[36] of the verb, only the simple form of the term will be studied because the "pregnant sense of following as discipleship is reserved for the simple form ἀκολουθέω."[37]

In the following sections, an observation and analysis of the relevant pericopes will be given in three steps to find out how the term ἀκολουθεῖν is employed. One, all the occurrences of the term in a metaphorical and spiritual sense in the Synoptics will be investigated in order to find out what spiritual implications are communicated. This will be done by examining what words and motifs are associated with ἀκολουθεῖν. Two, the rare occurrences of ἀκολουθεῖν outside of the Synoptics will be probed, focusing on the texts that reflect the spiritual meaning of following. Three, from the inquiries, we will infer the characteristics of the usages of the term in the other books of the New Testament. The resulting inference will provide the present study with the basis to discern how the Fourth Gospel uses the common term ἀκολουθεῖν in unique theological significance and what distinctive aspects of the Spirituality of "following Jesus" are imparted by ἀκολουθεῖν in the Gospel.

A. In the Synoptic Gospels

In Matthew, among 25 occurrences of ἀκολουθεῖν, the texts 4:20, 22; 8:19, 22; 9:9; 10:38; 16:24; 19:21, 27–28 use the term metaphorically in a spiritual sense, and the texts 4:25; 8:1, 10; 9:19, 27; 12:15; 14:13–14; 19:2; 20:29, 34; 21:9; 26:58; 27:55 in a literal sense, and 8:23 in an ambiguous sense.[38] In

---

36. ἐξακολουθέω (2 Pet 1:16; 2:2, 15); ἐπακολουθέω (Mark 16:20; 1 Pet 2:21; 1 Tim 5:10, 24); παρακολουθέω (Mark 16:17; Luke 1:3; 1 Tim 4:6; 2 Tim 3:10); συνακολουθέω (Mark 5:37; 14:51; Luke 23:49).

37. Kittel, " ἀκολουθέω," *TDNT* 1:216.

38. This analysis is based on the data from both Davies and Allison's commentary and Kingsbury's article, which performs a thorough survey on the verb ἀκολουθεῖν to shed a light on the view of the community of Matthew. In determining whether the term is used in a metaphorical or a literal sense, Davies and Allison note that "the metaphorical usage consistently involves at least two things: (1) Jesus is the speaker—he issues the

Mark, among 18 uses of the term, the texts 1:18; 2:14; 8:34; 9:38; 10:21, 28, 52; 15:41[39] use it in a metaphorical sense, and the texts 2:15; 3:7; 5:24; 6:1; 10:32; 11:9; 14:13, 54 in a literal sense. In Luke, among 17 occurrences of the term, the texts 5:11, 27–28; 9:23, 49, 57, 59, 61; 18:22, 28, 43 use it in a metaphorical connotation, and the texts 7:9; 9:11; 22:10, 39, 54; 23:27 in a literal sense.[40] We will examine the passages that use ἀκολουθεῖν in spiritual and discipleship connotation as presented in the below table.[41]

	Matthew	Mark	Luke
1	4:20, 22	1:18	5:11
2	8:19, 22		9:57, 59, 61
3	9:9	2:14	5:27–28
4	10:38		
5	16:24	8:34	9:23
6	19:21, 27–28	10:21, 28	18:22, 28
7		10:52	18:43

---

summons to follow—and (2) cost is involved: discipleship entails sacrifice." Davies and Allison, *Matthew*, 1:399. Their analysis follows Kingsbury's criterion. Acknowledging the difficulty in determining whether the verb is used in literal or metaphorical manner, Kingsbury ("The Verb *Akolouthein* ['to Follow']," 58) claims that "the presence or absence of these two factors in connection with Matthew's use of *akolouthein* in any given passage is the critical principle." The two factors are: one, "personal commitment" to Jesus; and two, "cost" and "personal sacrifice."

39. France supports use of the verb ἀκολουθεῖν in a discipleship connotation: "Moreover, these women had not only provided material help, but also ἠκολούθουν αὐτῷ; this is the language of discipleship, and suggests that they, like the Twelve, were regular members of the group." France, *Mark*, 663.

40. Bock also renders a similar list. Bock, *Luke 1:1—9:50*, 461.

41. Although the verb ἀκολουθεῖν is used in metaphorical manner, Mark 9:38 and Luke 9:49 are not included in the investigation because the object of ἀκολουθεῖν is not Jesus, but "us" as the band of the disciples most likely referring to the Twelve exclusively commissioned by Jesus. Here "following us" means not "so much personal allegiance and obedience to Jesus, but membership in the 'authorized' circle of his followers." France, *Mark*, 377.

1. *Matt 4:20, 22; Mark 1:18; Luke 5:11*

Texts	Associated words/motifs	Context
Matt 4:20, 22	19 "I will make you <u>fish for people</u>"	17 "**kingdom of heaven** has come near"
	20 "**left** their nets"	23 "teaching..., proclaiming ..., and curing..."
	22 "**left** the boat and their father"	
Mark 1:18	17 "I will make you <u>fish for people</u>"	14,15 "proclaiming the good news";
	18 "**left** their nets"	"**kingdom of God** has come near"
	20 "**left** their father"	
Luke 5:11	6 "caught so many fish"	43,44 "proclaim the good news of **the**
	10 "you will be <u>catching people</u>"	**kingdom of God**"
	11 "**left** everything"	

In the narrative of Jesus' initial calling of Peter and Andrew and the Zebedee's sons in Matt 4:20, 22; Mark 1:18; Luke 5:11, two elements characterize the significance of following Jesus. First, the word juxtaposed before ἀκολουθεῖν is the repeated aorist participle ἀφέντες—"*left* their nets," "*left* the boat and their father," and in the Lukan text, "*left* everything." By the juxtaposition of the word "*left*" before the motion of following (ἀκολουθεῖν), the Synoptic evangelists emphasize that "following Jesus" entails a decisive action of abandoning one's former way of life and disconnecting from one's own family responsibilities.[42] Second, by clearly showing that they are called to be fishers of men, the Synoptics diligently point out the centrality of mission in the life of following Jesus. Furthermore, in the Lukan text, not only Jesus' divine power over nature, but the abundance of future success in the mission of fishing for people is alluded to by the miraculous catching of fish. When it is viewed in the near context (Matt 4:17; Mark 1:14, 15; Luke 4:43, 44), following Jesus taking "precedence over livelihood and family" is an essential prerequisite for becoming the agents of the gospel of the kingdom of heaven.[43] The subsequent context (Matt 4:23, "Jesus went throughout

---

42. In both ancient Judaism and Greco-Roman culture, the renunciation of family relationship for the sake of religious commitment or philosophical quest is a commonly known notion as stated by Barton. For further discussion on this, see Barton, *Discipleship and Family Ties*, 23–56, 66–67.

43. France, *Mark*, 97. "The urgency and the radical nature of the call are based on the near approach of the kingdom of heaven (4:17); following Jesus has to do with his

Galilee, teaching in their synagogues and proclaiming the good news of the kingdom and curing every disease and every sickness among the people") also indicates that following Jesus means "carrying out the same activity as Jesus himself."[44]

2. Matt 8:19, 22; Luke 9:57, 59, 61

Texts	Associated words/motifs	Context
Matt 8:19	19 **"wherever you go"** (ὅπου ἐὰν ἀπέρχῃ) 20 "nowhere to lay his head" (οὐκ ἔχει ποῦ)	8:14–17 Jesus heals many
Matt 8:22	21 "first" 21 "bury my father" 22 "let the dead bury ..."	8:18–22 *the cost of following Jesus* 8:23–27 Jesus calms a storm
Luke 9:57	57 **"wherever you go"** 58 "nowhere to lay his head"	9:51–56 a Samaritan village rejects Jesus
Luke 9:59	59 "first" 59 "bury my father" 60 "let the dead bury ..." 60 "go and proclaim **the kingdom of God**"	9:57–62 *the cost of following Jesus*
Luke 9:61	62 "first" 61 "say farewell to those at my home" 62 "fit for **the kingdom of God**"	10:1–12 Jesus sends out the Seventy-two

In Matt 8:19–20 and Luke 9:57–58 the cost of following Jesus is expressed in both the would-be follower's statement and Jesus' reply to him. The statement, "I will follow you wherever you go," reflects a resolve to be his follower, no matter what the cost. Yet, Jesus warns him that if he will follow

---

significance for this kingdom." Nolland, *Matthew*, 179.

44. Nolland also suggests that the Matthean calling passage (4:18–22) is to be read looking "forward to verse 23" where Jesus' own ministry is condensed in three verbs: "Jesus went throughout Galilee, *teaching* in their synagogues and *proclaiming* the good news of the kingdom and *curing* every disease and every sickness among the people" (Matt 4:23).

him, he is to be ready for the rejection[45] of this world and the consequent homelessness of a wandering life.[46] In these texts, following Jesus involves, particularly, the loss of the basic human comforts of life in this world, the facing of hostility[47] and ostracism from the world. In the journey of following Jesus, the hostility and rejection of the world are as inevitable as facing constant waves and billows as one crosses the sea.[48]

To bury one's own father is one of the most important filial duties whether in ancient or contemporary culture, not to mention that it is so in Jewish context as linked to the fifth item of the Ten Commandments. Matt 8:21–22 and Luke 9:59–60, however, depict "the fiercely radical nature of the call to follow Jesus, with its priorities that displace even the most solemn and sacred of filial obligations."[49] Whether it is a request of permission for future burial of the aging parent or the primary mourning period or the secondary burial of the bones, and whether Jesus means spiritually or physically dead people in his reply of refusal, the focal point of the text is that following Jesus takes a matchless priority over any human responsibility and family ties.[50] Ironically, the word "first" (πρῶτον) that conveys priority is uttered in Matt 8:21 and Luke 9:59, 61 by those who need to have the spiritual priority of following Jesus. In Lukan text, the pressing duty that takes utmost precedence is identified as the proclamation of the kingdom of God (Luke 9:60) for which Jesus calls, ἀκολούθει μοι ("Follow me," Luke 9:59).

---

45. NET Bible study note (BibleWorks 9.0) on Matt 8:20 and Luke 9:58 says, "Jesus' reply is simply this: Does the man understand the rejection he will be facing? Jesus has no home in the world (*the Son of Man has no place to lay his head*)."

46. Davies and Allison, *Matthew*, 2:43.

47. In Matthew, the disciples will be warned to anticipate "not being welcomed (10:14), judicial persecution (vv. 16–20), and family and wider hostility (vv. 21–22, 34–36) and will be advised to flee from their persecutors (v. 23)." Nolland, *Matthew*, 366.

48. Nolland finds similitude between the demands of discipleship (Matt 8:20, 22) and the stresses of the voyage crossing the sea (Matt 8:18, 23–24).

49. Nolland, *Luke 9:21–18:34*, 541.

50. There have been various scholarly views and discussions on Jesus' refusal to the disciple's request. See Davies and Allison, *Matthew*, 2:56–58.

3. *Matt 9:9; Mark 2:14; Luke 5:27–28*

Texts	Associated words/motifs	Context
Matt 9:9	9 "sitting; got up"	Healing of the Paralytic (9:2–8)
	10 "sitting at dinner" (ἀνακειμένου)	
	10, 11 "tax collectors and sinners"	Fasting (9:14–17)
	13 "I desire mercy..."	
	13 "to call... sinners" (καλέσαι... ἁμαρτωλοὺς)	
Mark 2:14	14 "sitting; got up"	Healing of the Paralytic (2:1–12)
	15 "sitting at dinner" (κατακεῖσθαι)	
	15 "tax collectors and sinners"	Fasting (2:18–22)
	17 "to call... sinners" (καλέσαι... ἁμαρτωλοὺς)	
Luke 5:27–28	27 "sitting"	Healing of the Paralytic (5:17–26)
	28 "got up, left everything"	
	29 "great banquet" (δοχὴν μεγάλην)	Fasting (5:33–39)
	29 "tax collectors sinners"	
	32 "to call... sinners" (καλέσαι... ἁμαρτωλοὺς)	

In the calling account of Levi, the verb ἀκολουθεῖν is used by all Synoptic authors in both Jesus' authoritative summons (ἀκολούθει μοι) and in the response (ἠκολούθησεν αὐτῷ) of the one called. The contrastive action verbs of "sitting" at the tax booth and "got up" signify the decisiveness and radical abandonment of previous life in following Jesus. It is further added by the phrase, "left everything," in the Lukan text. However, the unique contribution of the account is the association of ἀκολουθεῖν with "sinners" and "banquet/sitting at dinner" and additionally "mercy" in the Matthean text. By calling sinners and having a banquet together with them, Jesus shows Levi that the life of following Jesus embraces "sinners" with mercy into the feast of the kingdom of heaven.[51] It adds a new light on the meaning of following Jesus; namely, that following Jesus has to do with being the agents

---

51. The term "sinners" in Matt 9:10 "creates a link back to 9:2, 5, 6." Nolland, *Matthew*, 386. The dinner table alludes to one's participation in the kingdom of God both in this life and in the eschatological dimension (Matt 26:29; Rev 3:29; cf. 2 Sam 9:7, 11, 13).

of mercy by calling sinners into the banquet of the kingdom. This is a true fulfillment of the spirit of fasting (cf. Isa 58:6–7).[52] Following Jesus not only calls for a complete change and severance from a former way of life, but also entails the newness[53] of the kingdom life following the Lord's mercy.

4. Matt 10:38 (Luke 14:27)[54]

Text	Associated words/motifs	Context
Matt 10:38	"take up the cross" "not worthy of me"	37 "love more than me" 39 "lose life" (ψυχή)

Thus far we have seen that following Jesus entails the renunciation of the former way of life (Matt 4:20; Mark 1:18; Luke 5:11), family ties and duties (Matt 4:22; 8:22; Mark 1:20; Luke 9:59–62), and of one's basic life of comfort in this world (Matt 8:19–20; Luke 9:57–58). Yet, the text Matt 10:38 goes into the deeper level of renunciation: the renunciation of self.[55] The abnegation of one's own self is an inevitable necessity in following Jesus: "whoever does not take up the cross and follow me is not worthy of me." Although there are other possible interpretations, taking up the cross is "in the first instance a vivid metaphor which stands for utter self abnegation (cf. the exposition of Calvin, *Ints*. 3.8)."[56] Davies and Allison rightly com-

---

52. The subsequent accounts following the account of Levi's calling demonstrate a sharp contrast between feasting and fasting. France, *Mark*, 136.

53. To follow Jesus is to become an agent of the new life of the kingdom of God by following the king. Nolland's summary of the larger context that includes Levi's calling narrative (Luke 5:27–32) supports it: "This fourth and central item in 5:1—6:16 offers important interpretive keys for the larger unit. The major emphasis is on the new state of affairs inaugurated by the coming of Jesus. It is a time of joyful celebration in which the pardoning hand of God reaches out to restore sinners. The new thing that God is doing is not to be treated as only a patch for the old, nor constrained within the limits of the old. As the new eschatological movement of God it must be allowed its own integrity." Nolland, *Luke 1:1—9:20*, 244.

54. The Lukan parallel text (Luke 14:27) employs ἔρχεται ὀπίσω μου instead of ἀκολουθεῖ ὀπίσω μου.

55. Matt 10:38 καὶ ὃς οὐ λαμβάνει τὸν σταυρὸν αὐτοῦ καὶ ἀκολουθεῖ ὀπίσω μου, οὐκ ἔστιν μου ἄξιος.

56. Davies and Allison, *Matthew*, 2:223. For the discussion of the various interpretations of the meaning of taking up the cross, see the list of six alternatives outlined by Davies and Allison (*Matthew*, 2:222–23) (i) to ready oneself for punishment by the Romans; (ii) martyrdom which is the same fate that befell Jesus; (iii) Jesus' original saying, "take up my yoke" (cf. Matt 11:29), which became "cross" after Easter; (iv) taking

ment, "For Matthew, the cross is, as 10:39 makes plain, the outstanding symbol of self-denial."[57] The fact that absolute self-denial in following Jesus is not optional is emphasized by Jesus' solemn saying, "is not worthy of me," which is asserted as "cannot be my disciple" in Luke 14:27. The subsequent verse Matt 10:39 as the immediate context further affirms the idea of self-renunciation that following Jesus must entail losing one's own life, which is "to die to oneself."[58]

Texts	Associated words/motifs	Context
Matt 16:24	24 "deny oneself"	21–23 Jesus' Messianic suffering prediction and Peter's objection
	24 "take up cross"	
	25 "lose life (ψυχή) for Jesus' sake"	27–28 the coming of the Son in glory
		17:1–8 the glorious Son
Mark 8:34	34 to "the crowd" and "his disciples"	31–33 Son of Man's suffering prediction and Peter's rebuke
	34 "deny oneself"	8:38—9:1 the coming of the Son in glory
	34 "take up cross"	
	35 "lose life (ψυχή) for Jesus' sake"	9:2–8 the glorious Son
Luke 9:23	23 "deny oneself"	21–22 Jesus' suffering
	23 "take up cross daily"	26–27 the coming of the Son in glory
	24 "lose life (ψυχή) for Jesus' sake"	28–36 the glorious Son and servants appeared in glory

the road of discipleship and self-denial; (v) the mark of the *Taw*, the last letter of the Hebrew alphabet (ת)—to dedicate oneself to God and to prepare oneself for the coming assize; (vi) originally the suffering of Isaac—to offer oneself up as a sacrifice like Isaac did.

For a discussion on cross-bearing in connection with a willingness to endure suffering, the pain of persecution or participating in Jesus' death by the active decision making and obedience in daily life as well as passively facing suffering, see Bruner, *Matthew*, 490-91; Bock, *Luke 9:51—24:53*, 1286-87.

57. Ibid., 2:221.

58. Losing one's life does not mean martyrdom in its literal sense (although it may be inferred as one of the forms of losing one's life as a result), but it means absolute self-denial; that is, hating one's life (cf. John 12:25). "To deny oneself—indeed to die to oneself—this is what it means to 'follow Jesus.'" Hagner, *Matthew 14–28*, 483.

5. Matt 16:24; Mark 8:34; Luke 9:23[59]

The texts (Matt 16:24; Mark 8:34; Luke 9:23) provide a fuller expression of what is said in Matt 10:38.[60] It is done by the association of ἀκολουθεῖν with the unique phrases "denying oneself" and "taking up one's cross." This association is found nowhere else but in these texts.[61] The verb ἀρνέομαι/ ἀπαρνέομαι (to deny) is used in Peter's denial of his Lord Jesus (Matt 26:34, 35, 75; Mark 14:30, 31, 72; Luke 22:57). In these usages, the meaning of the verb becomes obvious: "to disown somebody"[62] or "to dissociate oneself completely from someone."[63] The meaning of the phrase makes clear the implication of taking up the cross and following Jesus. To follow Jesus is the journey of life with constant "breaking of every link which ties a man to himself."[64] In other words, to follow Jesus renouncing oneself means to drastically disassociate oneself from one's own concerns, wishes, and desires. From the starting moment, as it were, the one who follows Jesus is not one's own, but Christ's (1 Cor 6:19). The Markan text says that this call is given not only to the disciples, but also to the crowd (Mark 8:34, "He called the crowd with his disciples, and said to them, 'If any want to become my followers, . . .'"). It means that anyone who wants to be a follower of Jesus must follow him in this way. By adding καθ' ἡμέραν ("daily"), the Lukan text adds that it must happen in every aspect of one's daily life. Yet, following Jesus in this way is not depressing or without reward because Jesus' followers will be welcomed by the Son who is coming in the dazzling glory and some of them will see the powerful presence of the kingdom even in this life (Matt 16:27—17:8; Mark 3:38—9:8; Luke 9:26–36).

---

59. "Matthew has followed Mark without alteration. Luke has inserted καθ' ἡμέραν (Luke 9:23) and dropped the ἀπ- prefix." Davies and Allison, *Matthew*, 2:670.

60. For the meaning of "take up the cross," see the previous discussion on Matt 10:38.

61. Matt 16:24 (par. Mark 8:34) ἀπαρνησάσθω ἑαυτὸν καὶ ἀράτω τὸν σταυρὸν αὐτοῦ καὶ ἀκολουθείτω μοι. Luke 9:23 ἀρνησάσθω ἑαυτὸν καὶ ἀράτω τὸν σταυρὸν αὐτοῦ καθ' ἡμέραν καὶ ἀκολουθείτω μοι.

62. Davies and Allison, *Matthew*, 2:670.

63. France, *Mark*, 340.

64. Davies and Allison, *Matthew*, 2:670. Cf. "Denying oneself," in Hebrew expression, is "hating one's own life."

6. *Matt 19:21, 27–28; Mark 10:21, 28; Luke 18:22, 28*[65]

Texts	Associated words/motifs	Context
Matt 19:21, 27–28	16 "eternal life" (ζωὴν αἰώνιον) 21 "go, sell, give, then come…" 23–26 impossibility for mortals to enter the kingdom and possibility of God 27 "have left everything…" 28 "at the renewal… when the Son of Man is seated on the throne of glory"; "you… will sit on twelve thrones" 29 "left," "receive a hundredfold," "will inherit eternal life" (ζωὴν αἰώνιον)	19:13–15 little children and the kingdom of heaven 20:1–16 hired laborers in the vineyard 20:17–19 Jesus' crucifixion and resurrection 20:20–23 the cup to drink
Mark 10:21, 28	17 "what must I do to inherit eternal life?" (ζωὴν αἰώνιον) 21 "go, sell, give, then come…" 23–27 impossibility for mortals to enter the kingdom and possibility of God 28 "have left everything…" 29 "who has left… for my sake and for the sake of the good news" 30 "receive a hundredfold in this age," "with persecution," "in the age to come eternal life" (ζωὴν αἰώνιον)	13–16 little children and the kingdom of God 32–34 Jesus' death and resurrection 35–40 the cup that I drink you will drink
Luke 18:22, 28	18 "what must I do to inherit eternal life?" (ζωὴν αἰώνιον) 22 "sell all, distribute, then come…" 24–27 impossibility for mortals to enter the kingdom and possibility of God 28 "we have left our homes…" 29 "who has left," "get back much more in this life," "in the age to come eternal life" (ζωὴν αἰώνιον)	15–17 infants and the kingdom of God 31–33 Jesus' death and resurrection 34 the disciples' inability to understand

---

65. The pericopes need to be interpreted as a coherent unit because the account of the rich young man and the dialogue between Jesus and Peter including the disciples are closely linked. For the detailed observation on the textual differences among the texts of the Gospels, refer to Bock, *Luke 9:51—24:53*, 1476–91.

The contribution of these texts to the significance of following Jesus is that ἀκολουθεῖν is associated with ζωὴν αἰώνιον ("eternal life"). Eternal life is identified as the ultimate goal of following in the dialogue between Jesus and the rich man, and as the reward in the subsequent conversation between Jesus and Peter.

Before paying attention to the fact that he is rich, the texts state that the man has made tremendous efforts to attain ζωὴν αἰώνιον (Matt 19:16, 20).[66] The urgency in his soul and the sincerity in his pursuit for eternal life are hinted at in the action that he "ran up and knelt before him" (Mark 10:17).[67] Jesus recognized the man's truthful and hard endeavor to enter God's kingdom.[68] Jesus wanted "him on board."[69] Yet, astonishingly the man failed to enter God's kingdom, but left grieving at Jesus' demand that he had to sell all his possessions, give to the poor, and follow him.[70]

Does the passage teach that affluence is the barrier to entering the kingdom of heaven? Is Jesus' command to sell all possessions and give to the poor universal for any follower of Jesus? As R. T. France comments, "[t]he following dialogue with the disciples leaves little room for concluding that this particular rich man was exceptional; Jesus' words are starkly universal, hence the disciples' dismay."[71] It is a universal command, not for this rich man or some spiritual elites only. Yet, wasn't it true that some followers of Jesus still retained their possessions while following Jesus, and Jesus was supported by their possessions? In fact, the question begins at the point of the man's approach for eternal life. Is eternal life obtainable by doing something good, by human works, such as by the reckless surrendering of all possessions? Does Jesus mean that the man can obtain eternal life by doing radically good deeds? Jesus' answer to him, "one thing you lack," which implies, do this and you will have treasure in heaven, appears to support that idea. But, that is not the case.

66. Matt 19:16, 20 διδάσκαλε, τί ἀγαθὸν ποιήσω ἵνα σχῶ ζωὴν αἰώνιον; . . . πάντα ταῦτα ἐφύλαξα· "Teacher, what good deed must I do to have eternal life? . . . I have kept all these."

67. In the Scriptures, this is the only person who knelt down before Jesus begging for the way to find eternal life. He petitioned like those who had tremendously painful human situations such as a man with leprosy or the fathers who had sick or dying children.

68. Scrutinizing his inner being with a careful searching look, Jesus is duly impressed and loves him (Mark 10:21). France, *Mark*, 403.

69. Ibid.

70. The young man's search for eternal life seems earnest. Yet, he fails to gain eternal life. Is it because he failed in renunciation of his possessions, or is it because he was approaching the matter of entering the kingdom of God with the wrong perspective?

71. Ibid., 400.

What applies universally to all followers of Jesus is not selling and giving one's possessions as a good work to inherit eternal life and the kingdom of God. What applies universally to all followers of Jesus is that it is impossible for mortals to attain eternal life by any good works, but possible only by God. It is already hinted by Jesus' initial reply that no one is good but God alone (Mark 10:18).

Jesus' immensely harsh demand to this sincere seeker of eternal life gives a whole different perspective on the kingdom of God and the way to inherit eternal life. It is never a matter of prioritization. The costs of following Jesus and the radical motions entailed in following Jesus, observed in the previous passages, never indicate that anyone can obtain ζωὴν αἰώνιον when one makes a radical decision and sacrifice to follow Jesus with precedence over former living or family ties. To have eternal life is not something human beings can attain by human will power and capability, or by making great efforts in the same way humans achieve things in this world (cf. John 1:13).

A camel passing through the eye of a needle (Matt 19:24; Mark 10:25) connotes not simply difficulty, but impossibility (παρὰ ἀνθρώποις τοῦτο ἀδύνατόν ἐστιν, Matt 19:26).[72] Whether rich or poor, for mortals to enter the kingdom of heaven is impossible by means of their own innate ability (παρὰ ἀνθρώποις ἀδύνατον, Mark 10:27).[73] Entering God's kingdom is something beyond the capacity of human prioritization or determination or making sacrifice for it. It is possible by God's own operation alone as is confirmed by Jesus' own statement (παρὰ δὲ θεῷ πάντα δυνατά, Matt 19:26; ἀλλ' οὐ παρὰ θεῷ· πάντα γὰρ δυνατὰ παρὰ τῷ θεῷ, Mark 10:27).[74]

The Synoptic texts, however, do not spell out further the details of the operation of divine power in God's own equation of the kingdom, unlike Pauline writings (cf. Rom 8:2–4), that how "For God all things are possible"

---

72. France (*Mark*, 404) explains its meaning: "The grotesque idea of a camel going through the eye of a needle is a proverbial way of stating the impossible: a rabbinic saying (*b. Ber.* 55b; cf. also *b. B. Mes.* 38b; *b. 'Erub.* 53a) uses an elephant going through the eye of needle (along with a date palm made of gold) as an image of the impossible . . ."

73. See Bock, *Luke 9:51—24:53*, 1486. "The disciples interpret Jesus' remark that the rich will find it impossible to enter the kingdom to mean that everyone will find it impossible to enter . . . Τίς (*tis*, who) is general, so the premise and implications of Jesus' remark is that it is not just rich people who are in trouble, but all people (Plummer 1896:426 and Fitzmyer 1985:1205 compare it to Num 24:23)."

74. As a theological insight, France (*Mark*, 406) comments on the mathematics of divine power beyond human calculation: "[I]t *is* impossible. But that impossibility is then placed on the debit side of the human/divine balance. What human beings cannot do, God can. They have considered the criteria for entering God's kingdom from a human perspective, and from that perspective those criteria, as Jesus has now set them out, cannot be met. But if it is *God's* kingdom, we are not limited to human calculation."

with regard to inheriting eternal life, and that how those who follow Jesus can inherit eternal life. Thus, we end further consideration except to mention that God's formula definitely works somehow in the life of those who follow Jesus. One certain thing is that inheriting eternal life by following Jesus is not a mathematical equation that humans can control. It is dependent on God's own mathematics of salvation because the kingdom and eternal life are, after all, his. Human decisive action in radical renunciation of one's possessions, former life, family ties and duties, and even one's own self is not the controlling factor. It is utterly dependent on God's own mysterious work that is exerted for the followers of Jesus (cf. Eph 1:20; 2:5, 6). With the insight of this point, the significance of following Jesus is lifted up to be a new and radically different dimension that goes beyond human capacity.

Although Matt 19:21, 27–28; Mark 10:21, 28; and Luke 18:22, 28 communicate the profound implication that entering the kingdom of God utterly depends on God's operation, these texts do describe what followers do and what recompense is for them. As to what humans must do, "left everything/homes" (Matt 19:27; Mark 10:28; Luke 18:28) is juxtaposed with "followed you" (ἠκολουθήσαμέν σοι) in Peter's saying, in contrast to the rich man's response. The verb "left" (ἀφίημι) is repeated in Jesus' affirmation with the list of the things the followers have left (καὶ πᾶς ὅστις ἀφῆκεν . . ., Matt 19:29). As for the recompenses, they are incomparable to what they left behind. "Much more" or "a hundredfold" will be paid back in this age, and in the age to come they will inherit eternal life (καὶ ζωὴν αἰώνιον κληρονομήσει, Matt 19:29), the very object which the rich man sought but failed to attain. In addition to these, the Matthean text adds the kingly privilege that those who have followed Jesus will sit on twelve thrones when the Son of Man will be seated on the throne of his glory (Matt 19:28; cf. 16:27). Yet, Jesus' followers will also face persecution in this life before they join their Master's glory (Mark 10:30).

Those who follow Jesus inherit ζωὴν αἰώνιον (Matt 19:29) which the rich young man failed to acquire (Matt 19:16, 22). It seems that the followers attain it by renunciation and because they left those things behind (Matt 19:27, 29), but as a matter of truth, according to the principle of the kingdom (Matt 19:26; Mark 10:27; Luke 18:27), it is God's work and power that enables them to surrender all the valuable things in this life, follow Jesus (ἡμεῖς ἀφήκαμεν πάντα καὶ ἠκολουθήσαμέν σοι, Matt 19:27), and receive ζωὴν αἰώνιον. It is what Jesus' followers receive as a gift of inheritance from God, not what they attain.

7. Mark 10:52; Luke 18:43[75]

Texts	Associated words/motifs	Context
Mark 10:52	47–48 "Son of David" 52 "gained sight," "on the way"	10:35–45 the disciples' desire to be great 11:1–11 Jesus' entry into Jerusalem
Luke 18:43	38–39 "Son of David" 43 "gained sight," "glorifying God"	18:31–34 final prediction of suffering of Son of Man 19:28–40 Jesus' entry into Jerusalem

The passages contribute to the implication of following Jesus: First, in the association of the term "follow" (ἀκολουθεῖν) with both "blindness" (τυφλός) and "gaining sight" (ἀναβλέπω); second, in the association of ἀκολουθεῖν with the critical phrase "on the way" (ἐν τῇ ὁδῷ) in the Markan text of 10:46–52.

The narrative of Jesus opening the eyes of the blind man plays a symbolic role "in relation to the 'blindness' of the disciples" (Mark 6:52; 8:17–18, 21).[76] The disciples have demonstrated their blindness in understanding the principle of the kingdom and the significance of Jesus' messianic suffering (the way of the cross).[77] Their eyes were closed because their interest was so human. One of the examples presented was their quarrelling over a greater seat in the earthly kingdom (Mark 10:35–45). Jesus was moving toward Jerusalem to fulfill the work of God by his suffering and death; the disciples were moving toward their own goal in their spiritual blindness. Though they were physically following Jesus, they were not following him in his way. Although they abandoned their former life for Jesus' sake, their eyes needed to be opened to follow Jesus as his followers. In this context, Jesus opened the blind man's eyes.[78] When his eyes were opened, the man began a new life of following Jesus, as an exemplary representative of all those who

---

75. Why is the parallel passage Matt 20:34 not included? It is because ἀκολουθεῖν in the Matthean text hardly conveys spiritual connotation as Nolland (*Matthew*, 830) states: "In Matthew this following puts them on a par with the crowd in v. 29: they have not necessarily become disciples in a more developed sense, but like the crowd they have behaved in a way that points towards discipleship (cf. Matt 4:25)."

76. France, *Mark*, 320.

77. As for the blindness and incomprehension of the disciples in relation to the way of the cross and Jesus' healing, see Watts, *Isaiah's New Exodus*, 221–57.

78. The literary context and positioning of the narratives are intriguing: the disciples' quarrel out of their blindness over seat (10:35–45)—the eye opening of the blind man (10:46–52)—the entry into Jerusalem (11:1–11).

find enlightenment and follow the Master.⁷⁹ Following Jesus is a spiritual journey of new life, possible only for those whose eyes are opened to grasp God's hidden kingdom values.

The association of ἀκολουθεῖν with ἐν τῇ ὁδῷ ("on the way") in Mark 10:52 indicates that following Jesus involves following him in his way to the cross. The recurring use of the phrase ἐν τῇ ὁδῷ in Mark (8:27; 9:33–34; 10:17, 32, 52) reflects not only geographical movement, but a specific way characterized by Jesus' journey to Jerusalem and eventual death on the cross. The phrase is found in the section of Jesus' journey to Jerusalem to take his cross. Beginning (8:27) and ending (10:52) with the phrase ἐν τῇ ὁδῷ, the pericope leads the narrative towards the cross. Therefore, it is implied by ἠκολούθει αὐτῷ ἐν τῇ ὁδῷ ("followed him on the way") that Bartimaeus followed Jesus in his way to the cross. Although the degree of Bartimaeus's understanding of Jesus' cross is questionable, it is hard to deny that, by the association of the two terms ἀκολουθεῖν and ἐν τῇ ὁδω, Mark intends to indicate that Bartimaeus followed Jesus' way to the cross.⁸⁰ Whereas others perceived him to be "Jesus of Nazareth," Bartimaeus twice called him by the special messianic title "Son of David," which is equivalent to χριστὸς (Christ).⁸¹ Furthermore, the first-century Jesus' followers consistently identified their own way of faith as "the Way" (ἡ ὁδός) (Acts 9:2; 16:17; 18:25–26; 19:9, 23; 22:4; 24:14, 22). Thus, in the narrative of Bartimaeus, it is implied that following Jesus is to follow him in the way of the cross.

To combine the two implications, to follow Jesus is to walk on the way of Jesus' cross by being freed from spiritual blindness, since God's way, wisdom, and power are hidden from and incomprehensible to natural human understanding (1 Cor 1:18–25).

---

79. For Best (*Following Jesus: Discipleship*, 136), Bartimaeus is a true and exemplary disciple. That Bartimaeus called Jesus ῥαββουνί also affirms that he became a follower of Jesus as it is what a disciple would do (cf. John 20:16). France, *Mark*, 424–25; Donahue and Harrington, *Mark*, 318; Stein, *Mark*, 497; cf. Lane, *Mark*, 389; Gundry, *Mark*, 595.

80. Ossandon, "Bartimaeus' Faith," 377–402.

81. The messianic title υἱὲ Δαυίδ appears only in the accounts of the blind man's eye opening in Mark and Luke (except Mark 12:35).

B. In the Book of Revelation (14:1–5)

Text	Associated words/motifs	Context
Rev 14:4	1 "standing with the Lamb on Zion"	The contrasts (13:1–18; 14:1–5)
	2 "sing a new song before the throne"	"follow": the beast (13:3) ↔ the Lamb (14:4)
	3 "been purchased"	"worship": the beast (13:4, 8, 12; cf. 14:9, 11) ↔ God (14:3; cf. 6–7)
	4b "not defiled"	
	4c "the Lamb—wherever he goes"	"mark on forehead": the beast's name (13:16–17; cf. 14:9, 11) ↔ the name of the Lamb and his Father's (14:1)
	4d "were purchased to be first fruits"	
	5 "no lie; blameless"	

Although it is used several times outside of the Gospels, the only usage of ἀκολουθεῖν with a spiritual connotation is found in Rev 14:4.[82] The text uniquely conveys the rich implications of "following Christ." It does so through an eschatological viewpoint by associating ἀκολουθεῖν with a few major motifs: "the Lamb" (14:1), "being purchased" (14:3), "first fruits" (14:4), and "not defiled and blameless" (14:4, 5).

Rev 14:1–5 begins with an eschatological "vision" of the Lamb standing on Mount Zion. Then there comes the "audition"; that is, the voice singing a new song before the throne of God in verses 2 and 3.[83] Though the Lamb stands in the center of the vision, the text quickly draws the readers' attention to the 144,000, those accompanying the Lamb.[84] The rest of the text is devoted to portraying the characterizations of the 144,000 in detail (14:4, 5). The diagram below shows the significance of ἀκολουθεῖν and how it functions as the center of the passage in relation to the others motifs.[85]

---

82. Acts 12:8, 9; 13:43; 21:36; 1 Cor 10:4; Rev 6:8; 14:4, 8, 9, 13; 19:14.

83. Fiorenza, "The Followers of the Lamb," 144.

84. As the 144,000 is the symbolic number of completeness, it is "the totality of God's people throughout the ages." Beale, *Revelation*, 733. Aune also comments, "It probably presents the complete number of the people of God: the twelve tribes of Israel times the twelve apostles (12 x 12 = 144) times 1,000 (representing completeness, totality and perfection) = 144,000." Aune, "Following the Lamb," 276.

85. For different views on the characteristics of the 144,000, see Fiorenza's fourfold characterization ("The Followers of the Lamb," 144); Mounce's three traits (Mounce, *Revelation*, 266–68); and Beale's two attributes emphasized by *inclusio*. Beale, *Revelation*, 738.

A: V3b having been purchased from
(οἱ <u>ἠγορασμένοι ἀπὸ</u>)

B: V4a were not defiled / they are virgins
(<u>οὐκ</u> ἐμολύνθησαν / παρθένοι γάρ <u>εἰσιν</u>)

> **C: V4b following the Lamb**
> (ἀκολουθοῦντες τῷ ἀρνίῳ)

A': V4c were purchased from
(οὗτοι <u>ἠγοράσθησαν ἀπο</u>)

B': V5 was not found a lie / they are unblemished
(<u>οὐχ</u> εὑρέθη ψεῦδος / ἄμωμοί <u>εἰσιν</u>)

The term ἀκολουθεῖν is located in the center of the unit C. Furthermore, while the other verbs in A and B are in aorist or perfect participle form, the text emphatically uses present participle form for ἀκολουθεῖν, even though the action of "following" happened in their past life on earth.[86] The 144,000 are those who are purchased from the earth/humankind (A and A'). Being purchased is not only the starting point but fountainhead from which their spiritual journey of "following" originated. They are eventually found to be virgins[87] in the condition of spiritual purity (B) and unblemished (B'). This is the final state of the 144,000 after the long journey of their life as Jesus' followers. Between being purchased and their final condition of purity and truthfulness lies the life of "following."[88] The contents of their whole life are identified in a single phrase: "following the Lamb" (C).

The weightiness of "following the Lamb" (14:4) as the central characteristic of the life of the 144,000 is reinforced by the contrast to the life of

---

86. Beale, *Revelation*, 741.

87. Virginity symbolizes that the 144,000 have kept their loyalty to God, not giving themselves to the idolatry of the beast in the way of the world. Beale (*Revelation*, 741) comments, "That the group described in 14:1–5 is in contrast with the beast-worshippers in 13:11–18 also suggests that the idea of virgins is figurative . . . virginity is one way of portraying that loyalty." Aune ("Following the Lamb," 274) also says, "It is also facilitated by the fact that in the Old Testament unchastity is a frequent metaphor for the act of turning away from the true worship of God and embracing the idolatrous worship of idols (cf. Jer 3:2; 13:27; Ezek 16:15–58; 23:1–49; 43:7; Hos 5:4; 6:10). Perhaps here too virginity is a metaphor for faithfulness to God." It is also supported by Paul's teaching of "a chaste virgin to Christ" in 2 Cor 11:2.

88. Swete rightly comments that "purity" and "truthfulness" are distinctive marks of the followers of Christ. Swete, *Apocalypse*, 180.

"following the beast" (13:3). What determines the quality of their life and their final destiny wholly depends on whom they "follow." The vision of the Lamb and his "followers" (14:1–5) is the "anti-vision" of the beast and the "followers" of the beast (13:2–4).[89] Even when all the inhabitants of the world follow the beast, bearing the beast's name on their foreheads (13:3) and worshipping him (13:4), the followers of the Lamb will not. Under the threat of death (cf. 13:8, 15), they will follow Jesus, the Lamb, keeping his name on their foreheads (14:1).

"Following the Lamb" is not sauntering with him as he "strolls" around in heaven. It is implied by the fact that ἀκολουθεῖν is closely associated with "the Lamb," whom they follow "wherever he goes," bears the mark of being slaughtered (5:6, 12; 13:8; cf. 7:14; 12:11).[90] It is one of the essential characteristics of the Lamb in Revelation. The Lamb went through suffering in service to God even to the point of being slain before he receives "divine adoration" with God (5:8, 13; 17:10; 15:3) and the authority (17:14; 19:16; 22:1, 3) and power of judgment (6:16; 14:10).[91] Thus, following the Lamb implies joining the suffering and death of the Lamb.[92] The reality is further supported by the phrase, "wherever he goes," which not only echoes the idea of "regardless of the cost" in the Synoptic tradition (Matt 8:19–20; Luke 9:57–58), but also, having in mind that the "where" the Lamb went is the way of death, suggests a dauntless life of facing death ("for they did not cling to life even in the face of death," Rev 12:11; cf. 2:10, 13; 18:24; 20:4). The implication of "following Jesus" to the point of death, which was indicated in the Synoptic tradition, is now clarified and bolstered up in Rev 14:4. Those who are following the Lamb at the risk of their life during the terrestrial life with spiritual purity and truthfulness will stand together with the Lamb in the celestial sanctuary of God.

C. Conclusion

Outside the Fourth Gospel, the theological implications and Spirituality of "following Jesus" evolved gradually by the term ἀκολουθεῖν, and, in

---

89. Fiorenza, "The Followers of the Lamb," 144–45, 152, 154.

90. Mounce, *Revelation*, 268. The term ἀρνίον is unique to Revelation (and John 21:15). Twenty eight of twenty-nine usages refer exclusively to Christ. As Mounce (*Revelation*, 132) comments, "[i]t should be noted that ἀρνίον is consistently used instead of ἀμνός, the word used of Christ in John 1:29, 36 (also in 1 Pet 1:19)."

91. Jeremias, "ἀμνός, ἀρήν, ἀρνίον," *TDNT* 1:338–41.

92. Mounce, *Revelation*, 268. Cf. Reading the text from the light of 7:17, Aune comments that following the Lamb means following the lead of the shepherd. Aune, *Revelation 6–16*, 812–13.

particular, through its association with various vocabularies and motifs in many passages. In the calling scene of the Synoptics, it started with the abandonment of the former life for the sake of the kingdom of God; that is, leaving behind one's human ties and filial responsibilities and making the kingdom mission the top priority. It further entails surrendering one's possessions, facing rejection from the hostility of the world, and embracing homelessness. As the Synoptic passages move toward the account of Jesus' cross, the Spirituality of following Jesus comes to mean walking the way of Jesus' cross, participating in his suffering, and taking up one's cross. It is a step further communicated in Rev 14:1–5 that to follow Jesus means to join the death of the Lord; it is conveyed by identifying that the one whom Christian disciples follow is "the Lamb" who was slain and still bears the mark of being slaughtered. In summary, the other books of the New Testament (other than the Fourth Gospel) employ ἀκολουθεῖν to convey the sacrifice and suffering inherent in following Christ, as one of the major implications.

Does the Fourth Gospel convey the same implications and Spirituality of following Jesus by the term ἀκολουθεῖν or communicate different (distinctive) aspects of following Jesus? Does the Gospel focus on the suffering and sacrifice in following Jesus like the Synoptics and Revelation? In the next several chapters, we will see, by investigating ἀκολουθεῖν in the Fourth Gospel, what unique implications of following Jesus are revealed in relevant texts, and into what distinctive aspects of Spirituality of following Jesus the fourth evangelist invites the readers.

PART II

Ἀκολουθεῖν in the Fourth Gospel

Introduction

THE PURPOSE OF PART II as the main body of the present study is to inquire into the Spirituality and theological implications of following Jesus according to the Fourth Gospel by investigating the term ἀκολουθεῖν (to follow) in relation to the associated motifs (where Jesus is/is going to; the light; death allusions; heaven opened/to the Father, etc.).

There are several distinguishing aspects (which will be articulated in this study) of the Spirituality of following Jesus communicated by the term ἀκολουθεῖν in the Fourth Gospel. These aspects converge on two words: directional and relational. The life of following Jesus is directional. It is a journey toward a destination. The destination is the place to which Jesus leads his followers, that is, the place where Jesus is, where Jesus is going to, and where Jesus will be. It is ultimately to the Father, and Jesus' own relationship of communion with the Father. Into this communion (destination), Jesus calls and leads men and women.

The idea that the life of following Jesus is both directional and relational is communicated by three levels of arrangement. First, it is arranged by the association of ἀκολουθεῖν and the ὅπου/ποῦ/πόθεν motif (where Jesus came from/where Jesus is/where Jesus is going to). In most texts in which ἀκολουθεῖν occurs, there the where (ὅπου/ποῦ) motif also appears. The where motif is presented in a few variant forms: "where he is from" (7:28; 8:14; cf. 9:29, 30), "where he is" (1:38, 39; 7:34, 36; 12:26; 14:3; 17:24), and "where he is going to" (8:14, 21, 22; 13:33, 36; 14:4, 5; 16:5)." It is not an overstatement to say that the where motif creates one of the major aspects of following Jesus in the Fourth Gospel, and thus it is implied that to follow Jesus is to follow him where he is, going together with him to where he is going, and will be with him where he will be.

Second, the idea of following Jesus in John is presented by the connection of ἀκολουθεῖν with death images. Death is the pathway through which Jesus is going to "where he will be" which is to the Father. The way Jesus is going to the Father is through the death of suffering and persecution, not a natural death. The death in the suffering of the cross is the pathway through which Jesus goes to the Father. It is also the same trail for his followers to take. In other words, following Jesus is a journey toward the destination where Jesus is going via the passage of death. This point is made by the reiterating appearances of death allusions near to the pericopes (1:35–51; 8:12; 10:1–42; 12:20–26; 13:36—14:3; 21:15–19) in which ἀκολουθεῖν is employed in the metaphorical sense. Yet, it is not always explicitly expressed, rather implicitly and progressively unfolded as the Johannine narrative proceeds from the calling of the first disciples in the first chapter to the commissioning narrative of Peter after the first Easter in the last chapter.

Third, the destination to which Jesus is leading his followers is God the Father himself and his relationship with the Father in glory. The Son was with the Father (1:1–2), was in the bosom of the Father (1:18), came from the Father, and is going back to the Father (13:3; 16:28). If I may borrow the "descent-ascent" motif,[1] the Son, who is descended from above (3:13, 31) which is the place where he was with the Father, is ascending to him (6:62; 20:17) to where he will be with the Father. When he came from the Father, he came alone, but when he goes back to the Father, he does not return to him alone. He goes back to the Father, taking his followers to the Father with him. That is the purpose for which he descended and is now ascending. Thus, by following Jesus, his followers are on the way of journey to the Father through and with Jesus.

To summarize the thesis of the present study, following Jesus according to the Fourth Gospel is a journey to enter the relationship with God the Father in glory through Jesus by being with him where he is, by taking the same pathway of suffering, persecution, and death which Jesus takes as his own pathway to go to the Father. Following Jesus in John means ultimately to be with the Father in the glory that Jesus had before

---

1. Sidebottom, "The Descent and Ascent of the Son of Man," 115–22; Meeks, "The Man from Heaven," 44–72; Talbert, "The Myth of a Descending-Ascending Redeemer," 418–40; Nicholson, *Death as Departure*, 60–62, 75–104; Pryor, "The Johannine Son of Man and the Descent-Ascent Motif," 341–51.

the beginning of the world and will have with the Father in eternity. In the course of the present study, we are going to investigate how the Johannine texts communicate this thesis.

The Texts to Investigate

The table below presents the texts in which ἀκολουθεῖν, ὅπου/ποῦ/πόθεν, and death allusions occur in the Fourth Gospel.[2] Among those listed, the pericopes in which ἀκολουθεῖν is employed in the spiritual/metaphorical sense are going to be explored. The pericopes are: (1) 1:35–51 which as the first relevant unit includes the verb ἀκολουθεῖν and "where" vocabulary and death allusion; (2) 8:12 is to be viewed in the wider context including chapter 7 because the chapter creates a thematic connection with 8:12 by reiterating the "where" motif; (3) 10:1–42 is the pericope where ἀκολουθεῖν appears with Jesus' intensive telling of his own death; (4) 12:26 (20–36) is the text where ἀκολουθεῖν occurs with the "where" motif accompanied by Jesus' speaking about his death within near context; (5) 13:21–14:3 is the text where all three elements of the verb ἀκολουθεῖν and the "where" motif and death image intensively occur;[3] (6) 21:1–19 as the closing account of the Gospel contains ἀκολουθεῖν twice, the "where" motif twice, and Jesus' prediction of the death that Peter will face as a follower of Jesus.

	ἀκολουθεῖν	ὅπου/ποῦ	πόθεν	death motif
Ch 1	37, 38, 40, 43	28, 38, 39	48	29, 36
Ch 2			9	19, 22
Ch 3		8*2	8	14
Ch 4		20, 46	11	
Ch 5				18

2. Van der Watt ("Johannine style," 90) also provides a brief analysis of the use of ἀκολουθεῖν in the Fourth Gospel with some interesting observations. He points out that: (1) The verb "follow" is mainly used for people following Jesus in the Gospel (chapter 1: his disciples; chapter 6: the crowd who saw the signs; chapter 8: those who believe; chapter 10: his sheep; chapter 12: the servant of Jesus; and from chapter 13 only Peter and the Beloved Disciple; (2) there are two exceptions: the mourners who followed Mary in chapter 11 and Peter followed the other disciple in chapter 20; (3) there are different reasons why people followed Jesus and they are called different names. Out of the analysis, he stresses that the term ἀκολουθεῖν is used "exclusively to signify the disciples of Jesus, following him" and "describes the actions of disciples in relation to Jesus."

3. The reason 14:1–3 is included in the investigation together with 13:21–38 as one semantic cluster is explained in footnote 6 of chapter 9.

	ἀκολουθεῖν	ὅπου/ποῦ	πόθεν	death motif
Ch 6	2	23, 62	5	
Ch 7		11, 34, 35, 36, 42	27*2, 28	1, 19, 20, 25, 30, 39
Ch 8	12	10, 14*2, 19, 21, 22	14*2	20, 28, 37, 40
Ch 9		12	29, 30	
Ch 10	4, 5, 27	40		11, 15, 17
Ch 11	31	30, 32, 34, 57		50–51, 53
Ch 12	26	1, 26, 35,		7, 10, 16, 23–24, 27, 32–34
Ch 13	36*2, 37	33, 36*2		1, 31, 37–38
Ch 14		3, 4, 5		
Ch 15				
Ch 16		5		2
Ch 17		24		1
Ch 18	15	1, 20		14, 32
Ch 19		18, 20, 41	9	6, 7, 15–42
Ch 20	6	2, 12, 13, 15, 19		
Ch 21	19, 20, 22	18*2		19

CHAPTER 5

Following Jesus to Where He Is and to See Heaven (1:35–51)

THE TEXT 1:35–51 OPENS with the Baptist's witness of Jesus which is an emphatic reiteration of the previous witness (1:29, 36). The two disciples of John heard him testifying about Jesus as the Lamb of God and started to follow Jesus (1:37). The main event of their movement of following Jesus was to follow him to where he was (1:39). Being with him where he is becomes central in the journey of discipleship. Having found, from the experience of being with Jesus, that he was the Messiah, one of the two disciples brought his own brother to Jesus (1:40–42). Another individual who was called directly by Jesus to follow him (1:43) also found that Jesus was the one whom Moses and the prophets had anticipated and thus led his friend to Jesus (1:45–46). Yet, the narrative does not end with their confession regarding who Jesus was or subsequent evangelism. It goes a step further to Jesus' prediction/promise for his followers that they would see heaven opened and experience God as the ultimate goal of the journey of following Jesus (1:51). The prediction/promise indicates heaven to be the destination of Jesus' followers.

John the Baptist who is sent from God turns people's attention to Jesus. Jesus, who descended from God, predicts/promises that the group of people, who follow him, will ultimately experience the heavenly reality of God. The narrative begins with a notion "of God" (1:36) and ends with looking "to God" (1:51). The narrative opens with John's witness that Jesus is the Lamb *of God*, and ends by intimating that Jesus will lead his followers to their destination—*to God*.

I. Literary Structure and Key Motifs

In this text 1:35–51 ἀκολουθεῖν appears four times (1:37, 38, 40, 43). It is used in connection with the "where" motif twice (1:38, 39), a death allusion including the Baptist's first witness from the prior context (1:29, 36), and the intimations related to God (1:29, 36, 51). Those key motifs which appear in the text are highlighted in the figure below.

V 29 ἴδε ὁ ἀμνὸς <u>τοῦ θεοῦ</u> (Behold, the Lamb <u>of God</u>)
V 36 ἴδε ὁ ἀμνὸς <u>τοῦ θεοῦ</u> (Behold, the Lamb <u>of God</u>)

    V 37 ἤκουσαν οἱ δύο μαθηταὶ (The two disciples *heard* him)
    <u>ἠκολούθησαν</u> τῷ Ἰησοῦ (they **followed** Jesus)
    V 38 θεασάμενος αὐτοὺς <u>ἀκολουθοῦντας</u> (saw them **following**)

        V 38 ῥαββί . . . <u>ποῦ μένεις</u>; (Rabbi . . . <u>where are you staying?</u>)
        V 39 εἶδαν <u>ποῦ μένει</u> (saw <u>where he was staying</u>)

    V 40 τῶν <i>ἀκουσάντων</i> παρὰ Ἰωάννου (who *heard* John speak)
    καὶ <u>ἀκολουθησάντων</u> αὐτῷ (and **followed** Jesus)
    V 43 <u>ἀκολούθει μοι</u> (<u>**Follow me**</u>)

V 50 μείζω τούτων <u>ὄψῃ</u> (You <u>will see</u> greater things)
V 51 <u>ὄψεσθε</u> <u>τὸν οὐρανὸν</u> ἀνεῳγότα (you <u>will see</u> <u>heaven</u> opened)

Three literary structures are outstanding. First, it magnifies the action of following Jesus. It is plainly stated in verse 37 first. Then in verse 38 by describing how Jesus "turned and saw them following," the text makes the readers with an imaginative eye see the action of the following of the two disciples. The action of following is magnified before the eyes of the readers with an effect similar to the replay of a climactic scene in a game of sport. And then, in verse 40 the action of following Jesus is reiterated. Second, the figure shows that all verbs and motifs converge on one motif "where Jesus is" (ποῦ μένεις; 1:38b; ποῦ μένει, 1:39). The movement of following Jesus is directed towards the place "where Jesus is." Third, the movement of following Jesus is encompassed with the intimations which relate to God (1:29, 36, 51). The commencement of following Jesus for the two disciples is triggered by hearing the proclamation that Jesus is the Lamb *of God*. And the journey of following Jesus moves *towards God*. As does the intimation of the image of the Lamb *of God*, so the motif of heaven opened invites the disciples to look to God as the goal of the journey.

With the purpose of finding out how and to what extent the text sustains the proposed thesis, we are going to take a look at the idea of following Jesus in association with the above mentioned key motifs under three headings: First, following Jesus of the two disciples; second, following Jesus and Philip's journey of discipleship; and third, following Jesus and seeing heaven opened.

II. Following Jesus of the Two Disciples (1:35–42)

A. Following Jesus and the Lamb of God

V 29 Τῇ ἐπαύριον βλέπει τὸν Ἰησοῦν ἐρχόμενον πρὸς αὐτὸν καὶ λέγει·
 ἴδε ὁ ἀμνὸς τοῦ θεοῦ ὁ αἴρων τὴν ἁμαρτίαν τοῦ κόσμου.
 (The next day he saw Jesus coming toward him, and said,
 "Behold, the Lamb of God, who takes away the sin of the world!")

V 35 Τῇ ἐπαύριον πάλιν εἱστήκει ὁ Ἰωάννης καὶ ἐκ τῶν μαθητῶν αὐτοῦ δύο
 (The next day again John was standing with two of his disciples)
V 36 καὶ ἐμβλέψας τῷ Ἰησοῦ περιπατοῦντι λέγει·
 ἴδε ὁ ἀμνὸς τοῦ θεοῦ.
 (and he looked at Jesus as he walked by and said,
 "Behold, the Lamb of God!")

V 37 καὶ ἤκουσαν οἱ δύο μαθηταὶ αὐτοῦ λαλοῦντος
 καὶ ἠκολούθησαν τῷ Ἰησοῦ.
 (The two disciples heard him say this,
 and they **followed** Jesus.)

For Jesus, the protagonist[1] of the Gospel, to appear on the stage and be revealed to men and women, John, the Witness, functions as the introducer. He was sent to bear witness about Jesus. His witness about Jesus is manifold. According to the witness, Jesus is the true light who is coming into the world (1:6–9); the one "whom you do not know" for the Jews (1:19–28; cf. 1:10); the Lamb of God who takes away the sin of the world (1:29); the one who baptizes with the Holy Spirit (1:33); the Son of God (1:34); and again the Lamb of God (1:36). In this manifold witness to Jesus, the fact that Jesus is the Lamb of God is the only part reiterated in the pericope. And this is the central proclamation that caused the two men to start the journey of following Jesus.

---

1. Culpepper, *Anatomy*, 106.

The first exclamation "Here is the Lamb of God who takes away the sin of the world" (1:29) assumes an audience that most likely includes the two disciples. Among the men who heard the witness were Andrew and an unidentified disciple. As the text states explicitly, when the same testimony "Look, here is the Lamb of God" (1:36) was proclaimed again, the two men were standing beside the Baptist, heard him testify, and decided to follow Jesus the Lamb of God. The repetitive witness[2] was powerful enough to change the direction of the lives of these two men.[3] There is no other catalyst that motivates them to follow Jesus (1:37) but "hearing" (1:37, 40) the pronouncement.[4] Beasley-Murray comments, "The cry, 'Look, the Lamb of God,' is a directive to the two disciples of John to follow Jesus."[5] In the introduction of Andrew it is made clear that because Andrew "heard" the Baptist's witness to the Lamb of God, he "followed" Jesus (1:40). As the result of hearing the proclamation that Jesus is the Lamb of God, the two men stopped following their master, the Baptist, and redirected their lives to following Jesus.

What did the title the Lamb of God mean to the two men? What did they understand from this title? Why is the fact Jesus is the Lamb of God powerful enough to draw them to Jesus? In order to discover the significance of the two disciples' action of "following Jesus" in connection with Jesus as the Lamb of God, a couple of questions have to be answered. Which image or allusion did they have in their minds when they heard the title from the Baptist? What implication of the title captured their mind that they might be attracted to Jesus and become his followers? What was the two disciples' understanding of the title the Lamb of God? Although the text does not explicitly give an explanation, there are clues within the text that, whatever the depth of their understanding might be, the two disciples understood it on the basis of the images of the Hebrew Scriptures. This is hinted by ample Hebraic terms, titles, and the names of geographical locales within the pericope: the title Rabbi (ῥαββι)[6] by which the two disciples called Jesus (1:38); the title the Messiah (τὸν Μεσσίαν) that Andrew exclaimed in the joy of encountering Jesus (1:41); " . . . about whom Moses in the law and also

---

2. Barrett (*John*, 180) comments on the purpose of the repetition of the witness, "The testimony of the Baptist is repeated in order to furnish a motive for the action of the two disciples." "'Following' is the appropriate consequence of John's μαρτυρία."

3. Brown (*John*, 1:76) remarks that "its purpose is to initiate a chain reaction which will bring John the Baptist's disciples to Jesus and make them Jesus' own disciples."

4. For a discussion on the relationship of hearing and faith, see Koester, "Hearing, Seeing, and Believing," 327–48.

5. Beasley-Murray, *John*, 26.

6. Lapin, "Rabbi," *ABD* 5:600–602.

the prophets wrote" (ὃν ἔγραψεν Μωϋσῆς ἐν τῷ νόμῳ καὶ οἱ προφῆται, 1:45) which is uttered by Philip; "truly an Israelite" (ἀληθῶς Ἰσραηλίτης, 1:47) which is used to refer to Nathaniel; "the King of Israel" (σὺ βασιλεὺς εἶ τοῦ Ἰσραήλ, 1:49) in Nathaniel's profession to Jesus; and the Jacob's ladder allusion (1:51) which Jesus used in speaking to them without any explanation, assuming that they were familiar with the text of Gen 28:12. These terms and titles from the Hebrew Scriptures are freely mentioned in the dialogues among the first disciples and with Jesus as if they are a part of their own natural language. It reflects the fact that the minds of the two disciples are soaked in Hebraic images and ideology, and thus supports the conclusion that they grasped the meaning of the title "the Lamb of God" against the backdrop of the Hebrew Scriptures.

The next question to be answered is, which allusions or images of the Hebrew Scriptures are behind the title the Lamb of God? Scholars have suggested several Old Testament allusions as the possible background. Hoskyns comments that the Baptist declared Jesus to be "a lamb without blemish" offered daily as sacrifice in the Temple (Exod 29:38–46).[7] Dodd views the title against the apocalyptic picture of the powerful conquering lamb, the messianic leader who will destroy evil in the world (Rev 7:17; 14:1–5; 17:14).[8] Brown and Schnackenburg see the Lamb of God in a combination of the images of the Paschal lamb and the Suffering Servant.[9] Beasley-Murray comments that the Baptist identifies Jesus as "the powerful Lamb of God," an image which is "modified" by that of the Lamb that brings "deliverance through submission to death as the Passover lamb," admitting a possible link with "the submissive lamb of Isa 53" and the lamb "provided by God at the intended sacrifice of Isaac" (Gen 22:10–13).[10] Leon Morris lists most of the possible Old Testament allusions in the widest range: (i) The Passover Lamb; (ii) the "lamb that is led to the slaughter" (Isa 53:6–7); (iii) the Servant of the LORD; (iv) the lamb of the daily sacrifices offered morning and evening in the Temple; (v) the gentle lamb (Jer 11:19); (vi) the scapegoat that was banished to the desert, symbolically bearing away the sins of the people (Lev 16); (vii) the triumphant Lamb of the apocalypses; (viii) the God-provided Lamb (Gen 22:8); (ix) the guilt offering (Lev 14:12–13; 21–25).[11] Then, he suggests that the Lamb of God is to be

---

7. Hoskyns, *The Fourth Gospel*, 176.

8. Dodd, *Interpretation*, 230–38. For arguments against this view, see Brown, *John*, 1:58–60; Keener, *John*, 1:452; Ridderbos, *John*, 72.

9. Brown, *John*, 1:60–63; Schnackenburg, *John*, 1:299–300.

10. Beasley-Murray, *John*, 24–25.

11. Morris, *John*, 144–47.

understood against almost all the listed images and allusions in the Old Testament, probably except for the gentle lamb figure and the apocalyptic triumphant lamb.[12]

No single allusion to the lamb in the Old Testament alone satisfactorily provides the full biblical background of the title Jesus as the Lamb of God.[13] The revelation of God has progressively unfolded the manifold aspects of the motif of the Lamb of God to point to Christ Jesus throughout redemptive history by various shadows and types ever since the first Book of the Hebrew Scriptures had introduced the motif. Every image and allusion foreshadowed in the Scriptures for the Lamb and named by the scholars is a part of the whole picture of the Lamb of God. Just as a picture with many puzzle pieces can be completed when all the pieces are put together, not one piece is to be ignored, though some pieces seem remotely related and some more explicitly related. Jesus' title as the Lamb of God is the all-encompassing title that fulfills[14] all the allusions and images of the lambs in the Old Testament as it has been gradually depicted in the Book of the Law, the Psalms, and the Prophets. It would not be erroneous to assume that the Baptist as the God-sent witness (1:6) and a prophet filled with the Spirit (Matt 11:7–11; Luke 1:16–17) was able to understand and declare Jesus the Lamb of God against the above mentioned multifaceted allusions to the Lamb of the Old Testament. And for the two disciples, it is most likely that as they heard the Baptist's witness, most of the above listed Old Testament lamb allusions would function as the backdrops of Jesus being the Lamb of God.[15]

Having confirmed that the Baptist's witness to Jesus as the Lamb of God was understood by the disciples against the backdrop of the Old Testament allusions to lambs, it is now necessary to consider what common denominators are found in these allusions and what aspects of the lamb are emphasized in the formulation of the Baptist's witness. Two common denominators are noteworthy in the Old Testament lamb images. First, the

---

12. Morris (ibid., 147–48) suggests, "The Lamb figure may well be intended to be composite, evoking memories of several, perhaps all, of the suggestions we have canvassed."

13. Barrett also mentions in the same tone that "no single Old Testament allusion is sufficient to account for it." Barrett, "The Lamb of God," 210–18.

14. Morris (*John*, 148) comments similarly, "All that the ancient sacrifices foreshadowed was perfectly fulfilled in the sacrifice of Christ."

15. It may not include the apocalyptic lamb image. It appears not in the Old Testament but in *1 Enoch* 89:46 and *Testament of Joseph* 19:8. It is developed in the Book of Revelation at a later date as Morris (*John*, 146) comments, "This is undoubtedly the meaning of 'the Lamb' in Revelation, . . . But it is more than difficult to see this as the reference." It is not within my scope to measure thoroughly the suggested options. For more scholarly discussions, see Carson, *John*, 149–51.

function of the lamb is the medium by which access to God is open, so that men and women, who are disconnected and far away from God, may approach him and enjoy him in his presence as the ultimate destination. Second, the function of the lamb is achieved by its death. These two predominant ideas are present in most of the listed lamb allusions. The lamb of the daily sacrifices was the medium, through whose death men and women were able to approach God. The Paschal lamb was the agent by whose blood the firstborn of Israel were saved from destruction and became able to join the journey of the Exodus into the land of God. The Servant of the LORD was the figure who through his suffering and death would vicariously obey and fulfill the call of God instead of the rebellious and disobedient Israel that could not but face the wrath of God and be cut off from God's presence. The guilt-offering animal was the means by whose death the barrier of sin between God and humankind was removed, so that men and women might come to God and have life. The dominant aspect, that the Lamb by its death is the agent through which men and women have access to God, is expressed repetitively in the lamb allusions by various forms. The ultimate goal to be accomplished by the provision of the Lamb of God is: to bring men and women to the presence of God by its sacrificial death. The Lamb of God is the divinely prepared agent that, by its death, connects the alienated human race to God himself.

In the uniquely formulated witness,[16] ἴδε ὁ ἀμνὸς τοῦ θεοῦ ὁ αἴρων τὴν ἁμαρτίαν τοῦ κόσμου (1:29) and ἴδε ὁ ἀμνὸς τοῦ θεοῦ (1:36), the Baptist proclaims that Jesus is the Lamb that "fulfills the reality to which the metaphor points,"[17] that he is in "an intensely personal relationship with God,"[18] and that he effects "the reconciliation of the world to God"[19] and brings people to God's presence by putting away the barrier between God and people through its vicarious sacrificial death. The whole idea of the ministry of sacrifice "as the foundation of communion between God and his people" is deeply embedded in the witness to Jesus as the Lamb. The Baptist's reiterated witness to Jesus as the Lamb of God eloquently testifies that Jesus is the one who opens "the way to God for the whole world" through his life-giving death.[20] Ridderbos rightly comments, "All that is said here in one

---

16. The word appears only five times in the canonical literature (Isa 53:7; John 1:29, 36; Acts 8:32; 1 Pet 1:19) and once Odes 14:17 in Deuterocanon. The formulation of ὁ ἀμνὸς τοῦ θεοῦ can be found nowhere in the canonical literature but the Fourth Gospel.

17. Dautzenberg, "ἀμνὸς," EDNT 1:71.

18. Brodie, John, 156-57.

19. Ridderbos, John, 73.

20. Ibid., 74.

splendid and comprehensive pronouncement is that from now on Jesus acts and answers for the reconciliation and indwelling fellowship between God and his people symbolized till now by the lamb—and does so for the whole world."[21]

Having heard the proclamation that Jesus was the Lamb of God, the two disciples (who were familiar with the allusions and images of the Hebrew Scriptures as we have confirmed above), realized that Jesus was the one who will lead them to God somehow through his death. The Jesus whom the disciples understood initially is the God-prepared-one who would lead them to the presence of God and ultimately connect them to God by removing, through his death, the barrier of sin which has separated them from the holy God. It is not possible to assess the depth of their understanding and determine to what degree they apprehended that Jesus was the one who would bring men and women to God himself through his death. Yet it is undeniable that their awareness was significant enough for them to leave their current master and decide to turn their life to following Jesus. That the Fourth Gospel mentions the spiritual dullness or misunderstanding of the disciples does not refute the possibility of the two disciples' initial apprehension from the Baptist's witness. The two disciples began to follow Jesus with some degree of awareness, a spiritual spark, in the anticipation that Jesus would lead them to the presence of God, in much the same way that the lamb had functioned between God and humankind.

Although it would be another matter for them to go deeper in their experience of the reality of Jesus' being the Lamb of God in their personal life, at least this initial perception was effective enough to cause them to begin the new journey of following Jesus. If it is true that the disciples commenced the journey of following Jesus in the understanding and expectation that Jesus the Lamb of God would connect them to God, then their act of following Jesus is ultimately theological (i.e., a journey into a relationship with God) as well as it is christological (i.e., a journey in relationship with Jesus). Through the act of following Jesus, they are being ushered into the theological experience (Spirituality) of encountering God. From this first pericope with ἀκολουθεῖν, the Fourth Gospel, by interweaving the theme of "following Jesus" together with "the Lamb of God," communicates that following Jesus implies the follower's journey into a relationship with God through the death of the Lamb Jesus. It is one of the major aspects of the Spirituality of following Jesus to which the evangelist invites his readers.

---

21. Ibid., 73–74.

B. Following Jesus and Where He Is

V 37 καὶ **ἠκολούθησαν** τῷ Ἰησοῦ.
(and they **followed** Jesus)

V 38 ῥαββί, ... <u>ποῦ μένεις</u>;
(Rabbi, . . . <u>where are you staying</u>?)

V 39 ἦλθαν οὖν καὶ εἶδαν <u>ποῦ μένει</u>
(So they came and saw <u>where he was staying</u>)

V 40 καὶ **ἀκολουθησάντων** αὐτῷ·
(and **followed** Jesus)

Motivated by the declaration that Jesus was the Lamb of God who would bring them into relationship with God by his own death like a lamb, the disciples started to follow him. Jesus' response to the disciples who were following him is interesting and draws our attention: "What are you looking for?" (τί ζητεῖτε;, 1:38). It is the first utterance from Jesus' own lips in the Fourth Gospel. Bultmann comments that it is "clearly the first question which must be addressed to anyone who comes to Jesus, the first thing about which he must be clear."[22] Although the question seems concerned about the "motivation of following him," Lincoln comments that for the "readers who are familiar with the later narrative, however, the formulation takes on deeper significance, since the verb used (ζητεῖν) is characteristic of the evangelist's vocabulary and will be employed to speak of people's attitude to Jesus and their deepest commitments."[23] In response to the question, they answered him with a question, "Where are you staying?" (ποῦ μένεις;). Did they reply to his question? Though in question form, they obviously expressed what they were seeking. They wanted "to be" with Jesus *where* he stayed for he was the one from God, so they asked *where* he was staying. An essential aspect of following Jesus is disclosed in the conversation. It is "to be" with Jesus *where he is*. Scholars have paid attention to ποῦ μένεις; and remarked that it has "theological overtones"[24] and "deeper dimensions are hinted."[25] It certainly conveys the deep significance of the relationship between Jesus and his followers. If closer attention is given to ποῦ (where) and it is considered in the light of the other uses of the "where" motif in the Fourth Gospel (where Jesus came from and where he is going to), it

---

22. Bultmann, *John*, 100.
23. Lincoln, *John*, 117.
24. Brown, *John*, 1:75.
25. Lincoln, *John*, 117.

will be found that the implication conveyed by ποῦ μένεις; extends to the ultimate relationship between God and Jesus' followers in and through Jesus beyond the relationship between Jesus and his followers. Chennattu fittingly remarks, "The literary and theological context of the story suggests that the query of the disciples ποῦ μένεις epitomizes the human drive for God or being in communion with God."[26]

To their inquiry, instead of informing them of the physical place where he stays, Jesus tells them to come and see (ἔρχεσθε καὶ ὄψεσθε, 1:39). It is not only an "invitation"[27] to *where Jesus is*, but both an invitation and a promise as Chennattu contends by translating it "come and you shall see."[28] It is an invitation for the followers not simply to a physical place, but to be with him where he is and in fellowship with him. Furthermore, it is a promise that he will lead them to see something beyond what they expect and pursue. Scholars have made attempts to identify what it was that they were seeking, such as "a long talk"[29] or "an undisturbed conversation"[30] with Jesus. Yet, the text does not say they had a longer conversation or heard an exposition of the Scriptures. Rather, the text maintains the attention of the text, focusing on the motif of *where Jesus is* by stating repetitively that they "came and saw where he was staying."[31]

The idea of being with Jesus is not completely absent from the Synoptics. The Gospel of Mark identifies one of the three purposes for which Jesus called and designated the twelve disciples as "to be with him" (ἵνα ὦσιν μετ' αὐτοῦ, Mark 3:14). However, while in the Markan Gospel, to be with Jesus is associated with mission ("to proclaim the message and to cast out demons," 3:14–15), the implication of being with Jesus *where he is* in this Fourth Gospel is different from this in that it aims at not any mission or task primarily, but being with Jesus per se as its objective. Unlike the first appearance of the term ἀκολουθεῖν in the Synoptic text where it is connected with "to be fishers of men" (Matt 4:20–22; Mark 1:17–18; Luke 5:10–11), the first appearance of ἀκολουθεῖν in the Johannine Gospel is associated not with any task, but with following Jesus to *where he is*, resulting in nothing but being with him *where he is*. For John, following Jesus is not primarily about doing any works

26. Chennattu, *Johannine Discipleship*, 31.
27. Morris, *John*, 157.
28. Chennattu, *Johannine Discipleship*, 31.
29. Morris, *John*, 157.
30. Schnackenburg, *John*, 1:308.
31. V 38 **Where** are you staying?
    V 39a Come and *see*.
    V 39b They came and *saw*.
    V 39c **Where** he was staying.

of mission such as proclaiming the message of the Kingdom or fishing for men, but about being with him *where Jesus is*. The movement of following Jesus culminates with "remaining with him that day" (1:39). In this way, the dwelling of the Father's only begotten Son among us (1:14) *is personally experienced* by the two disciples through being with him *where he is*. Schnackenburg notes that "it is not just that day but in permanent fellowship with him."[32] To be with him that day where he was is the commencement of a new journey as his followers. Here the uniqueness of the Johannine concept of following Jesus is characterized as relational. For John, following Jesus is a movement into a relationship with Jesus through going after him to *where he is*. We are not told the physical place where Jesus was staying because it is not the interest of the text. The attention of the text falls on the fact that following Jesus leads his followers *to be with him where he is*, so that they may permanently remain in relationship with him. It is a distinguishing quality of following Jesus in John.

Although Schnackenburg comments rightly to some extent that in John fellowship with the master is "characteristically modified to be 'there where Jesus is,'" to be with Jesus where he is implies something more profound than fellowship with the master.[33] It is because "where" Jesus is will be the place "where" the Jesus' followers will find their permanent dwelling, and there they will see the glory of the Father (12:26; 14:3–5; 17:24).[34] In this first Johannine pericope, in which the "where" motif first appears, the idea of "following Jesus" in association with "where Jesus is" is only introduced, and lifts the curtain up tantalizingly, hinting that more is behind the curtain. The Spirituality of following Jesus where he is in relation to God is yet to be unpacked. To put it another way, as the Gospel moves on, the spiritual connection between the "where" motif and following Jesus in a theological perspective (meaning, in relation to God the Father) will be gradually uncovered by the "hermeneutical spiral" of the repetition of the motifs "to follow" and "where" in the texts coming later in John's Gospel.[35]

---

32. Schnackenburg, *John*, 1:308.

33. Ibid.

34. Bultmann (*John*, 100) also noticed the importance of the motif "where Jesus is" in some degree as he briefly commented, "And it is essential to know where Jesus 'lives'; for in the place where Jesus is at home the disciple will also receive his dwelling (14.2)."

35. Van der Watt, "Johannine Style," 76, 94–95.

C. Following Jesus and Witnessing

After beginning to follow Jesus and being with him where he was, the first thing Andrew did was to bring another individual to where Jesus was. He found and brought his brother Simon to Jesus. Also the first thing Philip did after starting the journey of following Jesus was to invite another individual to Jesus. He found and brought his friend Nathaniel to Jesus. Interestingly, the text uses the same vocabularies with the similar arrangement in verses 41 and 45.

Andrew to Simon
V 40 ... **ἀκολουθησάντων** αὐτῷ·
  (... **followed** Jesus)
V 41 εὑρίσκει ... καὶ λέγει αὐτῷ· εὑρήκαμεν τὸν Μεσσίαν,
  (found ... and said to him, "We have found the Messiah")

Philip to Nathaniel
V 43 ... **ἀκολούθει** μοι.
  ("**Follow me**")
V 45 εὑρίσκει ... καὶ λέγει αὐτῷ· ... ὃν ἔγραψεν Μωϋσῆς ... εὑρήκαμεν,
  (found ... and said to him, "We have found him of whom Moses ...)

These are the first instances of evangelism in the Fourth Gospel. Two unique aspects of evangelism are noteworthy here. First, there is no explicit command of Jesus to the disciples to do evangelism or to preach the message of the Kingdom of God.[36] Rather, the evangelism happens as the natural effect of following Jesus and experiencing who Jesus is. Andrew "found" Jesus was the Messiah by being with him where he was. Although the text does not explicitly express Andrew's joy of encountering Jesus, it is implied beneath the text (1:40) that he was full of joy and excitement. Out of the overflowing joy of encountering the Messiah by being with him where he is, he spontaneously finds his brother and brings him to where Jesus is, so he might have the same experience. Though the command of doing the work of mission and preaching the message is important in the life of disciples, what is valued in this Johannine text is the power and impact of experiencing Jesus by being with him where he is. The impact is much more vivid and lively. In this pericope, the followers of Jesus are depicted not as those who should do the work of mission because they are enlisted,

---

36. That the disciples are to do the mission as Jesus did is implicit in 17:18 ("As you have sent me into the world, so I have sent them into the world") and 20:21 ("As the Father has sent me, so I send you").

but as the people who savor the elation of experiencing Jesus firsthand, and thus, spontaneously motivated by the experience, bring another individual to where Jesus is, so that they may also experience the same kind of jubilation of encountering Jesus. The spontaneous exultation of encountering Jesus that results in natural evangelism appears, not only in this text, but also in the account of the Samaritan woman. She was not commanded to do the work of evangelism at all by Jesus. She was not commissioned to be a witness. Having been motivated by her own joy of encountering the Messiah, however, the woman ran into the city and became a witness to Jesus for her own town people (4:28–30).

Second, the content of evangelism in the text is not primarily about delivering a message, but the person Jesus himself is at the center of evangelism. It is about inviting another to Jesus himself. In the Synoptic Gospels, the mission and evangelism of the followers of Jesus is focused on proclaiming the message of the good news. The first utterance from Jesus' lips in the Markan Gospel was the proclamation of the message of the good news of the Kingdom of God (Mark 1:15). The calling of the first four disciples is located in the near context of Jesus' mission of preaching the good news (Mark 1:38, 39). After starting to follow Jesus, the disciples in the Synoptics were not engaged in any activity of evangelism until they were sent to preach the message: "He called the twelve and began to send them . . . So they went out and proclaimed that all should repent" (Mark 6:7–13). It is the same in the Matthean Gospel. The disciples were called and commissioned to proclaim the message: "As you go proclaim the good news . . ." (Matt 10:7). However, in the text of John, evangelism happened in a different way. The firsthand experience of encountering Jesus is the driving force of evangelism, not the command of Jesus. Evangelism in John is associated not with receiving the good news, but with coming to Jesus to where Jesus is to experience him. To put it another way, evangelism in the Fourth Gospel is relational as following Jesus in John is. Therefore, the vocabulary related to evangelism in John is not "repent" (Mark 5:12) or "receive," but "come" and "see" (1:39, 46; 4:29). It is about "coming" to Jesus himself and "being" with Jesus where he is (4:40).[37]

---

37. As they appear in 1:35–51, the same vocabularies ("come" to Jesus; "stay" with him) are used in 4:40, ὡς οὖν ἦλθον πρὸς αὐτὸν οἱ Σαμαρῖται, ἠρώτων αὐτὸν μεῖναι παρ' αὐτοῖς· καὶ ἔμεινεν ἐκεῖ δύο ἡμέρας.

III. Following Jesus and Philip's Journey of Discipleship

A. The First Disciple to Whom "ἀκολούθει μοι" was Given

In the account of Jesus calling the first disciples (1:35–51), Philip is the only individual to whom Jesus gave his call of "Follow me" (ἀκολούθει μοι, 1:43). Later, in the last chapter of the Gospel, the same calling was given to Peter (21:19). Philip and Peter are the only two disciples who directly heard this important calling from Jesus' own lips. In this sense, both Philip and Peter take an important place in the study of the Spirituality of following Jesus. The examination of "following Jesus" communicated in Peter's case will be done in the reading of the texts of chapters 13 and 21. Here we will focus on Philip's case. For Philip, although the command of ἀκολούθει μοι is given in 1:43, there is no further development at all in this pericope about his journey of following Jesus, except that he brought Nathaniel to Jesus. Therefore, to expound the implication of "following Jesus" communicated in Philip's life, our attention on the current text alone is not sufficient. It is necessary to take into consideration the other texts where Philip appears.

Furthermore, Philip as a follower of Jesus takes on an important role in articulating the Johannine concept of following Jesus as considerable attention is given to him over several chapters in the Fourth Gospel (1:43, 44, 45, 46, 48; 6:5, 7; 12:21, 22[2x]; 14:8, 9), whereas in the Synoptics his name appears only once in the list of the twelve disciples (Matt 10:3; Mark 3:18; Luke 6:14). The implications and Spirituality of "following Jesus" depicted in the spiritual journey of Philip's life will be investigated by taking a look at chapters 6, 12, and 14 of John's Gospel.

There is a strange silence about what happened between Jesus' call for Philip (1:43) and his witnessing to Jesus (1:45). The silence leaves room to expect something more coming in the journey of Philip's following Jesus, which requires extra time and space to be unraveled. The silence not only makes the readers anticipate what is coming, but also invites us to listen attentively to the coming texts (6:5, 7; 12:21, 22; 14:8, 9). Although Philip's initial encounter with Jesus was inspiring enough to motivate him to bring another individual to Jesus, there are significantly further and deeper things that he needs to see, understand and digest fully, and in which he must grow.

B. Philip's Evangelism

As mentioned above, the text 1:43–46 does not state how Philip responded to Jesus' call "Follow Me." In verse 43 Jesus called him. Verse 44 inserts geographical information that he is "from Bethsaida, the city of Andrew and Peter."[38] Then, suddenly the text (1:45) states that Philip found Nathanael and gave a testimony to Jesus. It is quite a leap. We are not told what happened between the call and Philip's evangelism. What happened between Jesus and Philip and what motivated him to witness, we can only surmise from what he said to Nathanael, "We have found him about whom Moses in the law and also the prophets wrote, Jesus son of Joseph from Nazareth" (1:45). There must have been something between him and Jesus that convinced him to believe that Jesus was the long-awaited one whom God had promised to send in the Old Testament. As was the case for Andrew, this understanding (specifically that Jesus was the awaited Messiah) was a powerful spark for Philip's spiritual journey. Not many people have shouted this kind of confident profession in human history: "We have found him . . ." From what he said in witnessing, at least one thing became clear about Philip that he is a person who has paid close attention to what was written in the Book of Moses and the Prophets, and has been waiting for the one whom the Scriptures had prophesied.

When Philip saw his witness was not persuasive for Nathanael and it was about to raise a debate, Philip, instead of engaging in argumentation and thus, trying to persuade him about Jesus' town of origin, turned the focus to Jesus himself, and invited Nathanael to "come and see" him (1:46). Coming to Jesus himself and directly encountering him is exceedingly important in a disciple's spiritual journey, more so than any debate or argumentation about Jesus. This is the way Philip himself has reached the conviction of who Jesus is; and this is the way he expects his friend also will reach the same spiritual conviction. Once Philip invited Nathanael to experience Jesus himself, now the baton is in Jesus' hands (1:47), and it becomes a matter between Nathanael and Jesus. The task of witness is completed. Jesus deals with Nathanael directly, and through his own personal conversation with Jesus, Nathanael comes to confess Jesus as the Son of God and the King of Israel (1:49).

C. Philip as a Follower of Jesus in 1:43–46; 6:5–7; 12:20–22; 14:7–10

After the initial calling narrative in which he found Jesus to be the one about whom the Law and the Prophets wrote and as a consequence, brought

---

38. Brodie (*John*, 165) comments on the geographical reference from a theological perspective in relation to "Gentile world" and "the context of all-embracing church unity."

Nathaniel to Jesus (1:43–46), Philip's name appears in the miracle of feeding (6:5, 7). Jesus was with his disciples on a mountain at the other side of the Sea of Galilee (6:1, 3).[39] It was when the Passover was near (6:4). By identifying the fact that the feeding sign happened near the Passover, John locates it in the context of Jesus as the Paschal Lamb and his death.[40] When Jesus saw a large crowd coming toward him, Jesus said to Philip, "Where are we to buy bread for these people to eat?" (6:5).[41] It was to test his faith. Philip's response, based on his human calculation, only focuses on the impossibility and hopelessness of meeting the need of the crowd (6:7).[42] "Philip fails miserably."[43] He was not able to see things through the spiritual lens of who his master was and what he was able to do, although he has seen Jesus' power (2:1–11). Considering that this happened near the second Passover mentioned in the Gospel (cf. 2:13), at least a year has passed since Philip has begun to follow Jesus, but the progress of Philip's faith seems slow. Besides, after the miracle of feeding, the text doesn't mention that Philip came to understand who Jesus was or came to believe in him.

The next text where Philip appears is also near another Passover as it happened after Jesus' final entry into Jerusalem (12:12–20). Some Greeks who wished to see Jesus (12:21a) naturally first approached Philip whose name was a widely known Greek name. Philip, instead of coming to Jesus directly, went to and consulted Andrew first. Then "Andrew and Philip went and told Jesus" (ἔρχεται Ἀνδρέας καὶ Φίλιππος καὶ λέγουσιν τῷ Ἰησοῦ, 12:22). The text, by putting Andrew's name before Philip's, indicates that, though they went to Jesus and talked to him, Philip had Andrew tell Jesus that the Greeks wanted to see him.[44] Why did Philip first consult Andrew instead of directly coming to Jesus leading the Gentiles to him? Why did Philip let Andrew talk to Jesus, or why did he seem to need to rely on Andrew's assistance to talk to Jesus rather than speaking to Jesus directly? It was most likely because Philip "did not know" what Jesus would think about seeing the Gentiles.[45] Philip, who previously had not known what to

---

39. On the allusion of "the mountain" in relation to Moses and Mount Sinai, see Brown, *John*, 1:232; Schnackenburg, *John*, 2:14; Brodie, *John*, 259.

40. Brodie, *John*, 260. Cf. Barrett (*John*, 273–74) points out that it has "eucharistic significance, and the eucharist, like the last supper (cf. 13.1)."

41. To see the similarities of the question with that of Moses in Numbers, see Brown, *John*, 1:233.

42. In the Gospels the word πειράζω is mostly used in the negative sense, but here in John 6:6 it is used in the neutral sense. Barrett, *John*, 274; Brown, *John*, 1:233.

43. Lindars, *John*, 241.

44. Cf. For Philip's role as an intermediary of the Gentiles, see Lincoln, *John*, 349.

45. Morris, *John*, 592. For different views on the reason Philip consulted Andrew,

do facing Jesus' test, now again didn't know what to do with the request of the Gentiles. Even after spending three years with his master, Philip still was not confident what Jesus had in his heart towards the Gentiles. He has already heard that Jesus wants to gather the Gentiles into the fold of God (10:16) and has seen that he has accepted Gentiles (cf. Mark 7:24–30; Luke 7:1–10), but was still not confident about what Jesus had in his heart towards the Gentiles. Here we see a follower of Jesus who is pathetically slow to understand what his master has in his heart and what his master desires.

The last appearance of Philip occurs in the upper room dialogue (14:8–10). "Philip is attracted by the words about seeing the Father" when Jesus said, "From now on you do know him and have seen him" (14:7).[46] No one has ever seen the Father except the Son (1:18; 6:46) who was with the Father (1:1–2) and in the "bosom of the Father" (εἰς τὸν κόλπον τοῦ πατρὸς, 1:18) and came and made him known to his disciples during the past three years. Therefore, Philip should already have seen the Father in Jesus as it is said, "you . . . have seen him" (ἑωράκατε αὐτόν, 14:7) as an action in the perfect tense.[47] However, Philip's request "Lord, show us the Father" (14:8) reflects the fact that he has failed to see the Father in Jesus.[48] He has been unable to see the Father in Jesus, despite that revealing the Father to the disciples was what Jesus has been doing in his ministry and given that Philip has been with him for three years. Though he has been with Jesus for "so long" (τοσούτῳ χρόνῳ, 14:9), Philip has not really known Jesus[49] due to his "spiritual blindness."[50] The one who failed Jesus' test in the feeding of the crowd (6:6–7), and failed to know what Jesus had in his heart towards the Gentiles (12:20–22), once again appears to have miserably failed to see God in Jesus despite he has been with Jesus such a long time (14:9).

Through the accounts of following Jesus in Philip's life, it is communicated that the journey of following Jesus is a course of gradual growth. Philip is a representation of ordinary men and women who are slow in spiritual understanding and growth. The initial spark of spiritual perception about

---

see Brown, *John*, 1:470; Carson, *John*, 437.

46. Morris, *John*, 643.

47. "Seen" implies the lived experience (Spirituality) as well as understanding, even though it is without physical sight.

48. While Brown (*John*, 2:632) comments that what exactly Philip requests in verse 8 is not clear, Barrett (*John*, 459) and Carson (*John*, 494) say that it reflects "the universal longing of the religious man" and "the vision of God" as it is expressed in Moses' supplication in Exod 33:18.

49. Morris, *John*, 643. Spiritual blindness and dullness is not the problem of Philip alone, but the predicament of all humankind (Rom 3:11).

50. Carson, *John*, 494.

Jesus (1:45) does not demonstrate that Philip excels in spiritual capacity more than any other ordinary men and women. His fervor for evangelism does not denote that his journey of following Jesus reached a mature stage immediately. Following Jesus is a long journey into unexplored territory. The place where Jesus is taking his followers toward is more profound and glorious than what is expressed in the act of evangelism. As Jesus stated in the upper room discourse (14:1–24), it is a journey to the Father, to seeing and experiencing the Father, to a profound relationship with the Father through and with Jesus.

Despite the spiritual dullness and slow growth of his followers, the master will continue leading them toward that goal as he prays for it (17:24–26). A hope for Philip to grow as a follower of Jesus is not based on Philip himself or his capability. The hope comes from his Lord Jesus. The account about Philip in the Johannine text ends where his spiritual blindness is exposed. However, it is not the end. His Lord Jesus "will" continue making known the name of the Father to his spiritually dull follower. The Lord Jesus promised to come to him by the Holy Spirit (14:18) and lead him to understand everything, so that he may not only realize that the Father is in Jesus, but also experience the mystery of the mutual indwelling of the Father and the Son (14:20). The Spirit of truth from the Father and the Son will lead him into all these truths (16:13). For Philip as Jesus' follower, the possibility of spiritual growth and participation in the Jesus' fellowship with the Father depends not on his own ability or the power of his own personal volition, but on his master Jesus and the Spirit.

From this investigation into the accounts about Philip as a follower of Jesus, it can be inferred that the doctrine of sovereign grace applies to the life of following Jesus as well. Christian followers, despite their spiritual dullness and blindness, are able to follow Jesus, achieve spiritual growth, and experience a relationship with God not by their own human capability, but by the tenacious will, work, and grace of their Lord Jesus and the Spirit. To reiterate, the sovereign grace of God applies not only to the area of salvation or initial calling into the Christian journey, but also to the entire journey of following Jesus throughout the whole course of Christian life. Because there is the continuing grace and work of Jesus and the Spirit for them, the followers of Jesus may grow, attain spiritual understanding, and experience the divine reality and mystery. The same principle is communicated in Peter's journey of following Jesus, which will be considered by investigating 13:21—14:3 and 21:1–19.

IV. Following Jesus and Seeing Heaven Opened (1:51)

The motif of "seeing heaven opened" functions, by being stated with great solemnity in the double-amen formula, as the conclusion of the whole account, and thus, it takes the idea of following Jesus, communicated in the account of 1:35–51, to its climax.[51] At the beginning of the account Jesus invited the two disciples, Andrew and the unidentified person to "come and see" (ἔρχεσθε καὶ ὄψεσθε, 1:39). After hearing Nathaniel's confession, Jesus promised them, "You will see greater things than these" (μείζω τούτων ὄψῃ, 1:50). The whole pericope concludes with Jesus' promise that the disciples will see heaven opened (ὄψεσθε τὸν οὐρανὸν ἀνεῳγότα) and the angels of God ascending and descending upon the Son of Man (1:51). In addition to the solemn double-amen formula, by the increasing repetition of the motif of "to see," the text leads the whole story to the culmination which identifies the final destination toward which Jesus will be leading his followers. The destination to which Jesus is leading his followers according to the text is neither primarily the business of being fishers of men, nor the task of being preachers of the Gospel of the Kingdom of God, but to see something higher and greater through him.

What is that which Jesus leads his followers *to see* in the journey of following him? In the terse invitation of verse 39, what Jesus intends them *to see* is not fully identified yet. The subsequent verse (1:40) simply states that they came and saw where he was staying, yet a question arises here. Did Jesus simply mean they came and saw the physical place where he was staying? Rather, isn't it an invitation to something more than that, an invitation to a deeper experience of *seeing* something beyond seeing the physical place? Jesus' invitation is considered by scholars as an invitation to have faith in Jesus as the Messiah. In a general sense, that is not incorrect. Yet, it is indicated in verses 49 and 50 that what Jesus wants them to see is more than to come to believe Jesus as the Messiah. Nathaniel already came to faith in Jesus as the God-sent Messiah as his profession reflects, "Rabbi, you are the Son of God! You are the King of Israel!" His profession is phenomenal. However, Jesus neither expressed his contentment with Nathaniel's profession nor endorsed it, unlike the case where he acknowledged Peter's confession and blessed him in the Matthean Gospel (Matt 16:16, 17).

---

51. The Greek text ἀμὴν ἀμὴν is a transliteration of Hebrew אָמֵן ‖ אָמֵן. The double formula for special emphasis (cf. Num 5:22; Neh 8:6; Ps 41:44; 72:19) is particularly Johannine (25 times) that never occurs in the Synoptics (only single formula appears in Matthew 31 times, Mark 13 times, and Luke 6 times). The double amen formula is "the equivalent to his swearing an oath to the truth of his testimony." Lincoln, *John*, 122.

Instead, Jesus draws the disciples' attention to something greater (μείζω τούτων) that they must see and reach as their future destination. Here μείζω τούτων refers to something more profound than Nathaniel's faith in Jesus as the Messiah, the Son of God, and the King of Israel.[52] Then, what does μείζω τούτων indicate? What is greater than having faith in Jesus as the Messiah and the Son of God?

The final verse of the pericope uncovers in some degree what μείζω τούτων ("greater things") implies (καὶ λέγει αὐτῷ· ἀμὴν ἀμὴν λέγω ὑμῖν, ὄψεσθε τὸν οὐρανὸν ἀνεῳγότα καὶ τοὺς ἀγγέλους τοῦ θεοῦ ἀναβαίνοντας καὶ καταβαίνοντας ἐπὶ τὸν υἱὸν τοῦ ἀνθρώπου, 1:51). First, it is related to heaven (τὸν οὐρανὸν) and the one who is in heaven. What the followers of Jesus will see is not the heavenly things but God the Father himself in heaven (τοῦ θεοῦ).[53] Second, the greater things will be imparted to the followers through the Son of Man as the medium and the link between heaven and earth. In Jacob's vision the ladder was that which connected heaven and the earth.[54] It foreshadowed Jesus, and is now replaced by Jesus the divine ladder, as scholars agree that "Jesus is Jacob's ladder."[55] Jesus is the one who makes the connection between God and humankind, and the Way, through him, his followers come to the Father (14:6). Thus, *Jubilees* rightly calls him "the gate of heaven."[56] Does the experience of seeing the opened heaven[57] and the angels ascending and descending on the Son of man[58] only mean that Jesus' followers will recognize the glory of the Son of man as the glory of God in flesh? Does it exclude the personal experience of the presence of God in and through Jesus? Does the gate not exist for someone to en-

52. Bruner (*John*, 114) is of similar opinion that Jesus' personal relation with God is "greater things" beyond Nathaniel's personal relation with Jesus, whereas Lincoln's view (*John*, 121–22) on "greater things" is limited to "predominantly the signs Jesus will perform."

53. Bultmann, *John*, 106. "Thus the vision which is promised to the disciples is to be conceived . . . as the vision in faith of his Father (1:14), as the vision which sees in him the Father (14:9f)."

54. Gen 28:12 καὶ ἐνυπνιάσθη καὶ ἰδοὺ κλίμαξ ἐστηριγμένη ἐν τῇ γῇ ἧς ἡ κεφαλὴ ἀφικνεῖτο εἰς τὸν οὐρανόν καὶ οἱ ἄγγελοι τοῦ θεοῦ ἀνέβαινον καὶ κατέβαινον ἐπ' αὐτῆς. "And he dreamed that there was a ladder set up on the earth, the top of it reaching to heaven; and the angels of God were ascending and descending on it."

55. Keener, *John*, 1:489.

56. *Jub.* 27:27

57. "God is no longer only inscrutable mystery" (Bruner, *John*, 116), but became available for Jesus' followers to approach and experience in Jesus. Cf. For the opened heaven, see Mark 1:10; Luke 3:21; Isa 64:1.

58. Bultmann, *John*, 105–6. "The Evangelist understands the angels ascending and descending upon the 'Son of Man' as a mythological picture of the uninterrupted communion between Jesus and the Father."

ter and join the reality into which the gate leads? What Jesus promises is that his followers will enter into relationship with God through "the Son of Man as the link between heaven and earth found here and later in 3:13 and 6:62."[59] Brodie finds the similar implication that Jesus' followers could "entertain the prospect of the opening of heaven, in other words, the prospect of intimate communication with God."[60] In Johannine usage, to see does not merely mean a physical sight, but a spiritual experience of becoming a part of something. To see the opened heaven implies entering into the lived experience of communion with the Father. Third, the tense of the verbs of ascending and descending, which is present participle in 1:51 (and imperfect tense in Gen 28:12), reflects that the connection/communion between the Father and Jesus' followers in and through Jesus is not a static one time event, but a continuous communion in a manner similar to "the uninterrupted communion" which the Son of Man has with the Father.

From these considerations, it can be concluded that the life of following Jesus is not simply following the man Jesus, but ultimately the journey into communion with the Father through Jesus. Following Jesus is not only a journey into an experience of Jesus (christological), but also a journey into an experience of God (theological). It is implied from the beginning that the act of following is triggered by hearing that Jesus is the Lamb "of God" (1:36). It is also reinforced by the closing statement in the literary technique of *inclusio* (ὄψεσθε τὸν οὐρανὸν, 1:51).

V. Conclusion

We have seen in this chapter that the unique Johannine understanding of following Jesus is communicated in the text 1:35–51 by the association of the term ἀκολουθεῖν with the where motif, death allusion, and the images that refer to God. The focus of the text falls on two facts: First, to be with Jesus where he is takes on central importance in the life of following Jesus. The disciples stayed with Jesus himself where he was. Yet, the emphasis is not on the place where Jesus stayed as it is not even identified. The focus of the journey of following Jesus is Jesus himself. This is also explicitly stated elsewhere in the Gospel (14:3, "will take you to myself"; 17:24, "may be with me where I am"). To be with Jesus himself where he is certainly takes the place of central significance for the life of following Jesus. By communicating the centrality of "being with Jesus where he is" in the life of following Jesus, the fourth evangelist invites the readers to the Spirituality of being

59. Lincoln, *John*, 123.
60. Brodie, *John*, 168.

with Jesus where he is. To be with someone at the place where he/she is makes a huge difference to a person's life. How much greater a difference the experience of being with Jesus where he is will make in a person's life. It is beyond imagination. It will lead one to an utterly different level of life. To put it in other words, the experience of being with Jesus where he is will lead men and women to be like him, and to achieve authentic human life and self-transcendence.

Second, the text does not end there, but lifts the eyes of the readers toward heaven opened, the relationship with God through Jesus. It is communicated by the *inclusio* technique as the text is encompassed by the image that expresses God as the origin (1:36) and the allusion that points to God in heaven (1:51). It is also portrayed by Jesus' promise that his followers are to see "heaven opened" where God is. As one commentator similarly remarks, it "culminates in abiding with God."[61] The life of following Jesus is entering intimate fellowship with God the Father through being with Jesus where he is.

Jesus is the locus in which his followers experience the presence of God, the gate through which his followers can enter the once hidden but now open reality of heaven, and experience the Father and participate in the communion of the Son with the Father. It is no accident that Philip who first received Jesus' calling of "Follow me" (1:43) is also the one to whom the significant statement was given that whoever has seen Jesus has seen the Father (14:9). Yet, the glorious journey of ultimately experiencing God the Father by following Jesus requires the sovereign grace of the master as well as time, as reflected in the journey of Philip's life.

---

61. Ibid., 161.

CHAPTER 6

Following the Guiding Light to the Father (8:12)

IN JOHN 8:12 JESUS declares the important christological,[1] revelatory,[2] and soteriological[3] logion, "I am the light of the world" (ἐγώ εἰμι τὸ φῶς τοῦ κόσμου). Then he immediately invites men and women with a promise, "Whoever follows me (ὁ ἀκολουθῶν ἐμοὶ) will never walk in darkness (οὐ μὴ περιπατήσῃ ἐν τῇ σκοτίᾳ) but will have the light of life (ἀλλ᾽ ἕξει τὸ φῶς τῆς ζωῆς)."[4] Because Jesus is the light, his followers will not walk in darkness any more, but have the clear direction of life and will reach the destination Jesus leads to. Juxtaposed the two motifs, the light motif and the motif of following Jesus are closely connected. By the association of the two motifs, the unique implication of following Jesus in John is further developed and communicated to a deeper degree.

The present study investigates the Spirituality of following Jesus according to John. In this section we are going to study the Spirituality of following Jesus particularly as communicated by its connection with the motif of "following the light" in the text 8:12. In order to discover the implications of following the light, it is necessary to consider some points with a few questions. First, what is the immediate literary-theological context in which the text has to be interpreted? If it is chapters 7 and 8, how does the text 8:12 fit to the whole picture of the literary-theological context of the two chapters? Also, what have scholars mentioned about the cohesiveness of the two chapters? Second, how and in what background have scholars attempted to excavate the meaning of following the light in 8:12? These two questions lay a foundation for my own investigation on the text.

---

1. Keener, *John*, 1:739; Schnackenburg, *John*, 2:80, 88.
2. Schnackenburg, *John*, 2:80–81, 88, 189.
3. Ibid., 89, 189; Barrett, *John*, 337.
4. Schnackenburg, *John*, 2:191.

After considering the two previous questions, I will launch my own exploration on the connotations of following the light in 8:12 guided by several questions: First, what are the main motifs in the pericope of chapters 7 and 8 to be considered in relation to following Jesus? Second, what is the identity of the darkness? Is there any other text in John that exposes both the identity of the darkness and the meaning of walking in the darkness, and by doing so, sheds light on the interpretation of following the light? Third, what is the connotation of following the light, implied in 8:12, which is construed against the identity of the darkness and particularly viewed in the link with key motifs within the structure of the two chapters as the immediate context? Fourth, what contribution does the motif of following the light in 8:12 make to the main quest of the current study, which is the Johannine implication of following Jesus? Fifth, approaching from the Spirituality point of view, what experience of Christian faith are the readers invited to by Jesus' proclamation and promise of 8:12?

Here is a quick glance to what is coming in this investigation: Firstly, the research text 8:12 is neither a fragment nor an island, but fits to the literary-theological context of prior and subsequent pericope of chapters 7 and 8. Secondly, the implication of following the light is communicated by the recurring motifs of "where" in the context of the two chapters. Thirdly, the concept of following the light in 8:12 adds another substantial connotation to the Johannine concept of following Jesus by the association of the term ἀκολουθεῖν with the motifs of light and "where." In the current text of 8:12, the concept of following Jesus in association with the "where" motif ("from where" and "to where") is developed to a greater degree than in any other place in the Johannine literature.

I. The Text 8:12 within the Unity of the Two Chapters

The literary cohesiveness of chapters 7 and 8 that contain the research text of 8:12 is well established by scholars (excluding the story of the adulteress 7:53—8:11).[5] Brown reads the two chapters under one subtitle "Jesus at Tabernacles."[6] Schnackenburg remarks that the section 8:12–59 is

---

5. On excluding 7:53—8:11, see Beasley-Murray as he summarizes the nine bits of evidence with a comment, "It is universally agreed by textual critics of the Greek New Testament that this passage was not part of the Fourth Gospel in its original form." Beasley-Murray, *John*, 143.

6. Under the same title "Jesus at Tabernacles," Brown (*John*, 1:xii) views the pericope as one unit: Introduction (7:1–13); scene one (7:14–36); scene two (7:37–52); scene three (8:12–20); scene three (continued) (8:21–30); scene three (continued) (8:31–59).

"connected with the themes of the feast of Tabernacles," and further comments, "Internally, chapter 8 presupposes the state of affairs described in chapter 7."[7] Bruner, in dealing with 8:12–20 after posing the question, "Are we still at the Festival of Tabernacles?," answers in the affirmative that the setting of chapter 8 is the same as that of chapter 7.[8] In addition, he points out two factors which convinced him that chapter 8 is the continuation of chapter 7. They are "the absence of temporal or geographical relocation notices" at the beginning of 8:12ff and "the 'confrontational' continuity."[9] The simplest basis for supporting the continuity of the chapters is that most scholars view the light motif of 8:12 in the setting of the feast of Tabernacles.[10] In addition to these, the below outline of my observation on the key motifs that appear throughout chapters 7 and 8 supports why my reading 8:12 within the context of the two chapters is reasonable. That there is continuity between the two chapters provides a legitimate foundation to read the research text 8:12 within the literary and theological context of the chapters.

II. The Backgrounds Considered

Scholars have attempted to interpret the meaning of Jesus being the light of the world against various backgrounds, tracing them back to the places where the light motif appears in the Old Testament and other Judaic literature, the Dead Sea Scrolls or Hellenistic documents. As Barrett points out that "the background is complex," the difficulty of exploring the meaning of Jesus' being the light of the world lies not in the lack of its background data, but in its amplitude and complexity.[11] In this section we are going to survey scholarly opinion as to what backgrounds are considered and what inferences are drawn if any.

Barrett outlines four possible backgrounds of the light motif in 8:12. First, he begins with the ceremony of the first festival day of the feast of Tabernacles as it is described in *Sukkah* 5.2–4.[12] He also makes mention

7. Schnackenburg, *John*, 2:187.
8. Bruner, *John*, 516.
9. Ibid.
10. See the commentaries of the following scholars: Barrett, *John,* 335; Brown, *John,* 1:344; Schnackenburg, *John,* 2:189; Morris, *John,* 436; Carson, *John,* 337; Beasley-Murray, *John,* 127; Moloney, *John,* 266; Keener, *John,* 1:739; Lincoln, *John,* 264.
11. Barrett, *John,* 335.
12. Barrett, *John,* 335; Schnackenburg, *John,* 2:189. Beasley-Murray (*John,* 127) quotes as it is described in *Sukkah*: "Towards the end of the first day of the feast of Tabernacles, people went down into the court of the women, where precautions had

of a possible link with "Tabernacles *Haphtarah,*" quoting Zech 14:7, "there shall continuous day (it is known to the LORD), not day and not night, for at evening time there shall be light."

Second, starting with the "basic assumption of most Gnostic systems" that "God is light," Barrett points out that a "revealer-god was naturally a light to men," and remarks on the similarity between Gnostic understanding and the problem text that the "collocation of light and life, of the cosmological and revealing functions of the Word, who is the Son of God and the light of men, is very close to John's thought."[13]

Third, with regard to the Old Testament and Judaism as the background, he lists ample references of light: Light was the first thing created (Gen 1:3); "light frequently accompanies theophanies" (Gen 15:17); light is a "symbol of divine instruction" (Ps 119:105; cf. Prov 6:23); wisdom is identified with light (Prov 8:22; Wis 7:26, "she is a reflection of eternal light); Yahweh himself is the light ("The LORD is my light," Ps 27:1); the Law is considered "as a Lamp or light (Test. Levi 14.4: The light of the Law which was given for to lighten every man)."[14] Barrett further adds that one of the names of the Messiah is Light, and light is what the Messiah bestows on the righteous. As to the potential relation with the Qumran documents, he lists some passages (1 QS 2.3; 3.7.20f; 4.11) which might be relevant to John. Yet, Barrett closes with a comment that "whether these passages contribute anything to the understanding of the Fourth Gospel is doubtful."[15] Although John and the Qumran texts have a common aspect in their "acquaintance with the Old Testament," their connection is not more than that.[16]

Fourth, Barrett indicates that there are several metaphors of light in the Synoptic Gospels. The parable of the lamp (Mark 4:21–25), according to Barrett, might refer to the "revelation conveyed in the ministry of Jesus."

---

been taken [to separate the men from the women]. Golden lamps were there, and four golden bowls were on each of them, and four ladders were by each; four young men from the priestly group of youths had jugs of oil in their hands containing about 120 logs and poured oil from them into the individual bowls. Wicks were made from the discarded trousers of the priests and from their girdles. There was no court in Jerusalem that was not bright from the light of the place of drawing [water]. Men of piety and known for their good works danced before them [the crowd] with torches in their hands, and sang before them songs and praises. And the Levites stood with zithers and harps and cymbals and trumpets and other musical instruments without number on the 15 steps, which led down from the court of the Israelites into the court of the women and which corresponded to the 15 songs of the steps in the psalms."

13. Barrett, *John*, 335–36.
14. Ibid., 337.
15. Ibid.
16. Ibid.

Matt 4:16 indicates that the work of Jesus is the fulfillment of Isa 9:1. In Simeon's praise to God when he encountered the child Jesus, Luke 2:29–32 (φῶς εἰς ἀποκάλυψιν ἐθνῶν) echoes Isa 49:6 (εἰς φῶς ἐθνῶν). Barrett also recognizes that the words in Matt 5:14 are used by John.[17]

From the above outlined possible backgrounds, Barrett draws a conclusion that John stands within the primitive Christian tradition (cf. Acts 13:47; Phil 2:15; Col 1:12, 13; Eph 5:8; 1 Pet 2:9). Though he admits that there might be a probability that John was influenced both by Jewish thought about Wisdom and the Law, and by Hellenistic religion, Barrett believes that the light of the world in 8:12 has "essentially soteriological function rather than cosmological status."[18] Barrett, however, does not give any further effort to developing how the "soteriological function" works in Jesus' being the light of the world.

Similar to Barrett, Brown also considers the same sources as the backgrounds of 8:12 text: i) the lighting ritual of the ceremony of Tabernacles as depicted in Mishnah *Sukkah* 5:2–4; ii) Judaic literature that employs the image of light for the Law (Wis 18:3–4) or calls Wisdom "everlasting light" (Wis 7:26); iii) the resemblance of Johannine thought with the contrasted concepts of light and darkness in Qumran literature; iv) the image of a lamp for Jesus himself in the Synoptic Gospels. The background sources of 8:12 that Brown surveys are not much different from those of Barrett.[19]

There is only one point Brown adds further to Barrett's scope. It is his attempt to read 8:12 as linked with Exod 13:21, where "the imagery of flaming pillar that guided the Israelites through the darkness of the night" appears. At the end of the survey of the backgrounds, the theological reflection that Brown makes from 8:12 is noteworthy. Knitting together other Johannine texts that contain the light motif, Brown points out that God, who is the light (1 John 1:5), came into the world in Jesus to "dispel the darkness, for those who come to believe in him do not remain in darkness (12:46)."[20] He concludes, "[s]hining forth in him as the incarnate revealer, God's light irradiates human existence and gives man knowledge of the purpose and meaning of life."[21] Although Brown's theological reflection that Jesus is the light that gives men and women "knowledge of the purpose and meaning of life" is valuable in reading the text 8:12, it is limited and somewhat vague. Brown does not state specifically what is meant by "the purpose

17. Ibid.
18. Ibid.
19. Brown, *John*, 1:343–44.
20. Ibid., 344.
21. Ibid.

and meaning of life" in connection to the human predicament which is described in the context of chapters 7 and 8.

Moloney also views Jesus' being the light of the world as he "perfects" the liturgy of the feast of Tabernacles.[22] He further comments that Jesus' words in 8:12 are in line with "the Torah as the light" in Jewish wisdom tradition, providing a few more references (Wis 18:4; Sir 24:27; Bar 4:2) on top of Barrett's.[23] What Moloney adds to the interpretations of the text 8:12 is that he pays attention to the aspect of judgment, indicating that "light brings judgment."[24]

Lincoln begins to see the text "I am the light of the world" (8:12) as Jesus' "replacement of the significance of the Feast of Tabernacles, with its water and light imagery (cf. also 7.37–9)."[25] Similar to the previous scholars, he regards the symbolism of light as Jesus being the fulfiller of a "central feature of the Feast of Tabernacles."[26] Because of the connection of the light motif with the geographical name "Galilee" in 7:41, 52, Lincoln views 8:12 in association with Isa 9:1–2 (cf. Matt 4:14–16). As Moloney points out the aspect of judgment of the light, Lincoln also pays attention to the judgment function (cf. 3:19–21) of the light, as it was "provoked by the presence of the light," which is "the negative effect of revealing and condemning" those who belong to the darkness.[27] Lincoln also sees the positive effect of the light as the "illumination producing life, the salvific verdict in the cosmic trial."[28] Overall he does not bring any new light to the interpretation of 8:12, but he is unique in referring to a few less familiar Judaism texts, which previous scholars have not noticed, to see the light motif in 8:12 as connected to the life motif of Deut 30:15–20; Sir 17:11; and Pro 8:35.[29]

Bruner, as most scholars have done, interprets the text 8:12 against the festival of Tabernacles that "celebrated God's gracious providences during Israel's Wilderness Wandering."[30] After translating "the light of life" as "the Light of *real Life*," Bruner comments that Jesus is "the world's Enlightenment" that gives "the wisdom ('*the Light*') to live the "*real Life*."[31] Although

---

22. Moloney, *John*, 266.
23. Ibid.
24. Ibid.
25. Lincoln, *John*, 264–65.
26. Ibid.
27. Ibid.
28. Ibid.
29. Ibid.
30. Bruner, *John*, 516–17.
31. Ibid., 513.

it is not anything novel, Bruner's contribution in reading the text 8:12 is that he pays closer attention to the text's relationship with the Isaiah 9 passage. He states that Jesus' claim in 8:12 is "the fulfillment of an Isaian text that explicitly promises light from and on Galilee, Isaiah 9:1–2."[32]

Janzen in his article "'I Am the Light of the World' (John 8:12): Connotation and Context," gives a detailed examination of the text 8:12 in connection with Isaiah 8:1–22 and 9:1–7.[33] He begins with the consideration of the two images of "Messiah/Christ" and "the Son of God" in the purpose passage of the Fourth Gospel (20:30–31), and revisits the seven "I am" sayings because the 8:12 text is one of them. Then, he finds the structural similarity between the ending part of John 7 and that of Isaiah 8 as the passages that describe the dark situation of people, and John 8:12 and Isaiah 9:1 as the texts that introduce "the light" motif. Just as Isaiah 8:1–22 describes the situation of "gloom and darkness" of the prophet's opponents, the ending of John 7, particularly 7:52, describes the "taunt" of Jesus' opponents, "Are you from Galilee too? Search and you will see that no prophet is to rise from Galilee" (RSV). To the taunt of the Jews, according to Janzen, as the direct response, Jesus gives the "I am the light" saying in 8:12. This pattern is precisely the same as Isaiah 9:1 ("The people who walked in darkness have seen a great light") gives the "light" motif to the darkness depicted in Isaiah 8:22 ("into thick darkness"). Janzen concludes that "The pronouncement 'I am the light of the world' is, then, part and parcel of the primary theme of John's Gospel: that Jesus is the Messiah, the Son of God, whose coming, like the announced royal birth in Isaiah 9, brings light to those who walked in darkness."[34]

In the above survey we have seen what backgrounds and references from Judaism and Hellenistic documents are consulted by scholars and commentators. Those previous attempts to interpret the light motif in the text 8:12 do not exhaust the examination of the meaning of the text. They are only the starting point of the investigation into the connotation of Jesus' being the light of life. Beyond the efforts to interpret the text 8:12 in the light of distant and broad backgrounds of light motifs in Hellenistic or Judaic literatures, the meaning and implication of the text 8:12 is to be examined more closely in connection with the key motifs within the context of the literary and theological frame of chapters 7 and 8.

The theological inferences drawn by the commentators from the above scholarly attempts are fourfold. Jesus the light of the world functions, first,

32. Ibid., 512.
33. Janzen, "'I Am the Light of the World' (John 8:12)," 115–35.
34. Ibid., 129–30.

as the fulfiller of light motifs in the Old Testament; second, as the one who brings judgment on those who belong to the darkness; third, as the one who brings salvation (soteriological effect) to those who follow the light; and fourth, as the one who gives the purpose and meaning of life.

III. Following the Light in Association with the "Where" Motif

Having briefly surveyed the previous attempts of scholars to interpret the meaning of Jesus' logion in 8:12, now I launch an inquiry into the connotations of Jesus' being the light of the world, and the implications of following him. I am going to attempt to construe the 8:12 text in the association with the key motifs within the literary-theological context of chapters 7 and 8. A biblical text is to be interpreted primarily in the light of its immediate context. This section is devoted to investigating the implication of Jesus being the light that is particularly communicated by the involvement of the text 8:12 with key motifs within the literary-theological context of chapters 7 and 8.

What we are going to explore here are the following. First, the main motifs and the flow of logic within the pericope of chapters 7 and 8 will be probed. Second, as a spring board for examining the connotation of following the light, the identity and nature of walking in the darkness portrayed in connection with the main motifs of the pericope will be investigated. Third, once the nature of walking in darkness is identified, the function of the light and the connotation of having the light of life will be explored. Finally, we will conclude by considering the Spirituality of following Jesus in John conveyed by the light motif, and the contribution of the motif of "following the light" to the Johannine understanding of "following Jesus."

A. Key Motifs in Chapters 7 and 8 as the Context of 8:12

Chapters 7 and 8, as one literary-theological unit, create a peculiar environment for the research text 8:12. Death terminologies and allusions appear throughout the pericope (7:1, 19, 20, 25, 30, 32, 44, 45; 8:20, 28, 37, 40, 59).[35] The pericope begins with the Jews' intention of killing Jesus (7:1, "the

35. The continuity and cohesiveness of the two chapters are identified above, "I. The Text 8:12 within the Unity of the Two Chapters." Although the theme of the death of Jesus is looming in chapters 7 and 8, surrounding the motif of following the light in 8:12, the significance of the death motif to following Jesus is to be unveiled in the coming texts, thus elucidating how the death of Jesus is related to the journey of following Jesus.

Jews were looking for an opportunity to kill him"), and ends with an actual attempt to kill him (8:59, "they picked up stones to throw at him"). Underneath the intention of killing, there are hatred (7:7) and anger (7:23) at Jesus as the hostile emotion. The threats on the life of Jesus are also expressed in the attempts to arrest him (7:30, 32, 44, 45; 8:20). In this life threatening situation, Jesus spoke the important proclamation that he is the light of the world. When there are many threats of death, instead of withdrawing himself to safety, Jesus appears in the temple in the middle of the festival, confronts the Jews and speaks all the more about the Father ("he was speaking to them about the Father," 8:27) and his relationship with the Father (7:16, 17, 18, 28, 29, 33; 8:16, 18, 19, 28, 29, 38, 40, 42, 49, 54).

Ignorance and confusion are noticeable themes in the pericope of the two chapters. The people of Jerusalem are confused with the matter of who Jesus is. While some say he is a good man, others say he is a deceiver (7:12). Whereas some say Jesus is "the prophet," others say "the Messiah," still many say he cannot be the Messiah because he is from Galilee (7:40–43). About the crowd that are in confusion and ignorance, the Jewish religious leaders remark that they are accursed because they are ignorant of the law (7:49). Yet, these same leaders who utter that the crowd is accursed for ignorance are not in any better condition. They are also in the darkness of ignorance. They are in pathetic ignorance of Jesus and his relationship with God. The Jews claim that they know where Jesus is from (7:27), but know neither where Jesus is from nor where he is going to in a true sense. They neither know Jesus nor the Father (7:28; 8:19, 55; cf. 15:20–21; 16:2–3).[36] Although Jesus openly has said that he is from God and is going to him, and that they cannot come where he is, the Jews do not understand him at all (7:33–36; 8:27, 43). Rather, they continue remaining in the thick darkness of ignorance, and condemn Jesus, who is the giver of the Holy Spirit (7:37–39), to be someone who is possessed by a demon (7:20; 8:48–49, 52). Amongst the days of the festival when the city is bright due to the ritual of lighting, the Jews who are supposed to be in bright light (experiencing the Messiah's light), are in the darkness of ignorance.

The intense appearances of the motif of "where" (πόθεν/ὅπου/ποῦ) is outstanding in the pericope. It is continually repeated in various forms (πόθεν ἐστίν; ὅπου εἰμὶ ἐγώ; πόθεν ἦλθον; ποῦ ὑπάγω; πόθεν ἔρχομαι; ποῦ ὑπάγω): "Yet we know where this man is from" (7:27); "you know where I am from" (7:28); "where I am, you cannot come" (7:34, 36); "I know where

---

We will invesitgate this further in our study of the texts of chapters 10, 12, 13, and 21.

36. Ignorance lies underneath their desire to kill Jesus (chapters 7 and 8) and his followers (15:18—16:4).

I have come from and where I am going" (8:14a); "you do not know where I come from or where I am going" (8:14b); "where I am going, you cannot come" (8:21, 22). This important motif of "where" will be examined in the following subsection.

It is in this literary and theological context where Jesus' self revelatory logion "I am the light of the world" is proclaimed, and the pressing invitation to Jesus himself and the soteriological promise is given to those who are in darkness: "Whoever follows me will never walk in darkness but will have the light of life."

Below is the outline of the literary structure and the arrangement of the main motifs of the pericope. The research text 8:12 is located at the center of the pericope, surrounded by the motifs of "from where" and "to where," knowing/not knowing Jesus and the Father, and the looming threat of death.

> 7:1, 19, 20, 25 Death looms.
>
> 7:28 <u>You know neither</u> **where** I am from, nor me,
>   nor the one who sent me.
>
> 7:29, 33 <u>I know</u> **where** I am from, where I am going to,
>   and to whom I am going.
>
> 7:34, 36 **Where** I am, <u>you cannot come</u>.
>
> > 8:12 Whoever follows me will have the light of life,
> >   not walking in darkness.
>
> 8:14a <u>I know</u> **where** I come from, and where I am going to.
>
> 8:14b, 19 <u>You know neither</u> **where** I come from,
>   nor where I am going to, nor me, nor the Father.
>
> 8:21, 22 **Where** I am going, <u>you cannot come</u>.
>
> 8: 20, 28, 37, 40 Death looms.

Having recognized the main motifs and the flow of logic of the pericope, we are now ready to consider the implications of following the light in association with those motifs.

B. The Darkness and the "Where" Problem

Jesus' declaration that he is "the light" of the world does not come out of blue, but it is given in the midst of the darkness of the human predicament, which is described in the previous and subsequent chapters.[37] For the human beings in the darkness, Jesus proclaims that he is "the light of the world." If one follows him (the light), one will "never walk in the darkness, but will have the light of life" (8:12). What is the darkness of the human predicament they are walking in?[38] What is the identity of the darkness presented in chapters 7 and 8, in which the Jews and the people in Jerusalem dwell?[39] As Ridderbos rightly remarks that "the significance of 'light' is determined" by the Johannine "antithesis" of light versus darkness, once the nature and identity of the darkness in the context is identified, the task to grasp the connotation of having "the light of life" will become easier.[40]

As to the identity of the darkness, implied in "walking in darkness," Beasley-Murray assumes that the darkness is "death";[41] Ridderbos vaguely comments that it refers to "the conduct of life in a more comprehensive sense";[42] and Keener asserts that "walking in darkness" is a "standard depiction of humanity living in sin."[43] The general concept of darkness,[44] portrayed in the New Testament, is related with death (Matt 4:16; Luke 1:79), and death with sin (Rom 5:12, 21; 6:16, 23; 8:2; 1 Cor 15:56), and darkness of sin (1 John 1:5–7; 2:8–9, 11). In the pericope also the matter of sin and "dying in sins" briefly appears (8:21, 24, 34). Yet, the connotation of the darkness in 8:12 is to be construed in the "existential significance" because

---

37. It echoes the work of the light that it shines in the darkness as stated in 1:5, "The light shines in the darkness" (cf. Gen 1:2–3; Isa 8:22—9:1, 2).

38. Here the pronoun "they" includes almost all human beings that appear in the two chapters: the Jews (7:1, 11, 13, 15, 35; 8:22, 31, 48, 52, 57), the Pharisees (7:32, 45, 47, 48; 8:13), the people of Jerusalem (7:25), and the crowd (7:12, 20, 31, 32, 40, 43, 49).

39. As stated in the previous section, Bruner and Janzen recognized the light in 8:12 is in close connection with the darkness at the ending part of chapter 7. Brown only indirectly hints that the darkness is related to "purpose and meaning" of life, by pointing out that the light gives knowledge of purpose and meaning of life. Yet, no scholar probed the passages to identify the nature of darkness in this pericope. In this section, my task is to identify the nature of the darkness.

40. Ridderbos, *John*, 293.

41. Beasley-Murray, *John*, 128.

42. Ridderbos, *John*, 293.

43. Keener, *John*, 1:740.

44. Conzelmann, "σκότος, σκοτία," *TDNT* 7:423–45; Hahn, "σκότος," *NIDNTT* 1:421–25.

the proclamation of 8:12 is given in the existential condition of the human beings who appear in the pericope.[45]

The identity of the darkness, in my view, is to be understood in relation with the "where" motif, particularly "knowing where one's life is going." There are three supporting reasons we can see the identity of the darkness in this way. First, there is an important passage in the Fourth Gospel that discloses the identity of the darkness. It is 12:35, "If you walk in *the darkness*, you do not know *where* you are going" (emphasis added). The identity of the darkness in the pericope also is related to knowing the "from where" and "to where" issue of one's life. Schnackenburg comments on the identity of the darkness in the same sense, "Darkness characterizes the existential situation of the person who, lacking the light of saving revelation, leads a life without goal or direction and 'does not know where he goes' (12:35)."[46]

Second, the problem of the human condition in chapters 7 and 8 is portrayed in relation to the motif of "from where" and "to where." To put it another way, the existential darkness experienced by human beings in the pericope is depicted in the connection with the matter of knowing "where" Jesus is from and going and not being able to come to "where" Jesus is. Below is a summary outline of the literary structure of the occurrences of the motif "where." The expressions of "from where" and "to where" encircle the text 8:12 both before and after in a similar pattern.

    A. 7:27–28
    V 27 ἀλλὰ τοῦτον οἴδαμεν <u>πόθεν</u> ἐστίν·
       ὁ δὲ χριστὸς ὅταν ἔρχηται οὐδεὶς γινώσκει <u>πόθεν</u> ἐστίν.
       (But we know <u>where</u> this man comes <u>from</u>,
       and when the Christ appears,
       no one will know <u>where</u> he comes <u>from</u>.)
    V 28 καὶ οἴδατε <u>πόθεν</u> εἰμί·
       (and you know <u>where</u> I come <u>from</u>)

      B. 7:33, 34, 36
      V 33 ***ὑπάγω*** πρὸς τὸν πέμψαντά με.
        (***I am going*** to him who sent me.)
      V 34 **ὅπου εἰμὶ ἐγὼ** <u>ὑμεῖς οὐ δύνασθε ἐλθεῖν</u>
        (**Where I am** <u>you cannot come</u>.)
      V 36 **ὅπου εἰμὶ ἐγὼ** <u>ὑμεῖς οὐ δύνασθε ἐλθεῖν</u>
        (**Where I am** <u>you cannot come</u>)

---

45. As Ridderbos (*John*, 293) sees the meaning of the light of the world in "existential significance," so the meaning of the darkness is to be viewed in the same sense.

46. Schnackenburg, *John*, 2:191.

> C. 8:12
> ἐγώ εἰμι τὸ φῶς τοῦ κόσμου· ὁ ἀκολουθῶν ἐμοὶ οὐ μὴ περιπατήσῃ ἐν τῇ σκοτίᾳ, ἀλλ' ἕξει τὸ φῶς τῆς ζωῆς.
> (I am the light of the world. Whoever follows me will not walk in darkness, but will have the light of life.)

A''. 8:14
 ὅτι οἶδα <u>πόθεν</u> ἦλθον καὶ **ποῦ *ὑπάγω*·**
 ὑμεῖς δὲ οὐκ οἴδατε <u>πόθεν</u> ἔρχομαι ἢ **ποῦ *ὑπάγω*.**
 (for I know <u>where</u> I came <u>from</u> and **where *I am going*,**
 but you do not know <u>where</u> I come <u>from</u> or **where *I am going*.**)

B''. 8:21, 22
 V 21 **ὅπου *ἐγὼ ὑπάγω* <u>ὑμεῖς οὐ δύνασθε ἐλθεῖν</u>**
  (**Where *I am going*, <u>you cannot come</u>.**)
 V 22 **ὅπου *ἐγὼ ὑπάγω* <u>ὑμεῖς οὐ δύνασθε ἐλθεῖν</u>**
  (**Where *I am going*, <u>you cannot come</u>.**)

The literary structure shows that the identity of the darkness and the meaning of having the light are to be understood in association to the "where" motif because Jesus' proclamation, "I am the light of the world. Whoever follows me will not walk in darkness but will have the light of life" (8:12), is enclosed by the motifs of "from where" and "to where."

The issue of "from where" starts from the very moment when Jesus began to teach in the middle of the festival of Tabernacles (7:14) which is the setting of 8:12. The Jews question the origin ("from where") of Jesus' teaching: "How does this man have such learning, when he has never been taught?" Having failed to recognize the origin of Jesus' teaching (cf. 7:16, "my teaching is not mine but his who sent me"; 7:17, "the teaching is from God"), they only see Jesus' teaching from the standpoint of its earthly origin as a matter of human learning.

The "from where" motif continues to appear, as the main concern, around the matter of Jesus' origin to be the Messiah. The people of Jerusalem believe that they know "from where" Jesus came (7:27, "we know where this man is from"). Do they really know where Jesus is from? As a matter of fact, they do not know "from where" Jesus came in a real sense. They only recognize Jesus' earthly origin (cf. 7:41, 52, "Galilee"). That is why Jesus sarcastically cried out as he was teaching in the temple, "You know me, and you know where I come from?" (7:28, ESV).⁴⁷ Here it is implied that the reality of the darkness that overshadows the life of the Jews in the pericope is related to their ignorance in the matter of "from where" in approaching Jesus and his teaching.

Again in 7:40–52, for the crowd and the Pharisees their ignorance of Jesus' true origin ("from where") is the greatest barrier that keeps them from believing in Jesus. The crowd that sees Jesus only from the viewpoint of human origin is unable to believe his identity (7:41–42). Neither are the chief priests and the Pharisees, whose minds are occupied with Jesus' regional origin (7:52), able to perceive where Jesus really came from.

Despite the revelatory proclamation and soteriological promise of 8:12 directly given to them ("Again Jesus spoke to them, saying . . ."), they apprehend neither that Jesus is "from God," nor that the light of life came to them (1:5, 9) and is in front of them, nor that they are invited to the light of life. The Jewish religious leaders, as the people with substantial knowledge of the Scriptures (cf. 7:49–52), should be aware that the light is from God (Gen 1:3; Ps 27:1; Isa 9:1). They should have sensed that the one who proclaims "I am the light" is from God. But in the darkness of their spiritual blindness, they pathetically doubt the validity of Jesus' proclamation (8:13). To them, Jesus exposes that the identity of the darkness in which they are walking is related to the issue of "from where" in approaching Jesus: "you do not know where I come from" (8:14).

The darkness of ignorance in the issue of "from where" Jesus came does not end with recognizing Jesus' spiritual origin alone. It affects the matter of "to where." The matter of "to where" stems from that of "from where." The direction of one's existence is determined by the origin of one's existence. Because they are ignorant of "from where" Jesus came, there is no possibility that they can understand "to where" he is going.

The pericope, which first dealt with the matter of "from where" in the previous unit (7:14–31), now in the subsequent unit (7:32–36) deals with the matter of "to where" Jesus is going: "I will be with you a little while longer, and then I am going to him who sent me" (7:33). However, they pitifully reveal the darkness of their ignorance by thinking about "to where" Jesus is going only in the physical sense (7:35) just like they thought about "from where" Jesus came only in the same sense. The darkness which the Jews are in is that they do not know "to where" Jesus is going as well as "from where" Jesus came: "You do not know where I come from or where I am going" (8:14).

---

47. They should have reasoned rightly of Jesus' origin, of which Jesus has said over and over again (τοῦ πέμψαντός με, 7:16; ὁ πέμψας με, 7:28; παρ' αὐτοῦ εἰμι κἀκεῖνός με ἀπέστειλεν, 7:29; τὸν πέμψαντά με, 7:33).

The darkness of their ignorance of Jesus' origin ("from where") and destination ("to where") does not end with the problem in relation to Jesus alone. It affects the matter of "from where" and "to where" in the life of the people in the two chapters. Because they do not know where Jesus is from and where Jesus is going, there is no way they know where they are from and where they are going to in their own life.[48] The ignorance and unbelief about Jesus' "where" issue affects the "where" issue of their own life. The consequence is that they are not able to find out their own life's origin and direction. It results in a tragic end that they will not be able to come to where Jesus is going to: "Where I am, you cannot come" (7:34, 36). This dreadful result is reiterated in the succeeding chapter: "Where I am going, you cannot come" (8:21–22).

The identity of the darkness in which the Jews and the crowd are walking is not simply a matter of religious knowledge. It is an important matter for the existential direction of life. Because they do not accept that Jesus is from God ("from where") and going to him ("to where"), they are in the darkness of the ignorance about Jesus, and thus, in the darkness of the origin and direction of their own life also. Without the right knowledge about where Jesus came and where he is going to, there is no way they can figure out the direction of their life, that "from where" their life comes and "to where" their life is going. This is the darkness of the existential life situation in which the people of Jerusalem and the Jews are walking.

What is the essential root cause of the darkness? What is underneath the darkness portrayed in relation to the "where" problem? The nature of the darkness in this pericope goes deeper to its twofold roots. First, the root of the darkness is that they do not know God and Jesus, as is pointed out in the pericope a few times: "you do not know him" (7:28); "you know neither me nor my Father. If you knew me, you would know my Father also" (8:19); "you do not know him" (8:55).

Second, the texts 8:23, 39–47 reveal that the root cause of the darkness lies in the problem of the origin of their existence. What is the origin of the Jews in their existence? Where are they from? It is stated: "you are not from God" (8:47); "you are from below . . . you are of this world" (8:23); "you are from your father the devil" (8:44). The fundamental and deeper reason they are in the darkness is that they are from their own father, the devil. This is the opposite of being "born of God" (1:13). In other words, they were not

---

48. Why is the issue of knowing where Jesus is from and where he is going to inseparably connected to the same issue in the life of humankind? It is because Jesus is the origin and creator of humanity (1:3, 10), from whom the light of all people shines (1:4) that human beings may find the right sense of from where they came and to where they are going.

"born from above" (3:3, 5; cf. 8:23). Because they are neither from God nor born of God, they do not accept the one who is from God and are not able to believe that Jesus is from God and going to God, and thus are not able to learn where their life comes and where their life should go, and as the consequence they are not able to come to where Jesus is going to and cannot be with Jesus where he will be. This is the nature of the darkness in which the Jews and the crowd are walking.

In the profound insight of the darkness of human beings' existential predicament, Jesus proclaimed the revelatory and soteriological saying, "I am the light of the world. Whoever follows me will never walk in darkness but will have the light of life" (8:12).

C. To Have the Light of Life

As the identity of the darkness is established and it is evident that it is connected with the matter of "where" in life, the origin and "direction"[49] of life, now we are ready to consider the connotation of Jesus' being "the light of the world" and the implication of "having the light of life."

As to the meaning of the light "of the world," Ridderbos rightly comments: "That Jesus is the true light 'of the world' refers primarily not to the universal significance of the light but the existential significance of what in 1:4 is called 'the light of people' (cf. vs. 9: 'every person'), the light that humanity and the world need to exist, what is therefore called here 'the light of life.'"[50] Because the light of the world is the light which every human being needs for life and existence, it could be identified with the light of life. The function of Jesus as the light of the world is to give a light *for* life.[51]

What then is the connotation of having the light of life? What does it mean that whoever follows him will "have the light of life"? There are a few views on the meaning of "the light of life." For Barrett, the light of life

---

49. Schnackenburg, *John*, 2:191.

50. Ridderbos, *John*, 293. See also Conzelmann, "φῶς," *TDNT* 9:310–58; Hahn and Brown, "φῶς," *NIDNTT* 2:490–96.

51. Why is Jesus able to function as the light of the world for those who are in the darkness? There are two factors. First, specifically speaking, Jesus is able to be the light of life for humanity because Jesus himself has the definitive knowledge of the origin and direction of life. Jesus declares, "I know where I have come from and where I am going" (8:14). He knows from where he came (7:16, 28–29; 8:23, 29, 42) and to where he is going (7:33–34; cf. 8:21). The one who knows the definitive direction of life can be the "guiding light" of life (Brodie, *John*, 324). Second, generally speaking, Jesus is from God who is the Light (cf. 1 John 1:5). The one who came from the Light to be the light of humanity is the one who is able to function as the light of life for every human being (1:4, 9).

is the light that gives life, as he says, "the light has life in itself and gives life" (cf. 4:10, 14; 6:35, 51; 1:4).[52] For Ridderbos, similar to Barrett it is "life giving light."[53] For Lindars, it is the "illumination of men's mind by perfect knowledge of God" (1QS 3.1–9).[54] For Bruner, it is "real life," illuminated by the Wisdom (the Light).[55]

The text 8:12, however, is not concerned with elucidating the definition of the light of life and the meaning of having the light of life. It is left in the hands of the readers to figure out. It seems John trusts that his readers can grasp it in the context where 8:12 is located.

The light of life is neither simply a life-giving light though it might be correct in a broader concept as some of the above scholars comment, nor a light that illuminates life with wisdom or a knowledge about God in general. To have the light of life is neither living a morally elevated ethical life, nor simply living a life released from sin or death. What we are searching for is the particular meaning of having the light of life which is specifically portrayed in the immediate context.

The meaning of having the light of life is the opposite of the meaning of walking in the darkness. Examined and construed on the basis of the above considerations regarding the identity of the darkness, we can logically infer that to have the light of life means to have the right "direction" of life in the matter of "to where" one's life is going.[56] This is the particular meaning of having the light of life, communicated in the pericope by the association of the light motif together with the motifs of "from where" and "to where" and the nature of the darkness.

The connotation of "having the light of life" is that men and women who follow the light will have a sense of "direction" of life, knowing "from where" their own lives come and "to where" they are going. Schnackenburg's comment that the darkness characterizes the existential situation of the person who does not know the goal or "direction" of life and where one goes (12:35), conversely supports the conclusion that to have the light of life indicates having the "direction" of life knowing "where" one's life goes.[57] The right direction of life does not come from ones' own religious meditation, but comes from following the historic Jesus who is the creator of life and

---

52. Barrett, *John*, 337.
53. Ridderbos, *John*, 293.
54. Lindars, *John*, 314, 316.
55. Bruner, *John*, 513.
56. Schnackenburg, *John*, 2:191; Brodie, *John*, 324.
57. Schnackenburg, *John*, 2:191.

origin of their existence (1:3–4) and knowing that "from where" Jesus came and "to where" he is going.

D. Following the Light

The task of the present study is to expound the Johannine implication of following Jesus by investigating the term ἀκολουθεῖν in its connection with other motifs. We now need to consider what implication is communicated by the association of ἀκολουθεῖν with the motif of "having the light of life," and how it contributes to the Spirituality of following Jesus in John.

First, how does the verb ἀκολουθεῖν collaborate with the motif of "having the light of life" and create a unique implication of following Jesus? In proclaiming the logion and promise of 8:12, instead of receiving it, believing in it, or walking in it, the text uses the vocabulary ἀκολουθεῖν and thus employs the imagery of "following the light" that echoes what ancient Israel did in the wilderness.[58] Israel followed the guiding light of God. The pillar of fire by night and of cloud by day led them (Exod 13:21–22); and by *following* the light Israel *was led to* the Promised Land. Employing the imagery of following the light in the wilderness in 8:12 by the term ἀκολουθεῖν, Jesus makes himself "the guiding light" which leads his followers *to* a certain *destination*. As the light of God led Israel *to* the Promised Land, Jesus leads his follows *to the destination* where he is going to.

In 8:12 the light to follow is not a model that people are to imitate or emulate, but the guiding light which leads people to a certain place. Therefore, the theme of following Jesus communicated by the association of ἀκολουθεῖν with the motif of following the light is not to follow Jesus by doing what Jesus has done as mission nor to copy him, but *to be led by him to the final destination of life*. To state it again, the implication of following Jesus uniquely communicated in 8:12 is to be led to a certain destination where he leads to. This is one of the implications of following Jesus, specifically imparted by 8:12 in connection with the motif of following the light.

Second, what then is the destination Jesus leads his followers to? Does the immediate context of 8:12 help identify what it is? It is identified in the pericope of chapters 7 and 8: "I am going to him who sent me" (7:33; cf. 16:5). Who is the one who sent Jesus? It is God according to 7:16 and 8:42, "I came from God." It is also identified to be the Father according to 8:16, 18 "the Father who sent me" (cf. 5:36, 37; 6:44, 57; 12:49; 14:24; 17:21, 25; 20:21). The journey's end to which Jesus leads his followers is the God and Father of Jesus himself. That the Father is the destination is also identified

---

58. Beasley-Murray, *John*, 127–28.

in the broader context by 16:28, "I came from the Father and have come into the world; again, I am leaving the world and am going to the Father." Therefore, according to the Fourth Gospel, the movement of following Jesus is being led by Jesus *to* God the Father, who is the ultimate destination of the life journey of following Jesus.

Third, the implication of following Jesus depicted by 8:12 within the pericope is that the movement of following Jesus is *relational*. It is "relational" with God.[59] To follow Jesus is to be guided into a relationship with the Father because the Jesus whom men and women follow is not simply an isolated Jesus, but the Jesus who is *in relationship* with the Father. That Jesus is in a personal and profound relationship with the Father is an outstanding truth in the Fourth Gospel (1:1, 2, 18; 3:35; 5:17, 19–20, 36–37; 6:32, 40, 46; 8:28; 10:15, 17–18, 29, 37, 38; 12:27; 14:7, 10, 20, 23; 15:1, 8, 15, 23–24; 17:5; 20:17). The immediate context of 8:12 also states in various expressions that Jesus is in an intimate relationship with the Father: "my Father" (8:19, 49, 54); "I know him" (7:29; 8:55); "what I have seen in the Father's presence" (8:38); "the one who sent me is with me" (8:29). By following Jesus, his disciples enter a relationship with God and the Father of Jesus. Similar to my view, Brodie also insightfully comments, "[t]he light is not an isolated Jesus but a Jesus in relationship."[60] He further comments that when Jesus reveals himself "as a guiding light, a light to be 'followed' (8:12), he does so in the context of showing himself to be in union with the Father."[61] By following Jesus who is in the intimate relationship with God, his followers are being led into the same relationship he has with the Father. In this sense, the concept of following Jesus portrayed in John is unique in that the followers of Jesus will enter into an intimate relationship with the God and Father of Jesus by following him.

Fourth, from the viewpoint of Spirituality, following Jesus is a movement that entails for his followers to *experience* the unseen God whom no human has ever seen (1:18; 5:37; 6:46; 1 Tim 6:16; 1 John 4:12). They are able to *experience* the God and Father of Jesus both by seeing and experiencing Jesus (14:7, 9) in this life and eventually by entering the profound communion (relationship) that the Son has with Father in the life hereafter (cf. 14:3; 17:24), which will be a life reality experienced only by following Jesus and being with him where he is. According to Schnackenburg, it is to participate in God's own life, as he defines it, the light of life that the

---

59. Brodie (*John*, 324) understands the light to be *relational* as he comments, "What emerges then is that the concept of light, instead of being seen as something glaring, as coming from an abstract force, is seen as relational, as coming from a parent."

60. Ibid.

61. Ibid.

followers of Jesus will have is the life of "the sharing of God's eternal life."[62] The final and glorious destination of the life journey of following Jesus is to ultimately experience God's own eternal life together with Jesus. For this purpose, Jesus came from the Father and is going back to the Father, taking his followers to the Father.

IV. Conclusion

In the search of the Spirituality of following Jesus in John, I have investigated the text 8:12 in the following procedure to examine the implications of following Jesus which is communicated by the association of ἀκολουθεῖν with the motifs of light and "where." First, the literary cohesiveness of chapters 7 and 8 as one semantic cluster that provides the 8:12 text with the literary-theological context is confirmed. Second, the possible backgrounds and references for the text considered by scholars for interpreting the text 8:12 are surveyed. Third, key motifs and structure of the pericope of chapter 7 and 8 are outlined because the connotations of light and darkness need to be considered in connection with correlated motifs within the immediate literary and theological context. Fourth, acknowledging that the phrase "walking in darkness" is surrounded by the issue of "from where" and "to where," the nature of the darkness in which the Jews are walking identifies that the condition of the human predicament is people's ignorance of the direction ("to where") of life. The darkness of ignorance with regard to the direction of their own life is caused by their not accepting that Jesus is from God. Fifth, it is concluded that the connotation of having the light of life is to have the right "direction" of life that springs from the knowledge of "from where" Jesus came and "to where" Jesus is going. Knowing where Jesus came from and where he is going is not only a matter of knowing Jesus rightly, but also a matter of knowing one's own direction of life. Sixth, the Spirituality of following Jesus specifically imparted in the text 8:12 is reflected by considering how ἀκολουθεῖν is collaborated with the connotations of the imagery of "following the light."

On the basis of the above investigation, it is concluded that the Johannine concept of following Jesus is developed and expanded to a deeper degree by the text 8:12 in collaboration with the correlated motifs of light and "where" in the literary-theological context of chapters 7 and 8. The passage containing 8:12 makes an important contribution to the development of the Spirituality of following Jesus in John in terms of the three aspects. First, that the idea of following Jesus is *directional* is developed to a greater

---

62. Schnackenburg, *John*, 2:191.

degree than in any other pericopes of the Fourth Gospel. It is elaborated by the association of the motif of "following (ἀκολουθεῖν) the light" with the "from where" and "to where" issue. Second, that the journey of following Jesus has a definite *destination* is confirmed. The destination, which was only intimated to be God in 1:35–51 by the phrase of "you will see heaven opened" (1:51), is now disclosed that it is the God and Father of Jesus because that is where Jesus came from and is going, and where he will lead his followers. Third, that the life of following Jesus is *relational* is indicated by intense statements that Jesus, whom the disciples follow, is not an isolated Jesus, but is the Jesus who is in a relationship with the Father, and therefore following Jesus essentially means entering a relationship with the Father, the very relationship Jesus has with the Father. By communicating these particular aspects, the fourth evangelist draws the readers to the lived experience of God and the intimate communion with him by following Jesus the guiding light.

CHAPTER 7

Following the Good Shepherd who Acts for His Sheep (10:1–42)

THE TASK OF THE present study is to articulate the Spirituality of following Jesus portrayed in the Fourth Gospel. It is to be done by investigating what spiritual connotations are created by the association of ἀκολουθεῖν with other vocabularies and motifs within the pertaining pericope as a semantic cluster. Through surveying usages of ἀκολουθεῖν in Greco-Roman and Judaism documents in section one of chapter four, we have corroborated that the plain term ἀκολουθεῖν has been employed to convey a wide range of meanings from simple geographical or physical sense of following to ideological, religious, or spiritual connotations according to the literary context of what words or terms are interweaved with the term within the meaning units. Therefore, when the use of ἀκολουθεῖν in the pertinent texts of the Fourth Gospel is examined with regard to what vocabularies and motifs are associated with the term in each pericope, the distinctive Johannine understanding and implications of following Jesus can be detected.

In investigating the theme of following Jesus, much attention has been given by scholars to what the disciples are to do on their part as the followers of Jesus.[1] It is natural because after all it seems as though the act of following Jesus is all about what the followers do in their life. However, there is much more behind what the followers do in their own will and action in the course of following Jesus. Before the act of following emerges on the surface of the scene, there is a greater reality which is the thing that Jesus does, as the author and perfecter of the movement of following, for the followers as the indispensable and central factor which makes the journey of following Jesus possible and able to be realized.[2] Therefore, in

---

1. Refer to the works listed in footnote 71 of chapter 1 in the present study, and Köstenberger, *The Missions of Jesus and the Disciples*, 1998; van der Merwe, "Discipleship in the Fourth Gospel," 1996.

2. The life of following Jesus revolves around Jesus for he is at the center of the life

dealing with the Spirituality of following Jesus, the aspects and elements which Jesus does for his followers are to be considered with sufficient attention as far as biblical texts communicate them.

The above mentioned aspect of following Jesus is disclosed in a significant amount of detail in the Fourth Gospel. When it comes to chapter 10 of the Gospel, the fact that, in the life of following Jesus, there are more crucial works which Jesus (the author and perfecter of following) does for his followers before the followers do anything for him, is markedly communicated to a degree greater than one can find in any other Gospel accounts. It is presented in three distinguished points. First, the text makes use of varieties of linguistic expressions to highlight the intimacy of relationship between Jesus and his followers (10:3, 4, 14, 27; cf. 10:12, 26),[3] which had been initiated by Jesus and the Father *before* the disciples began to follow him. The relationship is the foundation from which the movement of following is generated, and is that which incessantly motivates and energizes them to continue the journey of following Jesus. Second, the text is dedicated to magnifying what the shepherd Jesus does for his own, leading in front of them (10:4) and protecting them (10:28; cf. 10:29), and more importantly as the central act, laying down his own life for his followers (10:11, 15; cf. 10:17). Third, the text indicates, by intentionally and repetitively mentioning the name of "the Father" (10:15, 17, 18, 25, 29, 30, 32, 36, 37, 38), that the acts of Jesus the shepherd for his sheep are not only the works of Jesus but also those of the Father. Before the followers do anything for Jesus, there are the divine works of Jesus and the Father behind and underneath the movement of following Jesus.

Having in mind the above outlined aspects of following Jesus, we are going to examine the text of 10:1–42 in the following procedure. First, the literary and historical context of the text will be briefly considered. Second, the three suggested respects as the distinct features of following Jesus will be elaborated by taking a closer look at the key vocabularies and motifs.

---

of following him, not the followers. The Spirituality of following Jesus is essentially characterized by who Jesus is, what he does for them, and where he leads them to.

3. V. 3 "He calls his own sheep by name." V. 4 "When he has brought out all his own, . . . because they know his voice." V. 14 "I know my own and my own know me." V. 27 "My sheep hear my voice. I know them, and they follow me." V. 12 "The hired hand, who . . . does not own the sheep." V. 26 "You do not belong to my sheep."

I. The Context: Literary and Socio-Historical

The current text 10:1–42 forms one larger literary unit together with chapter 9 and is the continuation of the previous text where Jesus' address to the Pharisees started in 9:40–41.[4] Jesus opened the born-blind man's eyes and healed his life from darkness to light, but the Pharisees drove the man out of the synagogue (9:34) "as if they have the authority to decide who does and who does not belong to the covenant people."[5] By doing this, the Jewish leaders who were responsible to take care of God's flock proved that they were false shepherds (cf. Ezek 34) who did not take care of the God-entrusted sheep. On the contrary, Jesus who came as the good shepherd, when the man was expelled out of the community, found him once again and revealed himself as the Son of Man (9:35–37), so that the man might have the gift of believing in and worshipping him (9:38) as well as physical healing. In order to present the true shepherd Jesus against the false shepherds, the fourth evangelist intentionally employed the same verb "to drive out" (ἐκβάλλω) for both cases where the Jews cast the man (ἐξέβαλον αὐτὸν ἔξω) out of the synagogue community (9:34, 35) and Jesus' bringing out his own sheep (10:4)—the same verb but in two opposite connotations.[6]

In the socio-historical context in which the followers of Jesus are being persecuted and driven out of the community (9:22, 34, 35; 12:42; 15:18–25; 16:2), Jesus reveals himself as the shepherd who knows, leads, and protects them, and furthermore the one who gives his own life for them (10:11, 15). Why does the fourth evangelist include the account of Jesus the good shepherd here after the persecution narrative of the blind man? Jesus as the good shepherd is not simply presented in a historical vacuum with a neutral tone of voice. The readers of the community of the fourth evangelist, who were in a similar socio-historical situation of persecution and harassment, needed to be reminded that their Lord Jesus, whom they were following in the midst of life threatening daily life, was the faithful and responsible shepherd, the one who had given his own life for them to the point of actual death, and who would continue defending and protecting them. It is certainly to give encouragement, comfort, and strength to the followers of Jesus, so they can continue the journey of following Jesus even amongst an adverse and

---

4. Lincoln, *John*, 291. Morris (*John*, 501) also points out that the expression ἀμὴν ἀμὴν (10:1) never opens a new discourse, but always follows up some previous teaching; thus, chapter 10 has "a connection with the preceding." For discussions on the relation between the two chapters, see Dodd, *Interpretation*, 359; Bruner, *John*, 615; Busse, "Open Questions on John 10," 1–17.

5. Keener, *John*, 1:797.

6. Lincoln, *John*, 292.

hostile socio-historical environment. This is why the fourth evangelist puts the narrative of chapter 9 together with chapter 10, and around the term of discipleship ἀκολουθεῖν (10:4, 27) places plenty of motifs that convey what the faithful shepherd does for his own (10:3, 4, 11, 15, 28, 29). The followers of Jesus in the evangelist's community needed to hear what their faithful Lord Jesus does and continues doing for his followers.

II. Following Jesus Implied in 10:1–42

In the first half (10:1–21) of the text 10:1–42, the fourth evangelist focuses on communicating that Jesus is the good shepherd (and the gate) *for* the sheep (10:7, 11, 14), describing his relationship with them (10:3, 14–15), including what he does for them as the shepherd (10:3, 4), and what benefits are given to the sheep from the shepherd's coming to them (10:9, 10).[7] In the second half (10:22–42) of the text that is placed in the context of hostile rejection by the Jews (10:31, 39), the evangelist continues presenting what Jesus does *for* his sheep (10:28), and more importantly what Jesus does is not only his works but the works of the Father at the same time (10:29, 30, 31, 37). The distinctive aspects of following Jesus communicated in 10:1–42 are: firstly, the commencement of the life of following is not what generates relationship with Jesus, but the followers come to follow him because Jesus already owns and knows them. Secondly, before it is the followers who work for Jesus, it is Jesus the shepherd who does many works for his sheep. That is the most fundamental and essential factor that makes the journey of following Jesus possible, and able to be sustained and realized. Thirdly, the life of following Jesus utterly depends on not only the works of Jesus, but also the Father's, which is the co-ministry of Jesus and the Father. All works Jesus does for his own are the works of the Father and from the Father. The journey of following Jesus is in the Father's hand as well as in Jesus'.

---

7. Even though there is a temporal indicator (10:22, "At that time the feast of Dedication took place in Jerusalem") that divides the text into two parts, the current study assumes 10:1–42 to be one semantic cluster because they hold thematic cohesiveness under the imagery of shepherd and sheep (10:1–16; 26–27). The fourth evangelist is more concerned about themes of the pericope, as Schnackenburg rightly comments, "the evangelist does not concern himself with chronological considerations of this kind but is wholly preoccupied with his themes." Schnackenburg, *John*, 2:278. For other suggestions on the literary structure of the text, refer to Bruner, *John*, 603–4; Brown, *John*, 1:cxli, 404; Keener, *John*, 1:775, 821.

A. Following Jesus Who Owns and Knows the Followers from Before

The vocabularies and motifs that indicate the intimate relationship between Jesus the shepherd and his sheep appear in two groups. The first group is "his own" (τὰ ἴδια, 10:3, 4), "my own" (τὰ ἐμα, 10:14), and "my sheep" (τὰ πρόβατα τὰ ἐμά, 10:27). The second group is "to call by name" (φωνεῖ κατ' ὄνομα, 10:3), "to know his voice" (οἴδασιν τὴν φωνὴν αὐτοῦ, 10:4), "I know my own and my own know me" (καὶ γινώσκω τὰ ἐμὰ καὶ γινώσκουσί με τὰ ἐμά, 10:14), and "I know them" (κἀγὼ γινώσκω αὐτά, 10:27).

1. His Own, My Own, My Sheep

Before the act of hearing the shepherd's voice (10:3, 27) and following him (10:4, 27) from the part of the sheep, there is the shepherd who already made the sheep "his own" (τὰ ἴδια/τὰ ἐμα, 10:3, 4, 14, 27; cf. 1:11; 13:1). There is the shepherd's ownership[8] over the sheep's life before any movement of following starts. That which makes it possible for the believers to follow Jesus the shepherd in confidence without fear is the pre-created ownership of Jesus (created by the covenant between Jesus and the Father) over the life of his own sheep. The point is conversely sustained by the fact (analogy) that the hired hand runs away because he *does not own* the sheep (10:12, οὗ οὐκ ἔστιν τὰ πρόβατα ἴδια). The Jews do not hear Jesus' voice because they *do not belong* to his sheep (10:26; cf. 8:47). What precedes the act of hearing[9] and following from the sheep's part is the bond of belonging (cf. Isa 43:1; Rom 1:6), the ownership of the shepherd which was somehow already wrought by the shepherd to make the sheep his own.[10] It is not what the sheep initiated or obtained by works on their end, but what the shepherd has done to purchase the sheep so that they might belong to him.

The text 10:1–42 is not absolutely silent as to how and by what procedure the shepherd made the sheep his own and how the inseparable bond was generated. By the statement in verse 29 ("My Father who has

---

8. "[B]elong to him as *owner*" as seen in 10:12 (cf. 1:11; 13:1). Schnackenburg, *John*, 2:282, 294. Keener also points out the ownership of the shepherd over the sheep's life by commenting that in 10:1–18 the fourth evangelist turns "to the question of the true and false *owners* of the sheep." Keener, *John*, 1:797.

9. "To hear the voice of Jesus one must be 'of God' (8:47) and 'of the truth' (18:37)." Brown, *John*, 1:406. Hearing the voice of the shepherd presupposes that the sheep belong to him.

10. Carson, *John*, 383.

given them to me"),[11] it is intimated that the ownership of Jesus over his sheep's life was formed by the transaction between the Father and the Son by which the Father[12] gave them to the Son.[13] This is also indicated in other places in the Fourth Gospel (cf. 6:37, 39, 44, 65). In chapter 17 it is indicated that before the creation of the world there was the divine compact between God and Jesus that made Jesus' followers to be "his own."[14] The followers of Jesus who were also the Father's (17:9, 10) were given Jesus from the Father to be Jesus' own, and it was done before any act of following started from the followers' part. The act of hearing Jesus the shepherd's voice, and following him, was generated by the pre-established "bond" between Jesus the shepherd and his sheep by the sheer divine act between the Father and the Son.[15]

Just as sheep follow a shepherd without fear under the shepherd's ownership over their life, the followers of Jesus are drawn to follow him in confidence on the basis of Jesus' ownership over their life. The life of following Jesus is neither due to their own preference, nor their innate ability to do so, but springs up out of the divine act of sovereignty. It is God's initiative that takes the central role over the entire life of following Jesus.

Furthermore, the shepherd's ownership over the sheep's life includes a full responsibility of the shepherd for the wellbeing and security of sheep's life. It will be discussed in the next section what the shepherd does *for* his sheep. It is not the followers of Jesus themselves who are responsible for the wellbeing and security of their life through their own capability, but Jesus the owner takes the full responsibility. This is the most reliable foundation on which Jesus' followers can launch the journey of following him without fear, and from which they can draw great assurance and comfort amongst the socially and historically hostile circumstances that threaten their identity as the followers of Jesus.

---

11. Reading of ESV, NAB, NAU, NET, NIV, and RSV. For discussions on the variants of the verse, see Barrett, *John*, 381–82; Schnackenburg, *John*, 2:307–8.

12. "[T]he inseparable bond uniting him with his sheep is established through the Father." Schnackenburg, *John*, 2:298.

13. Brown, *John*, 1:407; Carson, *John*, 393.

14. 17:6, 9 "those whom you gave me"; 17:24 "whom you have given me"; cf. 18:9 "those whom you gave me." Barrett writes, "The disciples belonged to God from the beginning, because from the beginning he had predestined them as his children. He gave them to Jesus to be his disciples as part of his gift of all authority." *John*, 505. Cf. Ephesians 1:4, 5 καθὼς ἐξελέξατο ἡμᾶς ἐν αὐτῷ πρὸ καταβολῆς κόσμου . . . προορίσας ἡμᾶς εἰς υἱοθεσίαν διὰ Ἰησοῦ Χριστοῦ εἰς αὐτόν.

15. Schnackenburg, *John*, 2:297–98. Brown (*John*, 1:407) refers it to as "predestination."

2. To Know

Before the sheep hear the shepherd's voice (10:3) and follow him (10:4), there is the shepherd who *knows* the sheep (10:14, 27). The word "to know" appears in two Greek verbs. First, οἶδα occurs in relation to "voice" that the sheep know the shepherd's voice (10:4) and do not know a stranger's voice (10:5). Why do the sheep follow the shepherd? "The sheep follow him because they know (ὅτι οἴδασιν) his voice" (10:4). Why do the sheep not follow a stranger? "They will not follow a stranger . . . because they do not know (ὅτι οὐκ οἴδασιν) the voice of strangers" (10:5). Knowing is the key factor. Because there is no bond of intimacy in knowledge, the sheep do not follow a stranger, which conversely upholds the idea that the sheep follow the shepherd on the basis of the bond of intimacy in knowing the shepherd's voice.

Second, the word γινώσκω also is used to describe the "bond" between Jesus and his sheep (10:14),[16] which is an expansion of the mutual bond in knowledge between the Father and Jesus (10:15).[17] The verb is repeated to emphasize Jesus' personal knowledge of his sheep (10:27).[18] The last use of γινώσκω appears to describe the fact that those who believe Jesus' works will obtain the knowledge and understanding of the "reciprocal immanence"[19] between the Father and Jesus (10:38).[20] Schnackenburg confirms that γινώσκω conveys the inseparable mutual bond between Jesus and his followers:

> He 'knows' them in the way that the owner of the flock knows his sheep. And the relationship between them is one of friendship and intimacy. The term γινώσκειν does not denote knowledge of the theoretical-rational kind but, in an O.T.-Semitic sense, a personal bond, a knowing that leads on to communion. Consequently it can also be said in the same breath that the sheep know him. It is a mutual bond whose whole meaning is straight away made clear by the imagery itself, but which thereupon takes on deeper implications, since those named 'mine' by Jesus

---

16. 10:14 "I know my own and my own know me" (καὶ γινώσκω τὰ ἐμὰ καὶ γινώσκουσί με τὰ ἐμά).

17. 10:15 "just as the Father knows me and I know the Father" (καθὼς γινώσκει με ὁ πατὴρ κἀγὼ γινώσκω τὸν πατέρα).

18. 10:27 "I know them, and they follow me" (κἀγὼ γινώσκω αὐτὰ καὶ ἀκολουθοῦσίν μοι).

19. Ridderbos, *John*, 560.

20. 10:38 "so that you may know and understand that the Father is in me and I am in the Father" (ἵνα γνῶτε καὶ γινώσκητε ὅτι ἐν ἐμοὶ ὁ πατὴρ κἀγὼ ἐν τῷ πατρί).

are given him by the Father, given him 'out of the world' (17:6)—
and hence the idea of election is conveyed in overtones.[21]

Even though it is recognized to be a "mutual bond of knowledge," the way this mutual knowledge is developed is not like that between two equal human beings. Jesus' knowledge of his followers is the foundation of his followers' knowledge of Jesus. Jesus' knowing them is first, and it generates the followers' knowledge of him. The former is the cause and foundation, the latter is the effect and fruit.

In 10:1–42 there are two places where the shepherd's knowledge of his sheep comes before the sheep's knowledge of the shepherd. Firstly, in verse 3 that the shepherd knows the sheep personally is implied in the phrase in which the shepherd calls his sheep by name (10:3), then comes the fact that sheep know the shepherd's voice in the following verse (10:4).[22]

Secondly, it is implied in verses 14 and 15 by the order in which Jesus' knowledge of the sheep is mentioned before their knowledge of him, just as the Father's knowledge of Jesus comes first, then Jesus' knowledge of the Father follows. Schnackenburg also points out the same important order:

> [B]ecause he 'knows' them and reveals himself to them (cf. 15:15), they are consequently enabled to know him in turn and to grow in fellowship with him. It is not without reason that Jesus' 'knowing' comes before the 'knowing' on the part of his own, as, too, the Father's 'knowing' comes before the Son's.[23]

It is also noted in the account of the calling of the first disciples that Jesus already knew Nathaniel before he comes to know Jesus and follows him (1:48). The shepherd first knows the sheep. As a consequence of the shepherd's knowing them, the sheep come to know the shepherd. Jesus' knowledge of his own is the foundation of the commencement of the life of following Jesus into intimacy. As they keep following him, they come to know him more and more in an ever increasing manner.

The relationship in mutual knowledge is not only the foundation but also the content and objective of the life of following Jesus. The journey of following is the voyage into a deeper knowledge, which is experiencing who Jesus is, knowing him and being known by him (cf. 14:9, 20; 21:17).

---

21. Schnackenburg, *John*, 2:297.

22. For the cultural background of Palestinian shepherds' calling their sheep by name, see Brown, *John*, 1:385; Keener, *John*, 1:805. On the meaning of "by name," Schnackenburg (*John*, 2:282) remarks that it implies "the shepherd's loving familiarity with his sheep." Cf. Its reading as "individually," see Dodd, *Tradition*, 384; Beasley-Murray, *John*, 169; Bultmann, *John*, 373, n. 1; Bruner, *John*, 610.

23. Schnackenburg, *John*, 2:297.

The journey is a movement into the profound experience of the mysterious relationship of immanence between the Father and the Son (cf. 10:38; 14:10, 11, 20; 17:21, 23). In the intimacy of being known by the shepherd and knowing him, the followers of Jesus are incessantly reenergized to continue the journey of following him.

What do the above findings connote about the Johannine understanding of following Jesus? By arranging the terms "my own," "his own," "my sheep," and "I know them" before and after the term ἀκολουθεῖν, 10:1–42 implies that the act of following Jesus is generated by the divinely pre-established "bond."[24] The followers of Jesus came to follow him, not because they first decided to follow him, but because the shepherd knows them first (10:27, "I know them, and they follow me") and has the full ownership over their existence. They are his, and known by him, therefore they are enlightened to know him and enabled to follow him. On the surface level it seems like the controlling factor that forms the life of following Jesus is the choice and determination of the followers, but as a matter of fact, the controlling energy and determining factor of the movement of following Jesus and the intimate bond of the shepherd-sheep relationship is that, before they hear and follow him (10:4, 27), they were already given to Jesus by the Father, came to belong to Jesus and became his own (10:3, 4, 27), and moreover are known (10:27) by Jesus the shepherd. Those who belong to him and are known by him follow him. This is the essential foundation and root of the movement of following. And this is the distinct and profound aspect of following Jesus communicated by the present Johannine text.

As Jesus' followers started the journey of following him on the foundation of his knowledge of them, they will come to know him more deeply in subjective experience, while continuing the journey. The life of following Jesus, triggered by the pre-established bond in the divine act between the Father and the Son, will be deepened and become richer from one degree to another in the intimacy of an ever intensifying inseparable bond as the movement of following continues even in the midst of adverse life situations (cf. 9:22, 34). That ever increasing knowledge and deepening bond of intimacy with Jesus and ultimately with the Father in and through Jesus, is the foundation, objective, and content of the journey of following Jesus.

---

24. Ibid., 2:297–98.

B. Following the Shepherd Who Acts
Many Works for His Sheep

While there are only two terms that describe the act from the sheep's part (to hear and follow, 10:3, 4, 27), John 10 is fully loaded with a linguistic feast regarding what the shepherd does for the sheep. It connotes that, just as the life of the Palestinian sheep utterly depends upon what the shepherd does for the sheep, the life of following Jesus absolutely depends on the many acts that Jesus does for his followers.[25] The vocabularies and motifs that indicate the acts which the shepherd does for his sheep are: leading them out (10:3); bringing them out (10:4); going ahead of them (10:4); laying his own life for the sheep (10:11, 15); giving them eternal life (10:14, 27); protecting them and not losing any of them (10:28–29). The structural diagram below shows how intentionally the movement of following is surrounded by the vocabularies that express Jesus' many acts for his sheep.

    ⌐ V 3 The shepherd **brings out** his own.
    └ V 4 The shepherd **leads** his own before them.

        V 4 The sheep *follow* the shepherd.

        ⌐ V 11 The shepherd **lays down his life** for his sheep.
        └ V 15 Jesus **lays down his life** for his sheep.

        V 27 The sheep *follow* him.

    ⌐ V 28 Jesus **protects** the sheep.
    └ V 29 The Father **protects** the sheep.

There are three major passages within 10:1–42 that communicate Jesus the shepherd's acts for his sheep.

    Passage 1: 10:3, 4
    καὶ τὰ ἴδια πρόβατα φωνεῖ κατ' ὄνομα καὶ ἐξάγει αὐτά.
    (He calls his own sheep by name and leads them out.)
    ὅταν τὰ ἴδια πάντα ἐκβάλῃ, ἔμπροσθεν αὐτῶν πορεύεται
    (When he has brought out all his own, he goes ahead of them)

---

25. That the acts of provision and protection of the shepherd for his sheep take an absolutely crucial role for the life of the sheep is widely known by the fact that the Palestinian sheep wholly depend on the shepherd's care. "Without the shepherd the sheep were helpless." Keener, *John*, 1:812. See also Ryken, Wilhoit, and Longman III, "Sheep, shepherd," 782–85.

Passage 2: 10:11, 15
ὁ ποιμὴν ὁ καλὸς τὴν ψυχὴν αὐτοῦ τίθησιν ὑπὲρ τῶν προβάτων·
(The good shepherd lays down his life for the sheep)
καὶ τὴν ψυχήν μου τίθημι ὑπὲρ τῶν προβάτων.
(And I lay down my life for the sheep)

Passage 3: 10:28, 29
καὶ οὐχ ἁρπάσει τις αὐτὰ ἐκ τῆς χειρός μου.
(No one will snatch them out of my hand)
καὶ οὐδεὶς δύναται ἁρπάζειν ἐκ τῆς χειρὸς τοῦ πατρός.
(no one can snatch it out of the Father's hand)

The first passage that describes Jesus' act for his sheep is 10:3, 4 which depicts a pastoral scene in which the shepherd brings his sheep out and leads them going before them.[26] Unlike western ranch culture where a great number of sheep are raised in wide grass pastures fenced by barbed wire, Palestinian shepherds take their sheep every morning along a narrow path through a wilderness to pasture by leading them, walking in front of them. In the dry Judean desert the Palestinian sheep can stay in good health only because the shepherds continue leading them to grass every day.

In the Old Testament, God appointed leaders such as Moses[27] and David[28] to deliver the people of Israel from enemies and dangers, and lead them to God's rest.[29] More importantly God himself was the shepherd who was leading his people in the wilderness throughout the journey of the Exodus.[30] He led the people by going ahead of them in the pillar of cloud and fire, so that they might know when to depart and stop, and where to camp and rest.[31] His leading continued until they arrived in the God-promised destination. *Because* God was leading them in front of them all the way through the journey, Israel was able to travel safely through the wilderness overcoming many dangers, and reach the Promised Land. Likewise, *because* Jesus the shepherd leads his own sheep every day, the journey of following

---

26. Among the major research texts of this study (1:35–51; 8:12–29; 10:1–42; 12:20–36; 13:31—14:3; 21:1–19), the current text 10:1–42 is the only one that lacks the term "where." However, the idea of "to where" for the life of following Jesus is implicitly reflected by the expression "he goes ahead of them" (10:4) because where Jesus the shepherd leads them going before them is where his followers go to.

27. Ps 77:20; 78:52; 80:1; Isa 63:11.

28. 2 Sam 5:2; 1 Chr 11:2; Ps 78:70–72; Ezek 34:23; 37:24.

29. Num 27:17; 1 Kgs 22:17; Jer 3:15.

30. Ps 78:52; 80:1; Isa 40:11; 63:14; cf. Exod 13:21; 15:13; Deut 8:2; Ps 78:14; 106:9; 136:16; Neh 9:12; Isa 48:21; Jer 2:6; Hos 11:3–4; Amos 2:10.

31. Num 9:15–23; cf. Exod 40:36–37.

Jesus can continue. What makes possible the journey of following is the fact of the shepherd's going immediately before them every day. Furthermore, *because* Jesus the shepherd is leading his followers to the Father, going (πορεύω) ahead of them, the followers of Jesus will be able to reach the place where the Father is safely.[32] It is the shepherd's act of going in front of the followers that guarantees their successful journey.

The second passage that portrays the shepherd's acts for his own sheep is 10:7–15. By twice repeating the "I am" saying (Ἐγώ εἰμι ὁ ποιμὴν ὁ καλός) in verses 11 and 14, Jesus identifies himself as the good shepherd.[33] Then he declares that, as the good shepherd, he lays down his life for his own sheep (10:11, 15).[34] "To lay down life" (τίθημι τὴν ψυχήν) is a peculiarly Johannine expression (10:11, 15, 17; 13:37; 15:13; 1 John 3:16).[35] "None of the Old Testament passages on the shepherd theme contains this striking feature."[36] Although there appeared shepherds who risked their life for their sheep in the Old Testament (1 Sam 17:34–35), Jesus is the only shepherd who actually sacrificed his life for his sheep. The preposition ὑπέρ (for) in the Fourth Gospel (as appears in the phrase ὑπὲρ τῶν προβάτων, 10:11) almost always conveys "the significance of death," which is "a sacrificial death for the benefit of others."[37]

Why does the evangelist closely juxtapose the idea of having an abundant life (10:10) and the expression of laying down life (10:11, 15)?[38] By doing so, the evangelist reveals that Jesus' act of laying down life is to give

---

32. The verb πορεύεται (which is employed to refer to "the shepherd's *going* before the sheep" in 10:4) appears 12 times in the Fourth Gospel (except for twice in 8:1–11). Among them, five occurrences are employed simply to state some movements in a geographical sense (4:50; 7:35, 53; 11:11; 20:17). However, the other six occurrences are noticeably employed for *one specific movement*, which is "Jesus' going to the Father" (14:2, 3, 12, 28; 16:7, 28). If the significance of the usages of the verb for this particular movement of Jesus' *going* to the Father is not ignored and the significance that Jesus' leading of his followers *going* before them continues throughout the journey of following him is considered, then it is not too big a leap to infer that, because there is Jesus who is leading them *going* ahead of them, they will be able to reach where the Father is.

33. The "noble" or "model" (ideal or model of perfection) shepherd (Brown, *John*, 1:386) can be read against the wicked shepherds in Ezek 34:2–4 (cf. Isa 56:10–12). For other discussions on the reading of "καλός," see Morris, *John*, 509; Keener, *John*, 1:813.

34. 10:11 τὴν ψυχὴν αὐτοῦ τίθησιν ὑπὲρ τῶν προβάτων. 10:15 τὴν ψυχήν μου τίθημι ὑπὲρ τῶν προβάτων.

35. Barrett, *John*, 374; Brown, *John*, 1:386; Morris, *John*, 509.

36. Lindars, *John*, 361

37. Barrett, *John*, 375. Jesus' death (6:51; 10:11, 15; 11:50–53; 18:14; cf. 17:19); Peter's death (13:37, 38); a person's death for one's friends (15:13).

38. UBS4 reads 10:7–18 as one semantic unit, although NA28 divides the text into several smaller units: 7–10; 11–13; 14–16; 17–18.

"life" to his own sheep.[39] "[T]he death of the Palestinian shepherd meant disaster for his sheep. The death of the good shepherd means life for his sheep."[40] The acts of Jesus the good shepherd for his sheep "culminate" in the act of actual redemptive giving of his own life.[41] It not only gives life to his followers, but also makes the journey of following Jesus possible all the way from commencement to continuation to completion. Furthermore, it is his death by which Jesus leads his followers to the Father just as it is reflected already in the image of the Lamb of God (1:29, 35–37) that the death of the Lamb leads the followers to heaven opened (1:51). Not the qualifications or competence of the followers, but Jesus' laying down his own life for them is the magnetic force that draws his own to follow him (cf. 12:32) and ultimately to the Father. Underneath the movement of following Jesus, there is the shepherd's act of laying down his own life for his followers.

The third passage that expresses the shepherd's act for his sheep is 10:28–29. Jesus knows his sheep and they follow him (10:27). He gives them eternal life (10:28) by the act of laying down his life (10:10–11, 15). His act for his sheep, however, does not end there. It continues in his act of protecting them: οὐχ ἁρπάσει τις αὐτὰ ἐκ τῆς χειρός μου (10:28).[42] The word ἁρπάζω (to snatch away) presupposes that there is an enemy that prowls around to snatch the followers of Jesus out of his hand and destroy.[43] The journey of following Jesus is open to dangers from the enemy's attack (10:12, "the wolf"). However, there is the χείρ (hand) of the shepherd that holds them securely in perfect safety and protection. They are in the shepherd Jesus'

---

39. The same idea is repeated in the Fourth Gospel. By being lifted up, the Son of Man will give eternal life (3:14–15); and by dying, a grain of wheat yields many fruits of life (12:23–24).

40. Morris, *John*, 510.

41. Schnackenburg, *John*, 2:294.

42. The two recurring terms ἁρπάζω and χείρ are employed for both Jesus and the Father in verses 28 and 29. The co-ministry of the Father and the Son in the work of protection of the followers will be discussed below. Also see 17:11, 12, 15.
17:11 πάτερ ἅγιε, τήρησον αὐτούς. "Holy Father, protect them."
17:12 ἐγὼ ἐτήρουν αὐτούς . . . καὶ ἐφύλαξα. "I protected them . . . I guarded them."
17:15 ἀλλ' ἵνα τηρήσῃς αὐτούς. "but I ask you to protect them."

43. In the Old Testament it represents "to take away or rob" (Lev 6:4; 19:13; Judg 21:23; Isa 10:2; and metaphorically Mic 3:2) and "to tear into pieces by beasts" (Gen 37:33; Amos 3:4; Hos 5:14; Ps 50:22; cf. Hos 6:1). Among the total 14 time appearances in the New Testament, two meanings are relevant to its usage in the current text of chapter 10. First, it means "to steal, carry off, drag away" (Matt 12:29; John 10:12); second, "to lead away forcibly" (John 6:15; 10:28, 29; cf. Acts 23:10; Jude 23). Tiedtke and Brown, "ἁρπάζω," *NIDNTT* 3:601–5. In the reality of the conflict between the kingdom of God and that of Satan (cf. Matt 12:29; Foerster, "ἁρπάζω," *TDNT* 1:472–73), the enemy Satan is trying to snatch and kill the followers of Jesus.

mighty grip.⁴⁴ Morris remarks, "[O]ur continuance in eternal life depends not on our feeble hold on Christ, but on his firm grip on us."⁴⁵ The followers of Jesus can continue the journey without falling away and reach the destination Jesus called to not depending upon their own spiritual ability or power of will, but depending upon the all-powerful protection of the shepherd Jesus.⁴⁶ The shepherd's act of protection is what makes the journey of following Jesus possible.

What is the intention of the fourth evangelist in arranging the text of chapter 10 with many words and motifs that articulate the acts of the shepherd Jesus for his sheep in association with the discipleship term ἀκολουθεῖν? What kind of Spirituality of the life of following Jesus is communicated to the readers? The evangelist wants the readers to find confidence from that, although their deeds of hearing and following are still important elements, there is the greater reality that enables and sustains their journey of following Jesus. By arranging the vocabularies of Jesus' many acts for his sheep in connection with ἀκολουθεῖν, the evangelist invites the readers to the lived experience of blessed assurance that comes from the fact that they are not having a lone journey but the shepherd Jesus is continually leading them every step right in front of them, that they came to have life and were drawn to follow him by his life-giving sacrifice, and that the shepherd Jesus who laid down his life for them will hold them tightly in his mighty grip until they reach the final destination.⁴⁷ From the commencement to reaching the final

---

44. In the Old Testament the hand (יָד) is a symbol of power. Thus, to fall into someone's hand means to come into their power (Gen 32:11; Judg 2:14; Jer 27:6f.). It is likewise a symbol for divine omnipotence (2 Chr 20:6; Ps 89:21). The hand of the Lord is used in the same way to express his loving care (Ezra 7:6; Job 5:18; Ps 145:16; Isa 49:16) and his divine protection (Isa 51:16). In the New Testament the word χείρ occurs 176 times with a few additional occurrences in variant readings. As in the Old Testament the hand of the Lord in the New Testament also means the embodiment of divine power. It is also applied to Christ in the Fourth Gospel (3:35; 10:28; 13:3). It expresses special care (Luke 1:66), security and protection (Luke 23:46; John 10:29). Laubac, "χείρ," *NIDNTT* 2:148–50. Also refer to Lohse, "χείρ," *TDNT* 9:424–34.

45. Morris, *John*, 521.

46. Ibid., 522.

47. Bruner (*John*, 637) fittingly remarks that Question and Answer 1 of the Heidelberg Catechism (1563) is an excellent commentary of 10:28–29. "Question 1: What is thy only comfort in life and in death? Answer: That I with body and soul, both in life and death, am not my own, but belong unto my faithful Savior Jesus Christ, who, with his precious blood, hath fully satisfied for all my sins, and delivered me from the power of the devil; and so preserves me that, without the will of my heavenly Father, not a hair can fall from my head; yea, that all things must be subservient to my salvation: and therefore, by his Holy Spirit, he also assures me of eternal life, and makes me sincerely willing and ready henceforth to live unto him." Ursinus, *Commentary on the Heidelberg Catechism*, 17.

destination, the journey of following Jesus is completely surrounded by the mighty acts of the shepherd Jesus. That is the firm foundation on which, and the abiding energy source by which they continue the journey of following him even in the midst of the most trying circumstances.

C. The Shepherd's Drawing Other Sheep

As to evangelism, the text of chapter 10 does not mention it as something the followers of Jesus are to do. Rather, it says that the ministry of evangelism (bringing other sheep that are outside of the sheepfold) is what the shepherd himself does: "I have other sheep that do not belong to this fold. I must bring (ἄγω) them also" (10:16). In the calling account of the first disciples, it was the followers of Jesus who did evangelism by bringing (ἄγω) others to Jesus (1:41–42, 45–46). It is the same in the case of the Samarian woman's evangelism for her own town people (4:28–30). It is the work of the followers of Jesus to invite and bring others to Jesus by telling who Jesus is. Yet, underneath of the ministry of evangelism of the followers of Jesus is the hand of Jesus the great shepherd who brings those who are outside of the fold (10:16; cf. 12:32). This distinctive aspect of evangelism that it is the shepherd Jesus who is working behind all human evangelical efforts is tersely yet clearly indicated in the text, as the life of following Jesus is portrayed from the point of view that what Jesus does for his followers is the greater controlling factor rather than what the followers do. The shepherd's own work of bringing people to his sheepfold is the definitive factor that operates behind every human effort of evangelism.

D. Co-Ministry of the Father and the Son for the Followers

The name "the Father" appears repetitively in various forms throughout the text of John chapter 10: "the Father" (10:15, 17), "my Father" (10:18, 29), "my Father's name" (10:25), "my Father's hand" (10:29), "works from the Father" (10:32), "works of the Father" (10:37). The text begins with who the shepherd is (10:2), what he does for his sheep (10:3, 4, 11, 15, 16, 28) and what he gives them (10:10, 28), but as the account advances, the text introduces the Father to the scene (10:15) and further states that the works which Jesus does for the sheep are from the Father. The act of laying down his life for the sheep, which is the most essential deed of Jesus the good shepherd, is not due to Jesus own individual plan, but a command he received from the Father (10:18). Not only does Jesus do the works in the Father's name (10:25), but they are the works of the Father himself (10:32, 37). Not only did the Father send Jesus into the world to do the many works for the sheep (10:36), but also he is doing the same works together with Jesus (10:28, 29).

The fourth evangelist employs the identical words ἁρπάζω and χείρ for both Jesus and the Father in the work of the protection of the sheep to indicate that the work is the co-ministry of Jesus and the Father (10:28, οὐχ ἁρπάσει τις αὐτὰ ἐκ τῆς χειρός μου; 10:29, οὐδεὶς δύναται ἁρπάζειν ἐκ τῆς χειρὸς τοῦ πατρός). Jesus protects his sheep holding them securely that no one may snatch (cf. 10:12) them out of his hand. God the Father also protects holding them securely that no one can snatch them out of the Father's hand. "Followers of Jesus are in one good pair of hands."[48] The Father and Jesus are one (10:30) in the co-ministry of protecting and preserving the followers.[49] It is once again underscored in Jesus' prayer that he has protected and guarded them (17:12, ἐγὼ ἐτήρουν αὐτοὺς ἐν τῷ ὀνόματί σου ᾧ δέδωκάς μοι, καὶ ἐφύλαξα) and asks the Father to protect them (17:11, πάτερ ἅγιε, τήρησον αὐτοὺς; cf. 17:15). The followers of Jesus are protected by both Jesus, to whom all authority in heaven and earth is given (3:35; 17:2; cf. Matt 28:18), and the Father who is stronger than all (10:29). The life of following Jesus is secure because of the co-ministry of the Father and the Son.[50]

Moreover, the text of John 10 ends with an expression that reflects "the mutual indwelling" of the Father and the Son which Jesus wants all to know and understand (10:38; 14:10–11).[51] By closing the account with the invitational exhortation, the evangelist reminds the readers that, as intimated

---

48. Bunner, *John*, 639.

49. Functional oneness in securing the safety of the sheep under their care is expressed in verse 30, not ontological oneness. Brown, *John*, 1:407; Brodie, *John*, 376; Lincoln, *John*, 306; Keener, *John*, 1:825. Although it is essentially true that the Son is equal to and one with the Father in substance, power, and eternity, the assertion in verse 30 is concerned not with the oneness in substance, but with "essential unity" that these two belong together in the divine works. The verse conveys the identification of Jesus with the Father in his works, as Barrett (*John*, 382) comments that "the actions and words of Jesus were veritably the actions and words of God." See also Bruner, *John*, 644. All the works that the shepherd Jesus does for his followers are essentially the works of the Father, as Jesus does his Father's will, speaks his Father's words, and carries out his Father's mission. Cf. 14:28 "The Father is greater than I." The statement is concerned with the relation between God the Father who is sending and commanding and the Son who is sent and obedient (Barrett, *John*, 468). In this statement, the fourth evangelist has the humiliation of the Son in his mind.

50. If the gatekeeper is the Holy Spirit as some scholars suggest (Brown, *John*, 1:391; Bruner, *John*, 617), the text of John 10 indicates that the life of following Jesus is under the trinitarian work of three Persons of the Godhead.

51. Morris, *John*, 529; Lincoln, *John*, 309.

in 1:51, the destination to which Jesus desires to take his followers is to the Father himself, so that they might participate in Jesus' intimate fellowship with the Father.[52] The followers of Jesus are to be incorporated into the oneness of the close fellowship between the Father and the Son (17:21).[53]

The life of following Jesus is a journey under the mighty hand of both the Father and the Son, initiated by the Father and the Son, being continually led by the shepherd whom the Father sent for them, and sustained by the co-ministry of the Father and the Son. The followers of Jesus are completely surrounded by the manifold acts of the Father and the Son, behind and before, underneath and above. The journey of following Jesus is the result of the sovereign act of the Father and the Son.

III. Conclusion

Before the movement of following comes to the surface, there are the multiple acts of Jesus the shepherd for his own as the greater factor that shapes the life of following. The life of following Jesus essentially springs up from what Jesus the shepherd does for his sheep before they do anything for him. The text of John chapter 10 is unique in the sense that it focuses on many acts that Jesus the shepherd does for his own sheep before it mentions anything about what the sheep must do. Under the imagery of shepherd-sheep relationship, the fourth evangelist employs several important words and motifs that express what the shepherd does for his sheep in association with ἀκολουθεῖν to communicate three unique aspects of the Spirituality of following Jesus.

First, before the movement of following begins from the sheep's end, there was the pre-established bond of relationship between Jesus and his sheep, which is Jesus' ownership over the life of his sheep. This bond was formed not by what the followers have done, but by the divine act between the Father and the Son. Out of the bond of relationship, his own are drawn to follow him. Jesus the shepherd knows his sheep before they begin to know him. By Jesus the shepherd's knowledge of the sheep, they are enabled to come to know him. The sheep follow the shepherd who already knows them and owns their life. The movement of following is not to earn the privilege of becoming sheep in his fold, but to experience as subjective realties what is already granted to them by the shepherd. This is the first aspect of the Spirituality that the fourth evangelist portrays in the text to invite the readers to

---

52. "[T]he sheep belong commonly to the Father and the Son (17:10) and are admitted into the fellowship of the Father and the Son (cf. 10:14; 17:21–23, 26)." Schnackenburg, *John*, 2:308.

53. Ibid., 2:313.

experience the pre-established bond of relationship between Jesus and them as the immovable foundation of their journey of following him.

Second, before there are any actions by the sheep, there are numerous acts of Jesus the shepherd for his sheep. The shepherd Jesus leads them always going before them. The shepherd lays his life down for his sheep. The shepherd protects them so securely, and to such a degree that no one can snatch them out of his hand. The followers of Jesus can take the journey of following him every day in confidence, and will be able to complete it because of the manifold acts of the shepherd for them. They are perfectly safe, absolutely protected, continually led, and incessantly reenergized by the manifold acts of the shepherd Jesus. This is another facet of the Spirituality of following Jesus that the evangelist draws the readers to experience in their life.

Third is the co-workmanship of the Father and the Son. The bond between Jesus and the sheep and the shepherd's multiple act for the sheep are not done alone, but in joint partnership with the Father. John presents the shepherding of the sheep (Jesus' own) as a Father-Son business. The Father, who gave the sheep to Jesus to be his own possession, who established the bond between Jesus and the sheep, and who sent and commanded him to carry out the work for the sheep, is in fact doing the work together with Jesus. The Father and Jesus are one in doing all the works for the sheep.[54] Therefore, the life of following Jesus is both Christ-centered and God-centered. The followers of Jesus not only come to know and experience Jesus more and more in the course of the journey, but also come to know and experience the Father himself more and more in and through Jesus. It is a journey into the Father as well as the Son. This is the third aspect of Spirituality to which the evangelist draws the readers to experience.

The three aspects of the Spirituality of following Jesus are presented to the readers neither in a vacuum nor in a friendly historical environment, but in the midst of adverse life settings where Jesus' followers are being driven out of their own community and exposed to hatred, persecution, and even the threat of death (9:22; 15:18–20; 16:2, 33; 17:14). It is to help the readers find comfort, strength, and assurance from the great shepherd and the Father, by whom their journey of following is engendered, sustained, led, and protected. Their first-hand experience of all these from the acts of the great shepherd will eventually enable the followers to do the same work for others when the shepherd entrusts his sheep to them (21:15–19).

---

54. "Jesus and his Father are perfectly one in action, in what they do: what Jesus does, the Father does, and vice versa." Carson, *John*, 394.

CHAPTER 8

Following Jesus on the Path of Death to Glory (12:26)

THE TEXT 12:20–36 IS a transitional passage (including 12:37–50) that bridges John 1–12 and John 13–20.[1] It concentrates the focus of the Gospel on the Passion of Jesus, drawing the readers' attention to the upcoming "hour" of Jesus' death, which is recognized as the "hour" of glorification. The text contains 12:24–26 which is the Johannine equivalent of Mark 8:34–38 (Matt 16:24–28; Luke 9:23–27), and 12:27 the Johannine version of Gethsemane prayer (Mark 14:32–36; Matt 26:38–39; Luke 22:39–44). Fully loaded with the motif of the "hour" that denotes Jesus' death and glorification more intensively than any other texts in the Gospel, 12:20–36 provides the logion of 12:26 with a rich literary and theological environment to communicate the Spirituality of following Jesus by ἀκολουθεῖν in association with other correlated motifs and vocabularies—the "death" motif, "to serve/servant," "to honor," and the "where" motif.[2] Positioned and formulated

---

1. Keener, *John*, 2:871; Lincoln, *John*, 348.

2. In the first research text (1:35–51), among the six major pericopes of the present study, the motif of death is only implicitly intimated by John the Baptist's pronouncement that Jesus is the Lamb of God (1:29, 36) that leads men and women to God's presence through its death. By starting to follow Jesus upon hearing the pronouncement, it is dimly hinted that following Jesus is related to Jesus' death. In the second research text (8:12–29) and its near context, the death motif is foretold by the term "to be lifted up" (8:27) as well as implied by the motif of the place where Jesus is going to is the Father (7:33; 8:14, 21, 27), yet the texts 7:30 and 8:20 state that Jesus' hour has not yet arrived. In the third research text (10:1–42) the death motif explicitly announces that Jesus the shepherd is going to lay down his life (10:11, 15, 7) for his own sheep, yet the text focuses on the many acts of Jesus the shepherd together with the Father that they do for the sheep. When it comes to the fourth research text 12:20–36, however, the death motif emerges as the central motif directly connected with ἀκολουθεῖν to impart the Spirituality of following Jesus as the radical life experience of walking on the path of death just as Jesus walked the road of death into glory. In this text, the implication of following Jesus is apparently communicated that the followers of Jesus are invited to follow Jesus' path of death, and the promise of future glory for those who follow the

within the unique context, 12:26 communicates "the original idea of following Jesus," and invites the readers to a distinctive Spirituality of following Jesus—to experience the mystery of the interconnectedness of Jesus' death and glory, as they are led toward their final destination, home to the Father.[3]

To articulate the Spirituality of following Jesus imparted by the association of ἀκολουθεῖν with correlated motifs in 12:20–36, I will explore 12:26 with the following questions. First, what is the literary and theological environment in which the fourth evangelist positioned ἀκολουθεῖν? How does the literary-theological context collaborate with ἀκολουθεῖν to communicate the distinctive experience of following Jesus? Also, what implication of following Jesus does the context give to the term ἀκολουθεῖν? Second, why does the fourth evangelist employ the rare words διακονέω (to serve) and διάκονος (servant) in connection with ἀκολουθεῖν? Where does this motif come from in the Fourth Gospel? And what Spirituality of following Jesus is communicated by associating ἀκολουθεῖν with διακονέω and διάκονος? Then third, what is the meaning of "where I am, there will my servant be also"? What significance does the "where" motif give to the life of following Jesus? What is the meaning of Jesus' pronouncement "the Father will honor"? What kind of future reward do the readers come to anticipate from reading the two motifs?

I. Death Motif as Literary-Theological Context of ἀκολουθεῖν

The motif of death permeated the immediate context of 12:26 with several vocabularies and expressions that denote Jesus' death, creating a unique literary-theological environment toward the Spirituality of following Jesus communicated by ἀκολουθεῖν. The below figure not only outlines the structure of its semantic relations, and identifies what vocabularies are interconnected with ἀκολουθεῖν, but also presents the rhetoric of the fourth evangelist that creates the distinctive Spirituality of following Jesus into which the author invites his readers.

---

path of Jesus' death is most clearly stated. In this sense, the fourth research text 12:26 makes a distinctive contribution to the development of the Johannine Spirituality of following Jesus.

3. 12:26 ἐὰν ἐμοί τις διακονῇ, ἐμοὶ ἀκολουθείτω, καὶ ὅπου εἰμὶ ἐγὼ ἐκεῖ καὶ ὁ διάκονος ὁ ἐμὸς ἔσται· ἐάν τις ἐμοὶ διακονῇ τιμήσει αὐτὸν ὁ πατήρ. "Nowhere as clearly as in this passage has John used the original idea of following." Schnackenburg, *John*, 2:386.

John 12:26 encircled by the motif of death

11:50 ὅτι συμφέρει ὑμῖν ἵνα εἷς ἄνθρωπος <u>ἀποθάνῃ</u> ὑπὲρ τοῦ λαοῦ — ·· — ·· ┐2
11:51 ὅτι ἔμελλεν Ἰησοῦς <u>ἀποθνῄσκειν</u> ὑπὲρ τοῦ ἔθνους   — — — — │
11:53 ἀπ' ἐκείνης οὖν τῆς ἡμέρας ἐβουλεύσαντο ἵνα <u>ἀποκτείνωσιν</u> αὐτόν ┐3 │

11:55 Ἦν δὲ ἐγγὺς τὸ <u>πάσχα</u> τῶν Ἰουδαίων ... πρὸ τοῦ <u>πάσχα</u> ─────┐1 │

12:1 πρὸ ἓξ ἡμερῶν τοῦ <u>πάσχα</u> ─────────────────────────────────────┘ │
12:7 ἵνα εἰς τὴν ἡμέραν τοῦ <u>ἐνταφιασμοῦ</u> μου τηρήσῃ αὐτό — · — · · 4   │

12:10 ἐβουλεύσαντο δὲ οἱ ἀρχιερεῖς ἵνα καὶ τὸν Λάζαρον <u>ἀποκτείνωσιν</u>   │

12:23 ἐλήλυθεν <u>ἡ ὥρα</u> ἵνα δοξασθῇ ὁ υἱὸς τοῦ ἀνθρώπου. — — — — — —┤ ┐5
12:24 ἀμὴν ἀμὴν λέγω ὑμῖν, ἐὰν μὴ ὁ κόκκος τοῦ σίτου πεσὼν εἰς τὴν γῆν │ │
      <u>ἀποθάνῃ</u>, αὐτὸς μόνος μένει· ἐὰν δὲ <u>ἀποθάνῃ</u>, πολὺν καρπὸν φέρει. ─┤ │

  ┌─────────────────────────────┐
  │ 12:26 ἐμοὶ ἀκολουθείτω   │   │
  └─────────────────────────────┘

12:27 καὶ τί εἴπω; πάτερ, σῶσόν με ἐκ <u>τῆς ὥρας</u> ταύτης; — — — — — ┤ │
      ἀλλὰ διὰ τοῦτο ἦλθον εἰς <u>τὴν ὥραν</u> ταύτην.   │

12:32 κἀγὼ ἐὰν <u>ὑψωθῶ</u> ἐκ τῆς γῆς ·· 6 │
12:33 τοῦτο δὲ ἔλεγεν σημαίνων **ποίῳ θανάτῳ** ─────── 7   │
      ἤμελλεν <u>ἀποθνῄσκειν</u>. — — — — — — — —   │
12:34 ὅτι δεῖ <u>ὑψωθῆναι</u> τὸν υἱὸν τοῦ ἀνθρώπου; ·····················   │

13:1 Πρὸ δὲ τῆς ἑορτῆς τοῦ <u>πάσχα</u> εἰδὼς ὁ Ἰησοῦς ὅτι ἦλθεν αὐτοῦ <u>ἡ ὥρα</u> ┐─ ─┘
     ἵνα μεταβῇ ἐκ τοῦ κόσμου τούτου πρὸς τὸν πατέρα,

John 12:26 encircled by the motif of death (ESV)

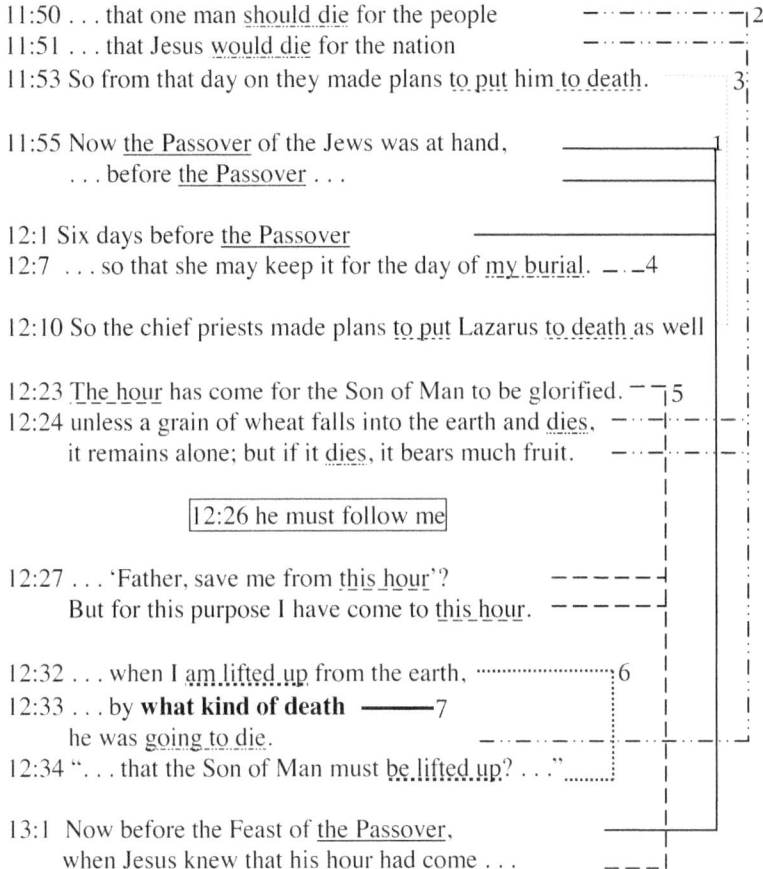

As presented in the analysis, seven vocabularies and terms are embedded in the discourse encompassing ἀκολουθεῖν to create an exceptional literary-theological environment and to communicate the Spirituality of following Jesus in connection with Jesus' death. First, as the temporal setting, the feast of the Passover (πάσχα, 11:55*2; 12:1; 13:1; cf. 12:20) is deliberately mentioned over and over again. It is the time when the Lamb of God is to be slaughtered for men and women to be freed and brought into the presence of God.[4] The readers are aware that Jesus is the Lamb of God (1:29, 36; 19:36; cf. Exod 12:46; Num 9:12), and that the time of Jesus' death is imminent as

---

4. Hoskins, "Deliverance from Death," 285–99.

this is the third Passover in his public ministry. It is in this context that the readers hear Jesus' demand to follow (ἀκολουθεῖν) him.

Second, ἀποθνήσκω (to die, 11:50, 51; 12:24, 33) in relation to Jesus' death occurs six times in the Fourth Gospel and among them four appearances (11:50, 51; 12:24, 33) are within the immediate context near 12:26. Besides, two other occurrences are virtually repetitions of what were mentioned already within the current context (11:50=18:14; 12:33=18:32). Thus, it can be said that in terms of content, all employments of ἀποθνήσκω in relation to Jesus' death appear within the immediate literary context of 12:26.

That Jesus is about to die (ἀποθνήσκω) for the nation is unconsciously prophesied by Caiaphas the high priest (11:50). The kindred idea is indicated by Jesus himself in the analogy of a grain of wheat that he is going to die (ἀποθνήσκω) in order to lead many people to life, as a grain of wheat bears much fruit by dying (ἀποθνήσκω, 12:24). Furthermore, as an application of what is said in 12:24 to the life of the disciples, the idea of laying down one's own life (ἀποθνήσκω) is implied by the expression of hating one's own life (12:25). It "looks ahead to the later missionary activity of the disciples, who will not only make Jesus' death bear fruit in their preaching of the word (v. 24), but also bear witness to it with their own."[5] When reading the pronouncement "Whoever serves me must follow me" within this literary context, the readers would hardly miss the connotation of following Jesus by walking in the path of death to bear the fruits of life.

Third, ἀποκτείνω (to kill, 11:53; 12:10)[6] in its total of twelve appearances in the Fourth Gospel, interestingly occurs all in relation to Jesus and his followers—ten times in relation to Jesus (5:18; 7:1, 19, 20, 25; 8:22, 37, 40; 11:53; 18:31) and the other two in reference to Jesus' disciples (12:10; 16:2). Until now the Jews have been seeking (ζητέω, 5:18; 7:1, 19, 20, 25; 8:37, 40) to kill (ἀποκτείνω) Jesus, but from the current pericope they resolved and began to make a plan (βουλεύω, 11:53) to put him to death (ἀποκτείνω). The Jews' evil desire to kill Jesus is no longer merely a threat, but a determined reality. Until now the verb ἀποκτείνω has been applied to Jesus only, but from the present pericope onwards it is applied to Jesus' followers also (12:10; 16:2). When stating the Jews' plot to kill Lazarus in 12:10, the evangelist employs the identical wordings and sentence pattern.[7] By doing so, the

---

5. Schnackenburg, *John*, 2:385.

6. Coenen, "ἀποκτείνω," *NIDNTT* 1:429–30. The verb appears a total of 74 times in the New Testament, mostly in the Gospels and Revelation, with only five occurrences in the Pauline epistles. When it appears, the verb almost always refers to the violent killing of God's messengers.

7. 11:53 ἀπ' ἐκείνης οὖν τῆς ἡμέρας ἐβουλεύσαντο ἵνα ἀποκτείνωσιν αὐτόν. 12:10 ἐβουλεύσαντο δὲ οἱ ἀρχιερεῖς ἵνα καὶ τὸν Λάζαρον ἀποκτείνωσιν.

evangelist visually shows that the followers of Jesus will face the same treatment from the world that it gave to Jesus their Lord (15:18–21; cf. 16:33; Matt 10:22; 24:9). This is the context in which the readers hear Jesus' call of following him in 12:26 (ἐμοὶ ἀκολουθείτω). And this is the reality that the life of following Jesus entails.

Fourth, ἐνταφιασμός (burial, 12:7) is employed once. Six days before the Passover, when Jesus came to Bethany, Mary anointed Jesus' feet with a pound of costly perfume made of pure nard and wiped them with her hair. According to the ancient custom, anointing the head of a guest is one way of honoring a guest (Ps 23:5; Luke 7:46). Keener grasps Mary's anointing as the royal anointing because it fits to the following unit (12:13–15).[8] However, this is unlikely because Jesus did not accept the royal acclamation of the crowd. Rather the anointing of the woman is from the motive of love, as Brown comments that it is "a culminating expression of loving faith."[9] The significance of the anointing that the evangelist imparts in the text is stated by Jesus' interpretation that she did it in preparation for his burial (12:7, ἵνα . . . τοῦ ἐνταφιασμοῦ μου). Therefore, Brown concludes that "Mary's action constituted an anointing of Jesus' body for burial, and thus unconsciously she performed a prophetic action" regarding Jesus' death.[10] By accepting her unconscious prophetic action as a preparation for his burial (ἐνταφιασμός), Jesus implicitly declares that his death is not only an impending event, but a fixed fact. It is in this definite environment that the imperative of ἐὰν ἐμοί τις διακονῇ, ἐμοὶ ἀκολουθείτω is given to the followers.

Fifth, ἡ ὥρα (the hour, 12:23, 27; 13:1) appears four times. At least four effects of the hour of Jesus' death are stated in 12:23–33. It is the hour i) when the Son may enter into glory through death (12:23); ii) when the Father's name is glorified (12:27–28) because the death of the Son is the pivotal point when the decree of God is fulfilled; iii) when the ruler of this world will be driven out (12:31); and iv) when all people will be drawn to Jesus (12:32) and thus to the Father. The effect of the hour of Jesus' death is truly decisive and pivotal, and cosmic in its scope. It is the moment of the completion of God's eternal plan, of the judgment of the adversary, the devil, and thus of the completion of redemptive history. What a glorious hour it is!

Some Greeks who went up to worship during the Passover came to see Jesus (12:20).[11] Jesus interpreted this as the arrival of the hour for the Son

---

8. Keener, *John*, 2:865.
9. Brown, *John*, 1:454.
10. Ibid.
11. It is a sign of the future realization of 10:16 and 11:52 (cf. Isa 49:6; Matt 8:11;

of Man to be glorified (12:23). Until now it has been stated that the hour had not yet come (οὔπω ἐληλύθει ἡ ὥρα αὐτοῦ, 7:30; 8:20; cf. 2:4; 4:21, 23; 5:25, 28), but seeing that the Gentiles are coming to him, Jesus now clearly declares that the hour has come (12:23; 17:1; cf. 12:27; 13:1). Furthermore, Jesus elaborates by using the analogy of a grain of wheat that as the result of his death there would be much fruit (12:24). Not only is it verbally declared that the hour of death has arrived, but also Jesus feels the gravity of the hour of death as expressed in the words, "Now my soul is troubled" (12:27). Yet, he does not withdraw himself from facing the severity entailed in redemptive death, but resolutely embraces *the hour*. Instead of asking God that *the hour* might pass away from him, Jesus determinedly accepts *the hour* declaring, "No, it is for this reason that I have come to this hour" (ἀλλὰ διὰ τοῦτο ἦλθον εἰς τὴν ὥραν ταύτην, 12:27).

Where is the imperative of ἐάν ἐμοί τις διακονῇ, ἐμοὶ ἀκολουθείτω ("Whoever serves me must follow me," 12:26) positioned? It is positioned between the two solemn declarations: the hour of death has arrived (12:23) and for this purpose I came to this hour (12:27). By this, the magnitude of the hour of death is effectively transmitted over the call of ἐάν ἐμοί τις διακονῇ, ἐμοὶ ἀκολουθείτω, and thus the inseparable connection between the life of following Jesus and walking the path of death after Jesus is markedly communicated.

Sixth and seventh, the mode of death ὑψόω (to lift up, 12:32, 34) and ποίῳ θανάτῳ (the kind of death, 12:33). The verb ὑψόω is a particular term of the Fourth Gospel. It appears only four times in the Gospel and is used only with respect to Jesus being lifted up (8:28; 12:32, 34) and the lifted serpent (3:14a; cf. Num 21:8, 9) which is the shadow of the lifted Son of Man on the cross (3:14b). According to Bertram, in John ὑψόω has "intentionally a double sense in all the passages in which it occurs, 3:14; 8:28; 12:32, 34. It means both exaltation on the cross and also exaltation to heaven."[12] Keener points out that "the Hebrew Bible already played on the double meaning of exalted or hanged (Gen 40:13, 19–22)."[13] Jesus' being lifted up "is not simply on the cross, but via the cross to the throne of heaven."[14]

Having acknowledged that ὑψόω denotes the double meaning of death and glorification, however, it is important to note that in 12:32 the death on the cross is in view in the first place. The evangelist directly interprets that

---

Eph 2:13; 1 John 2:2) that by his death Jesus is going to gather all people whom God called from all over the world beyond the limit of the nation.

12. Bertram, "ὑψόω," *TDNT* 8:610. See also Schnackenburg, *John*, 2:393; Beasley-Murray, *John*, 211; Ridderbos, *John*, 440.

13. Keener, *John*, 2:881.

14. Beasley-Murray, *John*, 214.

Jesus said this "to indicate the kind of death he was to die" (12:33). And the crowd also grasped it in the same way (12:34). Keener asserts in his comments on 3:14 that "'[l]ift up' certainly refers to the crucifixion here as elsewhere in the Gospel" and that "John clearly refers to Jesus' crucifixion (12:32–33)."[15] "Crucifixion is clearly in view."[16] By the direct interpretation of the evangelist in 12:33 that the meaning of "to be lifted up" is to die upon a raised cross, the death of Jesus is now visualized in the minds of the readers. The readers are most likely familiar with the horror of the Roman crucifixion that Jesus faced. The call of ἐάν ἐμοί τις διακονῇ, ἐμοὶ ἀκολουθείτω ("Whoever serves me must follow me") is given to the readers in this serious context where even the mode of Jesus' death is remembered.

What does the fourth evangelist specifically communicate about the Spirituality of following Jesus by associating the imperative ἐμοὶ ἀκολουθείτω ("must follow me") with the death motif presented by the above seven terms within the literary context? The evangelist communicates that the Spirituality of following Jesus embraces death as part of the journey to the Father.[17] The serious demand of following Jesus unto death is not the end of the call. The promise of the glorious reward for those who follow him unto death is also given in the same breath (12:26), which we will consider below.

II. To Serve/Servant and Following Jesus

Through this investigation of 12:26, other questions arise: Why does the fourth evangelist employ the word διακονέω (to serve) which is very rare in the Gospel? Why does he refer to Jesus' follower as διάκονος (a servant)? What image would the readers have in their minds when they read the words διακονέω and διάκονος? And, what implication does the evangelist bring into the life of following Jesus by juxtaposing ἀκολουθεῖν with διακονέω and διάκονος? To answer these questions, it is necessary to probe other occurrences of διακονέω/διάκονος in the Gospel.[18]

In the Fourth Gospel both terms διακονέω and διάκονος appear only three times each: διακονέω in 12:2 and 26 (twice); διάκονος in 2:5, 9 and 12:26. In 12:2 διακονέω is employed to state a service of love, that Martha served (διακονέω) in love, making a dinner for Jesus. The occurrence of

15. Keener, *John*, 1:565–66. See also Morris, *John*, 225, 598.
16. Beasley-Murray, *John*, 215.
17. Schnackenburg, *John*, 2:385.
18. No scholar has considered the literary significance of the words διακονέω and διάκονος to the Johannine readers, and that they might have recalled Jesus' servanthood of God in reading the vocabularies.

διάκονος in chapter 2 of the Gospel is noteworthy. The mother of Jesus said to the servants (τοῖς διακόνοις), "Do whatever he tells you" (ὅ τι ἂν λέγῃ ὑμῖν ποιήσατε, 2:5). Then they did all the things that Jesus told them to do (2:7, 8), and by doing them they served the work of Jesus' sign that revealed his glory (2:11). Although διάκονος is not directly used in reference to Jesus in the Gospel, the words ὅ τι ἂν λέγῃ ὑμῖν ποιήσατε (2:5; cf. 17:4) reflect the life of Jesus as the servant (διάκονος) of God who has faithfully done all things the Father commanded him to do. Jesus did nothing in his own will (5:30). His entire life was wholly devoted to doing what God commanded him to do (5:36; 14:31; 15:10). He glorified God by finishing the work that the Father gave him to do (17:4). Jesus himself was the servant (διάκονος) of God who served (διακονέω) God faithfully by completing all the things he gave him to do. Therefore, when the readers read the words διακονέω and διάκονος, it is likely that they naturally reflected upon Christ Jesus as the faithful servant of God.

One might raise a question whether διάκονος reflects Jesus' servanthood of God because the term in 12:26 is not δοῦλος (a slave), the commonly used term that refers to the servants of God and the Servant of Yahweh (עבד יהוה) in the LXX. However, considering the following five points, it is not impossible for διάκονος and διακονέω to convey Jesus' servanthood of God. First, in the Fourth Gospel (2:5, 9) servants in the Hebrew culture are referred to as διάκονος. Second, δοῦλος is not the only word that is employed to refer to the servants of God in a Hebrew setting in the LXX. Together with δοῦλος other words are used in the Old Testament to refer to the servants of God (παῖς in Josh 1:7 and Ps 18:1 [17:1, LXX]; θεράπων in Exod 33:11; δοῦλος in Josh 24:30 and Ps 36:1 [35:1, LXX]) and the Servant of Yahweh (δοῦλος and παῖς in Isa 42:1, 19 and 49:3). Third, the followers of Jesus are referred to by both terms in the Fourth Gospel (12:26, ὁ διάκονος ὁ ἐμός; 15:15, οὐκέτι λέγω ὑμᾶς δούλους). Fourth, there are instances in the Synoptic Gospels where the verb διακονέω is used in reference to Jesus' servanthood (Mark 10:45, ὁ υἱὸς τοῦ ἀνθρώπου οὐκ ἦλθεν διακονηθῆναι ἀλλὰ διακονῆσαι). Fifth, in the other books of the New Testament the word διάκονος is used for Christ Jesus (Rom 15:8)[19] and for the servants of Christ (2 Cor 3:6; Eph 3:7; 1 Tim 4:6). Therefore, there would be no difficulty for John's readers to consider Jesus' servanthood of God through the words διακονέω and διάκονος.

In the Fourth Gospel to a greater extent than in any other New Testament books, Jesus is depicted in detail as the perfect model of servanthood by being described as the one who uniquely does all the things the Father

---

19. Rom 15:8 λέγω γὰρ Χριστὸν διάκονον γεγενῆσθαι περιτομῆς ὑπὲρ ἀληθείας θεοῦ. "Christ has become a servant of the circumcised on behalf of the truth of God."

commanded him to do in both word and deed (5:19, 30; 10:18; 12:49, 50; 14:31; 15:10; 17:4; 19:30; cf. Rom 5:19; Phil 2:7-8; Heb 5:8). Doing the will of God and completing his work is the food and purpose of Jesus' life (4:34). When he pronounces the important logion of 12:26, Jesus is about to leave the world and go back to the Father. It is at this crucial moment, by calling the one who will follow him "my servant," Jesus declares that the one who follows him must do the same for him *just as* he has been the faithful servant of God by completing the Father's work. By the reiteration of "whoever serves me" in 12:26, Jesus emphatically demands that those who will follow him must *serve* him as his servants, doing the things he commands them to do.

Until now Jesus has never demanded that his followers do his work. But now at the moment when he is about to take the path of death (as copiously indicated by the previously discussed seven terms) in accordance with the Father's command, he manifestly reveals the meaning of following him and explicitly demands what they must do. Doing his will and completing his work as his servant is the life of following Jesus, unprecedentedly communicated by the current text 12:26. This is one unique facet of the Spirituality of following Jesus that the fourth evangelist delivers in 12:26 by the juxtaposition of ἀκολουθεῖν with διακονέω and διάκονος.

III. Following Jesus and the Promised Reward

12:26 is composed of two sentences that begin with the same clause: "Whoever serves me . . . Whoever serves me . . ." (ἐὰν ἐμοί τις διακονῇ, . . . ἐάν τις ἐμοὶ διακονῇ . . .). Both of them end with a promise of reward for those who serve Jesus as his servants.[20] They are stated in two different expressions: "where I am, there will my servant be also" (ὅπου εἰμὶ ἐγὼ ἐκεῖ καὶ ὁ διάκονος ὁ ἐμὸς ἔσται); and "the Father will honor him" (τιμήσει αὐτὸν ὁ πατήρ).

A. Where I Am, My Servant Also Will Be

In the first clause the reward is stated by the "where" motif, "Where I am, there will my servant be also" (ὅπου εἰμὶ ἐγὼ ἐκεῖ καὶ ὁ διάκονος ὁ ἐμὸς ἔσται). What does ὅπου εἰμὶ ἐγω (where I am) point to? There are two groups of scholars with differing views. One group takes it to include both suffering and glory. Barrett views it as "in life and death, humiliation and

---

20. 12:26 ἐὰν ἐμοί τις διακονῇ, ἐμοὶ ἀκολουθείτω, καὶ ὅπου εἰμὶ ἐγὼ ἐκεῖ καὶ ὁ διάκονος ὁ ἐμὸς ἔσται· ἐάν τις ἐμοὶ διακονῇ τιμήσει αὐτὸν ὁ πατήρ.

glory."[21] Beasley-Murray interprets it in the same way because "the Christ draws men to fellowship with himself alike in suffering and in the presence of God."[22] Keener also has both in mind as he remarks that "wherever Jesus would be, there his servants would be as well, both in death and in the Father's presence."[23] The other group of scholars recognizes ὅπου εἰμὶ ἐγω as the place where Jesus will be *in glory*, of which Bruner remarks, referring to Chrysostom, Henry, Meyer, and Bultmann, that it means "according to the almost unanimous interpretation of the church: 'where I am *in glory*, there my servant will be as well.'"[24]

In the wider perspective and the ultimate sense, it is not incorrect to say that ὅπου εἰμὶ ἐγω may include both places of suffering and glory because Jesus enters glory through suffering, that is by being in the place of death he enters the place of glory.[25] However, it is more likely that the fourth evangelist points specifically to the place of glory by the expression ὅπου εἰμὶ ἐγω. The other usages of the expression in the Gospel support this. The phrase ὅπου εἰμὶ ἐγω is a peculiar Johannine expression that appears only in four places in the Gospel: 7:34 (36); 12:26; 14:3 and 17:24.

To those who do not follow Jesus:

7:34 ζητήσετέ με καὶ οὐχ εὑρήσετέ [με], καὶ **ὅπου εἰμὶ ἐγὼ** ὑμεῖς οὐ δύνασθε ἐλθεῖν. (You will search for me, but you will not find me; and **where I am**, you cannot come)

To those who follow Jesus:

12:26 ἐάν ἐμοί τις διακονῇ, ἐμοὶ ἀκολουθείτω, καὶ **ὅπου εἰμὶ ἐγὼ** ἐκεῖ καὶ ὁ διάκονος ὁ ἐμὸς ἔσται· (Whoever serves me must follow me, and **where I am**, there will my servant be also.)

14:3 καὶ ἐὰν πορευθῶ καὶ ἑτοιμάσω τόπον ὑμῖν, πάλιν ἔρχομαι καὶ παραλήμψομαι ὑμᾶς πρὸς ἐμαυτόν, ἵνα **ὅπου εἰμὶ ἐγὼ** καὶ

---

21. Barrett, *John*, 424.
22. Beasley-Murray, *John*, 212.
23. Keener, *John*, 2:874–75.
24. Bruner, *John*, 715. See also Brown, *John*, 1:475; Moloney, *John*, 359; Lincoln, *John*, 351.
25. If ὅπου εἰμὶ ἐγὼ ἐκεῖ καὶ ὁ διάκονος ὁ ἐμὸς ἔσται is read as the continuation of Jesus' imperative (ἔσται as imperatival future) which begins with ἐμοὶ ἀκολουθείτω, the place where Jesus is could be the place of Jesus' death. However, it is unlikely because ἀκολουθείτω is imperative present active and ἔσται is indicative future middle. The sentence makes more sense when it is read as the resulting reward of serving and following him: "Whoever serves me must follow me, and *as the result* where I am, there will my servant be also."

ὑμεῖς ἦτε. (And if I go and prepare a place for you, I will come again and will take you to myself, so that **where I am**, there you may be also)

17:24 Πάτερ, ὃ δέδωκάς μοι, θέλω ἵνα **ὅπου εἰμὶ ἐγὼ** κἀκεῖνοι ὦσιν μετ' ἐμοῦ, ἵνα θεωρῶσιν τὴν δόξαν τὴν ἐμήν, ἣν δέδωκάς μοι … (Father, I want these whom you have given me to be with me **where I am**. Then they can see all the glory you gave me …)

In 7:34 (36) ὅπου εἰμὶ ἐγω refers to the place as where Jesus will be in the glory of the Father.[26] It is indicated by Jesus in the preceding verse, "I am going to him who sent me" (7:33). More explicitly in 14:3 ὅπου εἰμὶ ἐγω indicates that it is the place where Jesus will be with the Father in glory. It is identified by the combination of a few correlated phrases in 14:1–7: "In my Father's house there are many dwelling places" (14:1); "the place where I am going (14:4); "to the Father" (14:6). And most apparently in 17:24 ὅπου εἰμὶ ἐγω points to the place where Jesus will be in glory because it is the place where his followers will see the glory which God has given him before the foundation of the world. That ὅπου εἰμὶ ἐγω in 12:26 indicates the place where Jesus will be in glory is supported by these three other employments of the phrase in the Gospel.

In addition to the above, interpreting καὶ ὅπου εἰμὶ ἐγὼ ἐκεῖ καὶ ὁ διάκονος ὁ ἐμὸς ἔσται ("and where I am, there will my servant be also") as the promise of reward, Schnackenburg rightly comments that ὅπου εἰμὶ ἐγω means "the goal the disciples will reach through their deaths, the heavenly world … Jesus' sphere, his home."[27] Ridderbos also affirms that it refers, "as in 14:3 and 17:24, to Jesus' future glory."[28] To put it another way, it is for Jesus' followers to be "swept up into the oneness that unites the Father and the Son."[29]

Not all human beings will be there with Jesus where he is in glory in the presence of the Father. Those who refuse God's gracious invitation in Jesus, the one whom the Father sent, the one who is the power and wisdom of God (1 Cor 1:24) for salvation, cannot come to the place where Jesus is in glory (7:34; 8:21). But those who accept God's gracious invitation, follow Jesus, and serve him as his faithful servants, will be there with Jesus, participating in the glorious fellowship with the Father (12:26). This is the reward promised in 12:26 by the statement καὶ ὅπου εἰμὶ ἐγὼ ἐκεῖ καὶ ὁ διάκονος ὁ

---

26. Lindars, *John*, 296; "the return to the Father," Brown, *John*, 1:318; cf. Barrett, *John*, 325.
27. Schnackenburg, *John*, 2:385.
28. Ridderbos, *John*, 433.
29. Moloney, *John*, 359.

ἐμὸς ἔσται and the lived experience (Spirituality) of the journey of following Jesus into which 12:26 draws the readers.

B. The Father will Honor

In the second clause of 12:26 the reward to those who serve Jesus is stated by the unique expression, "Whoever serves me, the Father will honor him" (ἐάν τις ἐμοὶ διακονῇ τιμήσει αὐτὸν ὁ πατήρ). It is another way of putting the same idea of "where I am, there will my servant be also" (ὅπου εἰμὶ ἐγὼ ἐκεῖ καὶ ὁ διάκονος ὁ ἐμὸς ἔσται).[30] Apparently it means that the faithful servants of Jesus will be taken into heaven to share in the honor and glory of the Son[31] and they will be loved by the Father (14:21, 23).[32] Schnackenburg richly explains its meaning quoting Augustine:

> Just as the Father seeks Jesus' honor and glorifies him (cf. 8:50, 54; 13:32), in the same way he lets the disciples of Jesus share in it: 'honor' (τιμᾶν) means the gift of heavenly glory, the full revelation of the love of God (cf. 17:24–26). The Father loves the disciples because they have loved Jesus (16:27) and he will complete this love by taking them into perfect communion with himself and his Son. 'What greater honor could an adopted son receive than to be where the Only Son is, not equal to him in divine nature, but united with him in the eternal world?' (Augustine).[33]

The reward stated by τιμήσει αὐτὸν ὁ πατήρ ("the Father will honor him") is not only the ultimate prize human beings can receive from God, but also deals with the fundamental issue of human existence: honor and glory. To further probe into the matter of "to receive honor from the Father," the words glory (δόξα, δοξάζω) and honor (τιμή, τιμάω) in the Fourth Gospel need to be examined together because often they are used as synonyms. In the Gospel δόξα is used to convey the meaning of honor, for instance, 'to seek honor' in 7:18, 8:50, and 5:44, and 'to receive honor' in 5:41, 44.[34]

In the Fourth Gospel the word τιμή (honor) appears once (4:44) and τιμάω (to honor) thrice, and δόξα (glory) 19 times and δοξάζω (to glorify) 23 times. The following figures include all texts that contain τιμάω, and then

30. Schnackenburg, *John*, 2:386.
31. Ridderbos, *John*, 433.
32. Bultmann, *John*, 426.
33. Schnackenburg, *John*, 2:386.
34. Aalen, "glory, honor," *NIDNTT* 2:44–51. Also in Heb 2:9 (and 2:7; cf. Ps 8:6) referring to the honor and glory with which Jesus is crowned after his suffering, the two words δόξα and τιμή are employed as synonyms: τὸν δὲ βραχύ τι παρ' ἀγγέλους ἠλαττωμένον βλέπομεν Ἰησοῦν διὰ τὸ πάθημα τοῦ θανάτου δόξῃ καὶ τιμῇ ἐστεφανωμένον.

some texts that contain δόξα and δοξάζω that are pertinent to the current exploration.

Humanity in general

5:23 ἵνα πάντες **τιμῶσι** τὸν υἱὸν καθὼς τιμῶσι τὸν πατέρα. ὁ μὴ **τιμῶν** τὸν υἱὸν οὐ **τιμᾷ** τὸν πατέρα τὸν πέμψαντα αὐτόν. (so that all may **honor** the Son just as they **honor** the Father. Anyone who does not **honor** the Son does not honor the Father who sent him.)

The Jews

5:44 πῶς δύνασθε ὑμεῖς πιστεῦσαι **δόξαν** παρὰ ἀλλήλων λαμβάνοντες, καὶ τὴν **δόξαν** τὴν παρὰ τοῦ μόνου θεοῦ οὐ ζητεῖτε; (How can you believe when you accept **glory** from one another and do not seek the **glory** that comes from the one who alone is God?)

12:43 ἠγάπησαν γὰρ τὴν **δόξαν** τῶν ἀνθρώπων μᾶλλον ἤπερ τὴν **δόξαν** τοῦ θεοῦ. (for they loved human **glory** more than the **glory** that comes from God.)

8:49 καὶ ὑμεῖς **ἀτιμάζετέ** με. (And you **dishonor** me.)

Jesus himself

5:41 **Δόξαν** παρὰ ἀνθρώπων οὐ λαμβάνω, (I do not accept **glory** from human beings.)

8:50 ἐγὼ δὲ οὐ ζητῶ τὴν **δόξαν** μου· (Yet I do not seek my own **glory**.)

8:54 ἀπεκρίθη Ἰησοῦς· ἐὰν ἐγὼ **δοξάσω** ἐμαυτόν, ἡ **δόξα** μου οὐδέν ἐστιν· Jesus answered, (If I **glorify** myself, my **glory** is nothing.)

The disciples in relation with Jesus and the Father

17:10 καὶ τὰ ἐμὰ πάντα σά ἐστιν καὶ τὰ σὰ ἐμά, καὶ **δεδόξασμαι** ἐν αὐτοῖς. (All mine are yours, and yours are mine; and I have been **glorified** in them.)

15:8 ἐν τούτῳ **ἐδοξάσθη** ὁ πατήρ μου, ἵνα καρπὸν πολὺν φέρητε καὶ γένησθε ἐμοὶ μαθηταί. (My Father is **glorified** by this, that you bear much fruit and become my disciples.)

21:19 τοῦτο δὲ εἶπεν σημαίνων ποίῳ θανάτῳ **δοξάσει** τὸν θεόν. (He said this to indicate the kind of death by which he would **glorify** God.)

The Father to the disciples

12:26 ἐάν τις ἐμοὶ διακονῇ **τιμήσει** αὐτὸν ὁ πατήρ. (Whoever serves me, the Father will **honor**.)

17:24 Πάτερ, ὃ δέδωκάς μοι, θέλω ἵνα ὅπου εἰμὶ ἐγὼ κἀκεῖνοι ὦσιν μετ' ἐμοῦ, ἵνα θεωρῶσιν τὴν **δόξαν** τὴν ἐμήν, ἣν δέδωκάς μοι ὅτι ἠγάπησάς με πρὸ καταβολῆς κόσμου. (Father, I desire that those also, whom you have given me, may be with me where I am, to see my **glory**, which you have given me because you loved me before the foundation of the world.)

Between the Son and the Father

8:49–50 ἀπεκρίθη Ἰησοῦς· ἐγὼ δαιμόνιον οὐκ ἔχω, ἀλλὰ **τιμῶ** τὸν πατέρα μου, . . . ἐγὼ δὲ οὐ ζητῶ τὴν **δόξαν** μου· ἔστιν ὁ ζητῶν καὶ κρίνων. (Jesus answered, "I do not have a demon; but I **honor** my Father, . . . Yet I do not seek my own **glory**; there is one who seeks it and he is the judge.)

8:54 ἔστιν ὁ πατήρ μου ὁ **δοξάζων** με, (It is my Father who **glorifies** me.)

13:32 [εἰ ὁ θεὸς **ἐδοξάσθη** ἐν αὐτῷ,] καὶ ὁ θεὸς δοξ**άσει** αὐτὸν ἐν αὐτῷ, καὶ εὐθὺς δοξάσει αὐτόν. (If God has been **glorified** in him, God will also **glorify** him in himself and will **glorify** him at once.)

14:13 καὶ ὅ τι ἂν αἰτήσητε ἐν τῷ ὀνόματί μου τοῦτο ποιήσω, ἵνα **δοξασθῇ** ὁ πατὴρ ἐν τῷ υἱῷ. (I will do whatever you ask in my name, so that the Father may be **glorified** in the Son.)

17:1 πάτερ, ἐλήλυθεν ἡ ὥρα· **δόξασόν** σου τὸν υἱόν, ἵνα ὁ υἱὸς δοξ**άσῃ** σέ, (Father, the hour has come; **glorify** your Son so that the Son may **glorify** you,)

17:4, 5 ἐγώ σε **ἐδόξασα** ἐπὶ τῆς γῆς τὸ ἔργον τελειώσας ὃ δέδωκάς μοι ἵνα ποιήσω· καὶ νῦν **δόξασόν** με σύ, πάτερ, παρὰ σεαυτῷ τῇ **δόξῃ** ᾗ εἶχον πρὸ τοῦ τὸν κόσμον εἶναι παρὰ σοί. (I **glorified** you on earth by finishing the work that you gave me to do. So now, Father, **glorify** me in your own presence with the **glory** that I had in your presence before the world existed.)

All humanity is to honor the Son and the Father (5:23). However, the Jews dishonor the Son (8:49) by refusing him whom the Father sent and not believing in him (5:43, 44; cf. 1:11; 3:32). The reason they cannot believe in the Son is that they love human glory (12:43) and accept glory from one another (5:44). They neither love nor seek the glory that comes from God (12:43; 5:44) who is the true source of the abiding glory. This is one of the fundamental problems of humanity, in which they all have gone astray.

There came the true human Jesus from the Father for their rescue. He neither accepts glory from human beings (5:41) nor seeks his own glory (8:50). In Jesus the new epoch of human life in relation to the matter of honor and glory is inaugurated. Those who are given to the Son by the Father (17:2, 6) and follow him, give honor to the Son whom the Father sent—glory has come to the Son in them (17:10). Furthermore, glory and honor is given to the Father by the fruitful life of Jesus' followers (15:8) and some of them will give glory to God by death (21:19). As the reward for this, the Father, who glorifies the Son (8:50, 54) when he gives glory to the Father by obedience (17:4), will give honor to Jesus' followers for they give honor to the Son by serving him as his loyal servants (12:26). This will be done when the Son takes them to be with him, sharing in his glory and honor (14:3; 17:24; cf. Rom 8:17).

What kind of glory and honor is it with which the Father will honor those who serve Jesus? First, it is the glory and honor that the Father and the Son mutually give to and take from each other (13:32; 17:1, 4, 5). Second, it is the glory and honor that the Son will receive again from the Father, which he had in the presence of the Father before the world began (17:5) and will again enjoy forever with him. This is the very glory the servants of Jesus, who follow him by serving him, will see (17:24; 1 John 3:2), participate in, and join as the reward from the Father (12:26). Therefore, the remark that the faithful followers of Jesus will be "swept up into the oneness that unites the Father and the Son" in the eternal communion in glory with the Father and the Son is not an overstatement at all.[35] Into this glorious lived experience (Spirituality) of following Jesus the text 12:26 pulls the readers by the two particular phrases: "where I am, there will my servant be also" (ὅπου εἰμὶ ἐγὼ ἐκεῖ καὶ ὁ διάκονος ὁ ἐμὸς ἔσται) and "the Father will honor him" (τιμήσει αὐτὸν ὁ πατήρ).

---

35. Moloney, *John*, 359.

IV. Conclusion

In this chapter I have explored the distinctive aspects of the Spirituality of following Jesus communicated in 12:26. First, by examining the seven terms (πάσχα, ἀποθνῄσκω, ἀποκτείνω, ἐνταφιασμός, ἡ ὥρα, ὑψόω, and σημαίνων ποίῳ θανάτῳ) that indicate or point to Jesus' death, the immediate literary-theological context of 12:26 is considered, in which Jesus' call of following him (ἐάν ἐμοί τις διακονῇ, ἐμοὶ ἀκολουθείτω) is given. It is inferred from this investigation that, by reading Jesus' call in this literary-theological context, John's readers heard the call in the close relation to Jesus' death, that is, to follow him even by taking the path of their Lord's death.

Second, the two words διακονέω and διάκονος, which are employed in Jesus' logion, are proved to be significant. Not only are they employed to call the readers into discipleship, but also they function as the triggering motif that could help them to recall Jesus' servanthood of God. The motif of "to serve" takes the significant role as "Whoever serves me" is reiterated twice in the verse (ἐάν ἐμοί τις διακονῇ, . . . ἐάν τις ἐμοὶ διακονῇ . . .). By the rare wordings of διακονέω and διάκονος, the believers are invited to recollect their memory of Jesus as the faithful servant of God, and are called to serve Jesus as his faithful servants, just as the Lord Jesus is the faithful servant of God, completing the work God gave him to do. By these two terms, the fact that the Spirituality of following Jesus includes serving him as his servant is effectively communicated to the readers.

Third, the promised reward for those who serve Jesus by following him is investigated, as expressed in the two phrases: "where I am, there will my servant be also" (ὅπου εἰμὶ ἐγὼ ἐκεῖ καὶ ὁ διάκονος ὁ ἐμὸς ἔσται) and "the Father will honor him" (τιμήσει αὐτὸν ὁ πατήρ). Essentially the two expressions convey the same idea. They will be taken to the place where Jesus is in glory. The Father who is the true source of glory and honor will take them into the place of honor and glory to share with Christ the same glory and honor that the Father will give the Son. The honor that the Father will bestow on Jesus' faithful servants is for them to join permanently the eternal and glorious communion of the Son with the Father.

Both the demand and the reward of the life of following Jesus is efficiently communicated in 12:26: following Jesus as the journey of death and glory (through death to glory), being a faithful servant of Jesus and being with him in glory, being a partaker of both suffering and honor, both humiliation and glorification. This is the distinctive aspect of the Spirituality of following Jesus that 12:26 communicates in the most inclusive manner. To follow Jesus is to serve him by taking the way of suffering and death into glory, just as Jesus walked the path of death into glory, serving God as the servant, and being honored by God as the result.

Throughout the narrative of the Fourth Gospel runs an important focus on the death-glory of Jesus. It aims at not only presenting Jesus' death-glory as the redemptive historical truth, but also inviting Jesus' followers to the Spirituality of walking on the same path of death-glory. Through the path of death, the followers will reach the glorious place where Jesus is with the Father and experience the glory of the Son and the Father. This is the Spirituality of following Jesus communicated to the readers by the association of ἀκολουθεῖν with the motifs of "where," "death," and "to serve" that the faithful followers of Jesus will be experiencing in this life and in the life hereafter.

CHAPTER 9

Human Inability; Divine Ability (13:21—14:3)

JOHN 13:36–38 IS TYPICALLY known as the text that predicts Peter's denial.[1] On the surface, it is not incorrect to say that the text is about Jesus' prediction of Simon Peter's denial. However, the text imparts more than that. It communicates a profoundly theological significance as the Fourth Gospel characteristically does.[2] By the unprecedented association of ἀκολουθεῖν (to follow) with οὐ δύναμαι (not able) and the prediction of Peter's denial, the text invites the readers into a new horizon of the Spirituality of following Jesus.

In the quest of the Spirituality of following Jesus implied in 13:36–38, two levels of questions are going to be asked as a guide to approach the text. The first level is that of Jesus and his disciples; the second level is that of John's text and his readers.[3] The first level question is comprised of two sub-questions. One, why does Jesus say to Peter that he cannot follow him now

---

1. This text is given the titles, "Peter's Denial Foretold" (UBS4; Ridderbos, *John*, 473), the "Prediction of Peter's Denial" (Brown, *John*, 2:614; Beasley-Murray, *John*, 248), and "the Predictions of Simon Peter's Denial" (Schnackenburg, *John*, 3:55) by scholars who have viewed the text with a focus on Jesus' prediction of Peter's denial. On the contrary, Bultmann attempts to see the bright side of the text 13:36–38 by focusing on the significance of the word ὕστερον (13:36) and combining 13:36–38 with 14:1–4 as one meaning cluster, and gives it a title "The Promise of Discipleship." Bultmann, *John*, 595.

2. Brown comments that the text has "definite theological overtones." Brown, *John*, 2:616.

3. The current text conveys two-levels of Spirituality. One is that of the disciples, which revolves around Jesus; the other is that of John's readers, which is experienced in and through the Johannine text. At the center of the Spirituality of the disciples is the person of Jesus, his words and deeds; and at the center of the Spirituality of John's readers is the Johannine text. Therefore, by examining the current text, we are ushered into the two levels of biblical Spirituality, which are essentially correlative as the latter is an expansion of the former.

(νῦν, 13:36)?[4] Peter is more than willing to follow Jesus even unto death. Besides, Peter is convinced that he is able to follow Jesus whatever it takes, even risking his own life ("I will lay down my life for you," 13:37). Then, why can he not follow Jesus now? This is the question that Peter asked Jesus ("Lord, why can I not follow you now?" 13:37). Though it is the same question in its literal wordings, Peter's question is a question that arose from anxiousness, but ours is out of theological concern in pursuit of the spiritual significance implied. Two, what is implied in the fact that Peter will be able to follow Jesus afterward (ὕστερον, 13:36)? What makes it possible for the one who denied his own Lord three times to eventually be able to follow him? Isn't he a man who was not able to keep his words even for the next twenty-four hours? What happened between νῦν and ὕστερον? What is it that enables Peter to follow the Lord afterward?

The second level question is concerned of the Spirituality to which the fourth evangelist invites his readers by the text. What aspect of Spirituality does the evangelist communicate to his readers by the association of ἀκολουθεῖν with οὐ δύναμαι (13:31, 36, 37) and Peter's denial prediction (13:38) against the backdrop of another disciples' betrayal (13:21, 30)? What unique respect of the Spirituality of following Jesus is communicated by this?

While reading 13:36–38 with the two level questions in mind, it is expected that another important characteristic of the Spirituality of following Jesus, which has not been revealed so far in the Johannine text, may be excavated. Three steps will be taken in this study. Firstly, by comparing the text of Peter's denial prediction in the Fourth Gospel (13:36–38) with other pertinent texts in the Synoptic Gospels, the distinctiveness of the Johannine text will be presented. Secondly, the literary context of 13:36–38 as its semantic and interpretative environment will be examined by discourse analysis to find out the key linguistic components and their semantic relations as well as the rhetoric and argument of the author. Finally, as the main body, the theological implications and the Spirituality of the life of following Jesus imbedded in the text 13:21–14:3 (which includes 13:36–38 as a semantic cluster) will be explored.

---

4. The current text is one of the important texts about Peter and the implication of the life of following Jesus communicated by Peter's journey of faith (1:40–42; 6:68; 13:6–9, 24, 36–38; 18:10–11, 15–27; 20:1–10; 21:11, 15–22). Among them, 13:36–38 is the text where the term ἀκολουθεῖν is associated with Peter for the first time, though in a negative sense, and the second one is 21:15–19 where the call "Follow me" is given to him finally and directly. When 21:15–19 is dealt with, another important implication of following Jesus will be discussed.

I. An Unparalleled Association of ἀκολουθεῖν with the Denial Prediction

The first thing that draws attention is the fact that the fourth evangelist associates the discipleship term ἀκολουθεῖν with the prediction of Peter's denial. The connection appears only in the Fourth Gospel, as shown in the following comparison chart.

Matt 26:31-35	Mark 14:27-31	Luke 22:31-34	John 13:36-38
31 Τότε λέγει αὐτοῖς ὁ Ἰησοῦς· <u>πάντες ὑμεῖς σκανδαλισθήσεσθε</u> ἐν ἐμοὶ ἐν τῇ νυκτὶ ταύτῃ, γέγραπται γάρ· πατάξω τὸν ποιμένα, καὶ διασκορπισθήσονται τὰ πρόβατα τῆς ποίμνης.	27 καὶ λέγει αὐτοῖς ὁ Ἰησοῦς ὅτι <u>πάντες σκανδαλισθήσεσθε</u>, ὅτι γέγραπται· πατάξω τὸν ποιμένα, καὶ τὰ πρόβατα διασκορπισθήσονται.	31 Σίμων Σίμων, ἰδοὺ ὁ σατανᾶς ἐξῃτήσατο ὑμᾶς τοῦ σινιάσαι ὡς τὸν σῖτον·	36 Λέγει αὐτῷ Σίμων Πέτρος· κύριε, ποῦ ὑπάγεις; ἀπεκρίθη [αὐτῷ] Ἰησοῦς· ὅπου ὑπάγω οὐ δύνασαί μοι νῦν **<u>ἀκολουθῆσαι</u>**, **<u>ἀκολουθήσεις</u>** δὲ ὕστερον.
32 μετὰ δὲ τὸ ἐγερθῆναί με προάξω ὑμᾶς εἰς τὴν Γαλιλαίαν.	28 ἀλλὰ μετὰ τὸ ἐγερθῆναί με <u>προάξω ὑμᾶς εἰς τὴν Γαλιλαίαν</u>.	32 <u>ἐγὼ δὲ ἐδεήθην περὶ σοῦ</u> ἵνα μὴ ἐκλίπῃ ἡ πίστις σου· καὶ σύ ποτε ἐπιστρέψας στήρισον τοὺς ἀδελφούς σου.	37 λέγει αὐτῷ ὁ Πέτρος· κύριε, διὰ τί οὐ δύναμαί σοι **<u>ἀκολουθῆσαι</u>** ἄρτι; <u>τὴν ψυχήν μου ὑπὲρ σοῦ θήσω</u>.
33 ἀποκριθεὶς δὲ ὁ Πέτρος εἶπεν αὐτῷ· <u>εἰ πάντες σκανδαλισθήσονται ἐν σοί, ἐγὼ οὐδέποτε σκανδαλισθήσομαι</u>.	29 ὁ δὲ Πέτρος ἔφη αὐτῷ· <u>εἰ καὶ πάντες σκανδαλισθήσονται, ἀλλ' οὐκ ἐγώ</u>.	33 ὁ δὲ εἶπεν αὐτῷ· κύριε, <u>μετὰ σοῦ ἕτοιμός εἰμι καὶ εἰς φυλακὴν καὶ εἰς θάνατον πορεύεσθαι</u>.	38 ἀποκρίνεται Ἰησοῦς· τὴν ψυχήν σου ὑπὲρ ἐμοῦ θήσεις; ἀμὴν ἀμὴν λέγω σοι, οὐ μὴ ἀλέκτωρ φωνήσῃ ἕως οὗ ἀρνήσῃ με τρίς.
34 ἔφη αὐτῷ ὁ Ἰησοῦς· ἀμὴν λέγω σοι ὅτι ἐν ταύτῃ τῇ νυκτὶ πρὶν ἀλέκτορα φωνῆσαι τρὶς ἀπαρνήσῃ με.	30 καὶ λέγει αὐτῷ ὁ Ἰησοῦς· ἀμὴν λέγω σοι ὅτι σὺ σήμερον ταύτῃ τῇ νυκτὶ πρὶν ἢ δὶς ἀλέκτορα φωνῆσαι τρίς με ἀπαρνήσῃ.	34 ὁ δὲ εἶπεν· λέγω σοι, Πέτρε, οὐ φωνήσει σήμερον ἀλέκτωρ ἕως τρίς με ἀπαρνήσῃ εἰδέναι.	
35 λέγει αὐτῷ ὁ Πέτρος· <u>κἂν δέῃ με σὺν σοὶ ἀποθανεῖν, οὐ μή σε ἀπαρνήσομαι</u>. ὁμοίως καὶ πάντες οἱ μαθηταὶ εἶπαν.	31 ὁ δὲ ἐκπερισσῶς ἐλάλει· <u>ἐὰν δέῃ με συναποθανεῖν σοι, οὐ μή σε ἀπαρνήσομαι</u>. ὡσαύτως δὲ καὶ πάντες ἔλεγον.		

There are two common elements which appear in all four Gospels. One is the vehement expression from Peter that he will never desert Jesus and he is ready to die for him (Matt 26:33, 35; Mark 14:29, 31; Luke 22:33; John 13:37). The other is the firm utterance of Jesus that Peter will deny him three times before the cock crows (Matt 26:34; Mark 14:30; Luke 22:34; John 13:38).[5]

The elements appearing in only one or two books are these: In Matthew and Mark, it is distinctively stated that all disciples will desert Jesus and that he will see them in Galilee. By mentioning that he will go to Galilee, ahead of the disciples, Jesus hints that he will meet and restore them (Matt 26:32; Mark 14:28). In Luke, with the gloomy denial prediction, a message of comfort is given in the same breath that Jesus has prayed for Peter and a bidding is given to Peter that he is to strengthen the brothers after restoration (Luke 22:32).

In the Fourth Gospel, ἀκολουθεῖν appears uniquely within the account of Peter's denial prediction. It is an unparalleled employment of ἀκολουθεῖν in connection to the denial prediction. Then, naturally questions arise: What spiritual significance does the fourth evangelist intend to impart to his readers through the close association of ἀκολουθεῖν with Peter's denial prediction? What implication of the life of following Jesus is created by the association? What response, attitude, and experience does the evangelist expect his readers to have in the journey of following Jesus by reading 13:36–38 within this distinct literary context?

II. Literary Context and Semantic Relations

In order to find out answers to the above questions, it is necessary to read the text 13:36–38 in the light of its literary context first, then theological reflection can be yielded rightly. The whole pericope of the farewell discourse (chapters 13–17), the passion and resurrection (chapters 18–20), and the epilogue (chapter 21) provide a wider literary context for reading 13:36–38. However, in this section the scope of the literary context will be limited to the near and immediate context (13:21—14:3) because it is this that furnishes a rich environment for theological reflection. The main vocabularies and elements within 13:21—14:3 are going to be demonstrated first by discourse analysis, and then they will be discussed.[6]

5. The Johannine text employs the particularly solemn double ἀμὴν ἀμὴν, while the Matthean and the Markan texts use a single ἀμὴν and the Lukan text contains none.
6. The reason 14:1–3 is included together with 13:21–38 in the discourse analysis as one semantic cluster is that Jesus continues in 14:1–3 addressing the disciples who

Semantic Networks of 13:21–14:3

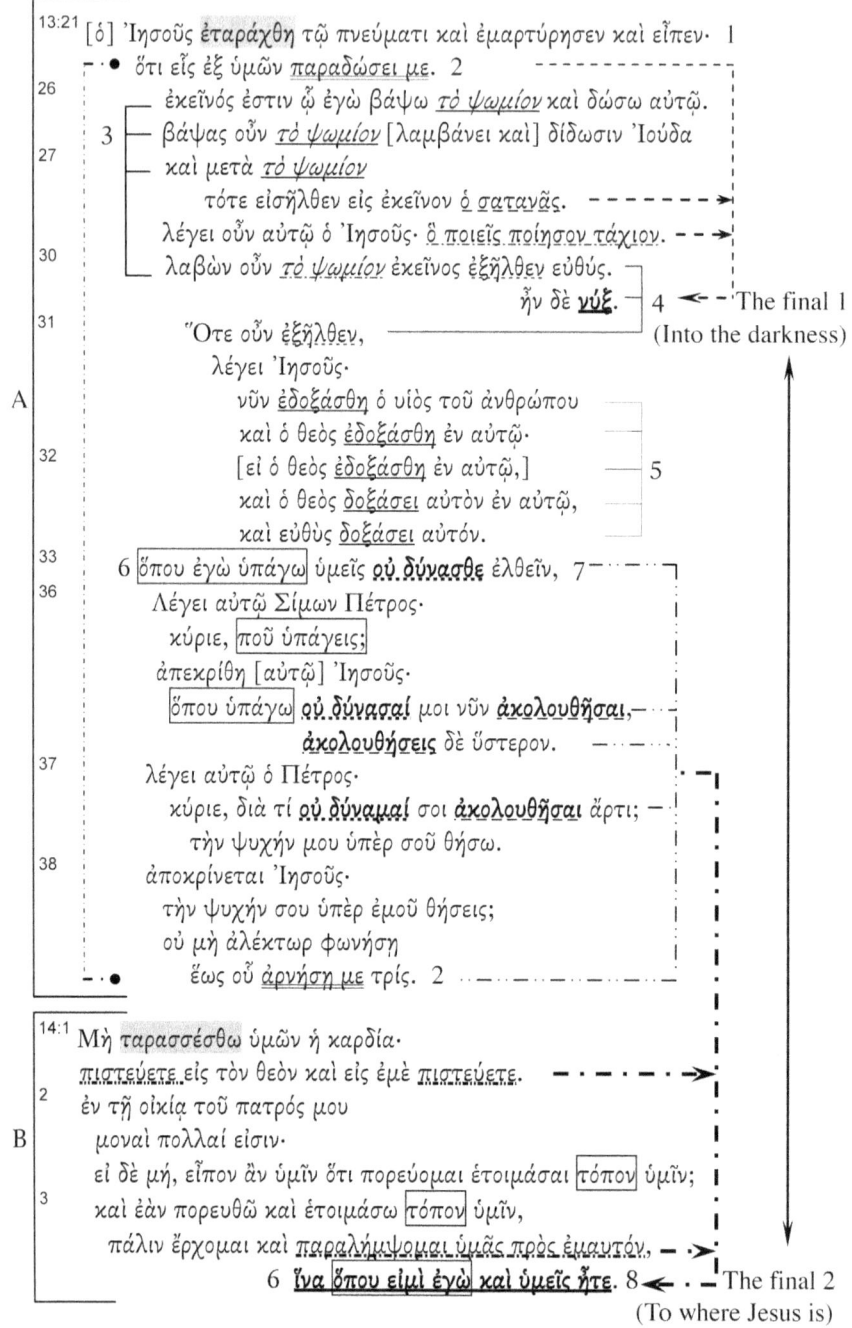

are troubled by what was said in 13:33–38, and that they are closely connected by the ὅπου motif and the term ταράσσω. Bultmann (*John*, 595) also combined 13:36–38 with 14:1–4 under the title "The Promise of Discipleship."

HUMAN INABILITY; DIVINE ABILITY (13:21—14:3)

Semantic Networks of 13:21–14:3 (ESV)

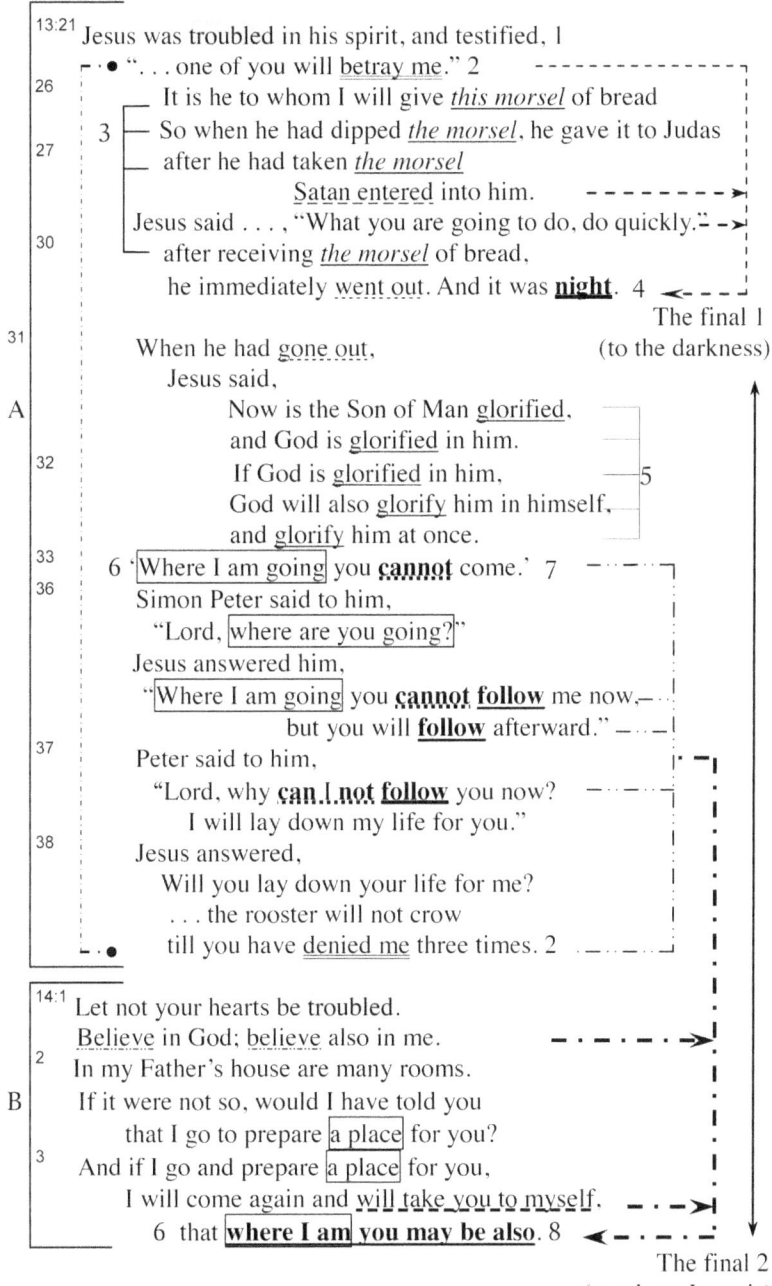

The semantic networks present the main ingredients of the pericope 13:21–14:3 and their semantic relations. First, ταράσσω (to stir up, to trouble, 13:21; 14:1): The pericope is comprised of two clusters. Each of them begins with a sentence that contains the same word ταράσσω. Cluster A begins with a statement that says, "Jesus was troubled in spirit" ([ὁ] Ἰησοῦς ἐταράχθη τῷ πνεύματι, 13:21). Jesus in his troubled spirit opens his mouth to address his disciple.[7] Cluster B starts with Jesus' address to the disciples who are now troubled in their hearts (Μὴ ταρασσέσθω ὑμῶν ἡ καρδία, 14:1). The one troubled in spirit comforts the disciples troubled in hearts.

Although both clusters A and B contain the same word ταράσσω at the very beginning of each of them, there is a great difference between them. The former deals with the human incapability of the disciples who can not follow Jesus to where he goes; the latter deals with what makes the incapable disciples able to come to where Jesus will be. We will have further reflection on this later.

Second, παραδώσει με (to betray me, 13:21) and ἀρνήσῃ με (to deny me, 13:38): Within cluster A is an *inclusio* of two appalling predictions, at the beginning and ending of the cluster, that one of the disciples will betray Jesus (εἷς ἐξ ὑμῶν παραδώσει με, 13:21) and another will deny him (ἀρνήσῃ με τρίς, 13:38). Is there any other passage in the Gospels where ἀκολουθεῖν is encircled by the horrific human failure accounts of both the betrayal and denial of the Lord? The current text is the only one. What significance does the author convey by employing ἀκολουθεῖν thrice within the human failure statements of παραδώσει με and ἀρνήσῃ με?

Third, τὸ ψωμίον (the piece of bread, 13:26*2, 27, 30): It seems like the fourth evangelist decided to reiterate τὸ ψωμίον as many times as he could in this short text (13:26–30). By the overwhelming repetition (four times within five verses) of τὸ ψωμίον, John demonstrates that Jesus extended "an offer of love to Judas" to give him an opportunity to change his mind and return.[8] Ironically and tragically, however, the opposite results follow the act of receiving the piece of bread: "After he received the piece of bread, Satan entered into him" (καὶ μετὰ τὸ ψωμίον τότε εἰσῆλθεν εἰς ἐκεῖνον ὁ

---

7. Cf. 11:33; 12:27

8. Keener, *John*, 2:918. Brown (*John*, 2:578) also takes it as "a special act of esteem" and the "sign of Jesus' affection, like the act of love." For different views on Jesus' act of giving the piece of bread, see Keener's footnote 216 on the same page. Whitacre takes it as Jesus sought to win Judas back (Whitacre, *John*, 335), while Stauffer views it in connection to the bitter herbs in which the bread was dipped with a curse (citing Deut 29:18–19), thereby prefiguring Judas' betrayal (Stauffer, *Jesus and His Story*, 116). Ridderbos (*John*, 470–71) differently comments that by expressly giving Judas a signal with the piece of bread, Jesus "not only unmasks Judas as the betrayer to the Beloved Disciple but also sets in motion a sequence of events in which Judas will play a decisive role."

σατανᾶς, 13:27). And "after receiving the piece of bread, he immediately went out. And it was night" (λαβὼν οὖν τὸ ψωμίον ἐκεῖνος ἐξῆλθεν εὐθύς. ἦν δὲ νύξ, 13:30).

Fourth, ὁ σατανᾶς (Satan, 13:27), ἐξῆλθεν (went out, 13:30, 31), and νύξ (night, 13:30): Despite the given sign of love and opportunity of repentance, when he received (λαμβάνω) the piece of bread (13:18; Ps 41:9),[9] Judas did not change his mind, rather he hardened his heart. When he refused Jesus' expression of love and rather embraced the devil's prompting (13:2),[10] Satan finally moved into action by entering into him (13:27).[11] Judas went out immediately (ἐξῆλθεν, twice in 13:30–31) to betray the Lord (παραδίδωμι, 13:21). And it was night (ἦν δὲ νύξ, 13:30).[12] Now one of the disciples went out into darkness outside and took the road of no returning. Linked, the three terms (ἐξῆλθεν, νύξ, and ὁ σατανᾶς) indicate the final place Judas reached.

Fifth, δοξάζω (to glorify, 13:31*2, 32*3): It is employed intensively, five times in two verses 31–32.[13] In the midst of the appalling event of being betrayed by one of his own, the Johannine Jesus sees it as the moment of glorification (glorifying/being glorified) for both the Father and the Son. At the death of Jesus on the cross (immediately triggered by the betrayal), the mystery of divine reciprocal immanence between the Father and the Son is dramatically manifested in the form of mutual glorification of the Father and the Son in each other (13:31–32).[14] The mutual glorification is that the

---

9. For different views on what λαμβάνω implies, see Barrett, *John*, 447 ("λαμβάνει may have been added to recall the notable action of Jesus at the last supper, repeated in the eucharist, of *taking* the bread before distribution") and Schnackenburg, *John*, 3:30 ("It is hardly possible, however, to presuppose a 'communion with Judas' here on the basis of the eucharistic overtones of the other texts").

10. Brown, *John*, 2:578.

11. Ridderbos, *John*, 470–71.

12. "When Judas goes out it is into the outer darkness (Matt 8:12; 22:13; 25:30). It is the hour of the power of darkness (Luke 22:53). John was of course aware that the hour was evening . . .; but his remark is far from being merely historical. In going into the darkness, Judas went to his own place" (Barrett, *John*, 449). "Night symbolized evil in other source as well (e.g., 4Q299 frg. 5, lines 1–4; cf. Aeschylus *Eumenides* 745)" (Keener, *John*, 2:920). In Acts 26:18 the dominion of Satan is named darkness in contrast to God's dominion light.

13. 7:39; 8:54*2; 12:16, 23, 28*3; 13:31*2, 32*3; 14:13; 15:8; 17:1*2, 4, 5, 10; cf. 16:14; 21:19

14. For an exegetical and historical study on 13:31–32, refer to Ensor, "The Glorification of the Son of Man," 229–52. The article argues "that Jesus is represented as saying, . . . that through his return to the Father by way of the cross his divine qualities would be revealed, that he would thereby fulfill the role of the one like a son of man of Daniel 7:13–14, and that God's own divine qualities would also thereby be revealed."

Son glorifies the Father by the death of obedience to his command; and the Father glorifies the Son with the glory they had in eternity (8:50, 54; 17:1, 5) and exalts him to be the head above all, bestowing on him all power and authority (Matt 28:18; Eph 1:20–22; Phil 2:6–11).

Sixth, ὅπου (where, 13:33, 36; 14:3), ποῦ (where, 13:36), and τόπον (a place, 14:2, 3): The terms that point to the place where Jesus is going to are significant ingredients as they appear most intensively in connection with ἀκολουθεῖν (13:36*2, 37) in the Fourth Gospel. They are ὅπου ἐγὼ ὑπάγω (13:33); ποῦ ὑπάγεις; (13:36); ὅπου ὑπάγω (13:36); ὅπου εἰμὶ ἐγὼ (14:3). The other expressions that indicate the same place are ἐν τῇ οἰκίᾳ τοῦ πατρός μου μοναὶ ("In my Father's house there are many dwelling places," 14:2); τόπον ("a place," 14:2, 3); πρὸς ἐμαυτόν ("to myself," 14:3). Because of the importance of the "where" motif in the present study, it calls for further consideration, which will be done later.

Seventh, οὐ δύναμαι (to be unable, 13:33, 36, 37): That the followers of Jesus are not able to come to where Jesus goes is addressed to all the disciples once (οὐ δύνασθε ἐλθεῖν, 13:33), and that Peter is not able to follow him is communicated emphatically (οὐ δύνασαί μοι νῦν ἀκολουθῆσαι, 13:36). To Peter's defiant question (κύριε, διὰ τί οὐ δύναμαί σοι ἀκολουθῆσαι ἄρτι; 13:37) in the strong refusal of what Jesus just said, Jesus, by uttering the shocking prediction of Peter's denial, reaffirms the fact that he *is unable to* come to where he is going to—not only is he unable to come where Jesus is going, but he will end up denying Jesus, by which he proves (18:27) that he is unable to follow Jesus to where Jesus is going.

Eighth, πιστεύετε ("believe," 14:2*2), παραλήμψομαι ὑμᾶς ("will take you," 14:3), and ἵνα ὅπου εἰμὶ ἐγὼ καὶ ὑμεῖς ἦτε ("so that where I am, there you may be also," 14:3): The account, however, does not end with the gloomy fact that Peter and the disciples are unable to follow Jesus to where he goes. It ends with the bright future promise that Jesus will take them to where he is, and thus eventually they will be with him where he is (14:3). Between the impossibility of the disciples' following Jesus to where he goes and the future fact that they will be there with him, there are two important phrases. One is that the disciples are called to believe in God and Jesus (πιστεύετε εἰς τὸν θεὸν καὶ εἰς ἐμὲ πιστεύετε, 14:1); and the other is what Jesus will do for them (ἔρχομαι καὶ παραλήμψομαι ὑμᾶς πρὸς ἐμαυτόν, 14:3).

III. Following Jesus Communicated in 13:21—14:3

Among the above noted linguistic ingredients interwoven in the semantic networking of 13:21—14:3, three points call for further development.

Firstly, the where (ὅπου/ποῦ) motif is to be inquired into since 13:33—14:3 is the pericope wherein it intensively appears in connection with ἀκολουθεῖν. Secondly, the theological significance communicated by the association of ἀκολουθεῖν with the two human failures (Judas and Peter: παραδώσει με and ἀρνήσῃ με) and inability (οὐ δύναμαι) of the disciples needs to be explored. Thirdly, what makes the incapable disciples become capable to follow Jesus to where he goes will be considered by investigating what has happened between νῦν (now) and ὕστερον (later).

A. The "Where" (ὅπου/ποῦ) Motif

Most pericopes that have been dealt with as the research texts of the present study commonly contain the where (ὅπου/ποῦ) motif in association with ἀκολουθεῖν.[15] In 1:35-51, it is communicated that the movement of ἀκολουθεῖν (1:37, 40) leads the first disciples to the place where Jesus stays, so they can be with him (ποῦ μένεις;, 1:38; ἦλθαν οὖν καὶ εἶδαν ποῦ μένει καὶ παρ' αὐτῷ ἔμειναν, 1:39), and it is further intimated that Jesus will eventually lead those who follow (ἀκολουθεῖν) him to heaven opened, thus to the Father (1:51).

In 8:12-29, the direction of life which is an existential matter of life is dealt with by the association of the where (ὅπου/ποῦ) motif with ἀκολουθεῖν (8:14, 21). Jesus, the light of the world (8:12) is the only one who is able to enlighten humanity with the problem of direction of life because he is the true one who knows from where he comes and to where he goes (8:14). By following Jesus the light of life (8:12), humans come to find the direction of their life and know where to go, not walking in the darkness (8:12; cf. 12:35).[16]

In 12:20-36, as discussed in the previous section on 12:26, the where motif (ὅπου εἰμὶ ἐγώ, 12:26) points to the place of glory where Jesus will reach, and thus the followers of Jesus will be as the reward from the Father (12:26).[17] This is the place where Jesus goes through the path of death, as

---

15. In 10:1-42, although the vocabulary ὅπου/ποῦ does not appear literally, the movement of following (ἀκολουθεῖν) is connected with going after him to the place "where" Jesus the good shepherd leads them to.

16. 8:12 ἐγώ εἰμι τὸ φῶς τοῦ κόσμου· ὁ ἀκολουθῶν ἐμοὶ οὐ μὴ περιπατήσῃ ἐν τῇ σκοτίᾳ, ἀλλ' ἕξει τὸ φῶς τῆς ζωῆς.

17. Bruner, *John*, 715. See also Brown, *John*, 1:475; Moloney, *John*, 359; Lincoln, *John*, 351.

indicated by the recurring death motifs within its literary context (11:50, 51, 53, 55; 12:1, 7, 10, 23, 24, 27, 32, 33, 34; 13:1).[18]

When it comes to the present text 13:31—14:3, the association of the where (ὅπου/ποῦ) motif with ἀκολουθεῖν appears in the arena once again, but this time it stands at the center of the text by its copious appearances, as shown in the above semantic network (ὅπου/ποῦ in 13:33, 36*2, 14:3) together with pertinent expressions that indicate the same place in 14:1-3. What does the place "where Jesus is going to" indicate?[19] In 13:31—14:3, it is identified as the dwelling place of the Father's house (ἐν τῇ οἰκίᾳ τοῦ πατρός μου μοναὶ πολλαί εἰσιν, 14:2) which is the place where Jesus will be with the Father and take his followers to be with him when he comes again (παραλήμψομαι ὑμᾶς πρὸς ἐμαυτόν, ἵνα ὅπου εἰμὶ ἐγὼ καὶ ὑμεῖς ἦτε, 14:3).[20] When Thomas asked in his spiritual crassness, "Lord, we do not know where you are going" (14:5), Jesus in his reply indicated, by mentioning the way of coming to the Father (ἔρχεται πρὸς τὸν πατέρα, 14:6), that the place he is going to is "to the Father." By Jesus' reiterated sayings in the Gospel that he is going "to the Father,"[21] it is also sustained that the locus is where Jesus will be with the Father in heaven. This is the final and ultimate destination of the journey of following Jesus.

---

18. For a detailed discussion, see my previous argument under the subheading: Where I Am My Servant also will Be, for the study of 12:26 in chapter eight of the present research.

19. 13:33 καὶ καθὼς εἶπον τοῖς Ἰουδαίοις ὅτι ὅπου ἐγὼ ὑπάγω ὑμεῖς οὐ δύνασθε ἐλθεῖν, καὶ ὑμῖν λέγω ἄρτι. 13:36 Λέγει αὐτῷ Σίμων Πέτρος· κύριε, ποῦ ὑπάγεις; ἀπεκρίθη [αὐτῷ] Ἰησοῦς· ὅπου ὑπάγω οὐ δύνασαί μοι νῦν ἀκολουθῆσαι, ἀκολουθήσεις δὲ ὕστερον. 14:4 καὶ ὅπου [ἐγὼ] ὑπάγω οἴδατε τὴν ὁδόν. 14:5 Λέγει αὐτῷ Θωμᾶς· κύριε, οὐκ οἴδαμεν ποῦ ὑπάγεις.

20. There are different opinions about "many dwelling places in my Father's house." Carson (John, 488-89) and Morris (John, 638) view it as heaven; Schnackenburg (John, 3:59-61) and Lincoln (John, 389) as the dwelling places in heaven; McCaffrey and Bryan as the heavenly temple. McCaffrey, The House with Many Rooms; Bryan, "The Eschatological Temple," 187-98. For the intended double meaning of the dwelling places in my Father's house (one, Jesus' continuing presence with the believers; the other, to be with Jesus in heaven where the Father is), refer to Gundry, "In my Father's house," 68-72.

21. 7:33 καὶ ὑπάγω πρὸς τὸν πέμψαντά με. 13:1 ὅτι ἦλθεν αὐτοῦ ἡ ὥρα ἵνα μεταβῇ ἐκ τοῦ κόσμου τούτου πρὸς τὸν πατέρα. 13:3 καὶ ὅτι ἀπὸ θεοῦ ἐξῆλθεν καὶ πρὸς τὸν θεὸν ὑπάγει. 14:12 ὅτι ἐγὼ πρὸς τὸν πατέρα πορεύομαι· 14:28 εἰ ἠγαπᾶτέ με ἐχάρητε ἂν ὅτι πορεύομαι πρὸς τὸν πατέρα. 16:5 ὑπάγω πρὸς τὸν πέμψαντά με, καὶ οὐδεὶς ἐξ ὑμῶν ἐρωτᾷ με· ποῦ ὑπάγεις; 16:10 ὅτι πρὸς τὸν πατέρα ὑπάγω καὶ οὐκέτι θεωρεῖτέ με. 16:17 ὅτι ὑπάγω πρὸς τὸν πατέρα. 16:28 πάλιν ἀφίημι τὸν κόσμον καὶ πορεύομαι πρὸς τὸν πατέρα. 17:11 κἀγὼ πρὸς σὲ ἔρχομαι. πάτερ ἅγιε, τήρησον αὐτοὺς ἐν τῷ ὀνόματί σου ᾧ δέδωκάς μοι. 17:13 νῦν δὲ πρὸς σὲ ἔρχομαι. 20:17 ἀναβαίνω πρὸς τὸν πατέρα μου καὶ πατέρα ὑμῶν.

From chapter 1 to 12 of the Fourth Gospel whenever the association of ἀκολουθεῖν with the where (ὅπου/ποῦ) motif appears, the destination of the journey of following Jesus has been revealed either implicitly or explicitly to some extent. But it is the current text 13:31–14:3 that most clearly identifies that the final and ultimate terminus of the journey of following Jesus is the heavenly place where Jesus will be with the Father. In this sense 13:31—14:3 makes a contribution to the Johannine understanding of following Jesus. However, its contribution does not end with an elucidation of the ultimate destination. More importantly, the text communicates a theologically significant point, by Jesus' firm statements, that the disciples are *not able to follow* him now to where he is going, but will follow him only afterward (13:33, 36). Why does Jesus need to give this firm pronouncement to his disciples who are willing to follow him to the point of death? What theological implication does the fourth evangelist communicate about the life of following Jesus and into what characteristic of the Spirituality of following Jesus does the evangelist draw the readers by the unique combination of ἀκολουθεῖν with οὐ δύναμαι and the where (ὅπου/που) motif?

B. Human Inability and ἀκολουθεῖν

The text 13:21–38 is peculiar in the sense that it correlates ἀκολουθεῖν with the reality of the disciples' inability. Firstly, it is that ἀκολουθεῖν appears in combination with οὐ δύναμαι (not able).[22] In verses 33 and 36–37, ἀκολουθεῖν and οὐ δύναμαι appear three times each. Jesus says to all of his disciples that they cannot follow him to where he is going (ὅπου ἐγὼ ὑπάγω ὑμεῖς οὐ δύνασθε ἐλθεῖν, 13:33).[23] Although ἀκολουθεῖν is replaced by ἔρχομαι, it conveys the same meaning. Peter asks Jesus of where he is going (κύριε, ποῦ ὑπάγεις;, 13:36), but instead of giving him an answer, Jesus repeats the same idea uttered in verse 33 that the disciple is unable to come to where Jesus goes (ὅπου ὑπάγω οὐ δύνασαί μοι νῦν ἀκολουθῆσαι, 13:36). Through the use of Peter's enquiry (κύριε, διὰ τί οὐ δύναμαί σοι ἀκολουθῆσαι ἄρτι; 13:37), which is a repetition of what Jesus just said, the fourth evangelist leads the

---

22. The preceding text 13:21–22, 27–28, as a pair, also demonstrates the similar condition of the disciples, the inability in the area of apprehension (the disciples' incomprehension).

    V 21 ἀμὴν ἀμὴν λέγω ὑμῖν ὅτι εἷς ἐξ ὑμῶν παραδώσει με.

       V 22 ἔβλεπον εἰς ἀλλήλους οἱ μαθηταὶ **ἀπορούμενοι** περὶ τίνος λέγει.

    V 27 λέγει οὖν αὐτῷ ὁ Ἰησοῦς· ὃ ποιεῖς ποίησον τάχιον.

       V 28 τοῦτο [δὲ] **οὐδεὶς ἔγνω** τῶν ἀνακειμένων πρὸς τί εἶπεν αὐτῷ·

23. The text is without the temporal adverb νῦν or ἄρτι.

readers to focus once again on what Jesus just said. In no other texts of the Gospels does Jesus reiterate so emphatically that his disciples are unable to follow him where he is going.

The grave reality of the disciples' impotence is clearly demonstrated by one concrete example, which is Peter's (who is the central figure among Jesus' disciples) complete denial of Jesus (13:38). At the very moment when he expressed his full readiness and willingness in strong self-confidence, "I will lay down my life for you" (13:37), Jesus mercilessly exposes how fragile and vain his human willingness and determination are. By firmly uttering his readiness to follow Jesus even to the point of death, Peter expresses that he is fully capable of following Jesus. By solemnly uttering Peter's nearing denial, Jesus nails down that he is never able to. Peter will prove his utter inability within the next twenty four hours.

Secondly, the text 13:21–38 arranges ἀκολουθεῖν (13:36*2, 37) between παραδώσει με (to betray me, 13:21) and ἀρνήσῃ με (to deny me, 13:38). The gravity of Jesus' statements that the disciples are unable to follow him is escalated by the two gloomy facts that one of the disciples will betray (13:21) and the other completely deny (13:38) Jesus.[24] The below figure displays that ἀκολουθεῖν is encircled by the two literary designs: One is the recurring οὐ δύναμαι in the link with ἀκολουθεῖν; the other is *inclusio* of dismal sentences of παραδώσει με (13:21) and ἀρνήσῃ με (13:38) which enclose ἀκολουθεῖν (13:36, 37).

---

24. The two announcements of the betrayal and the denial are accentuated by the solemn double amen saying (ἀμὴν ἀμὴν).

V 21 ἀμὴν ἀμὴν λέγω ὑμῖν ὅτι εἷς ἐξ ὑμῶν <u>παραδώσει με</u>.
(*Truly, truly*, I say to you, one of you will <u>betray me</u>.)

V 33 καὶ καθὼς εἶπον τοῖς Ἰουδαίοις
ὅτι ὅπου ἐγὼ ὑπάγω ὑμεῖς <u>οὐ δύνασθε</u> ἐλθεῖν,
(and just as I said to the Jews,
... "Where I am going you <u>cannot</u> come.")

V 36 Λέγει αὐτῷ Σίμων Πέτρος·
κύριε, ποῦ ὑπάγεις;
ἀπεκρίθη [αὐτῷ] Ἰησοῦς·
ὅπου ὑπάγω <u>οὐ δύνασαί</u> μοι νῦν **ἀκολουθῆσαι**,
ἀκολουθήσεις δὲ ὕστερον.
(Simon Peter said to him,
"Lord, where are you going?"
Jesus answered him,
"Where I am going you <u>cannot</u> **follow** me now,
but you will **follow** afterward.")

V 37 λέγει αὐτῷ ὁ Πέτρος·
κύριε, διὰ τί <u>οὐ δύναμαί</u> σοι **ἀκολουθῆσαι** ἄρτι;
τὴν ψυχήν μου ὑπὲρ σοῦ θήσω.
(Peter said to him, "Lord, why <u>can I not</u> **follow** you now?
I will lay down my life for you.")

V 38 ἀμὴν ἀμὴν λέγω σοι, οὐ μὴ ἀλέκτωρ φωνήσῃ ἕως οὗ <u>ἀρνήσῃ με</u> τρίς.
(*Truly, truly*, I say to you, the rooster will not crow
till you have <u>denied me</u> three times.)

The particular arrangement of ἀκολουθεῖν in the text raises questions. What is the intention of the fourth evangelist in positioning the term ἀκολουθεῖν between the two statements of the two disciples' failures? What significance does the evangelist convey and into what Spirituality of following Jesus does he pull the readers by employing ἀκολουθεῖν thrice within the *inclusio* structure of the two failure announcements, παραδώσει με (13:21) and ἀρνήσῃ με (13:38)? It is for the readers to see the journey of following (ἀκολουθεῖν) Jesus with a clear recognition of human inability, that human beings are not only open to failures, but also no one is able to follow Jesus and reach where he goes in their own ability.

The spiritual inability of following (ἀκολουθεῖν) Jesus for all the disciples is not a temporal matter. It is not right to say that the problem that hinders them from following Jesus now is only a matter of time even though they are fully capable to follow Jesus. The inability is not something that can be solved automatically as time changes. It is not that they cannot follow him, but that they are *unable* to follow him. The reason they are unable to follow Jesus is the lack of intrinsic spiritual ability. Jesus' firm saying to all the disciples, "Where I am going, you cannot come" (13:33), does not include the temporal qualification. When it is said in 13:36, "you cannot follow me now, but you will follow me afterward," the focus is not on time change, but on spiritual concern. The disciples need something from outside of their own beings. Something has to come into their existence from the above. Something has to be done by Jesus in the spiritual realm between now and afterward, and that spiritual something has to be appropriated in each individual follower's life, so that they may be able to follow Jesus to the place where the Father is.

The event of the denial is not only Peter's problem, but of all the disciples as Bultmann comments that "Peter's denial (13:38) is only a representative event."[25] The miserable experience of the denial is the life story and existential reality of all the disciples (16:32; Mark 14:27). Judas' failure as a disciple is not only one man's story. It could be any human being's story. There are many men and women whose journey of following Jesus is aborted (1 John 2:19; 1 Tim 1:19–20; 2 Cor 11:13; Acts 20:30; Heb 6:4–6).

Why do the disciples need to hear that they are unable to follow Jesus (13:33, 36)?[26] Why does Jesus allow Peter and the disciples to have the painful experience of denying/deserting Jesus? It is for the same reason, to let them know that the journey of following Jesus is impossible in their own ability. Their overconfidence (Matt 26:35) is futile and even dangerous for the journey of following Jesus, and thus it needs to be removed from the hearts of all the disciples, so that they may finish the race of following Jesus on the basis of what Jesus provides them.[27] The possibility is not in them. The ability is not in them. The supernatural divine intervention from Jesus and the Father has to come upon them.

Why does Jesus say to his disciples the same words that he told the Jews? Previously, Jesus told the Jews twice that they could not come to where Jesus was going (7:34; 8:21). The wordings in 7:34 and 8:21 spoken to the Jews and 13:33 to the disciples are exactly the same.

7:34 ὅπου εἰμὶ ἐγὼ ὑμεῖς οὐ δύνασθε ἐλθεῖν.

8:21 ὅπου ἐγὼ ὑπάγω ὑμεῖς οὐ δύνασθε ἐλθεῖν.

13:33 ὅπου ἐγὼ ὑπάγω ὑμεῖς οὐ δύνασθε ἐλθεῖν.

---

25. Bultmann, *John*, 597.

26. What Jesus says to Peter in 13:36 is "valid for all" the disciples as it is so in 14:1–4. Bultmann, *John*, 597; Bruner, *John*, 807.

27. Brown, *John*, 2:616; Ridderbos, *John*, 478. Carson (*John*, 486) calls it "a certain haughty independence."

HUMAN INABILITY; DIVINE ABILITY (13:21—14:3)

7:34 Where I am, you cannot come.

8:21 Where I am going, you cannot come.

13:33 Where I am going, you cannot come.

It is to let the disciples know that all human beings are the same in their spiritual ability in the sense that no one is capable enough to follow Jesus and reach where the Father is.[28] Are the disciples different from the Jews in their innate ability in terms of following Jesus? Were they born with spiritually superior DNA in their genes to be capable to follow Jesus? No, of course not. "The disciples must not suppose that they are better than the Jews."[29] All humans are the same in this sense, whether they are the Jews or the disciples (cf. Rom 3:9, 23; 11:32). All are unable to follow Jesus in their own inherent ability. Both John (1:13; 3:3, 5) and Paul (Rom 3:10-12; Eph 2:1; Col 2:13) give enough witnesses to the spiritual impotence of all humankind just as it is confirmed by Jesus' statement in the Synoptics (Matt 19:26; Mark 10:27)[30] as discussed in chapter 3 of the present study.[31] This is the predicament of the spiritual condition of humanity (including the followers of Jesus) to be taken care of by Jesus.

In interpreting the text 13:31–38, scholars have paid attention to this important spiritual point by naming it as spiritual incompetence,[32] weakness,[33] powerlessness,[34] impossibility,[35] or inability.[36] Barrett indicates that following Jesus is not possible by "a simple human possibility, waiting only upon a human decision" just "like entering the kingdom of God" (3:3–8) is impossible in human power and ability. Lincoln, in commenting on 13:36–38, remarks that here Jesus "focuses on Peter's present inability" in following him.[37] Bruner submits the same point that the access to God, i.e., following Jesus to the place where the Father is, is "utterly beyond all human

---

28. "We disciples, too, are deeply needy human beings, no less than the rest of the human race." Bruner, *John*, 794.

29. Barrett, *John*, 451.

30. Matt 19:26 παρὰ ἀνθρώποις τοῦτο ἀδύνατόν ἐστιν, παρὰ δὲ θεῷ πάντα δυνατά. Mark 10:27 παρὰ ἀνθρώποις ἀδύνατον, ἀλλ' οὐ παρὰ θεῷ· πάντα γὰρ δυνατὰ παρὰ τῷ θεῷ.

31. Also the Old Testament exposes the miserable spiritual inability of humanity in Gen 6:5; Ps 14:1–3; 53:1–3; Jer 17:9.

32. Bruner, *John*, 793.

33. Keener, *John*, 2:928; Carson, *John*, 486; Brown, *John*, 2:616.

34. Ridderbos, *John*, 479.

35. Segovia, *The Farewell*, 59; Bruner, *John*, 804.

36. Lincoln, *John*, 388; Ridderbos, *John*, 478.

37. Barrett, *John*, 453.

and even beyond all spiritual competence."[38] "[D]isciples are unable to get to Jesus, and, so, to God *on their own* or automatically."[39] Bruner continues that because "we are all hopeless creatures, disciples included," the disciples and the readers need to learn first of all that where Jesus is going we all are utterly unable to follow him on our own.[40]

Then, the next question is, what is it that makes the disciples of spiritual impossibility eventually able to follow Jesus (13:36) despite their inability?

C. What Makes Them Able to Follow (ἀκολουθεῖν)

The present text 13:21—14:3 does not end with just letting the readers know the spiritual inability in following Jesus in their own power and ability. Starting with the true recognition and honest acknowledgement of inability, one can take the journey of following Jesus on the foundation of the true and authentic source of power. When the disciples come to realize their own powerlessness in following Jesus and thus are deeply troubled in their hearts (14:1), Jesus presents that which will enable them to follow Jesus to where he is going. What is it that will enable the disciples of spiritual impossibility to follow Jesus and reach the final place where he is going, to the Father? It will be explored in two ways: First, by considering the larger literary context; second, by investigating the remaining portion (14:1–3) of the current research text.

First, it can be found in the rest of the Johannine Gospel as the larger context that follows the current text 13:21—14:3. What happens between νῦν (now) and ὕστερον (later), between "You are unable to follow me" (13:33, 36–37) and "Follow me" (21:19)?[41] In chapters 14-20 of the Fourth Gospel, Jesus' death and resurrection takes place (chapters 18–20) and the coming of the Holy Spirit, the Advocate is promised to the disciples (14:16–18, 26; 15:26–27; 16:5–15). Only when their sin is atoned for by the Lamb of God (1:29, 36; 1 John 2:2; 3:5; Rev 1:5), and only when the power of Satan and the power of the world is defeated by Jesus' resurrection and

38. Bruner, *John*, 794.
39. Ibid.
40. Ibid.

41. Cf. By interpreting that "ὕστερον implies that Peter first must become mature," Bultmann (*John*, 598) focuses on the need for growth of Peter's faith, which can be done by the "attainment of the decisive knowledge of faith." No one would deny the need for growth of Peter's faith in and knowledge of Jesus. However, there are more important and essential works that have to be done for Peter and the disciples from Jesus' end as the Savior and Lord, which is the absolutely critical factor that will enable them to follow Jesus.

HUMAN INABILITY; DIVINE ABILITY (13:21—14:3)

thus they are liberated from the grip of the death, will the disciples be delivered from spiritual inability and become able to follow Jesus in his going to the Father.[42] It is by the power of the atonement of Jesus and the enabling might of the Holy Spirit which will be granted them through the death and resurrection.[43] That which makes the life of following Jesus possible for the disciples despite their spiritual incompetence is the continuing appropriation of the redemptive work of Jesus by the Holy Spirit that comes from the Father and the Son.

Second, the last portion of the current research text 14:1-3 explicitly states that the entity, which makes the spiritually impotent disciples finally come to where Jesus goes, is the direct and personal work of Jesus that he will take them to himself and to the Father, so that they may be with him where he is (14:3). It is not what the disciples must do. In the matter of following Jesus to where he goes, there is nothing the disciples can contribute. What they need to do is only to believe (πιστεύετε εἰς τὸν θεὸν καὶ εἰς ἐμὲ πιστεύετε, 14:1). Jesus does everything for them (πάλιν ἔρχομαι καὶ παραλήμψομαι ὑμᾶς πρὸς ἐμαυτόν, ἵνα ὅπου εἰμὶ ἐγὼ καὶ ὑμεῖς ἦτε, 14:3). What they need to do is "to believe" in Jesus and the Father.

This essential factor that makes it possible for the disciples to follow Jesus to where he goes can be explained in another way by comparing Judas and Peter (and the disciples) in 13:21—14:3.

---

42. Brown, *John*, 2:616; Ridderbos, *John*, 479.

43. Barrett, *John*, 453. Just as the Holy Spirit was the power source for Jesus' Messianic life and ministry (3:34; cf. 1:33; Luke 3:16; Acts 1:5, 8), the followers of Jesus are in absolute need of being enabled by the same Spirit.

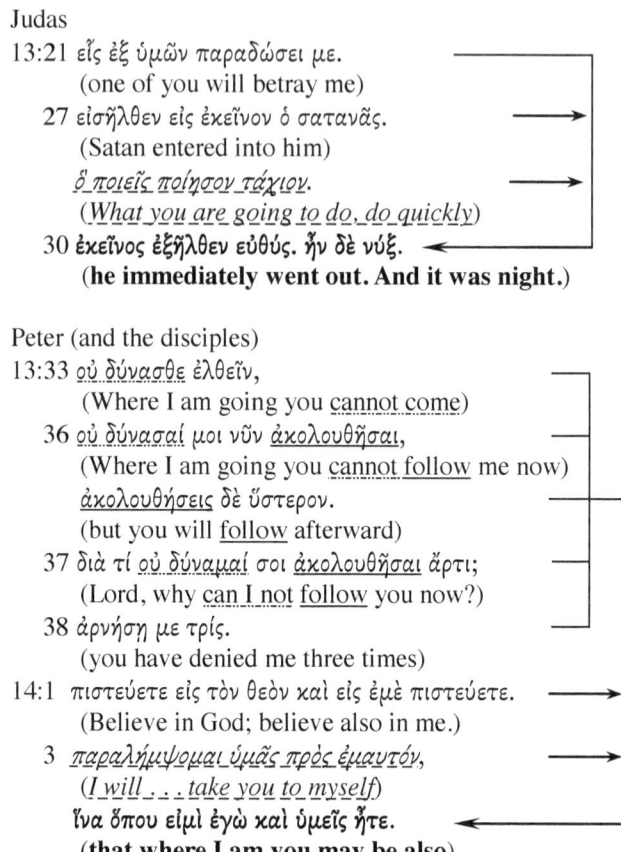

One disciple betrays Jesus (13:21); the other denies him (13:38). One ends his life with entering into the darkness (13:30; cf. 3:19, Luke 22:53) "symbolic of Satanic darkness";[44] the other ends with entering into the place where Jesus is (14:3). What brings in this difference? It depends on whether Jesus leaves them alone to act as they wish or continues upholding them. When Judas refuses the token of Jesus' love signified in giving the piece of bread,[45] Jesus leaves him to do quickly what he is going to do (ὃ ποιεῖς ποίησον τάχιον, 13:27). When Jesus lets him act in his own free will,[46] Judas

44. Brown, *An Introduction to the New Testament*, 352.

45. Bruner (*John*, 780) says that Judas went out into the darkness while "the Lord's gift bread" was still in his hand.

46. For discussion on the relation between divine sovereignty and human responsibility in the matter of Judas' betrayal and entering into the darkness of Satan, refer to Carson, *Divine Sovereignty and Human Responsibility*, 130–32. Carson remarks, "In the

under the influence of Satan takes the road from which he can never return. His life of following Jesus ends up miscarried. He went into the final place, the realm of Satan, which is signified by darkness (13:30).

Judas	Peter (and the disciples)
One of you will betray me (13:21)	You cannot follow me (13:33, 36); Peter will deny Jesus (13:38)
He refuses the token of love; and thus, Satan enters into him (13:27)	Jesus directs the disciples to believe in God and him (14:1)
Jesus lets him do as he wants (13:27)	*Jesus takes them to himself where he is (14:3)*
He went into the darkness of Satan (13:30)	**They will be with Jesus where he is (14:3)**

The reason Peter and the other disciples, despite the fact that they are no different than Judas in human ability and nature, can complete the journey of following Jesus, finally arriving at where Jesus is to be with him, is that Jesus does not leave them alone to live in their spiritual inability. Jesus died and was resurrected for them to bring them newness of life, and more importantly, he comes and takes them to himself where he is (14:3), not leaving them as orphans (14:18). As the result, they come to the final place where Jesus is (παραλήμψομαι ὑμᾶς πρὸς ἐμαυτόν, ἵνα ὅπου εἰμὶ ἐγὼ καὶ ὑμεῖς ἦτε, 14:3). The essential factor, to reiterate it, is whether Jesus leaves them alone to act according to their own wishes or takes them to the Father in his grace. The difference lies between ὃ ποιεῖς ποίησον τάχιον ("Do quickly what you are going to do," 13:27) and παραλήμψομαι ὑμᾶς πρὸς ἐμαυτόν ("I will take you to myself," 14:3).

The decisive act of Jesus for Peter and the disciples is portrayed by the term παραλαμβάνω (to take with). It is the same act of taking his own to Jesus himself at his *parousia* (Matt 24:39–40).[47] It is like the act that Joseph as the bridegroom "took (παραλαμβάνω) Mary home with him as his wife"

---

case of both Caiaphas and Judas, therefore, divine ultimacy even behind evil actions is presupposed. But divine ultimacy operates in some mysterious way so that human responsibility is in no way mitigated, while the divine being is in no way tarnished. In particular, Judas is responsible even when Satan is using him; but over both stands the sovereignty of God (132)."

47. Matt 24:39-40 "... so too will be the coming of the Son of Man. Then two will be in the field; one will be taken and one will be left." οὕτως ἔσται [καὶ] ἡ παρουσία τοῦ υἱοῦ τοῦ ἀνθρώπου. τότε δύο ἔσονται ἐν τῷ ἀγρῷ, εἷς παραλαμβάνεται καὶ εἷς ἀφίεται.

(Matt 1:20–24). The vital factor that changes the disciples' spiritual inability to follow Jesus to a new freedom to go where he goes is that Jesus will take (παραλήμψομαι) them to himself.

When Jesus leaves one alone to live in one's nature and ability, one is unable to reach the place where the Father is. Rather, one's journey of following Jesus will be aborted, and one will end in the darkness. Only when Jesus keeps sustaining and leading his followers by his mighty hand (10:28, 29), can they complete the journey of following Jesus and arrive at the place where the Father is (17:24).

That the power is not in the followers, but absolutely lies in Jesus' act and divine intervention is expressed by Jesus' exhortation, πιστεύετε εἰς τὸν θεὸν καὶ εἰς ἐμὲ πιστεύετε ("Believe in God, believe also in me," 14:1). Why does Jesus command them to believe in God and in him? To believe in God and Jesus presupposes the power is not in humans, but in God and Jesus.[48] "To believe in God and Jesus" begins with the humble acknowledgement of self-inability in their spiritual bankruptcy (Matt 5:3) and consequent utter dependence on God and Jesus. By commanding the disciples to believe in God and him, Jesus not only reaffirms the innate inability of the disciples, but also directs them to tap into the right source which they must utterly depend upon. The command of "Believe in God and believe in me" is a condensed expression of "It is God and I who will make you come to where I am. What you need to do is to believe. What you are unable to do, I will do for you."[49]

As discussed, the life of following Jesus is something beyond what the followers do for Jesus (although it is an important part of the journey of

---

48. "To believe" (πιστεύω) presupposes the incapability of the one who believes, as a spiritually bankrupt. Because one is absolutely unable to manage one's own life, one depends on someone else who is capable. Because one is utterly incapable of solving one's own predicament, one *believes in* someone else who is mightier than one and can save one from it. "To believe" begins with sheer recognition and admission of one's utter inability. Therefore, when it is commanded πιστεύετε εἰς τὸν θεὸν καὶ εἰς ἐμὲ πιστεύετε to the disciples, it conveys twofold significance: One, they are unable, so they must depend on God and Jesus; and two, what they are unable to do, God and Jesus will do for them. The command πιστεύετε εἰς τὸν θεὸν καὶ εἰς ἐμὲ πιστεύετε turns the eyes of the disciples from the despair of their total inability to the divine ability, from what they are unable to do to what Jesus and the Father will do for them.

49. The kindred idea is implied in the fact that Jesus prayed for Simon Peter (Luke 22:32 NET, "but I have prayed for you," ἐγὼ δὲ ἐδεήθην περὶ σοῦ) and for the disciples (17:24, Πάτερ, ὃ δέδωκάς μοι, θέλω ἵνα ὅπου εἰμὶ ἐγὼ κἀκεῖνοι ὦσιν μετ' ἐμοῦ). That Jesus prays to God that the disciples may come to where he goes means that they are not able to come to the place where he goes in their own ability, but it is God who will make it happen.

HUMAN INABILITY; DIVINE ABILITY (13:21—14:3)

following Jesus in this life).[50] Following Jesus is the life that ultimately aims at entering into the relationship of Jesus with the Father in glory (17:24).[51] No one is able to reach there. No one is able to come where Jesus goes to, unless Jesus takes him/her to where the Father is, just as no one is able to come to the Son unless the Father draws (6:44).[52]

Because Jesus who came from the Father takes his followers to the Father, their lives do not end in failures or darkness, but arrive in the glorious presence of the Son with the Father. The ability is not in human beings. It is utterly of the Father who sent Jesus for them and Jesus who takes them to the Father. The Jesus, who calls his followers to himself (1:43), leads ahead of them (10:4), prays for them (chapter 17), and protects them holding them tightly in his mighty grip (10:28, 29) that their journey may not fail, will in his grace, authority, and power take them "to himself" (πρὸς ἐμαυτόν, 14:3) to be with him in the glorious presence of the Father.[53]

The divine hand of drawing people to Jesus (6:44) is not only what humans need at the beginning of the journey of following Jesus, but also it is indispensable throughout the entire journey in every step of the way, to the very end until it reaches the final destination of their calling.

The one who calls his followers does not leave them alone to follow him on their own. The one who calls knows their powerlessness (13:38; cf. 10:14, 27; 21:17). Therefore, the one who calls dies for them (10:11, 15), comes to them and leads them by the Spirit (14:18), and takes them to himself where he is (14:3). This is the only true and authentic foundation on which the journey of following Jesus is to be established. This is the power source by which they can follow Jesus, not falling away in the middle entangled by their spiritual impotence. The life of following Jesus is launched by his gracious calling, sustained by his power and authority, and will be completed by the work of his mighty hand. The life of following Jesus is entirely under the theology of grace, from its beginning to completion. The text 13:21–14:3 draws the readers to this profound and gracious truth, so that the readers may experience this deep Spirituality in the journey of

---

50. What the followers must do in the life of following Jesus is considered by examining the words διακονέω and διάκονος in the previous chapter of this study where 12:26 is investigated. It will be further discussed in the study of 21:1–19 because that is the text where what the followers must do is dealt with.

51. 17:24 Πάτερ, ὃ δέδωκάς μοι, θέλω ἵνα ὅπου εἰμὶ ἐγὼ κἀκεῖνοι ὦσιν μετ' ἐμοῦ, ἵνα θεωρῶσιν τὴν δόξαν τὴν ἐμήν, ἣν δέδωκάς μοι ὅτι ἠγάπησάς με πρὸ καταβολῆς κόσμου.

52. 6:44 οὐδεὶς δύναται ἐλθεῖν πρός με ἐὰν μὴ ὁ πατὴρ ὁ πέμψας με ἑλκύσῃ αὐτόν.

53. According to Bruner (*John*, 811), the reason Jesus calls the place "where I am," "to myself (14:3)" is because the essence of what is called heaven is "most simply, the real presence of Jesus Christ himself *with* his people. This is the next life's most simple, compact, intimate, and adequate definition."

following Jesus, and though rough and bumpy the road of the journey may be, they may walk in great assurance on the authentic foundation and firm faith in Jesus and the Father.

IV. Conclusion

In search for the Spirituality of following Jesus uniquely communicated by 13:21—14:3, we have taken three steps. First, it is observed that unlike the Synoptics the discipleship term ἀκολουθεῖν (to follow) appears within the account of Peter's denial prediction and associated with οὐ δύναμαι (not able) in the Fourth Gospel. Second, as the literary and theological context of 13:36–38, the pericope of 13:21—14:3 is investigated by discourse analysis and the semantic network of correlated vocabularies are presented. Finally, as the main body, the implications of following Jesus embedded in 13:21—14:3 are considered. The theological implication communicated by the association of ἀκολουθεῖν with two human failures (Judas and Peter: παραδώσει με and ἀρνήσῃ με) and the inability (οὐ δύναμαι) of the disciples is that human beings, including the willing disciples, are unable to follow Jesus to reach the place where he is with the Father. Only by the divine work (in his power and grace) are the followers of Jesus able to come to where the Father is with the Son.

By arranging the employments of the discipleship term ἀκολουθεῖν within the immediate literary context where Peter, trusting in his own ability (13:37; Matt 26:33, 35; Luke 22:33), miserably ends up with completely denying Jesus and even knowing him (13:38; cf. 18:15–18, 25–27), together with the account of another disciple's failure who ends up with selling off Jesus and walking into the dominion of the darkness which is signified by night (13:21, 27, 30; cf. 18:3–5; Matt 27:3–5), the fourth evangelist leads his readers to understand the following implications: (i) that in their own ability humans are unable to follow Jesus and come to where he is with the Father; (ii) that which makes humans able to follow Jesus and enter the place where Jesus is with the Father is only the redeeming work of Jesus, its appropriation by the Holy Spirit, his continuing leading them through the Spirit, and his act of taking them to the place where he is with the Father.

Following Jesus is not what humans can do in their own will and ability, but possible because Jesus who calls them (1:43; 21:19) also dies for them to redeem them (10:11, 15), sends the divine Helper for them (14:16; 15:26; 16:13), protects them by the mighty power (10:28, 29), leads them onward walking before them (10:4), and will take them to where he goes (14:3). The movement of following Jesus is the journey that is possible by the grace and power of the Father and the Son. That is why Jesus commands his followers to believe in God and in Jesus (14:1).

The text 13:21—14:3 invites the readers to the Spirituality of humble recognition of human inability in following Jesus. With the existential recognition of their utter spiritual inability to reach where the Father is (where Jesus goes to), the readers are drawn to the Spirituality of absolute reliance on Jesus' redemptive work and the consequent gift of the Spirit (as presented in the larger context of chapters 14–20), and Jesus' act of taking them to where the Father is (as presented in 14:3 as an immediate context). In this unique Johannine text 13:21—14:3, the readers are attracted to a very distinguishing Spirituality of following Jesus that those who recognize that they are unable to follow Jesus, can follow him successfully by the power and work of the Father and the Son and the Spirit.

CHAPTER 10

Shepherd as the One Shepherded in Love (21:1–19)

FINALLY THE CALL TO follow Jesus, "Follow me" (ἀκολούθει μοι, 21:19), is given to Simon Peter in the epilogue which is the conclusion[1] of the Fourth Gospel.[2] In the first chapter of the Gospel, Simon was introduced to Jesus by his brother (1:41), and a new name Cephas (Peter) was given to him by Jesus (1:42). Yet, the Gospel does not use the discipleship term ἀκολουθεῖν (to follow) for Peter at the first encounter with Jesus although Jesus recognized him by renaming him. In the sixth chapter of the Gospel where Peter utters the important christological confession to Jesus, his remark does not receive any special attention from Jesus, and the call to follow Jesus is not given to him (6:68–69).[3]

In the thirteenth chapter where Peter passionately expresses his willingness to lay down his life for Jesus (13:37), Jesus does not say ἀκολούθει μοι to him either, but on the contrary to Peter's willingness to follow, Jesus says that he is unable to follow Jesus (13:33, 37). In the eighteenth chapter

---

1. "John 21 should be read as the conclusion of John 1–20 since it builds on earlier sections of the gospel and completes and resolves themes and plot issues that are unresolved in John 1–20." Culpepper, "Designs for the Church," 402.

Over against the view that chapter 21 is an appendix added later (Bultmann, *John*, 700; Barrett, *Essays*, 159–60; Schnackenburg, *John*, 3:350), for more arguments on the function of John 21 as the conclusion of the Fourth Gospel and its relation with the rest of the Gospel, see Minear, "The Original Function of John 21," 85–98; Beasley-Murray, *John*, 395–98; Breck, "John 21: Appendix, Epilogue or Conclusion?," 27–49; Ellis, "The Authenticity of John 21," 17–25; Franzmann and Klinger, "The Call Stories of John 1 and John 21," 7–15; Gaventa, "The Archive of Excess," 240–52; Brodie, *John*, 574–82; Bauckham, "The 153 fish and the unity," 77–88.

2. For discussions on Peter in the Fourth Gospel, refer to Droge, "The Status of Peter," 307–11; Domeris, "The Confession of Peter," 155–67; Blaine Jr., *Peter in the Gospel of John*; Culpepper, "Peter as Exemplary Disciple," 165–78.

3. 6:68–69 ἀπεκρίθη αὐτῷ Σίμων Πέτρος· κύριε, πρὸς τίνα ἀπελευσόμεθα; ῥήματα ζωῆς αἰωνίου ἔχεις, καὶ ἡμεῖς πεπιστεύκαμεν καὶ ἐγνώκαμεν ὅτι σὺ εἶ ὁ ἅγιος τοῦ θεοῦ.

the term ἀκολουθεῖν appears in a literal sense (18:15) for Simon's movement after Jesus at a distance, yet the account does not portray any positive outcome but ends with Peter's denial of Jesus (18:16–18, 25–27). Unlike the Synoptics where the term appears to describe Peter's commencement of following Jesus at the early stage of his faith journey (Mark 1:16–18),[4] the Fourth Gospel has reserved the use of the term ἀκολουθεῖν in a positive way and in the form of the calling "Follow me" until it reaches the closing chapter. In 21:15–19 the call ἀκολούθει μοι is given to Peter at last.

The text 21:1–19 contributes to the development of the Johannine Spirituality of following Jesus in the sense that it communicates both aspects of following Jesus, which are the aspect of what Jesus does for his followers and that which the disciples must do as Jesus' followers. It also communicates the centrality of love as the nucleus of Jesus' acts for his followers and their acts for him (and thus presents "love" as the central driving force of the Spirituality of following Jesus); the unique aspects of following Jesus by the "where" motif in contrast between ὅπου ἤθελες ("wherever you wished") and ὅπου οὐ θέλεις ("where you do not wish," 21:18); and an unparalleled idea of following Jesus by the fact that ἀκολούθει μοι (21:19) is given by the risen Jesus.

To put these points in question form, the text 21:15–19 imparts the following five points. One, what does Jesus do to recover the failed disciple so that he can follow him? How does Jesus restore the disciple, and enable him to follow Jesus anew? Two, what must the disciple do in the course of following Jesus after Jesus' ascension? What are the main contents of the life of following Jesus after Jesus' departure? Three, what is at the root of Jesus' act of rehabilitating his failed disciple? What is at the root of the disciple's commitment to the mission given by Jesus? What is the core energy that drives him to live a new life as a Jesus' follower? Four, what implication of following Jesus is conveyed by the "where" motif? Fifth, what distinctive aspect of the life of following Jesus is intimated by the fact that the call ἀκολούθει μοι is given by the risen Lord?

In the quest of the Spirituality of following Jesus communicated in 21:1–19 with the five questions, two steps will be taken. First, the linguistic and semantic constituents (images, terms, and motifs) correlated with ἀκολουθεῖν within 21:1–19 will be identified and presented by discourse analysis. Second, some unique aspects of the Spirituality of following Jesus that the fourth evangelist intends to communicate to his readers will

4. Mark 1:16–18 Καὶ παράγων παρὰ τὴν θάλασσαν τῆς Γαλιλαίας εἶδεν Σίμωνα καὶ Ἀνδρέαν τὸν ἀδελφὸν Σίμωνος ἀμφιβάλλοντας ἐν τῇ θαλάσσῃ· ἦσαν γὰρ ἁλιεῖς. καὶ εἶπεν αὐτοῖς ὁ Ἰησοῦς· δεῦτε ὀπίσω μου, καὶ ποιήσω ὑμᾶς γενέσθαι ἁλιεῖς ἀνθρώπων. καὶ εὐθὺς ἀφέντες τὰ δίκτυα ἠκολούθησαν αὐτῷ.

be explored by probing the semantic relations of the constituents with ἀκολουθεῖν.

I. Linguistic Constituents and Their Relations

There are reasons why 21:15–19 has to be investigated together with 21:1–14 as one semantic pericope. First, the process of Peter's rehabilitation to discipleship starts in verses 1–14 with Jesus' revealing himself by the events of catching the fish and the meal, and finishes with the dialogue between Jesus and Peter in verses 15–19.[5] As Brown remarks, verses 1–14 are incomplete without verses 15–19 for the latter concludes what is started in the former.[6] Second, the opening temporal phrase of verse 15, "When they had finished breakfast (ἀριστάω)" (cf. 21:12, δεῦτε ἀριστήσατε), invites the readers to read the text 21:15–19 in the backdrop of what has happened in 21:1–14.[7] Third, Keener also connects the two narratives by the "feeding" motif by subtitling 21:9–14 "Jesus Feeds His Sheep"[8] and 21:15–17 "Feed My Sheep," and further commenting, "Just as Jesus fed his disciples here (21:9–14), so Peter is to feed them after Jesus departs."[9]

The following discourse analysis presents the main linguistic constituents and their semantic relations within 21:1–19.

---

5. "It is better to speak of rehabilitation to discipleship than to apostleship: he was a disciple before; now he is rehabilitated as a disciple . . ." Brown, *John*, 2:1111. There is ample textual evidence that the focus of 21:1–19 is on the restoration of Peter as a disciple: the charcoal fire setting is for Peter (21:9; cf. 18:18); the scene of the catch of fish is reminiscent of the Lukan call of Peter (Luke 5:1–11); Peter's actions are highlighted with details (21:3, 7, 11); the dialogue is between Jesus and Peter (21:15–19); the call of "Follow Me" is given to Peter (21:19, 22). Although in verses 1–14 Jesus deals with seven disciples together, Peter is at the center of both scenes of catching fish and the meal.

6. Brown also concludes in favor of the argument that there is unity between verses 1–14 and 15–19. Brown, *John*, 2:1082–84, 1110.

7. Carson also sees it as a connection between verses 1–14 and 15–19. Carson, *John*, 675.

8. Keener, *John*, 2:1230.

9. Ibid., 2:1234.

SHEPHERD AS THE ONE SHEPHERDED IN LOVE (21:1–19)   199

Semantic Networks of 21:1–19

¹ Μετὰ ταῦτα ἐφανέρωσεν ἑαυτὸν πάλιν ὁ Ἰησοῦς τοῖς μαθηταῖς …
  ἐφανέρωσεν δὲ οὕτως.
³ … ὑπάγω ἁλιεύειν. … καὶ ἐν ἐκείνῃ τῇ νυκτὶ ἐπίασαν οὐδέν. ────┐(a)
  ⁴ … οὐ μέντοι ᾔδεισαν οἱ μαθηταὶ ὅτι Ἰησοῦς ἐστιν. ────(b)
⁵ … παιδία, μή τι προσφάγιον ἔχετε; ἀπεκρίθησαν αὐτῷ· οὔ.
⁶ … καὶ οὐκέτι αὐτὸ ἑλκύσαι ἴσχυον ἀπὸ τοῦ πλήθους τῶν ἰχθύων. ────(a')   A-i
  ⁷ … ὁ κύριός ἐστιν. (b')
⁸ … σύροντες τὸ δίκτυον τῶν ἰχθύων. ────(a')
  ⁹ … ἀνθρακιὰν κειμένην καὶ ὀψάριον ἐπικείμενον καὶ ἄρτον.
¹¹ … Σίμων Πέτρος καὶ εἵλκυσεν τὸ δίκτυον εἰς τὴν γῆν
  μεστὸν ἰχθύων μεγάλων ἑκατὸν πεντήκοντα τριῶν· ────(a')
  καὶ τοσούτων ὄντων οὐκ ἐσχίσθη τὸ δίκτυον. ────(a')
¹² λέγει αὐτοῖς ὁ Ἰησοῦς· **δεῦτε ἀριστήσατε.**   ────── B
  … εἰδότες ὅτι ὁ κύριός ἐστιν. (b")   A-ii
¹³ ἔρχεται Ἰησοῦς καὶ λαμβάνει τὸν ἄρτον καὶ δίδωσιν αὐτοῖς,
  καὶ τὸ ὀψάριον ὁμοίως.
¹⁴ … ἐφανερώθη Ἰησοῦς τοῖς μαθηταῖς ἐγερθεὶς ἐκ νεκρῶν.

¹⁵ Ὅτε οὖν **ἠρίστησαν**
  λέγει τῷ Σίμωνι Πέτρῳ ὁ Ἰησοῦς·
  Σίμων Ἰωάννου, ἀγαπᾷς με πλέον τούτων;   B'
  λέγει αὐτῷ· ναὶ κύριε, σὺ οἶδας ὅτι φιλῶ σε.
            λέγει αὐτῷ· βόσκε τὰ ἀρνία μου.
¹⁶ λέγει αὐτῷ πάλιν δεύτερον·
  Σίμων Ἰωάννου, ἀγαπᾷς με;   B'
  λέγει αὐτῷ· ναὶ κύριε, σὺ οἶδας ὅτι φιλῶ σε.
            λέγει αὐτῷ· ποίμαινε τὰ πρόβατά μου.   C-i
¹⁷ λέγει αὐτῷ τὸ τρίτον·
  Σίμων Ἰωάννου, φιλεῖς με;
  ἐλυπήθη ὁ Πέτρος ὅτι εἶπεν αὐτῷ τὸ τρίτον· φιλεῖς με;   B'
  καὶ λέγει αὐτῷ· κύριε, πάντα σὺ οἶδας,
            σὺ γινώσκεις ὅτι φιλῶ σε.
            λέγει αὐτῷ· … · βόσκε τὰ πρόβατά μου.

¹⁸ ἀμὴν ἀμὴν λέγω σοι,
  ὅτε ἦς νεώτερος, ἐζώννυες σεαυτὸν καὶ περιεπάτεις ὅπου ἤθελες·
  ὅταν δὲ γηράσῃς, ἐκτενεῖς τὰς χεῖράς σου,
            καὶ ἄλλος σε ζώσει καὶ οἴσει ὅπου οὐ θέλεις.   C-ii
¹⁹ τοῦτο δὲ εἶπεν σημαίνων ποίῳ θανάτῳ δοξάσει τὸν θεόν.

  καὶ τοῦτο εἰπὼν λέγει αὐτῷ·
            ἀκολούθει μοι.
            C

Semantic Networks of 21:1–19 (ESV)

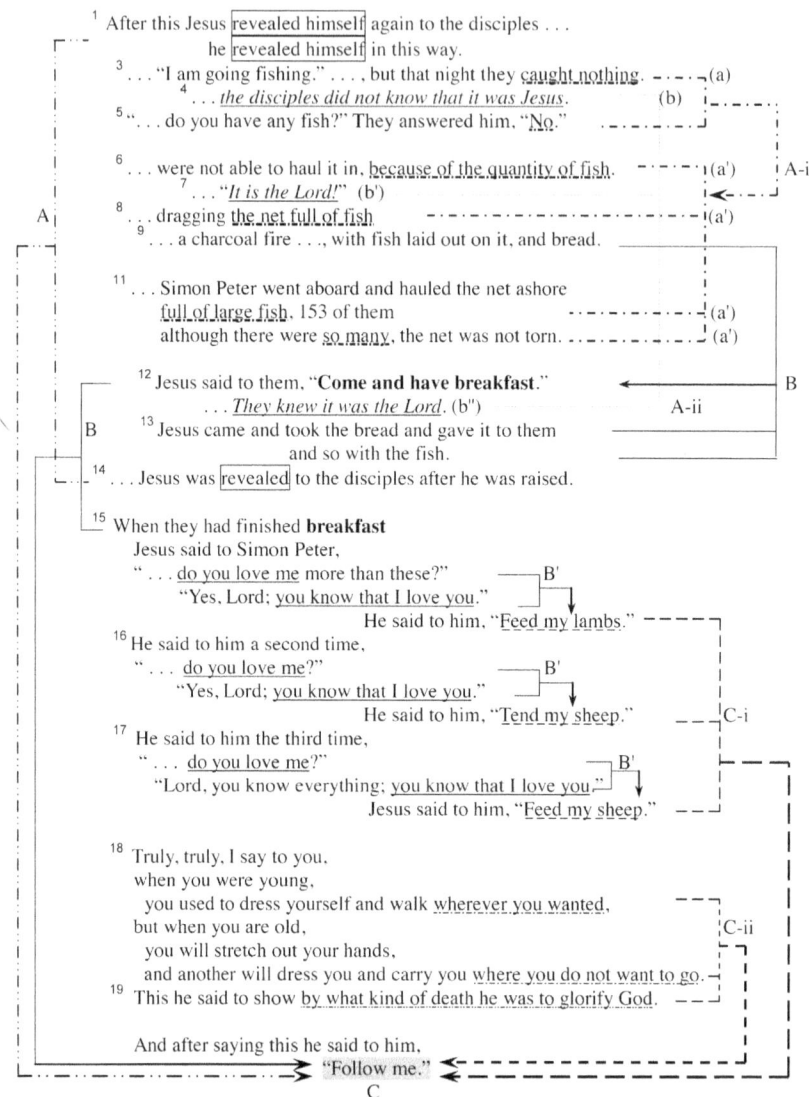

The noticeable vocabularies and motifs that comprise 21:1–19 are as follows. First, the motif of Jesus' manifestation (A): The verb φανερόω (to reveal), which appears twice in verse 1 (ἐφανέρωσεν ἑαυτὸν πάλιν ὁ Ἰησοῦς τοῖς μαθηταῖς; ἐφανέρωσεν δὲ οὕτως) and once again in verse 14 (ἐφανερώθη Ἰησοῦς τοῖς μαθηταῖς), draws the readers' attention to Jesus' appearance, not as simply coming to the disciples, but as an act of "revealing" himself for a special purpose.

Second, from emptiness to abundance (A-i): The fact that the disciples' effort to catch fish was futile, catching nothing (a) over the night is expressed in verses 3 (ἐπίασαν οὐδέν) and 5 (οὔ). In comparison to the emptiness (a) of the disciples' endeavor, fullness and abundance (a') in catching fish in Jesus' presence with them is emphatically reiterated by four different phrases (καὶ οὐκέτι αὐτὸ ἑλκύσαι ἴσχυον ἀπὸ τοῦ πλήθους τῶν ἰχθύων, 21:6; τὸ δίκτυον τῶν ἰχθύων, 21:8; μεστὸν ἰχθύων μεγάλων, 21:11a; καὶ τοσούτων ὄντων, 21:11b).

Third, recognition motif (A-ii): As the result of catching fish in miraculous fashion, the disciples who previously were not able to recognize Jesus (b), now come to recognize him (b'), and further come to know (οἶδα, 21:4, 12) that he is the Lord (b") when they are invited to the meal.

Fourth, banquet motif (B): Just as the motif of "from emptiness to abundance" in Jesus' presence is emphasized in the text by various expressions, the motif of having a meal with Jesus, which is prepared by Jesus, draws the readers' attention by describing it in many details—charcoal fire as the setting; that bread and fish were on it; that Jesus invited them to the meal; and that Jesus gave them the bread and fish (ἀνθρακιὰν κειμένην καὶ ὀψάριον ἐπικείμενον καὶ ἄρτον, 21:9; δεῦτε ἀριστήσατε, 21:12; ἔρχεται Ἰησοῦς καὶ λαμβάνει τὸν ἄρτον καὶ δίδωσιν αὐτοῖς καὶ τὸ ὀψάριον ὁμοίως, 21:13; ὅτε οὖν ἠρίστησαν, 21:15).

Fifth, love confession and relationship (B'), and shepherding mission (C-i): Three sets of dialogue after the meal between Jesus and Peter (21:15–17), in which Jesus purposefully repeated the same question and the same charge, stand at the center of the pericope. Here the important motifs of love and the disciple's mission of feeding Jesus' sheep are highlighted, and do not allow the readers' attention to move away hurriedly, but rather call for lingering over them in serious reflection.

Sixth, the "where" motif and the path of death (C-ii): In Jesus' prediction of Peter's future life (death), the "where" motif appears in contrast of two opposite patterns (21:18): "where you wished" (ὅπου ἤθελες) versus "where you do not wish" (ὅπου οὐ θέλεις). Here again we see that ἀκολουθεῖν is associated with the ὅπου motif as it has appeared in previous research pericopes of this study.

Seventh, at the end of the pericope as its pinnacle (C), Jesus gives the grand call, "Follow me" (ἀκολούθει μοι, 21:19). It is this call that powerfully recapitulates the pastoral charge (21:15–17), and concludes the whole purpose for which Jesus has revealed himself to the disciples (21:1–14).

Taken as a whole, all Jesus' actions in the text (revealing himself, helping the disciples to catch fish, preparing the meal, feeding them, and having a conversation) run toward one goal which is to give the call "Follow Me" to all the disciples represented by Simon Peter.[10] And the Jesus who calls the disciples to follow him also explicitly and specifically pronounces the contents of "following" him, which is what to do in "following" him in life and death (21:15–19).

II. Spirituality of Following Jesus implied in 21:1–19

Keeping in mind the motifs and linguistic constituents outlined above, we are going to devote the current investigation to articulating some unique aspects of the Spirituality of following Jesus under the five subheadings: A. Following Jesus and Jesus' Presence and Provision; B. Following Jesus and the Centrality of Love; C. Following Jesus and Feeding his Sheep; D. Following Jesus and the Where Motif; and E. Following Jesus and the Guaranteed Victory.

A. Following Jesus and His Presence and Provision

By denying the Lord Jesus (13:38; 18:17, 25, 27), Peter became like a broken branch, severing himself from the vine (cf. 15:1–8). What is it that brings him back and reunites him to the vine? What is it that leads him to overcome the fatal wound of denying the Lord Jesus and be rehabilitated to function as a faithful follower of Jesus? What is it that restores the failed disciple, Simon Peter, and enables him to follow Jesus anew? We have considered this point in the previous chapter where 13:21–14:3 was dealt with. However, it is necessary to revisit it here because 21:1–19 presents it in a different tone with different vocabularies within a different setting.

In the previous chapter on 13:21–14:3, it is discussed what enables the powerless and incapable disciples to follow Jesus—it is the appropriation of Jesus' redeeming death and resurrection, subsequent coming of the Spirit, and his grand act of taking his own to where he is with the Father. This is articulated in the perspective of the redemptive history.

In the current text of 21:1–19, that which enables the failed disciple to follow Jesus anew is presented within the setting of daily life, to put it another way, in the vocabularies of flesh and blood. They are the wordings of seeing, smelling, touching, eating, and conversing. They are in the actions of throwing and pulling net (21:6, 11), jumping into water (21:7), gathering around foods (21:12), dining together (21:13), and talking and walking with

---

10. Culpepper notes, "Peter is a representative character who dramatically confirms God's forgiving love and defines the connection between love for Jesus and care for the community." Culpepper, "Peter as Exemplary Disciple," 165.

Jesus side by side (21:15–17; cf. 21:20).[11] We will consider what aspects of the Spirituality of following Jesus are implied in the terms: revealing himself, catching many fish, and "Come and have breakfast (21:12)."

1. Revealing Himself (φανερόω)

21:1–14 begins with φανερόω (to manifest, twice in verse 1) and ends with the same term (once in verse 14).[12] The restoration of Simon Peter was possible because there was this act of revealing (φανερόω) himself to the disciple from Jesus' part.

It is not the disciple, who has put himself into the predicament, that restores himself, but Jesus who comes and reveals himself to the failed disciple. If Jesus had not come to him, Simon might have remained for the rest of his life in his failure and unforgettable wound, remaining like a broken branch.[13] To the fallen, Jesus came. To the broken, Jesus revealed (φανερόω) himself. The restoration starts with Jesus' revealing himself (21:1, 14) to him.

As noted by Barrett, φανερόω is a Johannine word (1:31; 2:11; 3:21; 7:4; 9:3; 17:6; 21:1, 4).[14] In 2:11 Jesus revealed (φανερόω) his glory to his first disciples, changing water to vintage wine, and they came to believe in him.[15] In 9:3 Jesus revealed (φανερόω) God's work in the blind man, and consequently the man's life was changed from an incurable condition (9:32) into a man who can see both physically and spiritually, and believe in and worship the Son of Man (9:35–38). As the act of Jesus' revealing (φανερόω) has brought radical changes where human condition is impossible, again by

---

11. Carson, *John*, 675.

12. 21:1 Μετὰ ταῦτα ἐφανέρωσεν ἑαυτὸν πάλιν ὁ Ἰησοῦς τοῖς μαθηταῖς ἐπὶ τῆς θαλάσσης τῆς Τιβεριάδος· ἐφανέρωσεν δὲ οὕτως. 21:14 τοῦτο ἤδη τρίτον ἐφανερώθη Ἰησοῦς τοῖς μαθηταῖς ἐγερθεὶς ἐκ νεκρῶν.

13. Hoskyns comments, "One has betrayed the Lord to death, all, except the Beloved Disciple had fled, and now, at the suggestion of Simon, the seven who remain together go back to their fishing. The scene is one of complete apostasy, and is the fulfilment of xvi. 32." Hoskyns, *The Fourth Gospel*, 552. Brown remarks, "McDowell, pp. 430 ff., argues that the present tense of the verb 'to go' expresses more than momentary intention: Peter is going back to his earlier way of life and will stay with it." Brown, *John*, 2:1068–69. If Hoskyns and McDowell are not utterly incorrect in interpreting the nature of Simon's going fishing in verse 3, his restoration would be impossible if there had not been Jesus' gracious revealing himself to Peter.

14. Barrett, *John*, 578. Among the Synoptic Gospels, the verb appears only in Mark 16:12, 14 for Jesus' manifestation after resurrection (and in 4:22 for another use).

15. Lincoln (*John*, 515) also pays an attention to φανερόω in 21:1, 14 in connection with 2:11, where an abundant supply of wine was just as an abundant supply of fish occurred in the present text.

the act of revealing (φανερόω) a change (by a transforming grace) occurs in the life of the failed disciple Simon Peter, and he is brought back to the privilege of following Jesus. A revolutionary change by the transforming grace is a gift that comes when Jesus reveals (φανερόω) himself to men and women in the midst of their human despair and impossibility.[16] The readers are invited into the live experience (Spirituality) of being radically changed by the transforming grace that comes in Jesus' revealing (φανερόω) presence.

In revealing himself to the disciples, Jesus does two things: helping them to catch fish abundantly and feeding them with a meal.

2. Catching Fish Abundantly

Why does Jesus choose to reveal himself in the particular setting of fishing for this third time manifestation? Why not when the disciples are at the house (20:19, 26) or on the road (Luke 24:13–16, 32)? Why specifically in the situation when they are fishing? Why at the particular moment when all their effort to catch fish have been proven fruitless? What does Jesus want to show to them by the miraculous catch? What does it intimate about the future journey of following Jesus? To what kind of Spirituality of following Jesus does the evangelist invite his readers by the narrative of the abundant catching of fish performed by Jesus for his fruitless followers?

The fourth evangelist is diligent in underlining the contrast between nothingness (οὐδέν) and fullness (πλῆθος, μεστός). As pointed out above, the disciples' effort to catch fish was futile, catching nothing over the whole night (21:3, ἐπίασαν οὐδέν; 21:5, οὔ). When there was no presence of Jesus among them, despite their hard endeavor as skilled fishers, the result was in vain.[17] It intimates that the disciples' effort in their best endeavor would be fruitless if there is no presence of Jesus with them. It is already indicated

---

16. There are more Johannine usages of φανερόω. When Jesus reveals himself, his followers will become like him (1 John 3:2 ἐὰν φανερωθῇ, ὅμοιοι αὐτῷ ἐσόμεθα). The eschatological transformation by the effect of Jesus' revealing himself will happen to his followers (cf. Col 3:4). When Jesus was revealed, the sins of the world were taken away (1 John 3:5 ἐκεῖνος ἐφανερώθη, ἵνα τὰς ἁμαρτίας ἄρῃ), and thus men and women who see his manifestation are freed from the bondage of sin. When Jesus revealed himself, the works of the devil were destroyed (1 John 3:8 εἰς τοῦτο ἐφανερώθη ὁ υἱὸς τοῦ θεοῦ, ἵνα λύσῃ τὰ ἔργα τοῦ διαβόλου), and as the result men and women who put their life in his powerful hands are delivered from the devil, moved into the Son's kingdom (cf. Col 1:13; John 5:24), and come to serve the living God (cf. Luke 1: 74).

17. Lincoln, *John*, 511. "In Jesus' absence the disciples' fishing has met with no success."

in 15:5. The disciples can do nothing (15:5)[18] without Jesus' presence with them, just as "the Son can do nothing on his own" (5:19, 30).[19]

Yet, the narrative does not give the primary focus to the emptiness. The fullness in catching fish with Jesus' presence is more emphasized in the text.[20] The evangelist untiringly employs various phrases to accentuate how abundantly the disciples caught fish (21:6, "there were so many fish"; 21:8, "the net full of fish"; 21:11a, "full of large fish"; 21:11b, "there were so many") when they were in Jesus' presence. Jesus' presence is what brings a radical change to the life of his followers, from nothingness to fullness.[21] Following Jesus through human effort and skill would be ineffective; following Jesus with his personal presence means abundance in results (cf. 10:10; 15:11; 16:24).

By the abundant catching of fish, it is intimated that the disciples are invited to the life of following Jesus in abundance in the coming ministry of leading people to Jesus, and also implicitly predicting that their ministry will be abundant. When they are in the presence of the risen Lord Jesus continually, the abundant outcome in the journey of following Jesus will be their experience. To demonstrate this tangibly and that they may have a foretaste of it, Jesus reveals himself to the empty disciples intentionally in this specific setting of fishing, and leads them to catch abundantly. Jesus' revealing (φανερόω) himself is not only for the restoration of the fallen disciple, but also to show that the restored disciples' journey of following him will be abundant after all. By this narrative of abundant catching of fish, the readers are drawn to the lived experience (Spirituality) of abundance and fruitfulness (21:6, 8, 11; cf. 10:10; 15:16) in the life of following Jesus when they are in his presence and of earnest pursuit of Jesus' presence in their journey.

---

18. 15:5 χωρὶς ἐμοῦ οὐ δύνασθε ποιεῖν οὐδέν.

19. 5:19 οὐ δύναται ὁ υἱὸς ποιεῖν ἀφ' ἑαυτοῦ οὐδέν. 5:30 οὐ δύναμαι ἐγὼ ποιεῖν ἀπ' ἐμαυτοῦ οὐδέν·

20. Note that their fullness is mentioned four times (21:6, 8, 11a, 11b) whereas their emptiness is mentioned two times (21:3, 5).

21. The great number of fish echoes Ezek 47:10. With respect to the symbolism of the number 153, Lincoln (*John*, 513) remarks that "the 153 fish most likely suggest the full amount of those who will be drawn in through the mission of Jesus' disciples." For further discussions on 153, refer to Brown, *John*, 2:1074–76; Keener, *John*, 2:1231–33; Kiley, "Three More Fish Stories," 529–31; Bauckham, "The 153 fish and the unity," 81–85.

3. Feeding the Hungry Followers

Jesus who has filled the empty net of the disciples now fills them in their hunger. The feeding scene is depicted with great details.[22] It is portrayed in threefold details: preparation, invitation, and distribution. The atmosphere of the whole process of the meal on the beach is full of affectionate and loving care.

As the disciples arrive at the shore, they see a charcoal fire with bread and fish on it (21:9), the meal the risen Lord Jesus prepared for the hungry and exhausted.[23] The disciples see the glowing fire, and smell the pleasant smoke of burning charcoal, the smell of warm bread and roasted fish. Yet, the disciples, who denied or deserted Jesus just a few days ago, cannot come near to him because of what they have done to him. To those who are standing in constrained silence, Jesus utters the loving invitation, "Come and have breakfast" (δεῦτε ἀριστήσατε, 21:12). To those who cannot come to the meal easily, Jesus first comes (ἔρχεται Ἰησοῦς)[24] and takes the bread (λαμβάνει τὸν ἄρτον) and gives it to them (δίδωσιν αὐτοῖς), and the fish in the same way (21:13; cf. 6:11).[25] The disciples see the food Jesus prepared for them (21:9), hear his tender voice of invitation (21:12), and receive the bread and fish from his hands (21:13)—the hands once nailed on the cross for their brokenness.

With the narration that Jesus gives the bread and fish to the disciples, verses 1–14 suddenly stops, and states that this is the third time that Jesus revealed himself to them, resonating what is said in verse 1, "in this way."[26]

---

22. Jesus filled the empty jars at the wedding at Cana with vintage wine and saved the celebration from a serious consequence (2:1–11).

23. Cf. 18:18, 25

24. All three verbs in verse 13 are employed in the historical present tense. The first verb ἔρχεται is seemingly unnecessary as it is considered as a pleonasm (Brown, *John*, 2:1077). As a matter of fact, the superfluous verb ἔρχεται seems to be a literary device that draws the readers' attention to Jesus' movement like a slow motion video effect, magnifying his movement, and thus, the readers are attracted to focus on Jesus' next movement of approaching more closely to the disciples with the food.

25. There are unsettled discussions on the nature of the meal whether it is a eucharistic meal or an agape meal. For the contention against a eucharistic meal (Barrett, *John*, 582; Brown, *John*, 2:1077, 1098–1100; Lincoln, *John*, 514), refer to Witherington's comment, "This meal that they share is not a eucharistic meal. There is no mention of a cup or drinking, of breaking bread or giving thanks. Rather this is to be seen as a fellowship meal, a family reunion of a sort." Witherington III, *John's Wisdom*, 354; see also Keener, *John*, 2:1231. For the argument that regards it as an agape meal, see Gray, "The Last Chapter," 696–97.

26. The phrase "in this way" possibly implies "in this loving and affectionate way" which is beyond the simple narration of "in the way of helping them to catch fish and

Though the narrative stops, the effect of the scene, the reverberation of the affectionate attention of Jesus lingers in the minds of the readers. Just like the disciples who were there at the scene, the readers, by reading the text, could have the vicarious experience of seeing the glowing charcoal fire, smelling the bread and roasted fish, hearing Jesus' voice of invitation, and sensing the warmth of Jesus' hands that passed the bread to the dispirited followers. By the detailed depictions of the scene appealing to various senses, the fourth evangelist invites the readers to the presence and spiritual experience of the risen Lord Jesus, so that they may also have the similar experience that the disciples experienced (cf. 1 John 1:1–3).[27]

Why does Jesus feed them? We know that it is not simply to fill their hungry stomach, so that they may go back to the Sea for another fishing trip. The purpose of the feeding is at least twofold. First, it is to demonstrate Jesus' love for them tangibly, so that they may know that they are embraced by his unfailing love.[28] It is to reveal that they are loved in his infinite love despite their desertion of him (13:38; 18:27; 16:32; Mark 14:27), so that they may love other followers of Jesus in the same way (cf. 13:34; 15:12).

Second, it is to nourish and equip the disciples to follow Jesus (21:19). In commenting on verse 13 "Jesus . . . took the bread and gave it to them, and in the same way the fish," Lincoln remarks, "Jesus has empowered the disciples for their mission of fishing, enabling them to make their catch, and he now provides nourishment for them in their task."[29] The feeding of the meal is *directional* in that it is to enable and strengthen the weary disciples to do the mission in Jesus' provision and nourishment.

What does it imply about the Spirituality of following Jesus? It implies that the journey of following Jesus is possible by being continually fed and nourished by the enabling grace of the Lord's nourishment. The same spiritual principle and experience is implied in the equipping nourishment of the dejected Elijah by the angel of the LORD with a bread baked on hot coals and a jar of water (1 Kgs 19:5–8) for the journey ahead to the mountain of God to receive the mission he is to accomplish (1 Kgs 19:15–16). The followers of Jesus must first and continually be nourished by Jesus' presence and provision to do his mission.[30] Without it no one can do the mission.

---

feeding them."

27. With respect to the religious experience through physical senses, see van der Merwe, "Early Christian Spirituality," 3–4.

28. Cf. Brown (*John*, 2:1099) remarks that "Jesus wished to share the intimacy of his messianic banquet table."

29. Lincoln, *John*, 514.

30. Keener (*John*, 2:1234) notes that Peter is invited to feed others *only after* Peter has himself *first* eaten.

All Jesus' actions of revealing himself to the disciples (ἐφανερώθη Ἰησοῦς τοῖς μαθηταῖς, 21:1, 14), helping them to catch fish abundantly (21:4-8, 11), and feeding at the beach (21:9, 12-13) run towards the final call to follow Jesus (21:19). That which restores the failed disciple to follow Jesus afresh overcoming failure and woundedness, is the sovereign act of Jesus' revealing himself to them. That which equips the feeble disciple to follow Jesus is Jesus' gracious presence and provision. The risen Lord continually manifests himself to his followers today, and "graciously supplies the need of his followers in their mission through his continuing empowering presence and through his nourishment of them."[31] This is the essential factor that makes the journey of following Jesus possible for men and women, being freed from the burden of their own brokenness and overcoming their own incapability and fragility. By reading this narrative, the readers are pulled towards having the lived experience of Jesus' continuing manifestation, empowering presence, and nourishment. Whenever they come to this narrative in their defectiveness, the readers have the spiritual experience of restoration in the presence of Jesus and get refreshed to continue the journey of following Jesus despite their frailty.

B. Following Jesus and the Centrality of Love

The text 21:15-17 contains three sets of dialogues of which the main terms are: to love (ἀγαπάω and φιλέω), to know (οἶδα and γινώσκω), to feed/tend (ποιμαίνω and βόσκω), and sheep/lamb (ἀρνίον and πρόβατον).[32] There are

---

31. Lincoln, *John*, 515.

32. In the dialogues, four pairs of vocabularies appear: ἀγαπάω and φιλέω; οἶδα and γινώσκω; ποιμαίνω and βόσκω; ἀρνίον and πρόβατον. The verb ἀγαπάω appears twice (vv. 15, 16) and φιλέω five times (vv. 15, 16, 17). In his answers Peter replies in the form of "You know . . ." using the term οἶδα (vv. 15, 16, 17) and in the third set using both οἶδα and γινώσκω. Each set of dialogue ends with Jesus' commanding Peter to feed Jesus' sheep, which are expressed by two pairs of terms for "feed/tend" and "lamb/sheep": ποιμαίνω once (v. 16) and βόσκω twice (vv. 15, 17); ἀρνίον once (v. 15) and πρόβατον twice (vv. 16, 17).

In regard to the interchangeability of φιλέω and ἀγαπάω in verses 15-17, just like most ancient Greek commentators (Chrysostom, Cyril of Alexandria) and the scholars of the Reformation period (Erasmus, Grotius), the majority of modern scholars consider them as synonymous in that they are employed without distinction in meaning (Bultmann, *John*, 711; Barrett, *John*, 584; Brown, *John*, 2:1103; Schnackenburg, *John*, 3:362-63; Morris, *John*, 871-74; Ridderbos, *John*, 665-66; Keener, *John*, 2:1235-36; Lincoln, *John*, 517), contrary to some scholars: Westcott, Lenski, Plummer, and Temple as listed in Morris, *John*, 872. Also refer to Evans, "The Verb ἀγαπᾶν," 64-71.

Furthermore, there are many usages wherein the two verbs are employed interchangeably in the Fourth Gospel (the Father loves the Son: both φιλέω 5:20 and

two main components in the dialogue. One is Jesus' questions to Peter and Peter's answers to Jesus, revolving around the love theme;[33] the other is Jesus' commands to Peter.[34] In this section Jesus' love question will be explored, and Jesus' command in the next section.

Why does Jesus question Peter, "Simon son of John, do you love me?"? First, the primary purpose is to give Simon Peter opportunities to confess love for Jesus. As hinted in the action of jumping into the water to come to Jesus as quickly as possible (21:7), Peter's "zealous love for Jesus" is flaring up within his heart.[35] By asking three times, Jesus gives him three opportunities to avow his love for him.[36] It is not to give him a chance to repent.[37] Peter has already repented in deep remorse (Mark 14:72).[38] That his sin of denying Jesus is washed away by the water is intimated (21:7) if "the water of John 21 may also recall the water of John 13, which may recall the salvific-water motif in earlier narratives."[39] That he is forgiven and embraced already by Jesus' forgiving grace is implied by the fact that Jesus has the fellowship meal with Peter at the table Jesus prepared for him in love (21:12, 13).[40] The question is not meant to double check "whether he is ready to lay down his

---

ἀγαπάω 10:17; Jesus loves Lazarus: both φιλέω 11:3 and ἀγαπάω 11:5; Jesus loves the Beloved Disciple: both φιλέω 20:2 and ἀγαπάω 21:7). In the LXX also the two verbs are used synonymously, for instance, to state Jacob's love for Joseph in Gen 37:3, 4 "Ιακωβ δὲ ἠγάπα τὸν Ιωσηφ παρὰ πάντας τοὺς υἱοὺς αὐτοῦ . . . ἰδόντες δὲ οἱ ἀδελφοὶ αὐτοῦ ὅτι αὐτὸν ὁ πατὴρ φιλεῖ ἐκ πάντων τῶν υἱῶν αὐτοῦ ἐμίσησαν αὐτὸν . . ."

For the interchangeability of the other terms (οἶδα and γινώσκω; ποιμαίνω and βόσκω; ἀρνίον and πρόβατον), refer to Bruce, *John*, 404; Brown, *John*, 2:1104–5; Schnackenburg, *John*, 3:363; Bruner, *John*, 1235.

33. V. 15 Σίμων Ἰωάννου, ἀγαπᾷς με πλέον τούτων;
   ναὶ κύριε, σὺ οἶδας ὅτι φιλῶ σε.
   V. 16 Σίμων Ἰωάννου, ἀγαπᾷς με;
   ναὶ κύριε, σὺ οἶδας ὅτι φιλῶ σε.
   V. 17 Σίμων Ἰωάννου, φιλεῖς με;
   κύριε, πάντα σὺ οἶδας, σὺ γινώσκεις ὅτι φιλῶ σε.

34. V. 15 βόσκε τὰ ἀρνία μου.
   V. 16 ποίμαινε τὰ πρόβατά μου.
   V. 17 βόσκε τὰ πρόβατά μου.

35. Keener, *John*, 2:1229.

36. "Most commentators have found in Jesus' thrice-repeated question 'Do you love me?' and in Peter's threefold 'You know that I love you' a symbolic undoing of Peter's threefold denial of Jesus." Brown, *John*, 2:1111. See also Carson, *John*, 678.

37. Cf. Schnackenburg, *John*, 3:364.

38. Mark 14:72 "At that moment the cock crowed for the second time. Then Peter remembered that Jesus had said to him, 'Before the cock crows twice, you will deny me three times.' And he broke down and wept."

39. Keener, *John*, 2:1230, n. 38.

40. Witherington III, *John's Wisdom*, 354. Cf. Brown, *John*, 2:1112.

life for Jesus, to be a good shepherd," either.[41] As alluded to in 21:7 and expressed in 13:37, Peter loves Jesus and is willing to lay down his life for him. The love confession "Lord, you know that I love you" is what Simon needs to speak out, not primarily for Jesus but for Peter himself, for he denied Jesus verbally (18:17, 25, 27). It is so that Peter may escape the traumatic memory, being healed of the abysmal wound, and thus from now on he may live a new life of expressing love for Jesus in action by doing the mission that Jesus is going to entrust to him.

In Peter's confession of love for Jesus, a significant change in Peter's life attitude is demonstrated. Before his love and loyalty for Jesus was based on his own eagerness and will. In his strong protestation, "Lord, why can I not follow you now? I will lay down my life for you" (13:37), there is none of the trace of self-awareness of his own fragility and the need of Jesus' sovereign grace upon his life. Peter's mind was full of self-confidence. However, after the heartbreaking experience of denying Jesus contrary to his own will, Peter now has come to have necessary despair of himself and be mindful of Jesus' Lordship in everything, even in his utterance of confessing love for Jesus. It is demonstrated by the way how he answers, "Lord (κύριε), you know (σὺ οἶδας/γινώσκεις) that I love you (φιλῶ σε)." It is to be noted that the recurring σὺ (you) in Peter's answers is emphatic. Especially, the additional phrase in the third confession, "Lord, you know everything" (κύριε, πάντα σὺ οἶδας), indicates that Peter has now come to depend on Jesus alone absolutely and humbly.[42] "Peter has given up all self-confidence and entrusted himself humbly to his Lord."[43] It is not a protestation.[44] How can a man who has undergone the hellish misery and disappointment in denying his own Lord three times protest (18:27)? How can a man who has seen how fragile he himself is and how unreliable the words that come from his own mouth are, protest to the Lord, asserting that he is certain that he loves Jesus? How can a man who has just experienced Jesus' forgiving and unchanging love in his manifestation through the catch and meal protest (21:1–14)? How can a man who has learned that Jesus knows everything including his fragility and the exact timing of the rooster crowing in connection with his denial (13:38; Matt 26:75) protest to the Lord? "Lord, you know everything" (κύριε, πάντα σὺ οἶδας). It is a humble acknowledgement of Jesus' Lordship over his existence and a submissive confession of the

---

41. Culpepper, "Peter as Exemplary Disciple," 170.

42. In Peter's third confession in verse 17 σὺ appears twice. There is no "I" but "You." "Peter no longer appeals to his own self-confidence." Bruner, *John*, 1227.

43. Schnackenburg, *John*, 3:363.

44. Contrary to Brown, *John*, 2:1106.

absolute need of the risen Lord's sovereign grace over his entire life. Peter's repeated confession depending on Jesus' Lordship (κύριε, πάντα σὺ οἶδας) is in line with the confessions of humble servants of the LORD in the biblical tradition (Ps 139:1–6).

If Peter is ready to follow Jesus finally, it is in this sense he is ready to follow Jesus and tend Jesus' flock.[45] Not by his own competency, but by his humble and total dependency (cf. 1 Pet 5:6).[46] Perhaps for this purpose Jesus needed to allow Peter to go through the painful experience of utter self-despair by denying the Lord contrary to his assertion (13:37). When Peter comes to know his own willingness and assertion is nothing but futility, and begins to depend on Jesus' Lordship over everything, he is finally ready to shepherd Jesus' flock by his sovereign grace in his presence and provision alone.

Second, the deeper purpose that Jesus leads Simon Peter to confess love for him is to draw him to the mysterious web of divine love. In Jesus' repeated questions and Peter's constant confessions is implied the centrality of love as the deepest motivation and driving energy of the life of following Jesus.[47]

In reading the love dialogue of 21:15–17, the readers may recall the love motif recurring throughout the Hebrew Scriptures and Johannine documents, and find the significance of the love questions and confessions within the ideological frame of love. First of all, the demand of love for God, to love him with all their being (Deut 6:5; 10:12; cf. 11:1, 13, 22; 13:3; Josh 22:5; 23:11; Ps 31:23) would come to the readers' minds. The reciprocal love between God and his people is at the heart of the covenant relationship (Exod 20:6; Deut 7:9; Neh 1:5).[48] Love in the covenant bond demands love.[49] Yet, the God who knows human incapability, that they are not able to love him as required, promises to change their heart by spiritual circumcision, so that they may become able to love him as he demands (Deut 30:6). Thus, the

---

45. Cf. Lincoln, *John*, 520.

46. Bruner (*John*, 1230) states what Peter has in his heart, "I can't appeal to my own convictions or conscience anymore, Lord; I don't trust myself; but I do appeal to your knowledge of me and of every human heart (cf. Acts 1:24)."

47. In the last dialogue of Jesus with his disciple, the love theme (21:15–17), which does not appear in any Synoptic Gospels, takes the center before any mission is mentioned.

48. As for the role of the covenant motif as a literary paradigm of the Fourth Gospel, see Brown, "Gift upon Gift."

49. The gravity of the demand of love in the covenant relationship between God and his people is poignantly expressed in St. Augustine's confession, "What am I to you that you command me to love you, and that, if I fail to love you, you are angry with me and threaten me with vast miseries?" Augustine, *Confessions*, 5.

Psalmist has become able to confess love for the LORD (Ps 18:1).[50] In addition to the pervasive truth that love is the essence of relationship between God and his people, the readers would remember that love is the controlling motivation of all divine actions for his people. Out of love God chose his own people (Deut 4:37; 10:15). Out of love he redeemed them (Deut 7:8). Out of love he turned the curse of Balaam into a blessing for them (Deut 23:5). At the root of all God's acts for his people is love.

The readers may also look at the love dialogue of 21:15–17 in connection with the ample love sayings permeating in the Johannine documents. It is very likely that the readers will recognize that "love" is that which exists between God and Jesus as an unbreakable bond that binds the Father and the Son, before it is what Jesus asks of Peter. Love stands at the center of the relationship between the Father and the Son. Love, as the deepest motivation of all divine acts, is the nucleus that moves the Father and the Son in everything they do for each other. Because he loved the Son, the Father gave him glory before the foundation of the world (17:24). Because he loved the Son, the Father placed all things in his hands (3:35). Because he loves the Son, the Father shows him all things he himself is doing (5:20). The Son also does all for the Father out of love. The Son obeys the Father since he loves the Father (14:31). At the heart of the relationship between the Father and the Son is love. Love is the driving force of all divine actions between the Father and the Son for each other.

The same love formula is working in the acts of the Father and the Son towards his own people. In love and out of the love between the Father and the Son, the Father chose his own (Eph 1:4–5). In love the Father gave them to the Son to be his own (17:6). The love within the circle of the Father and the Son overflows to his own. As the Father has loved the Son (17:23), the Father himself loves his own (16:27; Eph 2:4). The Son loves his own to the end (13:1). Out of love God gave his own Son to them by sending him into the world, so that men and women might live through the Son (3:16; 1 John 4:9). In love God made them his own children (1 John 3:1). Just as the motivation of God's every act for Jesus' followers is love, the Son also does all for them in love. Out of love the Son laid down his own life for them (15:13–14; 1 John 3:16; Gal 2:20; Eph 5:2). In love the Son freed his own from their sins by his blood (Rev 1:5). Love is the core of the relationship of the Father and the Son and the followers, and the energy of all actions of the Father and the Son for the followers. The followers of Jesus are drawn into this marvelous interconnectedness of the divine reciprocal love (14:21, 23).[51]

50. Ps 18:1 (17:2 LXX) καὶ εἶπεν ἀγαπήσω σε κύριε ἡ ἰσχύς μου.

51. 14:21, 23 "Those who love me will be loved by my Father, and I will love them

The purpose for which Jesus has the love dialogue with Peter in 21:15–17 is not merely to have him engage in mission or perform certain works for Jesus. Although it is true as most scholars have remarked that the dialogue basically aims at restoring Peter to feed Jesus' flock after his departure, in the dialogue is implied much more than that. By the love conversation, Jesus is pulling Peter into the web of divine love, into the dynamic power of love, into the mysterious and profound relationship of love. It is an invitation into wondrous communion with Jesus and through him with the Father to be participants in the circle of love, loving and being loved. Jesus who has thrown the net of love around Peter by revealing (φανερόω) himself to him by helping him to catch fish and having the fellowship meal (21:1–14), now by the question, "Do you love me?," pulls him onto the boat of the divine love to join the circle of love with Jesus and the Father. Although Peter may not fully apprehend now the centrality of love and the high call toward which Jesus is drawing him by the repeated love questions, he may grasp it someday when he will give his life for the risen Lord and his flock, in the power of the love of the Father and the Son. By reading the love dialogue of 21:15–17 the readers are being invited into the mysterious lived experience (Spirituality) of being participants in the communion of love.

What aspect of the Spirituality of following Jesus is communicated by the association of love questions (21:15–17) with the call "Follow me" (ἀκολούθει μοι, 21:19)? It is communicated that following Jesus is the journey of living in the relationship of divine love and experiencing its profundity. Following Jesus is the course of experiencing the love of the Father and the Son, participating in it, continually expressing it by taking care of Jesus' people, and expanding the circle of the love wider and wider. In the course of following Jesus captured in the web of divine love, Jesus' followers will come to know the Father and his love deeper and deeper (its breadth and length and height and depth, Eph 3:18–19), and the love with which the Father loves the Son will ever increasingly abide *in* the life of the followers and their band of love (17:26) as a lived experience in daily realities.[52]

In addition, to deal with the love theme of 21:15–17 more precisely in the theological perspective as the central motivation and driving force of doing Jesus' works, it is not Peter's love on which Jesus entrusts his sheep to him.[53] It is on Jesus' own love. If there is any follower of Jesus who can do

---

and reveal myself to them. Those who love me will keep my word, and my Father will love them, and we will come to them and make our home with them."

52. 17:26 "I made your name known to them, and I will make it known, so that the love with which you have loved me may be in them, and I in them."

53. In regard to love as the driving force, Ridderbos also in a similar vein remarks when he comments on 13:15 and 15:9. Ridderbos, *John*, 463, 519.

Jesus' work faithfully to the end, it is not out of his or her own love for Jesus, but out of Jesus' love for him or her. The Apostle Paul makes it clear that it is Christ's love that continually motivates and compels him (2 Cor 5:14) to move on and holds him fast not to fall away from serving Christ with the utmost integrity.[54]

As the nature of all human beings (including the believers) cannot be depended upon (2:23–25), a human's love for Jesus is never to be trusted as the foundation for doing missionary and pastoral works.[55] If anyone assumes that Jesus expected here in 21:15–19 that Peter would be able to do Jesus' mission on the basis of Peter's own love, one goes back to Peter's mindset expressed in 13:37 which depends on human ability for following Jesus. Because Jesus' love for his followers never changes even though their love for him ebbs and flows, the followers of Jesus will be able to do the mission of Jesus faithfully to the end even in the midst of their changeability.[56] Because Jesus' love will sustain his followers to the end (13:1), they will be able to complete the journey of following Jesus, doing his work. It is by his love, not by their own fragile love.

C. Following Jesus and Feeding His Sheep

Each of three set love dialogues (21:15–17) ends with Jesus' thrice-repeated commands to Peter, and immediately Jesus' prediction of Peter's future destiny follows (21:18). Then the whole pericope culminates in the decisive calling, ἀκολούθει μοι ("Follow me," 21:19). To put it differently, 21:15–18 unfolds the particular constituents of the life of following Jesus (21:19).

So far, in the pericopes researched in the present study (1:35–51; 8:12; 10:1–42; 12:26; 13:21—14:3), what Jesus' followers must do has not been

---

54. 2 Cor 5:14 ἡ γὰρ ἀγάπη τοῦ Χριστοῦ συνέχει ἡμᾶς. "For the love of Christ controls us" (ESV). See that the meaning of the word συνέχω includes "to exercise continuous control over someone" (Louw and Nida, *Greek-English Lexicon*), and "to hold together; any whole, lest it fall to pieces or something fall away" (Thayer, *A Greek-English Lexicon*). It is Christ's love that controls and holds fast his followers to continue his mission.

55. 2:23–25 "When he was in Jerusalem during the Passover festival, many believed in his name because they saw the signs that he was doing. But Jesus on his part would not entrust himself to them, because he knew all people and needed no one to testify about anyone; for he himself knew what was in everyone."

56. Bruner (*John*, 1229) also notes that the love of Jesus' followers for him "is always flawed and incomplete," and thus needs the continuing grace of sustaining from him. Although he does not say that it is Jesus' love on which the disciples are to feed his sheep, his understanding is in a similar vein to my opinion in the sense that the foundational source energy (love) of doing the given task is from Jesus, not from the followers themselves.

concretely commanded in direct association with ἀκολουθεῖν. That following Jesus entails evangelism (bringing people to Jesus) as the result of being with Jesus is implicitly indicated by Andrew and Philip's invitation (1:41–42, 45–46), and that whoever follows Jesus must serve him as his servant is mentioned in 12:26. However, there has been no entrusting or commission from Jesus with respect to what his followers must do practically. Finally here in 21:15–19, what the followers must do, which is one of the major contents of the life of following Jesus is communicated explicitly in the close association with ἀκολουθεῖν.

V. 15 βόσκε τὰ ἀρνία μου. (Feed my lambs.)

V. 16 ποίμαινε τὰ πρόβατά μου. (Tend my sheep.)

V. 17 βόσκε τὰ πρόβατά μου. (Feed my sheep.)

V. 19 ἀκολούθει μοι. (Follow me.)

Jesus has shepherded Peter and the other six disciples in the previous section (21:1–14). Now they are commanded to shepherd Jesus' sheep (21:15–17). By the commands to Simon Peter as a representative of all Jesus' disciples, Jesus commissions all his followers with what they must do. With regard to the universal application of ἀκολούθει μοι (21:19) to all followers of Jesus, Lindars remarks that the command is addressed to all the readers.[57] Bruner also agrees to it by quoting what Calvin mentioned, "[I]n these words [of Jesus to Peter] there was nothing given to Peter that is not common to all ministers of the Gospel."[58] Ridderbos expresses the same sentiments, "As such it [feeding his sheep] is not typically 'apostolic' but rather characteristic of every task or ministry in the church (cf. Acts 20:28; Eph 4:11; 1 Pet 5:1ff.)."[59]

How do Peter and the readers grasp Jesus' commands to feed his sheep? Against what backdrops do they understand the commands? These are at least threefold: First, the biblical data of shepherding imagery in the Old Testament; second, the model of the good shepherd in John 10; and third, how Jesus has looked after the disciples in 21:1–14.

First, it is very likely that Jesus' commands to tend/feed his sheep are understood against the copious data of the imagery of shepherding in the Old Testament, especially in the intertextuality of 21:15–17 and the LXX by

---

57. "The command is addressed to the reader as much as it is to the Apostle." Lindars, *John*, 638.

58. Bruner, *John*, 1236.

59. Ridderbos, *John*, 666.

the two terms: βόσκω and ποιμαίνω.⁶⁰ The term βόσκω appears in the LXX most intensively in Ezekiel 34 where God says that he will feed his people with rich pasture and shepherd them (Ezek 34:13, 14*2, 15, 16) after condemning the unfaithful shepherds who have neglected their duty as shepherds (Ezek 34: 2*2, 3, 8*2, 10; cf. Jer 31:10).⁶¹ And in the New Testament in relation to feeding sheep, the term appears only in John 21:15, 17.⁶² It is quite certain that the evangelist turns the readers' eyes to "God being the shepherd" of his own flock by employing βόσκω in 21:15, 17.⁶³ Therefore the readers likely understand Jesus' commands in the backdrop of God being the shepherd of his flock, who feeds his people in a rich pasture.

The synonymous term ποιμαίνω is employed in significant portions of the LXX where God himself will shepherd his people and he will give shepherds who will shepherd them just as God does. God is the shepherd who leads his people (Ps 23:1; 48:14; 80:1). "He will feed his flock like a shepherd (ὡς ποιμὴν ποιμανεῖ τὸ ποίμνιον αὐτοῦ); he will gather the lambs in his arms, and carry them in his bosom, and gently lead the mother sheep" (Isa 40:11). God fed his people in the wilderness (Hos 13:5). David prays that God would be the shepherd of his people and carry them (Ps 28:9). The prophet Micah petitions God to be the shepherd his people: "Shepherd your people with your staff, the flock that belongs to you" (ποίμαινε λαόν σου ἐν ῥάβδῳ σου πρόβατα κληρονομίας σου, Mic 7:14). God promised that he would raise up shepherds like David over his people (Ezek 34:23; cf. Jer 23:4) and give them shepherds: "I will give you shepherds after my own heart, who will feed you with knowledge and understanding" (καὶ δώσω ὑμῖν ποιμένας κατὰ τὴν καρδίαν μου καὶ ποιμανοῦσιν ὑμᾶς ποιμαίνοντες μετ' ἐπιστήμης, Jer 3:15). According to the promise, the coming Messiah will shepherd his flock in the strength of the LORD (καὶ ποιμανεῖ τὸ ποίμνιον αὐτοῦ ἐν ἰσχύι κυρίου, Mic 5:3). By the employment of the term ποιμαίνω, John leads his readers to read Jesus' commands of 21:15-19 in the idea that God himself is the shepherd and that those whom God appoints to shepherd his flock are to feed them after God's heart (κατὰ τὴν καρδίαν μου, Jer 3:15).

60. Although βόσκω and ποιμαίνω are used interchangeably in 21:15-17, in their nuances the term βόσκω focuses on feeding the animals, whereas ποιμαίνω includes such duties toward the flock as guiding, guarding, and feeding. Brown, *John*, 2:1105; Keener, *John*, 1236-37.

61. In Gen 29:7, 9; 37:12, 16, it is used for pasturing the flock.

62. Other occurrences of the term in the New Testament are in the context of feeding swine in Matt 8:30, 33 (par. Mark 5:11, 14; Luke 8:32, 34) and Luke 15:15.

63. That God is the shepherd of his people is imparted by the term πρόβατον (Ps 77:20; 78:52; 79:13; 80:1; 100:3; Isa 63:11, etc.). See Preisker and Schulz, "πρόβατον," *TDNT* 6:689-92. And also refer to the term ποιμήν (Isa 40:11) for God being the shepherd of his people. Jeremias, "ποιμήν," *TDNT* 6:485-99.

Second, Jesus' commands are naturally grasped in connection with Jesus being the good shepherd, as portrayed in John 10 because there is a rich intertextuality between 10:1–18, 26–30 and 21:15–19. Scholars have paid attention to the intertextuality between the two passages. Among them are Bishop Cassian,[64] Moloney,[65] Beasley-Murray,[66] Lewis,[67] Culpepper,[68] and Lincoln.[69] Although ποιμήν does not appear in John 21, it is obvious that the texts of John 10 and 21 are inter-related by the terms πρόβατον (10:1, 2, 3, 4, 7, 8, 11, 12, 13, 15, 16, 26, 27; 21:16, 17) and ποιμήν (10:2, 11, 12, 14, 16) considering the fact that in the LXX ποιμαίνω and ποιμήν belong to the word group of רעה (to pasture). Jesus already hinted in John 10 what "feeding the sheep" is by describing what he does as the good shepherd for his sheep and his relationship with them. The shepherd knows his own sheep (10:14, 27) and calls them by name (10:3). He leads them out (10:3) and goes ahead of them (10:4). As the only gate and source of life everlasting, he provides his sheep with rich nourishment and an abundant life (10:9, 10, 28).[70] He protects them from the enemies (10:13, 28, 29). He lays down his life for them (10:11, 15, 17, 18). As Culpepper remarks, "This rich web of texts suggests that when Jesus commands Peter to tend his sheep, he is exhorting him to follow Jesus' example as the good shepherd."[71]

Third, the commands to feed Jesus' sheep could be grasped in the light of what Jesus has just done for Peter and the disciples as described in 21:1–14. The readers have seen how Jesus the good shepherd was watching them from the shore although they did not recognize him (21:4), tended them (21:5–6), and fed them (21:9–13). To tend and feed Jesus' sheep is to take care of them just as Jesus has done with Peter and the disciples in 21:1–14. Those who have been *shepherded* by the good shepherd in 21:1–14 are now commanded to *shepherd* others (21:15–17) just as they have been shepherded by the shepherd. Furthermore, *only when* they are continually shepherded by the risen Lord, can they continue shepherding others.

---

64. Besobrasoff, "John XXI," 134–36.
65. Moloney, *John*, 555.
66. Beasley-Murray, *John*, 406.
67. Lewis, "'Shepherd My Sheep,'" 320–22.
68. Culpepper, "Peter as Exemplary Disciple," 168.
69. Lincoln, *John*, 518.
70. Barrett, *John*, 373. "There is only one means of entering the fold; there is only one source of knowledge and life; there is only one way to obtain spiritual nourishment; there is only one way to heaven. And the single means of access to all that is good is Jesus."
71. Culpepper, "Peter as Exemplary Disciple," 168.

From the above considerations, two aspects of following Jesus emerge with respect to doing the mission of shepherding Jesus' sheep: *continuation* and *just as*. Firstly, continuation: the mission of Jesus' disciples to shepherd his flock is not anything novel, but the continuation of what God has done as the shepherd and what Jesus has done as the good shepherd. Moreover, the disciples' shepherding mission is not their own work in their own best skills, but the continuing work of the Father and the Son *through* Jesus' followers as Lincoln comments that it is "the continuation of Jesus' mission through that of the disciples."[72] Secondly, the mission of shepherding Jesus' flock is to be done "just as" (καθὼς) the good shepherd has done for his own.[73] The principle of "just as" (καθὼς) is imparted to the disciples in 13:34 when they are commanded to follow his model (ὑπόδειγμα, 13:35).[74] Although there is no appearance of καθὼς in 21:15–19, the principle of "just as" (καθὼς) is also applied to the area of shepherding because Jesus' followers are his sub-shepherds who are to follow his example.

D. Following Jesus and the "Where" Motif

The "where" (ὅπου/ποῦ) motif has appeared close to ἀκολουθεῖν in the research pericopes of the present study.

---

72. Lincoln, *John*, 515. The same idea of "continuation" of Jesus' work "through" his disciples is expressed by Köstenberger in his comment on John 10:16. "[T]he statement in John 10:16 is one of a few sayings by Jesus recorded in this Gospel that clearly refer to the future mission of the exalted Lord through his disciples (see 4:34–38; 14:12; 17:20; 20:21–23; 21:15–19)." Köstenberger, "Jesus the Good Shepherd," 71. Lewis also notes that the disciples' feeding Jesus' sheep is "the ongoing activity of the shepherd by the disciples—the sheep—toward greater works than these." Lewis, "'Shepherd My Sheep,'" 322.

73. For a discussion on καθὼς as the "disciples' new way of life" in God-Jesus-disciples relationship under the concept of *imitatio Christi*, see van der Merwe, "*Imitatio Christi*," 139–40.

The Johannine theology implied by "as" (καθὼς) needs to be investigated further by probing the pericopes where καθὼς appears in relation to the Father-the Son relationship or Jesus-the followers relationship (5:23, 30; 6:57; 8:28; 10:15; 12:50; 13:15, 34; 14:31; 15:9 10, 12; 17:11, 14, 16, 18, 21, 22, 23; 20:21). The καθὼς theology lays an essential foundation for disciples of Jesus of all times because the pattern of the life of Jesus' followers is formulated by and springs from the pattern of relationship between the Father and the Son in every aspect of life, relationship, and mission.

74. 13:34 ἵνα ἀγαπᾶτε ἀλλήλους, καθὼς ἠγάπησα ὑμᾶς.

ἀκολουθεῖν	ὅπου/ποῦ
1:37, 38, 40, 43	1:38, 39
8:12	7:34, 35, 36, 42; 8:14*2, 21, 22
12:26	12:26, 35
13:36*2, 37	13:33, 36*2
21:19	21:18*2

In each pericope different aspects of the Spirituality of following Jesus have been communicated by the association of ἀκολουθεῖν and ὅπου/ποῦ. Then, what distinguishing Spirituality of following Jesus is conveyed by the association of the two motifs in 21:18–19?

In interpreting 21:18–19, scholars have given their thoughts to whether Jesus' utterance refers to Peter's death by crucifixion or not. Bultmann comments that it is a wrong interpretation to view it as pointing to crucifixion.[75] Yet, most scholars seem to agree that it refers to Peter's crucifixion.[76] Barrett notes as evidence for the reference of this expression ἐκτενεῖς τὰς χεῖράς σου to crucifixion: "Isa 65:2 (ἐξεπέτασα τὰς χεῖράς μου) is taken as foreshadowing the crucifixion by Barnabas (12.4), Justin (1 Apol., 35), Irenaeus (Demonstratio of the Apostolic Preaching, 79), and Cyprian (Test. II, 20); similarly Moses' outstretched hands (Exod 17:12) by Barnabas (12.2) and Justin (Trypho, 90f.)."[77]

---

75. Bultmann, John, 713, n. 7. "'Ετενεῖς τὰς χεῖράς σου therefore is neither to be related to crucifixion . . . nor does it relate to a criminal, who has to stretch out his hands in order to become fettered. These two interpretations are wrong because ζώννυναι means 'to gird,' and not 'to bind' in the sense of 'fetter.'"

76. Barrett, John, 585; Schnackenburg, John, 3:366–67; Ridderbos, John, 667; Keener, John, 2:1238. For an extensive discussion, see Beasley-Murray, John, 408–9; and for the earliest evidence about Peter's death outside of the canonical writings, see Lincoln, John, 518–19.

77. Barrett, John, 585. Barn. 12.4 Καὶ πάλιν ἐν ἑτέρῳ προφήτῃ λέγει Ὅλην τὴν ἡμέραν διεπέτασα τὰς χεῖράς μου πρὸς λαὸν ἀπειθοῦντα καὶ ἀντιλέγοντα ὁδῷ δικαίᾳ μου. (All day long I have stretched forth my hands to an unbelieving people, and one that gainsays my righteous way.) 1 Apol., 35 And again the same prophet Isaiah, being inspired by the prophetic Spirit, said, "I have spread out my hands to a disobedient and gainsaying people, to those who walk in a way that is not good. They now ask of me judgment, and dare to draw near to God." And again in other words, through another prophet, He says, "They pierced My hands and My feet, and for My vesture they cast lots." And indeed David, the king and prophet, who uttered these things, suffered none of them; but Jesus Christ stretched forth His hands, being crucified by the Jews speaking against Him, and denying that He was the Christ. Barn. 12.2 Τίθησιν οὖν Μωϋσῆς ἓν ἐφ᾽ ἓν ὅπλον ἐν μέσῳ τῆς πυγμῆς καὶ σταθεὶς ὑψηλότερος πάντων ἐξέτεινεν τὰς χεῖρας καὶ

It is to be noted, however, that the interpretation of 21:18 that it refers to crucifixion is done from the perspective of the time *after* Peter's death occurred. It is the perspective of the fourth evangelist who is aware of Peter's death on a cross as something that has already happened. Thus, when he writes the Fourth Gospel, the evangelist adds verse 19 ("He said this to indicate the kind of death (σημαίνων ποίῳ θανάτῳ) by which he would glorify God") to Jesus' utterance in verse 18. This explanatory addition naturally has influenced commentators to read verse 18 more confidently in connection with Jesus' crucifixion in its intertextual link with 12:33 (σημαίνων ποίῳ θανάτῳ) and 18:32 (σημαίνων ποίῳ θανάτῳ).[78] When verse 18 is read from the perspective of the time *after* Peter's death, there is no a substantial difficulty in saying that it communicates the fact that the Spirituality of following Jesus is to take the road of death in the same way Jesus did, and moreover, following Jesus unto death after him is a way of glorifying God, just as Neyrey comments.[79] It is a way of reading it from the fourth evangelist's perspective.

There is another possible way of reading verse 18. It is from the perspective of the time *before* Peter's death on a cross occurred. It is Peter's perspective at the moment when he hears it from Jesus. It is hard to say definitively that when Jesus speaks to Peter what is written in verse 18, Peter perceives it in connection with his future death especially in the form of crucifixion.

If it is considered that there is a similarity between the wordings of Jesus' saying in 21:18 (ἐκτενεῖς τὰς χεῖράς σου, . . . ὅπου οὐ θέλεις) and the wordings in Sir 15:16 (stretch out your hand for whichever you choose, οὗ ἐὰν θέλῃς ἐκτενεῖς τὴν χεῖρά σου), which is given in the context of "freedom of choice" (Sir 15:11–20), Jesus' saying of Peter's future may impart a different indication by *a contrast* between an action of one's own choice and an action of surrendering oneself to another's will (choice).

οὕτως πάλιν ἐνίκα ὁ 'Ισραήλ Εἶτα ὁπόταν καθεῖλεν πάλιν ἐθανατοῦντο. (Moses therefore placed one weapon above another in the midst of the hill, and standing upon it, so as to be higher than all the people, he stretched forth his hands, and thus again Israel acquired the mastery. But when again he let down his hands, they were again destroyed.)

78. Schnackenburg, *John*, 3:366–67; Beasley-Murray, *John*, 408–9; Keener, *John*, 2:1238; Lincoln, *John*, 519.

79. Neyrey, *John*, 340. "'Follow' strongly suggests complete imitation of Jesus, especially by a death that will give God glory, just as Jesus did."

John 21:18 ἐκτενεῖς τὰς χεῖράς σου, ... ὅπου οὐ θέλεις
(you will stretch out your hands,
... carry you where you do not wish ...) (RSV)

Sir 15:16 οὗ ἐὰν θέλῃς ἐκτενεῖς τὴν χεῖρά σου
(stretch out your hand for whichever you wish) (RSV)

What, then, is a possible understanding of Jesus' saying from Peter's perspective at that moment when Peter heard it? What was Peter's understanding about Jesus' utterance about his future? Especially, when he heard the repeating word ὅπου (where) twice in the contrast of ὅπου ἤθελες (wherever you wished) and ὅπου οὐ θέλεις (where you do not wish), how would he grasp Jesus' saying?

21:18 ὅτε ἦς νεώτερος, ... **ὅπου ἤθελες·**
(when you were younger, ... **wherever you wished,**)
ὅταν δὲ γηράσῃς, ... **ὅπου οὐ θέλεις.**
(But when you grow old, ... **where you do not wish** to go.)

In contrast by the repetition of the "where" motif, there lies the possibility that Peter might grasp it that, until now he has gone to wherever he wishes to go (ὅπου ἤθελες) in his own will, but from now on after receiving the call to be a sub-shepherd of Jesus, he should even go to where he does not wish to go (ὅπου οὐ θέλεις). Brown rightly comments, "Peter is no longer his own master and is to serve Jesus,"[80] after stating what Schwartz proposes in comparison, "When you were young, you girded yourself and walked where you wished, but now I gird you and I will take you where I wish."[81] Until now Peter was the master of his own life, but from now on having been called to be Jesus' sub-shepherd, he must go where his master orders him to go. It can imply a total submission to Jesus' will and leading in the coming days of Peter's life. If this reading is not utterly impossible, the Spirituality of following Jesus communicated by the association of the repeated ὅπου motif in verse 18 and Jesus' command to follow him ἀκολούθει μοι in verse 19 can be that in the life of following Jesus there is no insisting on one's own preference or will, but total submission to the master. Following Jesus is a matter of *lordship* in total obedience, surrendering to his leading and turning down one's own choice.

80. Brown, *John*, 2:1107.
81. Ibid.

Whereas it is communicated in the previous pericopes (1:51; 12:26) that the journey of following Jesus ultimately leads to where Jesus is with the Father in heaven, it is imparted in 21:18 that while they are here on earth, the place where Jesus' followers should go is the place where Jesus leads them to go, not the place where they wish to go. The text of 21:18–19, by the association of ἀκολουθεῖν and the ὅπου/ποῦ motif, draws the readers to the Spirituality of total submission in the journey of following Jesus.

E. Following Jesus and the Guaranteed Victory

Another unparalleled aspect of the Johannine idea of following Jesus implied in 21:15–19 is found in the fact that Jesus' command "Follow me" (ἀκολούθει μοι, 21:19) is given by the risen Jesus *after* his resurrection. Among the four Gospels, this is the only appearance that the calling ἀκολούθει μοι is given after Jesus' resurrection happened. What does it imply about the life of following Jesus that the calling ἀκολούθει μοι is given by the risen Lord, the Lord of resurrection, who not only was crucified, but conquered death by the resurrection? It is that the journey of following Jesus is the way to the ultimate victory, the triumph over death, which is guaranteed by the risen Lord's resurrection. This unique aspect is pointed out by Calvin and reiterated by Bruner, "And we notice *who* says them: the *crucified (martyred) but now risen (conquering) Lord!* Jesus is saying to Peter, in effect, 'I came out the other side of an awful cross, Peter; you will too; just *follow me!*'"[82] "Jesus' words 'Follow me' [is] not only the call to the courage of martyrdom but also Jesus' courage-enabling promise of death-defeating resurrection."[83] The life of following Jesus is a wondrous journey of being ushered into the life of the guaranteed final victory in the power of the Lord of resurrection (Rev 21:4; cf. Isa 25:8; Hos 13:14; 1 Cor 15:54–57; Heb 2:14–15).

III. Conclusion

The current chapter started with a discourse analysis of 21:1–19 arguing that several motifs are associated with ἀκολουθεῖν in order to impart some important aspects of the Spirituality of following Jesus. Firstly, 21:1–14 communicates that what restores the failed disciples and strengthens them

---

82. Bruner, *John*, 1232. "This one consideration greatly soothes all the bitterness in death[:] when the Son of God presents Himself before our eyes with His blessed resurrection, which is our triumph over death." Calvin, *The Gospel according to St. John 11–21*, 223.

83. Bruner, *John*, 1237.

to follow Jesus anew is Jesus' gracious presence and provision. In reading 21:1–14, the readers are pulled to the Spirituality of being recovered, refreshed, and reenergized by Jesus' presence and provision in the midst of their weakness in the journey of following him. The followers of Jesus are first and continually to be nourished by Jesus' presence and provision, then they will be able to achieve abundant result in doing his mission, overcoming their own brokenness and frailty.

Secondly, 21:1–19 draws the readers to the Spirituality that the life of following Jesus is the journey of living within the powerful web of divine love and experiencing its profundity. Following Jesus is the journey of experiencing the love of the Father and the Son, participating in it, expressing it by taking care of Jesus' people, and expanding the circle of love wider in the world. In the process of following Jesus, the followers of Jesus will come to experience the profound love of Jesus and the Father deeper and deeper, and share it wider as the lived experience in daily realities.

Thirdly, in Jesus' repeated commands to shepherd/feed his sheep which is given in connection with the call to follow him (21:15–19), two particular aspects of the mission of shepherding are communicated: (i) that the work of shepherding Jesus' sheep is to be done *just as* the Father has shepherded them and Jesus has done for them (10:1–39; 21:1–14); (ii) that the life of following Jesus is not what Jesus' followers do in their own skills and ability, but the *continuation* of Jesus' own ministry through them.

Fourthly, by the contrast of ὅπου ἤθελες (wherever you wished) and ὅπου οὐ θέλεις (where you do not wish, 21:18), an unique aspect of the Spirituality of following Jesus is intimated that the life of following Jesus is not a journey in one's own choice or preference, but a total submission to the leading of the Lord that one must go even to the place where one does not wish to go. The text draws the readers to the Spirituality of total submission to the living Lord's leading in the journey of following him.

Fifthly, by the fact that the call ἀκολούθει μοι ("Follow me," 21:19) is given from the risen Lord Jesus after his resurrection of triumph over death, it is communicated that the journey of following Jesus is not only a way of suffering but the guaranteed journey to the ultimate triumph. The lived experience that Jesus' followers will have is not the sorrow of defeat, but the victory over death and all trials, for they follow the Lord of resurrection who stands on the other side of death as the Son of God in power (cf. Rom 1:4).

PART III

Conclusion

CHAPTER 11

Summary and Reflections

IN THE QUEST FOR the Spirituality of following Jesus according to the Fourth Gospel communicated by the association of ἀκολουθεῖν (to follow) with correlated motifs, pertinent Johannine texts that employ ἀκολουθεῖν in a figurative sense have been investigated. This closing chapter is comprised of two sections. Firstly, what has been discussed, presented, or investigated in both Part I (Preliminaries) and Part II (ἀκολουθεῖν in the Fourth Gospel) of the present study will be summarized chapter by chapter. Secondly, the distinct aspects of the Spirituality of following Jesus, which are imparted by ἀκολουθεῖν and its association with correlated motifs, will be arranged in the (redemptive) historical framework.

I. Summary by Chapter

Chapter 1: In the Literature Review section, scholarly works are surveyed and a conclusion is made that there has been neither scholarly literature that investigates the whole profile of ἀκολουθεῖν in the Fourth Gospel as biblical studies, nor any substantial studies in the Spirituality of following Jesus communicated by the association of ἀκολουθεῖν with "ὅπου/ποῦ" (where Jesus is/where Jesus goes to) or other correlated motifs in the Gospel. The presumption that ἀκολουθεῖν might be a particular term of the Synoptics and there would be no distinctive implication delivered by it in the Fourth Gospel probably lies underneath the scarce attention to ἀκολουθεῖν in the Gospel and the lack of studies in the Spirituality of following Jesus created by ἀκολουθεῖν.

In the Problem Statement section, it is pointed out that the much neglected ἀκολουθεῖν functions as an important term in the Fourth Gospel and is pervasive throughout the Gospel and thus calls for an investigation. In the section of Limitations and Points to be Studied Further, it is stated that the present study is neither concerned with pursuing or interacting with the spiritualities from a historical or psychological approach or other religious views, nor interested in textual criticism and the establishment of the Johannine text, but that the study will focus on the Spirituality of following Jesus imparted in the present canonical final form of the Gospel as it is as a narrative unity. The reasons ὑπόδειγμα (an example) and καθώς (just as) in 13:15 and the role of the Holy Spirit for the life of following Jesus are not discussed in the study are explained briefly, and the points and terminologies to be investigated further beyond the present study are suggested. In the Methodology section, it is presented that the current study will employ the literary-theological approach.

Chapter 2: As a part of the preliminary work, in this chapter a working definition of the term "spirituality" is suggested, after surveying understandings and definitions of spirituality offered by prominent scholars and writers. The relation of spirituality with theology is discussed as a mutually supporting and completing correlation. Lastly, it is mentioned that the present study will explore the Spirituality *in* the text, neither *behind* nor *before* the text.

Chapter 3: As the social and historical life setting of Jesus' followers in the Fourth Gospel, after scholarly theories of the Johannine community are briefly introduced, the textual evidences that facing social expulsion, suffering, and death were their daily experiences are presented. The key texts examined are 5:15–18; 7:1, 7, 19, 25; 8:37–47; 9:22, 34; 15:18—16:4, and the terms probed are διώκω (to persecute), ἀποκτείνω (to kill), μισέω (to hate), ἀποσυνάγωγος (expelled from the synagogue), and φόβος (fear).

Chapter 4: A survey of ἀκολουθεῖν outside the Fourth Gospel is done in the chapter. First, the usages of ἀκολουθεῖν in Greco-Roman literature and Judaism documents are observed only by looking into some exemplary cases, and it is concluded that the meaning and implication imparted by ἀκολουθεῖν are determined by the juxtaposed or associated words and motifs, as well as the development of the logic of the text. Second, the occurrences of ἀκολουθεῖν used in a spiritual/figurative sense in the other books of the New Testament are investigated, and it is inferred (at the risk of overgeneralization) that the implications and Spirituality of following Jesus delivered by ἀκολουθεῖν outside the Fourth Gospel mainly circle around self-commitment breaking all others former ties, the life of sacrifice and suffering for Christ, or doing his mission, as the common characteristics.[1]

---

1. (1) Matt 4:20, 22; Mark 1:18; Luke 5:11; (2) Matt 8:19, 22; Luke 9:57, 59, 61; (3) Matt 9:9; Mark 2:14; Luke 5:27–28; (4) Matt 10:38; (5) Matt 16:24; Mark 8:34; Luke 9:23; (6) Matt 19:21, 27–28; Mark 10:21, 28; Luke 18:22, 28; (7) Mark 10:52; Luke 18:43; (8) Rev 14:1–5.

Chapter 5: It is asserted that in 1:35–51 four aspects of the Spirituality of following Jesus are communicated. First, the fact that the first two disciples began to follow Jesus upon hearing the pronouncement that Jesus is the Lamb *of* God (1:29, 35–37) intimates that the life of following Jesus is a journey into the lived experience of Jesus who leads men and women to God the Father by his death just as the lamb of God opens an access to the presence of God by its death. Second, by the association of ἀκολουθεῖν with the "where" motif (ποῦ μένεις, 1:38; εἶδαν ποῦ μένει, 1:39), the text invites the readers to the lived experience of being with Jesus where he is, in appreciation that at the center of the life of following Jesus is Jesus himself, and that the journey is entering the relationship with Jesus. From that relationship stem service and obedience, mission and evangelism. Third, by presenting Philip as the first follower who was called by Jesus with the call ἀκολούθει μοι (1:43) and his spiritual blindness and dullness and miserable failure in understanding Jesus' intent and seeing the Father in Jesus (6:5–7; 12:20–22; 14:7–10), the Fourth Gospel invites the readers to the lived experience of the humble self-awareness of their spiritual dullness and absolute need of sovereign grace of the Lord for their maturity in following Jesus. Fourth, by presenting the future promise that the followers will see heaven opened and the Son of Man as the ladder that connects heaven and earth (1:51), the text draws the readers to the Spirituality of having fellowship with the Father in and through Jesus the bridge.

Chapter 6: Given the literary-theological context that communicates the human predicament of walking in darkness in which people do not know where their lives are going (12:35) which is essentially connected to their ignorance of where Jesus came from and where he goes (7:28, 29, 33, 34, 36; 8:14, 19, 21, 22), the text of 8:12 first leads the readers to the existential recognition that they are in need of the light of life. Then, by the important invitation ὁ ἀκολουθῶν ἐμοὶ οὐ μὴ περιπατήσῃ ἐν τῇ σκοτίᾳ, ἀλλ' ἕξει τὸ φῶς τῆς ζωῆς ("Whoever follows me will never walk in darkness but will have the light of life," 8:12), the fourth evangelist encourages the readers to the lived experience of being guided by Jesus, the guiding light, just as the ancient people were guided to the Promised Land by the pillar of cloud and fire in the wilderness. The Spirituality that the evangelist intends to create in the life of the readers by the text is that they may have the lived experience of being led to the ultimate destination of life (that is, to the Father) by Jesus the guiding light of life.

Chapter 7: Forming one literary-theological pericope together with chapter 9 and located within the hostile socio-historical situation where the man born with blindness (a representative of Jesus' followers of all time) was cast out of the synagogue for the reason of professing faith in Jesus, the text

10:1–42 leads the readers to the Spirituality of being encouraged by the fact that their journey of following Jesus is being sustained and protected by the good shepherd who knows them from before the beginning of the world just as the Father knows him and that they are unbreakably bound to Jesus (10:14, 15; cf. 10:3, 4, 27; 17:6, 9, 10, 24) who gives his own life for them (10:11, 15) and holds them in his mighty grip together with the Father (10:28, 29). By the text the fourth evangelist guides the followers of Jesus, who are under harassment and persecution, to the Spirituality of the blessed assurance of their eternal safety and being strengthened by the good shepherd to continue the journey however antagonistic their life circumstances may be.

Chapter 8: Surrounded by ample motifs and expressions that indicate Jesus' imminent death and given just before his death (12:23, ἐλήλυθεν ἡ ὥρα), the text of 12:26, highlighting the two most prominent characteristics, invites the readers to the lived experience of following Jesus by serving him as his servants (ἐὰν ἐμοί τις διακονῇ, . . . ὁ διάκονος . . . ἐάν τις ἐμοὶ διακονῇ . . .), just as Jesus was the faithful servant of the Father (10:18; 12:49; 14:31; 15:10; 17:4; cf. Rom 5:19; Phil 2:7–8; Heb 5:8).[2] The first prominent characteristic is to take the path of suffering and death as it is implied by the fact that Jesus pronounced the words of 12:26 when he was about to take the path of death. The second is the glorious reward of being with Jesus where he is (ὅπου εἰμὶ ἐγὼ ἐκεῖ καὶ ὁ διάκονος ὁ ἐμὸς ἔσται) in glory with the Father, which is being honored by the Father (τιμήσει αὐτὸν ὁ πατήρ). By reading 12:26, the readers are ushered into the two most essential attributes of the Spirituality of following Jesus (suffering and honor; death and glory).

Chapter 9: Within the context where Simon Peter insists, full of self-confidence, that he is more than willing and able to follow Jesus, by the literary design of the unprecedented association of ἀκολουθεῖν (to follow) with οὐ δύναμαι (not able, 13:36, 37) and the prediction of his denial of Jesus (13:38), the text of 13:36–38 draws the readers to the lived experience of humble recognition of human inability in following Jesus.[3] Upon the existential recognition of their utter spiritual inability to reach where the Father is (where Jesus goes to) and safeguarded against vain and dangerous self-confidence, the readers are guided into the Spirituality of absolute reliance on Jesus' redemptive work and the consequent gift of the Spirit (as presented in the larger context of chapters 14–20) and Jesus' act of taking

---

2. πάσχα (11:55*2; 12:1; 13:1); ἀποθνήσκω (11:50, 51; 12:24, 33); ἀποκτείνω (11:53; 12:10); ἐνταφιασμός (12:7); ἡ ὥρα (12:23, 27; 13:1); ὑψόω (12:32, 34); ποίῳ θανάτῳ (12:33).

3. In the entire Gospel narratives, John 13:36–38 is the only text where the term ἀκολουθεῖν is associated with the negative pronouncement οὐ δύναμαι and Peter's denial prediction.

them to where the Father is (as presented in 14:3 as an immediate context). It includes the lived experience of having faith in Jesus and the Father as an imperative need for the journey of following Jesus (14:1). By the unique text 13:36–14:3, the readers are attracted to the distinguishing Spirituality of following Jesus that those who recognize the spiritual-existential fact that they are unable to follow Jesus, can follow him, just as those who are aware that they do not see, can see by the power of his grace (cf. 9:41).

Chapter 10: The important call "Follow me" (ἀκολούθει μοι) is given to Simon Peter, neither at the beginning of his journey, nor in the middle when he utters the important christological confession (6:68–69), but at the very last chapter of the Fourth Gospel (21:19) when Peter was in complete self-despair in his awareness of inadequacy after he denied Jesus and went back to his former life. By giving the call in this dramatic moment and associating the call ἀκολούθει μοι with Jesus' multiple acts for the disciples (21:1–14) and some motifs (love, shepherding, where) in the dialogue between Jesus and Simon (21:15–19), the evangelist draws the readers to five unique qualities of the Spirituality of following Jesus. First, by the text that puts the calling to follow Jesus (ἀκολούθει μοι) in the context where Simon's (the representative of all followers) inadequacy and inability is demonstrated (13:38; 18:17, 25, 27; 21:3) and Jesus' gracious feeding and provision restores the failed disciples (21:1–14), the readers are invited to the Spirituality that the life of following Jesus truly starts upon the basis of total despair of oneself and is possible by Jesus' sheer grace and continuing provision. Second, together with Simon Peter being asked "Do you love me?" (ἀγαπᾷς με;/φιλεῖς με;, 21:15–17), the readers are not only invited to the life of following him in love as Jesus loves them (13:1), but also drawn to the lived experience (Spirituality) of love within the circle of love between the Father and Jesus, so that they may experience the divine love of the Father and the Son in their daily lives together with fellow followers and to expand the circle of divine love. Third, by linking the repeated imperative "Feed my lambs/Tend my sheep/Feed my sheep" (21:15–17) with ἀκολούθει μοι ("Follow me," 21:19), John the evangelist leads the readers to the lived experience of the privileged mission of shepherding Jesus' sheep (cf. Acts 20:28; Eph 4:11; 1 Pet 5:1–4) as one of the essential works of the journey of following Jesus just as Jesus the good shepherd (10:11, 14) and the Father (Ps 23:1; Isa 40:11; Ezek 34:11–16) have been shepherding them. Fourth, by associating ἀκολούθει μοι with Jesus' prediction of the kind of death by which Peter would glorify God and with the contrast of ὅπου ἤθελες (wherever you wished) and ὅπου οὐ θέλεις (where you do not wish, 21:18–19), John ushers the readers to the lived experience of glorifying God in the same way Jesus did by death and the Spirituality of total submission to the Lord's leading, even though he takes him to where he does not wish to go. Fifth, by letting the readers hear the call ἀκολούθει μοι from the Lord of resurrection, the fourth evangelist draws the readers to the lived experience (Spirituality) of the triumphant life of resurrection that nullifies the power of the world, darkness and death which used to pull them down, and to walk the road of following Jesus as the suffering-yet-triumphant journey toward the guaranteed victory.

II. Following Jesus Arranged in the (Redemptive) Historical Framework

The journey of following Jesus can be understood in the framework of divine economy that began from eternity within the circle of the Father and the Son (and the Holy Spirit) (1:1, 2) and will be consummated in eternity when Jesus' followers participate in the Son's communion with the Father (17:24). The life of following Jesus is a pilgrimage that originates from the eternal compact and communion of love between the Father and the Son which was before the foundation of the world (*from* eternity) and moves into the eternal communion with the Father and the Son in this life as the commencement and in the life to come as the consummation (*into* eternity).

A. *From* Eternity

In eternity before time and space came to existence,[4] there was a relationship of love—the fellowship between the Father and the Son (and the Holy Spirit) (1:1, 2).[5] The relationship within the circle of the Father and the Son, specifically expressed by the twice repeated "intimate" preposition πρὸς (1:1, 2),[6] has been recognized as the Son's "close fellowship" with God.[7] The relationship is a profoundly intimate and loving communion between the Father and the Son (cf. 1:18; 17:21). The Son (the Logos) was with God not

---

4. 1:1 Ἐν ἀρχῇ

5. By stating "the Word was with God (πρὸς τὸν θεόν), . . . He was in the beginning with God (πρὸς τὸν θεόν)" (1:1, 2) not "with the Father," the fourth evangelist possibly indicates that the relationship is among the three Persons of the Divine Trinity including God the Holy Spirit.

6. 1:1, 2 Ἐν ἀρχῇ ἦν ὁ λόγος, καὶ ὁ λόγος ἦν πρὸς τὸν θεόν, καὶ θεὸς ἦν ὁ λόγος. οὗτος ἦν ἐν ἀρχῇ πρὸς τὸν θεόν. As to πρὸς Bruner comments, "The word used for the usual English translation 'with' in the Greek is not one of the two major Greek words for 'with' (*syn* and *meta*) but the more intimate preposition *pros*, 'toward,' which is difficult to render in English." Bruner, *John*, 11. For further discussion on πρὸς in John 1:1, see Caragounis and van der Watt, "A Grammatical Analysis of John 1:1," 100–10.

7. Bruner, *John*, 11.

merely sitting side by side with him in silence and inactivity, but dynamically looking to and conversing with each other. The Son was in fellowship with the Father facing "toward" the Father and the Father "toward" the Son (1:1, 2), taking delight in and giving to each other (Prov 8:30; cf. Isa 42:1; Matt 3:17; 17:5), loving and being loved by each other (cf. 3:35; 5:20; 15:9; 17:24; 1 John 4:8, 16), and giving glory to and receiving from each other (cf. 17:5, 24).[8] This intimate and loving relationship of communion is the eternal matrix from which the movement of following Jesus is generated.

Within the divine intimate communion of love before the creation of the universe, there was a divine covenant between the Father and the Son (17:4, 5; cf. Prov 8:23; 1 Pet 1:20).[9] The Father chose a group of men and women in the Son before the foundation of the world in love (Eph 1:4); the Son made a covenant with the Father that he would give his life and shed his blood for them (cf. 10:18; 1 Pet 1:18–20); and the Father gave them to the Son to be his (10:29; 17:6, 9, 24; cf. 6:37, 39; 18:9). The followers of Jesus do not become Jesus' own at the moment or because they begin to follow him, but they have already been given to the Son as a gift from the Father in eternity. Long before the movement of following Jesus starts in time and space by the decision from the followers' end to follow Jesus, they already belonged to both the Father and the Son (16:15; 17:10).[10] There was a pre-established ownership of Jesus over his followers' lives which was wrought by the divine pact between Father and the Son and is expressed by Jesus' claims "my own" (10:14, τὰ ἐμα; 10:4, τὰ ἴδια) and "my sheep" (10:27, τὰ πρόβατα τὰ ἐμά; 10:3, τὰ ἴδια πρόβατα). This pre-established ownership is the starting point of following Jesus.

The Son's ownership over his own (τὰ ἴδια) is not merely a legal proprietorship, but a "personal bond" that entails Jesus' intimate and absolute knowledge of them (10:14, 27; cf. 2 Tim 2:19).[11] Just as the Father knows the Son and the Son knows the Father from eternity, Jesus already knew his own even before the universe was created. Those whom he has known the Son calls to come to him. The divine knowledge of the Son for his own is the basis that the Son calls them and the magnet that pulls them to himself, and that they come to know him.

---

8. "John's statement, 'God is love,' refers first to all to the intratrinitarian relationship within the eternal God. God is love within himself: The Father loves the Son; the Son reciprocates that love; and this love between the Father and the Son is the Holy Spirit." Grenz, *Theology for the Community of God*, 72.

9. Turretin, *Institutes of Elenctic Theology*, 2:177–78.

10. Schlatter, *The History of the Christ*, 104.

11. Schnackenburg, *John*, 2:297–98.

To put it in other words, before the act of following Jesus emerges in history, it was designed by the Father and the Son in eternity. The act of following Jesus finds its origin in the eternity of God. The fellowship between the Father and the Son before the beginning of the world is the genesis of the act of following Jesus (cf. 1:1, 2, 18). The pre-established bond of ownership wrought by the divine transaction between Father and the Son is the incubator from which the life of following Jesus ensues (cf. 6:37, 39; 10:29; 17:2, 6, 9, 10, 24).

B. *To* the Father

The movement of following Jesus is ultimately theological as it journeys towards the Father. Jesus came from the Father (16:28) and returns to the Father (20:17). When he descended from the Father, he came alone, but when he ascends to the Father, he does so together with his followers, taking them to the Father. *To the Father*—this is the objective for which the Father sent the Son; this is the purpose for which Jesus calls men and women to himself and to follow; this is the goal for which the Son makes the Father known to his followers; this is the destination of the journey of following Jesus. Following Jesus is the God-ward theological movement.

That the journey of following Jesus is the theological God-ward movement is implied in 1:35–51 by two expressions. The first is that Jesus is the Lamb *of God* (1:29, 36). The role of the Lamb of God, that is from God and is in a close personal relationship with God, is to open an access to God and lead men and women to the presence of God by his death just as the lamb of the Hebrew Scriptures functions to open the way to God by removing the barrier of sin (Lev 14:12–13, 21–25; Isa 53:6–7).[12] That the two disciples begin to follow Jesus upon hearing the Baptist's pronouncement that Jesus is the Lamb of God, implies that their act of following Jesus is the God-ward theological movement.

The second is Jesus' promise to his first followers that they will see heaven opened and that the Son of Man will function as the bridge connecting God and humanity just as the Ladder of Jacob's vision connects heaven the place where God is and earth where humankind is. No matter whether they decide to follow Jesus by hearing the proclamation (1:37) or are invited to Jesus by someone else (1:42, 46) or called to follow him by Jesus himself (1:43), all the followers of Jesus are being led to have the lived experience of the ultimate reality of heaven opened and to enter into the relationship with

---

12. Brodie, *John*, 156–57.

God (1:51). God is the destination to whom Jesus leads the followers as the end of the journey of following Jesus.

In 8:12–29, the problem of existential darkness of humanity that they do not know the direction of life, from where they came and to where they are to go, is exposed (12:35). As the solution of the problem, Jesus the light of the world comes and calls men and women to follow him, so that they may have the light of life, the clear direction of life (8:12). The light of life that they will have by following Jesus is not only having the direction of life, but also, just as the light of God in the wilderness led ancient people to the Promised Land (Exod 13:21–22), being guided by the light to the final destination, to the Father himself, from whom Jesus came (8:42; 16:28) and to whom he is going (7:33; 13:1; 14:12, 28; 16:10, 17, 28; 17:11, 13; 20:17) and by whom humanity is created through the Son (1:3).

Encircled by many terms and motifs that convey the impending death of Jesus, the text of 12:26, for the first time and as the only case in the Fourth Gospel, states Jesus' serious call for his followers to serve him as his servants just as Jesus himself was the servant of God.[13] For those who follow him by serving him as his servant, twofold rewards are promised: they will be with him where Jesus is and the Father will honor them. The place where Jesus is and the servants will be with him refers to the "heavenly world . . . Jesus' sphere, his home" where he is in glorious communion with the Father.[14] The honor with which "the Father will honor" those who serve Jesus is the honor and glory that the Father and the Son share with each other, and thus being honored by the Father is to join the eternal glory of the Father and the Son. Both rewards point to the same state of glory in and with God. It is once again recapitulated that following Jesus is the God-ward movement that the final destination of the journey of following Jesus is to participate in the glory of the Father together with Jesus.

In the Upper Room discourse (13:31—4:3) given on the night before he was crucified, finally the destination of the movement of following Jesus, the place where Jesus goes is plainly stated that it is the dwelling place in the Father's house (ἐν τῇ οἰκίᾳ τοῦ πατρός μου μοναὶ πολλαί εἰσιν, 14:2). The terminus of the journey of following Jesus to which Jesus takes his own when he returns (παραλήμψομαι ὑμᾶς πρὸς ἐμαυτόν, ἵνα ὅπου εἰμὶ ἐγὼ καὶ ὑμεῖς ἦτε, 14:3) is God himself that they may have the permanent communion with him.[15]

13. πάσχα (11:55*2; 12:1; 13:1); ἀποθνῄσκω (11:50, 51; 12:24, 33), ἀποκτείνω (11:53; 12:10); ἐνταφιασμός (12:7); ἡ ὥρα (12:23, 27; 13:1); ὑψόω (12:32, 34); ποίῳ θανάτῳ (12:33).

14. Schnackenburg, *John*, 2:385.

15. Barrett, *John*, 457.

That the movement of following Jesus is ultimately a theological God-ward journey is repeatedly communicated by the prominent association of ἀκολουθεῖν and the where (ὅπου/ποῦ) motif in the Fourth Gospel. The deepest and most fundamental craving of humanity is to see, experience, and have unceasing communion with God in both this life and the life hereafter (14:8). Following Jesus who came from (descended) and goes back (ascends) to God and will take his followers to God, is the sole and surest God-given way (14:6) to satisfy the longing.

C. *With* Jesus

Although the life of following Jesus is in the ultimate sense a theological God-ward movement, it is essentially a christological movement because in a practical sense being with Jesus where he is, being led by Jesus, serving Jesus, and doing what Jesus commands to do, are the contents of the journey of following him.

Upon hearing the Baptist's witness that Jesus is the Lamb of God that will lead them to the presence of God (1:29, 36), the first thing that the disciples do and Jesus invites them to do is to be with Jesus where he is (1:39).[16] Their being *with* Jesus where he is does not end as a one time incident, but continues throughout the journey. It is not merely accompanying him physically, but having permanent fellowship with him.[17] Developing and deepening permanent fellowship with Jesus by being with him where he abides is the most essential component of the journey of following according to the Fourth Gospel.

After the initial experience of abiding *with* Jesus where he was (1:39), despite the fact that there is no direct command from Jesus to them to do the work of evangelism within 1:35–51, the followers naturally and most voluntarily do evangelism out of the jubilance of having fellowship with Jesus.[18] By stating two instances of evangelism in both groups of disciples (1:41–42, 45–46), the evangelist indicates that doing the work of evangelism in the Fourth Gospel is one of the natural activities of the life of following Jesus as a consequence of experiencing and enjoying fellowship with Jesus.

The importance of *being led* by Jesus' guidance and walking after him is not to be neglected. It is expressed in at least two places. In 8:12 when he declares that he is the light of the world and invites men and women to the

---

16. 1:39 ἦλθαν οὖν καὶ εἶδαν ποῦ μένει καὶ παρ' αὐτῷ ἔμειναν τὴν ἡμέραν ἐκείνην.

17. Schnackenburg, *John*, 1:308.

18. In the Samaritan woman's account, a similar voluntary evangelism happens (4:28–29, 39) out of the sheer jubilance of encountering Jesus (being *with* Jesus).

light of life, Jesus urges neither to receive it nor to walk in it, but to "follow" the light. Just as the people in the wilderness travelled by "following" the pillar of fire and cloud, moving forward when it rose and stopping when it stopped (cf. Exod 13:21, 22; Deut 1:33; Ps 78:14), the life of following Jesus is to be guided by Jesus the guiding light.[19] In 10:4 the importance of following closely the shepherd's guidance is implied (ἔμπροσθεν αὐτῶν πορεύεται καὶ τὰ πρόβατα αὐτῷ ἀκολουθεῖ), just as the guaranteed way to wellbeing of the Palestinian sheep utterly depends on following the shepherd's leading. Following Jesus is *being led* by Jesus' guidance throughout the journey.

Although the concrete content of serving Jesus is not mentioned in it, 12:26 employs the rare and unexpected vocabularies "to serve" (διακονέω)[20] and "servant" (διάκονος)[21] in association with ἀκολουθεῖν to communicate the important point that the act of following Jesus necessarily entails dedicated service for Jesus as his servants. Jesus himself lived the life of a perfect servant of God by fully serving him and completing all the things he commanded him to do (5:36; 10:18; 14:31; 15:10; 17:4). By calling those who follow him "my servant" and emphatically repeating the phrase twice ἐὰν ἐμοί τις διακονῇ, ... ἐάν τις ἐμοὶ διακονῇ ("Whoever serves me ... Whoever serves me ...," 12:26), it is made clear that the life of following Jesus is living as Jesus' servant, obeying him and completing the things that he commands to do just as he has lived a servant life to the Father.

What Jesus' followers must do is specifically communicated in 21:15–19 in connection with ἀκολουθεῖν.[22] Whereas the task of bringing other sheep outside sheepfold to Jesus is stated as Jesus' own work in 10:16 and the mission to reach out to the world is only hinted by the miracle of fish catch in 21:6, 11, the commission of particularly feeding Jesus' sheep is given to all Jesus' followers represented by Simon Peter (21:15–17). Following the examples that God has been the shepherd of his flock demonstrated in the wider Scriptural context (Ps 78:52; 80:1; Isa 40:11; 63:14), that Jesus

19. Beasley-Murray, *John*, 128.
20. It occurs only three times in the Fourth Gospel: 12:2, 26*2.
21. Also only three occurrences in the Gospel: 2:5, 9; 12:26.
22. Although what is commanded by the new commandment of love, modeled by foot washing (13:14–15, 34–35), is important for Jesus' followers to do in the life of following him, it is not included in the present study because in 13:31–14:3 the term ἀκολουθεῖν is directly associated with the where motif (13:33, 36, 37: Where I am going, you cannot follow me) in order to convey the inability of the disciples, not with the new commandment and the foot washing model, which are rather associated simply with "just as" (καθώς, 13:15, 34) without the employment of ἀκολουθεῖν. In the context where the followers' inability is the focus of the employment of ἀκολουθεῖν, connecting the term with what they must do is out of logic and coherence when there is no separate employment of ἀκολουθεῖν for the new commandment or foot wash modeling.

is the good shepherd as depicted by the model shepherd (10:11, 14, 15), and that the risen Jesus has fed the weary disciples in the immediate context (21:1–14), the followers of Jesus must feed his sheep in the course of following him as one of the major contents of the life of following Jesus and as a tangible expression of love for Jesus.

The final occurrence of the where motif in association with ἀκολουθεῖν implies what Jesus' followers must do in the twofold sense (21:18–19). From the perspective of the evangelist who already knew the mode of Peter's death by which he glorified God by taking the same kind of path of death wherein Jesus had glorified God, taking the passage of death (12:33; 18:32; cf. 13:31–32) is a way of following Jesus. From the perspective of Peter, who might grasp 21:18 in the sharp contrast of ὅπου ἤθελες (wherever you wished) and ὅπου οὐ θέλεις (where you do not wish), the life of following Jesus is a total surrender to the Master's leading, denying one's own wish to go to where one wishes to go (just as one has lived until now) and (from that moment on) going to wherever he leads even though it is where one does not wish to go. Those who are privileged to be with Jesus where he is and invited to have the glorious communion with the Father, are also to be with Jesus where he is in the place of humility, trouble, and affliction.

Therefore, the lived experience of following Jesus by being with him where he is includes both the life of *going down with* Jesus to the cross and *going up with* him to the Father's presence, both humility and honor, both death and glory. Yet, while the former is a transitory and temporal experience, the latter is the final and ultimate experience because the Jesus whom they follow is not the one who ended up in sorrow and defeat, but the one who won the victory over death, the Lord of triumphant resurrection.

D. *By* the Works of the Father, the Son, and the Holy Spirit

What is it that makes the journey of following Jesus possible in all the above mentioned aspects—the journey to God into communion with him (cf. 1:51; 12:26; 14:2–3; 17:24), the lived experience of being with Jesus where he is (1:39), doing the work of mission and feeding Jesus' sheep (21:15–17; cf. 15:16), serving him as his servants and as a result being honored by the Father (12:26), following the guiding light (8:12), total submission to his leadership by being led even to the place where one does not wish to go (21:18), walking the passage of death, and thus giving glory to God (21:18–19)? What is the most essential factor that makes the life of following Jesus realized?

In Philip's repeated failures—the failure to Jesus' test in feeding the crowd (6:6-7),[23] the failure in knowing Jesus' heart toward the Gentiles (12:20-22),[24] and the failure in seeing the Father in Jesus despite the time he has spent with him for three years (14:8-11)—the spiritual dullness and blindness of Jesus' followers is demonstrated. Human capacity in spiritual understanding is not what makes following Jesus viable in knowledge (cf. Ps 14:2; Rom 3:11; Matt 13:13-14).[25] Not only the dullness and blindness, but spiritual inability[26] and impossibility[27] in following Jesus is the dismal reality of human existence no matter whether they are the Jews or the disciples (7:34; 8:21; 13:33). That no human being is capable of following Jesus by one's own inherent ability is also expressed in Peter's denial of Jesus against his willingness and self confidence to follow him and even lay down his own life (13:36-38).

What is that which makes it possible for the incapable and fragile disciples to follow Jesus? It is the sovereign work of the Father and Jesus. As the spiritually dead can be quickened by the sovereign work of the Spirit (cf. 3:3, 5), the life of following Jesus can be started, sustained, and completed by the work of the Father and Jesus. Because Jesus gives his life for them first (10:11, 15, 17), they become alive and able to give their life for him afterward (cf. 13:36-37; 21:18-19). Because the Father draws them to Jesus, they are able to come to him (6:44; 12:32). Because the Son makes the Father's name known to them and enables them to understand, they come to know him (15:15; 17:6, 26; 1 John 5:20). Because the Father and the Son hold them in their mighty hands and protect them (10:28-29; 17:11, 15), they are able to finish the journey of following, not falling away in the middle of the journey like Judas (cf. 13:21, 27, 30; 18:2-3). Because Jesus comes and restores them when they fail, they are able to continue following him, overcoming their fragility and brokenness (21:1-19). Because Jesus feeds and sustains them continually, they become able to feed Jesus' sheep (21:1-17; cf. 1 Kgs 19:5-8).[28] Because the ascended Jesus does his own work in and through them continually, they are able to perform his mission.[29] Neither ability nor possibility is in the followers. The manifold

---

23. Lindars, *John*, 241.
24. Morris, *John*, 592.
25. Carson, *John*, 494.
26. Lincoln, *John*, 388; Ridderbos, *John*, 478.
27. Segovia, *The Farewell*, 59; Bruner, *John*, 804.
28. Keener, *John*, 2:1234.
29. Köstenberger, "Jesus the Good Shepherd," 71; Lewis, "'Shepherd My Sheep,'" 322; Lincoln, *John*, 515.

work of the Father and the Son for, in, and through them is that which makes the entire journey of following Jesus possible from commencement to completion. The journey of following Jesus is possible only by the sovereign work of the Father and the Son.

The term ἀκολουθεῖν is not associated with the role of the Holy Spirit within an immediate context.[30] However, by locating the coming of the Holy Spirit (14:16, 17, 26; 15:26; 16:13) after Peter and the disciples' inability to follow Jesus (13:33, 36–38) and Philip's dullness in seeing the Father in Jesus (14:8, 9), it is implied that the journey of following Jesus is possible by the work of the Holy Spirit. The spiritual inability and incompetence of human beings (including Jesus' followers) are not the final words. Another advocate, the Holy Spirit, whom the Father will send, is coming to them to open their spiritual senses, and teach and lead them to understand and experience all truths (16:13). The journey of following Jesus and participation in Jesus' fellowship with the Father by being where Jesus is, depends not on the ability of the disciples, but on the work of the Holy Spirit together with the Father and the Son.

E. *Into* Eternity

The ultimate destination of the journey of following Jesus is the union with the Father together with Jesus, just as it is never an overstatement that Jesus' followers will be "swept up into the oneness that unites the Father and the Son" (17:20–23).[31] The Son who came from eternity goes back into eternity taking his followers with him. Jesus who descended from heaven (from the Father) ascends to heaven (to the Father) taking his followers with him into the communion with the Father.[32] The Son who came out of the bosom of the Father (1:18) goes back leading his followers into the bosom of the

---

30. It is mentioned in the section on Limitations of the Study and Points to be Studied Further that the role of the Holy Spirit is indispensable for the life of following Jesus and the subject needs to be studied further to fully develop the theme of following Jesus. In this study, consideration of the works of the Holy Spirit in the life of following Jesus is limited because the purpose of the present research is to investigate the pericopes where ἀκολουθεῖν appears and the correlated motifs closely associated with ἀκολουθεῖν.

31. Moloney, *John*, 359.

32. The descent-ascent schema in the Fourth Gospel has been recognized by scholars in different perspectives and emphases. As for the function of the schema within the literary structure of the Gospel and the Johannine community in its relationship to its environment, see Meeks, "The Man from Heaven," 44–72; Sidebottom, "The Descent and Ascent of the Son of Man," 115–22. For the schema with a focus on "lifting up" sayings (3:14; 8:28; 12:32–34), see Nicholson, *Death as Departure*. For the schema in Jesus' mission perspective, see Köstenberger, *The Missions of Jesus and the Disciples*, 126–30.

Father, so that they may participate in the intimate loving communion with the Father together with him. There the followers of Jesus will experience the wondrous mystery of being the "co-lovers"[33] of God. When Jesus' followers commune with the Father, together with Jesus, participating in the inner life of the Father and the Son, the final objective of the journey of following Jesus will be completed (17:24). Toward this end, to invite the readers into this incomparably glorious lived experience (Spirituality) of following Jesus, the fourth evangelist communicates the unique aspects of following Jesus in the Johannine text.

---

33. Torrance and Walls, *John Duns Scotus*, 8–9.

Bibliography

Aalen, Sverre. "glory, honor." *NIDNTT* 2:44–51.
Abogunrin, Samuel O. "The Three Variant Accounts of Peter's Call: A Critical and Theological Examination of the Texts." *New Testament Studies* 31 (1985) 587–602.
Agourides, Savas. "The Purpose of John 21." In *Studies in the History and Text of the New Testament—in Honor of Kenneth Willis Clark, PhD*, edited by Boyd L. Daniels and M. Jack Sugg, 127–32. Studies and Documents 29. Salt Lake City: University of Utah Press, 1967.
Alexander, Patrick H., et al., eds. *The SBL Handbook of Style: For Ancient Near Eastern, Biblical, and Early Christian Studies*. Peabody, MA: Hendrickson, 1999.
Appold, Mark L. *The Oneness Motif in the Fourth Gospel: Motif Analysis and Exegetical Probe into the Theology of John*. Wissenschaftliche Untersuchungen zum Neuen Testament 2/1. Tübingen: Mohr, 1976.
Ashton, John. *Understanding the Fourth Gospel*. Oxford: Clarendon, 1993.
Athanasius. *On the Incarnation*. Accessed 3 January 2012. http://www.ccel.org/ccel/athanasius/incarnation.pdf.
Augustine. *Confessions*. Translated by Henry Chadwick. Oxford: Oxford University Press, 1991.
Aumann, Jordan. *Spiritual Theology*. London: Sheed and Ward, 1980.
Aune, David E. *The Cultic Setting of Realized Eschatology in Early Christianity*. Novum Testamentum Supplements 28. Leiden: Brill, 1972.
———. "Following the Lamb: Discipleship in the Apocalypse." In *Patterns of discipleship in the New Testament*, edited by Richard N. Longenecker, 269–84. McMaster New Testament Studies 1. Grand Rapids: Eerdmans, 1996.
———. *Revelation 6-16*. WBC 52B. Waco: Word, 1998.
Aune, David E., ed. *The Blackwell Companion to the New Testament*. Malden, MA: Blackwell, 2010.
Bacon, Benjamin W. "The Motivation of John 21.15–25." *Journal of Biblical Literature* 50 (1931) 71–80.
Baltzer, Klaus. *The Covenant Formulary in Old Testament, Jewish, and Early Christian Writings*. Translated by David E. Green. Philadelphia: Fortress, 1971.
Balz, Horst, and Gerhard Schneider, eds. *Exegetical Dictionary of the New Testament*. 3 vols. Grand Rapids: Eerdmans, 1990–1993.
Barclay, William. *New Testament Words*. Louisville: Westminster, 1974.
Barosse, Thomas. "The Seven Days of the New Creation in St. John's Gospel." *Catholic Biblical Quarterly* 23 (1959) 507–16.

Barr, James. "Words for Love in Biblical Greek." In *The Glory of Christ in the New Testament: Studies in Christology in Memory of George Bradford Caird*, edited by L. D. Hurst and N. T. Wright, 3–18. Oxford: Clarendon, 1987.

Barrett, C. K. *The Gospel according to St. John: An Introduction with Commentary and Notes on the Greek Text*. 2nd ed. Philadelphia: Westminster, 1978.

———. *The Gospel of John and Judaism*. London: SPCK, 1975.

———. "Jews and *Judaizers* in the Epistles of *Ignatius*." In *Jews, Greeks, and Christians: Religious Cultures in late Antiquity*, edited by Robert Hamerton-Kelly, and Robin Scroggs, 220–44. Leiden: Brill, 1976.

———. "John 21.15–25." In *Essays on John*, 159–67. Philadelphia: Westminster, 1982.

———. "The Lamb of God." *New Testament Studies* 1 (1954–1955) 210–18.

Barrosse, Thomas. "The Relationship of Love to Faith in St. John." *Theological Studies* (1957) 538–59.

Bartholomew, Gilbert L. "Feed my Lambs: 21:15–19 as Oral Gospel." *Semeia* 39 (1987) 69–96.

Barton, Stephen C. *Discipleship and Family Ties in Mark and Matthew*. Society for New Testament Studies Monograph Series 80. Cambridge: Cambridge University Press, 1994.

———. "New Testament Interpretation as Performance." In *Life Together: Family, Sexuality and Community in the New Testament and Today*, 223–50. Edinburgh: T. & T. Clark, 2001.

———. *The Spirituality of the Gospels*. Peabody, MA: Hendrickson, 1992.

Bauer, Walter, et al. *A Greek-English Lexicon of the New Testament and Other Early Christian Literature*. 2nd ed. Chicago: University of Chicago Press, 1979.

Bauer, Walter, et al. *A Greek-English Lexicon of the New Testament and Other Early Christian Literature*. 3rd ed. Chicago: University of Chicago Press, 2000.

Bauckham, Richard. "The 153 Fish and the Unity of the Fourth Gospel." *Neotestamentica* 36 (2002) 77–88.

———. "The Beloved Disciple as Ideal Author." *Journal for the Study of the New Testament* 49 (1993) 21–44.

———. "For Whom Were the Gospels Written?" In *The Gospels for All Christians: Rethinking The Gospel Audiences*, edited by Richard Bauckham, 9–48. Grand Rapids: Eerdmans, 1998.

———. *Jesus and the Eyewitnesses: The Gospels as Eyewitness Testimony*. Cambridge: Eerdmans, 2006.

———. *The Testimony of the Beloved Disciple: Narrative, History, and Theology in the Gospel of John*. Grand Rapids: Baker Academic, 2007.

Beale, G. K. *The Book of Revelation: A Commentary on the Greek Text*. NIGTC. Grand Rapids: Eerdmans; Carlisle, UK: Paternoster, 1999.

Beasley-Murray, George R. *John*. WBC 36. Waco: Word, 1987.

Beck, David R. *The Discipleship Paradigm: Readers and Anonymous Characters in the Fourth Gospel*. Biblical Interpretation Series 27. Leiden: Brill, 1997.

———. "The Narrative Function of Anonymity in Fourth Gospel Characterization." *Semeia* 63 (1993) 143–58.

Beirne, Margaret M. *Women and Men in the Fourth Gospel: A Genuine Discipleship of Equals*. Journal for the Study of the New Testament: Supplement Series 242. Sheffield: Sheffield Academic, 2003.

Bennema, Cornelis. "The Identity and Composition of *OI IOYΔAIOI* in the Gospel of John." *Tyndale Bulletin* 60, no. 2 (2009) 239–63.
Berkhof, Louis. *Systematic Theology.* Edinburgh: Banner of Truth, 2000.
Bernard, John H. *A Critical and Exegetical Commentary on the Gospel according to St. John.* 2 vols. ICC. Edinburgh: T. & T. Clark, 1928.
Bertram, G. "ὑψόω." *TDNT* 8:606–13.
Besobrasoff, S. (Bishop Cassian). "John XXI." *New Testament Studies* 3 (1956–1957) 132–36.
Best, Ernest. "Discipleship in Mark: Mark 8.22—10.52." *Scottish Journal of Theology* 23 (1970) 323–37.
———. *Following Jesus: Discipleship in the Gospel of Mark.* Journal for the Study of the New Testament: Supplement Series 4. Sheffield: JSOT, 1981.
———. "The Role of the Disciples in Mark." *New Testament Studies* 23 (1976–1977) 377–401.
Beutler, Johannes. "The Use of 'Scripture' in the Gospel of John." In *Exploring the Gospel of John: In Honor of D. Moody Smith*, edited by R. Alan Culpepper and C. Clifton Black, 147–62. Louisville: Westminster John Knox, 1996.
Blaine, Brad B., Jr. *Peter in the Gospel of John: The Making of an Authentic Disciple.* Academia Biblica 27. Atlanta: Society of Biblical Literature, 2007.
Blendinger, C. "ἀκολουθέω." *NIDNTT* 1:480–83.
Bock, Darrell L. *Luke 1:1—9:50.* Baker Exegetical Commentary on the New Testament. Grand Rapids: Baker, 1994.
———. *Luke 9:51—24:53.* Baker Exegetical Commentary on the New Testament. Grand Rapids: Baker, 1996.
Boismard, Marie E. *Moses or Jesus: An Essay in Johannine Christology.* Translated by Benedict T. Viviano. Minneapolis: Fortress, 1993.
Borgen, Peder. "God's Agent in the Fourth Gospel." In *Religions in Antiquity*, edited by Jacob Neusner, 137–48. Leiden: Brill, 1968.
Bornkamm, Gunther. *Early Christian Experience.* New York: Harper & Row, 1969.
Bouyer, Louis. *The Spirituality of the New Testament and the Fathers.* New York: Seabury, 1963.
Bowe, Barbara E. *Biblical Foundations of Spirituality: Touching a Finger to the Flame.* Lanham: Rowman and Littlefield, 2003.
Bowen, Clayton R. "Love in the Fourth Gospel." *Journal of Religion* 13 (1933) 39–49.
Breck, John. "John 21: Appendix, Epilogue or Conclusion?" *St. Vladimir's Theological Quarterly* 36 (1992) 27–49.
Bream, Howard N. "No Need to be Asked Questions: A Study of John 16:30." In *Search the Scriptures: New Testament Studies in Honor of Raymond T. Stamm*, edited by Jacob M. Myers, Otto Reimherr, and Howard N. Bream, 49–74. Gettysburg Theological Studies 3. Leiden: Brill, 1969.
Brodie, Thomas L. *The Gospel according to John: A Literary and Theological Commentary.* New York: Oxford University Press, 1997.
———. *The Quest for the Origin of John's Gospel: A Source-Oriented Approach.* New York: Oxford University Press, 1993.
Brouwer, Wayne. *The Literary Development of John 13–17: A Chiastic Reading.* Atlanta: Society of Biblical Literature, 2000.
Brown, Colin, ed. *New International Dictionary of New Testament Theology.* 4 vols. Grand Rapids: Zondervan, 1975–1985.

Brown, Jeannine K. "Creation's Renewal in the Gospel of John." *Catholic Biblical Quarterly* 72 (2010) 275–90.

Brown, Raymond E. *The Community of the Beloved Disciple: The Life, Loves, Hates of an Individual Church in New Testament Times.* New York: Paulist, 1979.

———. *The Gospel according to John.* 2 vols. New York: Doubleday, 1966–1970.

———. *An Introduction to the Gospel of John.* Edited by Francis J. Moloney. New York: Doubleday, 2003.

———. *An Introduction to the New Testament.* New Haven: Yale University Press, 1997.

———. *New Testament Essays.* London: Chapman, 1967.

———. "Other Sheep Not of This Fold: The Johannine Perspective on Christian Diversity in the Late First Century." *Journal of Biblical Literature* 97 (1978) 5–22.

———. "The Qumran Scrolls and the Johannine Gospel and Epistles." In *The Scrolls and the New Testament*, edited by Krister Stendahl, 183–207. New York: Crossroad, 1992.

Brown, Sherri. "Gift upon Gift: Covenant through Word of the Gospel of John." PhD diss., Catholic University of America, 2008.

Bruce, F. F. *The Gospel of John: Introduction, Exposition, and Notes.* Grand Rapids: Eerdmans, 1983.

Bruner, Fredrick D. *The Gospel of John: A Commentary.* Grand Rapids: Eerdmans, 2012.

———. *Matthew: A Commentary.* Vol. 1, *The Christbook, Matthew 1–12.* Rev. and exp. ed. Grand Rapids: Eerdmans, 2004.

Bruns, J. Edgar. Review of *John's Gospel in New Perspective: Christology and the Realities of Roman Power*, by Richard J. Cassidy. *Catholic Biblical Quarterly* 56 (1994) 134–35.

Bryan, Steven M. "The Eschatological Temple in John 14." *Bulletin for Biblical Research* 15, no. 2 (2005) 187–98.

Bultmann, Rudolf. *The Gospel of John: A Commentary.* Translated by George R. Beasley-Murray, Rupert W. N. Hoare, and John K. Riches. Philadelphia: Westminster, 1971.

———. *Theology of the New Testament.* 2 vols. Translated by Kendrick Grobel. New York: Scribner's Sons, 1955.

Burge, Gary. *The Anointed Community: The Holy Spirit in the Johannine Tradition.* Grand Rapids: Eerdmans, 1987.

Busse, Ulrich. "Open Questions on John 10." In *The Shepherd Discourse of John 10 and its Context*, edited by Johannes Beutler and Robert T. Fortna, 1–17. Society for New Testament Studies Monograph Series 67. Cambridge: Cambridge University Press, 1991.

Byrne, Brendan. "The Faith of the Beloved Disciple and the Community in John 20." *Journal for the Study of the New Testament* 23 (1985) 83–97.

Caird, G. B. *New Testament Theology.* Edited by L. D. Hurst. Oxford: Clarendon, 1994.

Calvin, John. *The Gospel according to St. John 11–21 and the First Epistle of John.* Translated by T. H. L. Parker. Grand Rapids: Eerdmans, 1961.

———. *Institutes of the Christian Religion.* 2 vols. Edited by John T. McNeill. Translated by Ford Lewis Battles. LCC 20–21.Westminster John Knox, 1960.

Caragounis, Chrys C., and Jan van der Watt. "A Grammatical Analysis of John 1:1." *Filologia Neotestamentaria* 21 (2008) 91–138.

Carson, D. A. "Current Source Criticism of the Fourth Gospel: Some Methodological Questions." *Journal of Biblical Literature* 97 (1978) 411–29.

———. *Divine Sovereignty and Human Responsibility: Biblical Perspectives in Tension.* Atlanta: Knox, 1981.
———. *The Gospel according to John.* Grand Rapids: Eerdmans, 1991.
Cassidy, Richard J. *John's Gospel in New Perspective: Christology and the Realities of Roman Power.* Maryknoll, NY: Orbis, 1992.
Catholic University of America staff, ed. *The New Catholic Encyclopedia.* New York: McGraw-Hill, 1967–1979.
Charlesworth, James H. *The Beloved Disciple: Whose Witness Validates the Gospel of John?* Valley Forge, PA: Trinity, 1995.
———. "The Dead Sea Scrolls and the Gospel according to John." In *Exploring the Gospel of John: In Honor of D. Moody Smith*, edited by R. Alan Culpepper and C. Clifton Black, 65–97. Louisville: Westminster John Knox, 1996.
Charlesworth, James H., ed. *The Old Testament Pseudepigrapha.* 2 vols. New Haven: Yale University Press, 1983, 1985.
Charry, Ellen T. "Spiritual Formation by the Doctrine of the Trinity." *Theology Today* 54, no. 3 (1997) 367–80.
Chennattu, Rekha M. "On Becoming Disciples (John 1:35–51) Insights from the Fourth Gospel." *Salesianum* 63 (2001) 467–98.
———. *Johannine Discipleship as a Covenant Relationship.* Peabody, MA: Hendrickson, 2006.
Chilton, Bruce, and Edwin M. Yamauchi. "Synagogue." In *Dictionary of New Testament Background*, edited by Craig A. Evans and Stanley E. Porter, 1145–53. Downers Grove, IL: InterVarsity, 2000.
Claussen, Carsten. "The Role of John 21: Discipleship in Retrospect and Redefinition." In *New Currents through John: A Global Perspective*, edited by Francisco Lozada Jr. and Tom Thatcher, 55–68. Atlanta: Society of Biblical Literature, 2006.
Clement, Olivier. *The Roots of Christian Mysticism: Texts from the Patristic Era with Commentary.* Edited by Jeremy Hummerstone. Translated by Theodore Berkley. Hyde Park, NY: New City, 1993.
Coenen, L. "ἀποκτείνω." *NIDNTT* 1:429–30.
Collins, Raymond F. "The *Berith*-Notion of the Cairo Damascus Covenant and Its Comparison with the New Testament." *Ephemerides Theologicae Lovanienses* 39 (1963) 555–94.
———. "Discipleship in John's Gospel." *Emmanuel* 91 (1985) 248–55.
Coloe, Mary L. *Dwelling in the Household of God: Johannine Ecclesiology and Spirituality.* Collegeville, MN: Liturgical, 2007.
———. *God Dwells with Us: Temple Symbolism in the Fourth Gospel.* Collegeville, MN: Liturgical, 2001.
Conway, Colleen M. "The Production of the Johannine Community: A New Historicist Perspective." *Journal of Biblical Literature* 121 (2002) 479–95.
Conzelmann, H. "σκότος, σκοτία." *TDNT* 7:423–45.
———. "φῶς." *TDNT* 9:310–58.
Cullmann, Oscar. *Early Christian Worship.* London: SCM, 1953.
———. *The Johannine Circle: Its Place in Judaism, among the Disciples of Jesus and in Early Christianity: A Study in the Origin of the Gospel of John.* London: SCM, 1976.
———. *Prayer in the New Testament.* Minneapolis: Fortress, 1995.
Culpepper, R. Alan. *Anatomy of the Fourth Gospel: A Study in Literary Design.* Philadelphia: Fortress, 1983.

———. "Anti-Judaism as a Theological Problem." In *Anti-Judaism and the Fourth Gospel: Papers of the Leuven Colloquium 2000*, edited by Reimund Bieringer, Didier Pollefeyt, and Frederique Vandecasteele-Vanneuville, 68–91. Assen, The Netherlands: Royal Van Gorcum, 2001.

———. "Designs for the Church in the Imagery of John 21:1–14." In *Imagery in the Gospel of John: Terms, Forms, Themes and Theology of Johannine Figurative Language*, edited by Jorg Frey, Jan G. van der Watt, and Reuben Zimmermann, in collaboration with Gabi Kern, 370–402. Wissenschaftliche Untersuchungen zum Neuen Testament 200. Tubingen: Mohr/Siebeck, 2006.

———. *The Gospel and Letters of John*. Nashville: Abingdon, 1998.

———. *The Johannine School: An Evaluation of the Johannine-School Hypothesis Based on an Investigation of the Nature of Ancient Schools*. Society of Biblical Literature Dissertation Series 26. Missoula, MT: Scholars, 1975.

———. *John, the Son of Zebedee: The Life of a Legend*. Minneapolis: Fortress, 1994.

———. "Peter as Exemplary Disciple in John 21:15–19." *Perspectives in Religious Studies* 37 (2010) 165–78.

Curtis, Edward M. Review of *The Missions of Jesus and the Disciples according to the Fourth Gospel: With Implications for the Fourth Gospel's Purpose and the Mission of the Contemporary Church*, by A. J. Köstenberger. *Journal of the Evangelical Theological Society* 43, no. 1 (2000) 142–43.

Dahl, Nils A. *Jesus in the Memory of the Early Church*. Minneapolis: Augsburg, 1976.

Dautzenberg, G. "ἀμνὸς." *EDNT* 1:71.

Davies, Williams D. "Reflections on Aspects of the Jewish Background of the Gospel of John." In *Exploring the Gospel of John: In Honor of D. Moody Smith*, edited by R. Alan Culpepper and C. Clifton Black, 43–64. Louisville: Westminster John Knox, 1996.

Davies, William D., and Dale C. Allison. *A Critical and Exegetical Commentary on The Gospel according to Saint Matthew*. 3 vols. ICC. Edinburgh: T. & T. Clark, 1988–1997.

De Jonge, Marinus. *Jesus: Stranger from Heaven and Son of God*. Edited and translated by John Steely. Missoula, MT: Scholars, 1977.

———. "Jewish Expectations about the 'Messiah' according to the Fourth Gospel." *New Testament Studies* 19 (1973) 246–70.

Diodorus Siculus. *Bibliotheca Historica*. Accessed 30 June 2012. http://penelope.chicago.edu/Thayer/E/Roman/Texts/Diodorus_Siculus/13D*.html.

Diogenes Laertius. *Lives of Eminent Philosophers*. Volume 2, Books 6–10. Translated by R. D. Hicks. Loeb Classical Library 185. Cambridge, MA: Harvard University Press, 1925. Accessed 30 June 2012. http://www.perseus.tufts.edu/hopper/text?doc=Perseus%3Atext%3A1999.01.0258%3Abook%3D9%3Achapter%3D3.

Dodd, C. H. *Historical Tradition in the Fourth Gospel*. Cambridge: Cambridge University Press, 1965.

———. *The Interpretation of the Fourth Gospel*. Cambridge: Cambridge University Press, 1953.

Domeris, William R. "The Confession of Peter according to John 6:69." *Tyndale Bulletin* 44, no. 1 (1993) 155–67.

Donahue, John R. "Growth in Grace: Discipleship and the Life of Grace." *Southwestern Journal of Theology* 28, no. 2 (1986) 73–78.

———. "The Quest for Biblical Spirituality." In *Exploring Christian Spirituality: Essays in Honor of Sandra M. Schneiders*, edited by Bruce H. Lescher and Elizabeth Liebert, 73–97. New York: Paulist, 2006.
Donahue, John R., and Daniel J. Harrington. *The Gospel of Mark*. SP 2. Collegeville, MN: Liturgical, 2002.
Donaldson, James. "Called to Follow, A Twofold Experience of Discipleship in Mark." *Biblical Theology Bulletin* 5 (1975) 67–77.
Downey, Michael, ed. *The New Dictionary of Catholic Spirituality*. Collegeville, MN: Liturgical, 1993.
———. *Understanding Christian Spirituality*. New York: Paulist, 1997.
Droge, Arthur J. "The Status of Peter in the Fourth Gospel: A Note on John 18:10–11." *Journal of Biblical Literature* 109, no. 2 (1990) 307–11.
Du Rand, J. A. "Narratological Perspectives on John 13:1–38." *Hervormde Teologiese Studies* 46 (1990) 367–89.
———. "Perspectives on Johannine Discipleship according to the Farewell Discourse." *Neotestamentica* 25 (1991) 311–25.
———. "Reading the Fourth Gospel like a Literary Symphony." In *"What is John?" Vol. II: Literary and Social Readings of the Fourth Gospel*, edited by F. F. Segovia, 5–18. Society of Biblical Literature Symposium Series 7. Atlanta: Scholars, 1998.
———. "A Story and A Community: Reading the First Farewell Discourse (John 13:31—14:31) from Narratological and Sociological Perspectives." *Neotestamentica* 26 (1992) 31–45.
———. "A Syntactical and Narratological Reading of John 10 in Coherence with Chapter 9." In *The Shepherd Discourse of John 10 and its Context*, edited by Johannes Beutler and Robert T. Fortna, 94–115. Society for New Testament Studies Monograph Series 67. Cambridge: Cambridge University Press, 1991.
Duke, Paul D. *Irony in the Fourth Gospel*. Atlanta: Knox, 1985.
Dunn, James D. G. "Spirit and experience." In *Unity and Diversity in the New Testament: An Enquiry into the Character of Earliest Christianity*, 174–202. London: SCM, 1990.
Ebel, G. "διώκω." *NIDNTT* 2:805–7.
Ellis, Peter F. "The Authenticity of John 21." *St. Vladimir's Theological Quarterly* 36 (1992) 17–25.
———. *The Genius of John: A Composition-Critical Commentary on the Fourth Gospel*. Collegeville, MN: Liturgical, 1984.
———. "Understanding the Concentric Structure of the Fourth Gospel." *St. Vladimir's Theological Quarterly* 47 (2003) 131–54.
Ensor, Peter. "The Glorification of the Son of Man: An Analysis of John 13:31–32." *Tyndale Bulletin* 58, no. 2 (2007) 229–52.
Evans, Ernest. "The Verb ἀγαπᾶν in the Fourth Gospel." In *Studies in the Fourth Gospel*, edited by F. L. Cross, 64–71. London: Mowbray, 1975.
Farelly, Nicolas. *Disciples in the Fourth Gospel: A Narrative Analysis of their Faith and Understanding*. Wissenschaftliche Untersuchungen zum Neuen Testament 290. Tubingen: Mohr/Siebeck, 2010.
Fee, Gordon D. *New Testament Exegesis*. 3rd ed. Louisville: Westminster John Knox, 2002.
Fernando, G. Charles A. "The Relationship between Law and Love in the Gospel of John." PhD diss., Saint Paul University, 2001.

Fiorenza, Elizabeth S. "The Followers of the Lamb: Visionary Rhetoric and Social-Political Situation." In *Discipleship in the New Testament*, edited by Fernando F. Segovia, 144–65. Philadelphia: Fortress, 1985.
Foerster, W. "ἁρπάζω." *TDNT* 1:472–73.
Fortna, Robert T. *The Fourth Gospel and Its Predecessor*. Philadelphia: Fortress, 1988.
———. *The Fourth Gospel: From Narrative Source to Present Gospel*. Philadelphia: Fortress, 1988.
———. *The Gospel of Signs: A Reconstruction of the Narrative Source underlying the Fourth Gospel*. Cambridge: Cambridge University Press, 1970.
France, R. T. *The Gospel of Mark: A Commentary on the Greek Text*. NIGTC. Grand Rapids: Eerdmans, 2002.
Franzmann, Martin H. *Follow Me: Discipleship according to Saint Matthew*. Saint Louis: Concordia, 1961.
Franzmann, Martin H, and M. Klinger. "The Call Stories of John 1 and John 21." *St. Vladimir's Theological Quarterly* 36 (1992) 7–15.
Freed, Edwin D. *Old Testament Quotations in the Gospel of John*. Novum Testamentum Supplements 11. Leiden: Brill, 1965.
———. "Samaritan Influence in the Gospel of John." *Catholic Biblical Quarterly* 30 (1968) 580–87.
Freedman, David N., ed. *Anchor Bible Dictionary*. 6 vols. New York: Doubleday, 1992.
———. "Divine Commitment and Human Obligation." *Interpretation* 18 (1964) 419–31.
Fuglseth, Kare S. *Johannine Sectarianism in Perspective: A Sociological, Historical, and Comparative Analysis of Temple and Social Relationships in the Gospel of John, Philo, and Qumran*. Novum Testamentum Supplements 119. Leiden: Brill, 2005.
Furnish, Victor P. *The Love Command in the New Testament*. London: SCM, 1973.
Ganss, George. Introduction to *Ignatius of Loyola: Spiritual Exercises and Selected Works*. Edited by George E. Ganss. New York: Paulist, 1991.
Gaventa, Beverly Robert. "The Archive of Excess: John 21 and the Problem of Narrative Closure." In *Exploring the Gospel of John: In Honor of D. Moody Smith*, edited by R. Alan Culpepper and C. Clifton Black, 240–51. Louisville: Westminster John Knox, 1996.
Gloer, W. Hulitt. "'Come and See': Disciples and Discipleship in the Fourth Gospel." In *Perspectives on John: Methods and Interpretation in the Fourth Gospel*, edited by Robert B. Sloan and Mikeal C. Parsons, 269–301. NABPR Special Studies Series 11. Lewiston, NY: Mellen, 1993.
Gray, Arthur. "The Last Chapter of St. John's Gospel as Interpreted by Early Christian Art." *Hibbert Journal* 20 (1921–1922) 696–97.
Grech, Prosper. *An Outline of New Testament Spirituality*. Grand Rapids: Eerdmans, 2011.
Green, Joel B. *The Way of the Cross: Following Jesus in the Gospel of Mark*. Nashville: Discipleship Resources, 1991.
Grenz, Stanley J. *Theology for the Community of God*. Grand Rapids: Eerdmans, 2000.
Grossouw, William K. "A Note on John XIII 1–3." *Novum Testamentum* 8 (1966) 124–31.
Gundry, Robert H. "In My Father's House are Many μοναί (John 14:2)." *Zeitschrift für die neutestamentliche Wissenschaft und die Kunde der älteren Kirche* 58 (1967) 68–72.

———. *Mark: A Commentary on His Apology for the Cross*. Grand Rapids: Eerdmans, 1993.
Haenchen, Ernst. *John*. Translated by Robert W. Funk. 2 vols. Hermeneia. Philadelphia: Fortress, 1984.
Hägerland, Tobias. "John's Gospel: A Two-Level Drama?" *Journal for the Study of the New Testament* 253 (2003) 309-22.
Hagner, Donald A. *Matthew 14-28*. WBC 33B. Waco: Word, 1995.
Hahn, H. C. "σκότος." *NIDNTT* 1:421-25.
Hahn, H. C., and C. Brown. "φῶς." *NIDNTT* 2:490-96.
Hartman, Lars. "An Attempt at a Text-Centered Exegesis of John 21." *Studia Theologica* 38 (1984) 24-45.
Harvey, A. E. *Jesus on Trial: A Study in the Fourth Gospel*. London: SPCK, 1976.
Hay, David. "Experience." In *The Blackwell Companion to Christian Spirituality*, edited by Arthur Holder, 419-41. Malden, MA: Blackwell, 2005.
Heil, John P. *Blood and Water: The Death and Resurrection of Jesus in John 18-21*. Washington, DC: Catholic Biblical Association, 1995.
Hengel, Martin. *The Charismatic Leader and His Followers*. Translated by James Greig. New York: Crossroad, 1981.
———. *The Johannine Question*. Philadelphia: Trinity, 1989.
Herbermann, Charles G., et al., eds. *The Catholic Encyclopedia*. New York: Encyclopedia, 1913-1922.
Hillmer, Melvyn R. "They Believed in Him: Discipleship in the Johannine Tradition." In *Patterns of Discipleship in the New Testament*, edited by Richard N. Longenecker, 77-97. Grand Rapids: Eerdmans, 1996.
Hitchcock, F. R. M. "Is the Fourth Gospel a Drama?" In *The Gospel of John as Literature: An Anthology of Twentieth-Century Perspectives*, selected and introduced by Mark W. G. Stibbe, 15-24. Leiden: Brill, 1993.
Holder, Arthur, ed. *The Blackwell Companion to Christian Spirituality*. Malden, MA: Blackwell, 2005.
Hooker, Morna. *Endings: Invitations to Discipleship*. Peabody, MA: Hendrickson, 2003.
Horbury, William, and Brian McNeil, eds. *Suffering and Martyrdom in the New Testament: Studies Presented to G. M. Styler by the Cambridge New Testament Seminar*. Cambridge: Cambridge University Press, 1981.
Horsley, Richard A. *Bandits, Prophets and Messiahs: Popular Movements in the Time of Jesus*. Harrisburg, PA: Trinity, 1999.
Hoskins, Paul M. "Deliverance from Death by the True Passover Lamb: A Significant Aspect of the Fulfillment of the Passover in the Gospel of John." *Journal of the Evangelical Theological Society* 52, no. 2 (2009) 285-99.
Hoskyns, Edwyn C. *The Fourth Gospel*. Edited by Francis N. Davey. London: Faber & Faber, 1947.
Hunter, Macbride. *According to John: The New Look at the Fourth Gospel*. Philadelphia: Westminster, 1968.
Hurtado, Larry W. *Lord Jesus Christ*. Cambridge: Eerdmans, 2003.
———. "Religious Experience and Religious Innovation in the New Testament." *Journal of Religion* 80 (2000) 183-205.
Janzen, J. Gerald. "'I Am the Light of the World' (John 8:12) Connotation and Context." *Encounter* 67, no. 2 (2006) 115-35.
Jeremias, J. "ἀμνός, ἀρήν, ἀρνίον." *TDNT* 1:338-41.

———. "ποιμήν." *TDNT* 6:485–99.
Johnson, Luke T. *Religious Experience in Early Christianity: A Missing Dimension in New Testament Studies*. Minneapolis: Fortress, 1998.
Kasemann, Ernst. *The Testament of Jesus: A Study of the Gospel of John in the Light of Chapter 17*. Translated by G. Krodel. Philadelphia: Fortress, 1968.
Keener, Craig S. *The Gospel of John: A Commentary*. 2 vols. Peabody, MA: Hendrickson, 2003.
Kierspel, Lars. *The Jews and the World in the Fourth Gospel: Parallelism, Function, and Context*. Wissenschaftliche Untersuchungen zum Neuen Testament 220. Tubingen: Mohr/Siebeck, 2006.
Kiley, Mark. "Three More Fish Stories (John 21:11)." *Journal of Biblical Literature* 127 (2008) 529–31.
Kinerk, Edward. "Toward a Method for the Study of Spirituality." *Review for Religious* 40, no. 1 (1981) 3–19.
Kingsbury, Jack D. "On Following Jesus: the 'Eager' Scribe and the 'Reluctant' Disciple (Matthew 8:18–22)." *New Testament Studies* 34 (1988) 45–59.
———. "The Verb *Akolouthein* ('to Follow') as an Index of Matthew's View of His Community." *Journal of Biblical Literature* 97 (1978) 56–73.
Kittel, Gerhard. "ἀκολουθέω." *TDNT* 1:210–16.
Kittel, Gerhard, and Gerhard Friedrich, eds. *Theological Dictionary of the New Testament*. 10 vols. Translated by G. W. Bromiley. Grand Rapids: Eerdmans, 1964–1976.
Koester, Craig R. *The Dwelling of God: The Tabernacle in the Old Testament, Intertestamental Jewish Literature, and the New Testament*. Catholic Biblical Quarterly Monograph Series 22. Washington, DC: Catholic Biblical Association of America, 1989.
———. "Hearing, Seeing, and Believing in the Gospel of John." *Biblica* 70 (1989) 327–48.
———. "Messianic Exegesis and the Call of Nathanael (John 1:45–51)." *Journal for the Study of the New Testament* 39 (1990) 23–34.
———. *Symbolism in the Fourth Gospel: Meaning, Mystery, Community*. Minneapolis: Fortress, 1995.
———. *The Word of Life: A Theology of John's Gospel*. Grand Rapids: Eerdmans, 2008.
Köstenberger, Andreas J. "Jesus as Rabbi in the Fourth Gospel." *Bulletin for Biblical Research* 8 (1998) 97–128.
———. "Jesus the Good Shepherd Who Will Also Bring Other Sheep (John 10:16) The Old Testament Background of a Familiar Metaphor." *Bulletin for Biblical Research* 12 (2002) 67–96.
———. "The Missions of Jesus and the Disciples according to the Fourth Gospel: With Implications for the Fourth Gospel's Purpose and the Mission of the Contemporary Church." PhD diss., Trinity Evangelical Divinity School, 1993.
———. *The Mission of Jesus and the Disciples according to the Fourth Gospel: With Implications for the Fourth Gospel's Purpose and the Mission of the Contemporary Church*. Grand Rapids: Eerdmans, 1998.
Kysar, Robert. "Anti-Semitism and the Gospel of John." In *Anti-Semitism and Early Christianity: Issues of Polemic and Faith*, edited by Craig A. Evans and Donald A. Hagner, 113–27. Philadelphia: Fortress, 1993.
———. "Community and Gospel: Vectors in Fourth Gospel Criticism." *Interpretation* 31 (1977) 355–66.

———. *John*. ACNT. Minneapolis: Augsburg, 1986.
———. *John: The Maverick Gospel*. Louisville: Westminster John Knox, 2007.
Lacomara, Aelred. "Deuteronomy and the Farewell Discourse (John 13:31—16:33)." *Catholic Biblical Quarterly* 36 (1974) 65–84.
Ladd, George E. *A Theology of the New Testament*. Edited by Donald A. Hagner. Rev. ed. Grand Rapids: Eerdmans, 1993.
Lane, William L. *The Gospel according to Mark*. NICNT. Grand Rapids: Eerdmans, 1974.
Lapham, Fred. *An Introduction to the New Testament Apocrypha*. London: T. & T. Clark, 2003.
Lapin, H. "Rabbi." *ABD* 5:600–602.
Lash, Nicholas. "Performing the Scriptures." In *Theology on the Way to Emmaus*, 37–46. London: SCM, 1986.
Laubac, F. "χείρ." *NIDNTT* 2:148–50.
Lee, Dorothy A. "Abiding in the Fourth Gospel: A Case-Study in Feminist Biblical Theology." *Pacifica* 10 (1997) 123–36.
———. *Flesh and Glory: Symbolism, Gender and Theology in the Gospel of John*. New York: Crossroad, 2002.
———. "Partnership in Easter Faith: The Role of Mary Magdalene and Thomas in John 20." *Journal for the Study of the New Testament* 58 (1995) 37–49.
———. *The Symbolic Narratives of the Fourth Gospel*. Sheffield: JSOT, 1994.
Leech, Kenneth. *Experiencing God: Theology as Spirituality*. San Francisco: Harper & Row, 1985.
Lescher, Bruce H., and Eilzabeth Liebert, eds. *Exploring Christian Spirituality: Essays in Honor of Sandra M. Schneiders*. New York: Paulist, 2006.
Lewis, Karoline M. *"Shepherd Discourse": Restoring the Integrity of John 9:39—10:21*. Lang, 2008.
———. "'Shepherd My Sheep': Preaching for the Sake of Greater Works than These." *Word and World* 28, no. 3 (2008) 318–24.
Lightfoot, Robert H. *St. John's Gospel*. Edited by C. F. Evans. Oxford: Oxford University Press, 1956.
Lincoln, Andrew T. "The Beloved Disciple as Eyewitness and the Fourth Gospel as Witness." *Journal for the Study of the New Testament* 85 (2002) 3–26.
———. "From Writing to Reception: Reflections on Commentating on the Fourth Gospel." *Journal for the Study of the New Testament* 29 (2007) 353–72.
———. *The Gospel according to Saint John*. Black's New Testament Commentaries. London: Continuum, 2005.
———. *Truth on Trial: The Lawsuit Motif in the Fourth Gospel*. Peabody, MA: Hendrickson, 2000.
Lincoln, Andrew T., J. Gordon McConville, and Lloyd K. Pieterson, eds. *The Bible and Spirituality: Exploratory Essays in Reading Scripture Spiritually*. Eugene, OR: Cascade, 2013.
Lindars, Barnabas. *The Gospel of John*. NCB. Grand Rapids: Eerdmans, 1981.
———. "The Persecution of Christians in John 15:18—16:4a." In *Suffering and Martyrdom in the New Testament: Studies presented to G. M. Styler by the Cambridge New Testament Seminar*, edited by William Horbury and Brian McNeil, 48–69. Cambridge: Cambridge University Press, 1981.
Loader, R. G. "The Central Structure of Johannine Theology." *New Testament Studies* 30 (1984) 188–216.

Lohse, E. "χείρ." *TDNT* 9:424–34.
Lombaard, Christo. "Spirituality: Sense and Gist. On meaning, God and Being." In *The Spirit that Empowers: Perspectives on Spirituality*, edited by P. G. R. de Villiers, Celia Kourie and Christo Lombaard, 94–107. Acta Theologica Supplementum 11. Bloemfontein: University of the Free State Press, 2008.

———. "What Is Biblical Spirituality? Perspectives from a Minor Genre of Old Testament Scholarship." *Journal of Theology for Southern Africa* 135 (2009) 85–99.

Lombard, H. A., and W. H. Oliver. "A Working Supper in Jerusalem: John 13:1–38 Introduces Jesus' Farewell Discourses." *Neotestamentica* 25 (1991) 357–78.

Longenecker, Richard N., ed. *Patterns of Discipleship in the New Testament*. Grand Rapids: Eerdmans, 1996.

Lossky, Vladmir. *The Mystical Theology of the Eastern Church*. Crestwood, NY: St. Vladimir's Seminary Press, 2002.

Louw, Johannes P., and Eugene A. Nida. *Greek-English Lexicon of the New Testament Based on Semantic Domains*. 2nd edition. New York: United Bible Societies, 1989.

Lozada, Francisco, Jr. "Social Location and Johannine Scholarship: Looking Ahead." In *New Currents through John: A Global Perspective*, edited by Francisco Lozada Jr. and Tom Thatcher, 183–97. Atlanta: Society of Biblical Literature, 2006.

Lunde, Jonathan. *Following Jesus, The Servant King: A Biblical Theology of Covenantal Discipleship*. Grand Rapids: Zondervan, 2010.

Macquarrie, John. *Paths in Spirituality*. New York: Harper & Row, 1972.

Mahoney, Robert. *Two Disciples at the Tomb: The Background and Message of John 20:1–10*. Theologie und Wirklichkeit 6. Frankfurt: Lang, 1974.

Malatesta, Edward. *Interiority and Covenant: A Study of eivai ev and meneiv ev in the First Letter of Saint John*. Analecta Biblica 69. Rome: Biblical Institute, 1978.

Malina, Bruce J., and Richard L. Rohrbaugh. *Social-Science Commentary on the Gospel of John*. Minneapolis: Fortress, 1998.

Martyn, J. Louis. *The Gospel of John in Christian History: Essays for Interpreters*. New York: Paulist, 1978.

———. *History and Theology in the Fourth Gospel*. 3rd ed. Louisville: Westminster John Knox, 2003.

Marrow, Stanley B. *John 21—An Essay in Johannine Ecclesiology*. Rome: Gregorian University, 1968.

McBrien, Richard P. *Catholicism*. Rev. ed. San Francisco: HarperCollins, 1994.

McCaffrey, James. *The House with Many Rooms: The Temple Theme of John 14:2–3*. Rome: Biblical Institute, 1988.

McCarthy, Dennis J. "Notes on the Love of God in Deuteronomy and the Father–Son Relationship between Yahweh and Israel." *Catholic Biblical Quarterly* 27 (1965) 144–47.

McDowell, Edward A., Jr. "'Lovest Thou Me?' A Study of John 21:15–17." *Review and Expositor* 32 (1935) 422–41.

McGinn, Bernard, John Meyendorff, and Jean Leclercq, eds. *Christian Spirituality: Origins to the Twelfth Century*. New York: Crossroad, 1987.

McGrath, Alister E. *Christian Spirituality: An Introduction*. Malden, MA: Blackwell, 1999.

McKay, K. L. "Style and Significance in the Language of John 21:15–17." *Novum Testamentum* 27 (1985) 319–33.

Meeks, Wayne A. "Equal to God." In *The Conversation Continues: Studies in Paul and John: In Honor of J. Louis Martyn*. Edited by Robert T. Fortna and Beverly R. Gaventa, 309–21. Nashville: Abingdon, 1990.

———. "The Man from Heaven in Johannine Sectarianism." *Journal of Biblical Literature* 91 (1972) 44–72.

———. *The Prophet-King: Moses Traditions and the Johannine Christology*. Novum Testamentum Supplements 14. Leiden: Brill, 1967.

Meier, John P. "Love in Q and John: Love of Enemies, Love of One Another." *Mid-Stream* 40 (2001) 42–55.

———. *A Marginal Jew: Rethinking the Historical Jesus*. Vol. 1, *The Roots of the Problem and the Person*. Anchor Bible Reference Library. New York: Doubleday, 1991.

———. *A Marginal Jew: Rethinking the Historical Jesus*. Vol. 2, *Mentor, Message and Miracles*. Anchor Bible Reference Library. New York: Doubleday, 1994.

———. *A Marginal Jew: Rethinking the Historical Jesus*. Vol. 3, *Companions and Competitors*. Anchor Bible Reference Library. New York: Doubleday, 2001.

Menken, Maarten J. J. *Old Testament Quotations in the Fourth Gospel: Studies in Textual Form*. Contributions to Biblical Exegesis and Theology 15. Kampen: Kok Pharos, 1996.

Mercer, Calvin. "*APOSTELLEIN* and *PEMPEIN* in John." *New Testament Studies* 36 (1990) 619–24.

———. "Jesus the Apostle: 'Sending' and the theology of John." *Journal of the Evangelical Theological Society* 35, no. 4 (1992) 457–62.

Meye, R. P. "Spirituality." In *Dictionary of Paul and his Letters*, edited by Gerald F. Hawthorne et al., 906–16. Downers Grove, IL: InterVarsity, 1993.

Meyer, Marvin. "Taking Up the Cross and Following Jesus: Discipleship in the Gospel of Mark." *Calvin Theological Journal* 37 (2002) 230–38.

Michaels, J. Ramsley. *The Gospel of John*. NICNT. Grand Rapids: Eerdmans, 2010.

Minear, Paul S. *John: the Martyr's Gospel*. New York: Pilgrim, 1984.

———. "The Original Function of John 21." *Journal of Biblical Literature* 102 (1983) 85–98.

Minor, Mitzi. *The Spirituality of Mark: Responding to God*. Louisville: Westminster John Knox, 1996.

Moloney, Francis J. "The Fourth Gospel and Jesus of History." *New Testament Studies* 46 (2000) 42–58.

———. *The Gospel of John*. SP 4. Collegeville, MN: Liturgical, 1998.

———. "'The Jews' in the Fourth Gospel: Another Perspective." *Pacifica* 15 (2002) 16–36.

———. *The Johannine Son of Man*. 2nd edition. Rome: LAS, 1978.

———. "John 21 and the Johannine Story." In *Anatomies of Narrative Criticism: The Past, Present, and Futures of the Fourth Gospel as Literature*, edited by Tom Thatcher and Stephen D. Moore, 237–51. Atlanta: Society of Biblical Literature, 2008.

———. "The Structure and Message of John 13:1–38." *Catholic Biblical Quarterly* 34 (1986) 1–16.

Moloney, Francis J., and Anthony J. Kelly. *Experiencing God in the Gospel of John*. New York: Paulist, 2003.

Morris, Leon. *The Gospel according to John*. NICNT. Grand Rapids: Eerdmans, 1984.

———. *Jesus Is the Christ: Studies in the Theology of John.* Grand Rapids: Eerdmans, 1989.

———. *Testaments of Love: Study of Love in the Bible.* Grand Rapids: Eerdmans, 1981.

Moule, C. F. D. "A Note on 'under the Fig Tree' in John 1.48, 50." *Journal of Theological Studies* 5 (1954) 210–11.

Mounce, Robert H. *The Book of Revelation.* Rev. ed. NICNT. Grand Rapids: Eerdmans, 1998.

Muilenburg, James. "The Form and Structure of the Covenantal Formulations." *Vetus Testamentum* 9 (1959) 347–65.

———. "Form Criticism and Beyond." *Journal of Biblical Literature* 88 (1969) 1–18.

Mukasa, Edoth. "The Blind Man of Jericho (Mark 10:46–52) Following Jesus on the Way." *Hekima Review* 29 (2003) 38–45.

Naumann, P. S., SJ. "The Presence of Love in John's Gospel." *Worship* (1965) 369–71.

Neirynck, Frans. "The Anonymous Disciple in John 1." *Ephemerides Theologicae Lovanienses* 66 (1990) 5–37.

Newsome, James D. *Greeks, Romans, Jews: Currents of Culture and Belief in the New Testament World.* Philadelphia: Trinity, 1992.

Neyrey, Jerome H. *The Gospel of John.* Cambridge: Cambridge University Press, 2007.

———. "The Jacob Allusions in John 1:51." *Catholic Biblical Quarterly* 44 (1982) 586–89.

———. "The 'Noble' Shepherd in John 10: Cultural and Rhetorical Background." *Journal of Biblical Literature* 120 (2001) 267–91.

Nicholson, Godfrey C. *Death as Departure: The Johannine Descent-Ascent Schema.* Society of Biblical Literature Dissertation Series 63. Chico, CA: Scholars, 1983.

Nielsen, Heige K. "Johannine Research." In *New Readings in John: Literary and Theological Perspectives: Essays from the Scandinavian Conference on the Fourth Gospel Arhus 1997*, edited by Johannes Nissen and Sigfred Pedersen, 11–30. Journal for the Study of the New Testament: Supplement Series 182. Sheffield: Sheffield Academic, 1999.

Nissen, Johannes. "Community and Ethics in the Gospel of John." In *New Readings in John: Literary and Theological Perspectives: Essays from the Scandinavian Conference on the Fourth Gospel Arhus 1997*, edited by Johannes Nissen and Sigfred Pedersen, 194–212. Journal for the Study of the New Testament: Supplement Series 182. Sheffield: Sheffield Academic, 1999.

Nolland, John. *The Gospel of Matthew: A Commentary on the Greek Text.* NIGTC. Grand Rapids: Eerdmans, 2005.

———. *Luke 1:1—9:20.* WBC 35A. Waco: Word, 1998.

———. *Luke 9:21—18:34.* WBC 35B. Waco: Word, 1998.

Nygren, Anders. *Agape and Eros.* London: SPCK, 1953.

Okure, Teresa. *The Johannine Approach to Mission: A Contextual Study of John 4:1–42.* Wissenschaftliche Untersuchungen zum Neuen Testament 2/31. Tubingen: Mohr/Siebeck, 1988.

Osborne, Grant R. "John 21: A Test Case for History and Redaction in the Resurrection Narratives." In *Gospel Perspectives II: Studies of History and Tradition in the Four Gospels*, edited by R. T. France and David Wenham, 293–328. Sheffield: JSOT, 1981.

Ossandon, Juan C. "Bartimaeus' Faith: Plot and Point of View in Mark 10,46–52." *Biblica* 93 (2012) 377–402.

Outka, Gene. *Agape: An Ethical Analysis*. New Haven: Yale University Press, 1972.
Packer, J. I. *A Quest for Godliness: The Puritan Vision of the Christian Life*. Wheaton: Crossway, 1990.
Painter, John. "The Church and Israel in the Gospel of John: A Response." *New Testament Studies* 25 (1978–1979) 103–12.
———. *The Quest for the Messiah: The History, Literature and Theology of the Johannine Community*. 2nd ed. Edinburgh: T. & T. Clark, 1993.
Palatty, Paul. "Discipleship in the Fourth Gospel: An Acted Out Message of Disciples as Characters." *Bible Bhashyam* 25 (1999) 285–306.
Parsenios, George L. *Departure and Consolation: The Johannine Farewell Discourses in Light of Greco-Roman Literature*. Novum Testamentum Supplements 117. Leiden: Brill, 2005.
Parson, Mikeal C. "Reading a Beginning/Beginning a Reading: Tracing Literary Theory on Narrative Openings." *Semeia* 52 (1990) 11–31.
Pazdan, Mary M. "Discipleship as the Appropriation of Eschatological Salvation in the Fourth Gospel." PhD diss., University of St. Michael's College, 1982.
———. "Nicodemus and the Samaritan Woman: Contrasting Models of Discipleship." *Biblical Theology Bulletin* 17 (1987) 145–48.
Perkins, Pheme. *Love Commands in the New Testament*. New York: Paulist, 1982.
Perrin, David B. "Mysticism." In *The Blackwell Companion to Christian Spirituality*, edited by Arthur Holder, 442–58. Malden, MA: Blackwell, 2005.
———. *Studying Christian Spirituality*. London: Routledge, 2007.
Plato. *Republic*. Accessed 2 July 2012. http://perseus.uchicago.edu/perseus-cgi/citequery3.pl?dbname=GreekTexts&getid=0&query=Pl.Resp. 474c.
Pourrat, Pierre. *Christian Spirituality*. Translated by W. H. Mitchell et al. 4 vols. Westminster, MD: Newman, 1953–1955.
Powell, Mark A. "Narrative Criticism." In *Hearing the New Testament: Strategies for Interpretation*, edited by Joel B. Green, 239–55. Grand Rapids: Eerdmans, 1995.
———. *What is Narrative Criticism?* Minneapolis: Fortress, 1990.
Preisker, and Schulz. "πρόβατον." *TDNT* 6:689–92.
Prescott-Ezickson, R. "The Sending Motif in the Gospel of John: Implications for Theology of Mission." PhD diss., Southern Baptist Theological Seminary, 1986.
Principe, Walter. "Toward Defining Spirituality." In *Exploring Christian Spirituality*, edited by Kenneth J. Collins, 43–59. Grand Rapids: Baker, 2000.
Pryor, John W. "Covenant and Community in John's Gospel." *Reformed Theological Review* 47 (1988) 44–51.
———. *John: Evangelist of the Covenant People, The Narrative and Themes of the Fourth Gospel*. Downers Grove, IL: InterVarsity, 1992.
———. "The Johannine Son of Man and the Descent–Ascent Motif." *Journal of the Evangelical Theological Society* 34, no. 3 (1991) 341–51.
Quast, Kelvin. *Peter and the Beloved Disciple: Figures for a Community in Crisis*. Journal for the Study of the New Testament: Supplement Series 32. Sheffield: Sheffield Academic, 1989.
Ramelli, llaria. "'Simon Son of John Do You Love Me?' Some Reflections on John 21:15." *Novum Testamentum* 50 (2008) 332–50.
Reim, Gunter. "Jesus as God in the Fourth Gospel: The Old Testament Background." *New Testament Studies* 30 (1984) 158–60.

Reinhartz, Adele. *Befriending the Beloved Disciple: A Jewish Reading of the Gospel of John.* New York: Continuum, 2001.

———. "The Johannine Community and Its Jewish Neighbors: A Reappraisal." In *"What is John?" Vol II: Literary and Social Readings of the Fourth Gospel*, edited by Fernando F. Segovia, 111-38. Society of Biblical Literature Symposium Series 7. Atlanta: Scholars, 1998.

———. "Judaism in the Gospel of John." *Interpretation* 63 (2009) 382-93.

Rensberger, David. *Johannine Faith and Liberating Community.* Philadelphia: Westminster, 1988.

———. "Sectarianism and Theological Interpretation." In *"What is John?" Vol II: Literary and Social Readings of the Fourth Gospel*, edited by Fernando F. Segovia, 139-56. Society of Biblical Literature Symposium Series 7. Atlanta: Scholars, 1998.

Resseguie, James L. *The Strange Gospel: Narrative Design and Point of View in John.* Leiden: Brill, 2001.

Ricci, Carla. *Mary Magdalene and Many Others: Women Who Followed Jesus.* Translated by Paul Bums. Tunbridge Wells, UK: Bums & Oates, 1994.

Ricoeur, Paul. "The Hermeneutics of Testimony." In *Essays on Biblical Interpretation*, edited by Lewis S. Mudge, 119-54. Philadelphia: Fortress, 1980.

———. *Interpretation Theory: Discourse and the Surplus of Meaning.* Fort Worth: Texas Christian University Press, 1976.

Ridderbos, Herman. *The Gospel of John: A Theological Commentary.* Translated by John Vriend. Grand Rapids: Eerdmans, 1997.

Ringe, Sharon H. *Wisdom's Friends: Community and Christology in the Fourth Gospel.* Louisville: Westminster John Knox, 1999.

Robbins, Vernon. *Exploring the Texture of Texts: A Guide to Socio-Rhetorical Interpretation.* Harrisburg, PA: Trinity, 1996.

Robinson, John A. T. "The Destination and Purpose of St. John's Gospel." *New Testament Studies* 6 (1959-1960) 117-31.

Romeo, Joseph A. "Gematria and John 21:11, The Children of God." *Journal of Biblical Literature* 97 (1978) 263-64.

Russell, Norman. *The Doctrine of Deification in the Greek Patristic Tradition.* New York: Oxford University Press, 2009.

Ryken, Leland, James C. Wilhoit, and Tremper Longman III. "Sheep, Shepherd." In *Dictionary of Biblical Imagery*, 782-85. Downers Grove, IL: InterVarsity, 1998.

Saliers, Don A. "Spirituality." In *A New Handbook of Christian Theology*, edited by Donald W. Musser and Joseph L. Price, 460-62. Nashville: Abingdon, 1992.

Schlatter, Adolf. *The History of the Christ.* Translated by Andreas J. Köstenberger. Grand Rapids: Baker, 1997.

Schnackenburg, Rudolf. *The Gospel according to St. John.* 3 vols. Translated by David Smith et al. New York: Crossroad, 1982.

Schneider, G. "ἀκολουθέω." *EDNT* 1:49-52.

Schneiders, Sandra M. "Biblical Spirituality." *Interpretation* 56 (2002) 133-42.

———. "Biblical Spirituality: Text and Transformation." In *The Bible and Spirituality: Exploratory Essays in Reading Scripture Spiritually*, edited by Andrew T. Lincoln, J. Gordon McConville, and Lloyd K. Pieterson, 128-50. Eugene, OR: Cascade, 2013.

———. "The Johannine Resurrection Narrative: An Exegetical and Theological Study of John 20 as a Synthesis of Johannine Spirituality." PhD diss., Pontificia Universitas Gregoriana, 1975.

———. "Johannine Spirituality." In *The New Westminster Dictionary of Christian Spirituality*, edited by Philip Sheldrake, 385–87. Louisville: Westminster John Knox, 2005.

———. "John 21:1–14." *Interpretation* 43 (1989) 70–75.

———. "Religion and Spirituality: Strangers, Rivals, or Partners?" *The Santa Clara Lectures* 6, no. 2 (2000) 1–26.

———. *The Revelatory Text: Interpreting the New Testament as Sacred Scripture*. Collegeville, MN: Liturgical, 1999.

———. "Scripture and Spirituality." In *Christian Spirituality: Origins to the Twelfth Century*, edited by Bernard McGinn and John Meyendorff, 1–20. New York: Crossroad, 1985.

———. "Spirituality in the Academy." *Theological Studies* 50 (1989) 676–97.

———. "Theology and Spirituality: Strangers, Rivals, or Partners?" *Horizons* 13 (1986) 253–74.

———. *Written That You May Believe: Encountering Jesus in the Fourth Gospel*. New York: Crossroad, 1999.

Schnelle, Udo. "Recent Views of John's Gospel." *Word & World* 21 (2001) 352–59.

Schrage, W. "συναγωγή, ἀποσυνάγωγος." *TDNT* 7:798–852.

Schweizer, Eduard. "Discipleship and Church." In *The Beginnings of the Church in the New Testament*, by Ferdinand Hahn, August Strobel, and Eduard Schweizer, translated by Iain and Ute Nicol, 85–104. Minneapolis: Augsburg, 1970.

———. *Lordship and Discipleship*. London: SCM, 1960.

Scorgie, Glen G., et al. *Dictionary of Christian Spirituality*. Grand Rapids: Zondervan, 2011.

Scott, John A. "The Words for 'Love' in John XXI.15ff." *The Classical Weekly* 39, no. 9 (1945) 71–72.

———. "The Words for 'Love' in John XXI.15ff. Second Note." *The Classical Weekly* 40, no. 8 (1946) 60–61.

Scott, Martin. *Sophia and Johannine Jesus*. Journal for the Study of the New Testament: Supplement Series 71. Sheffield: JSOT, 1992.

Segovia, Fernando F. *The Farewell of the Word: The Johannine Call to Abide*. Minneapolis: Fortress, 1991.

———. "The Final Farewell of Jesus: A Reading of John 20:30—21:25." *Semeia* 53 (1991) 167–90.

———. "The Journey(s) of the Word of God: A Reading of the Plot of the Fourth Gospel." *Semeia* 53 (1991) 23–54.

———. "The Love and Hatred of Jesus and Johannine Sectarianism." *Catholic Biblical Quarterly* 43 (1981) 258–72.

———. *Love Relationships in the Johannine Tradition: Agape/Agapan in 1 John and the Fourth Gospel*. Society of Biblical Literature Dissertation Series 58. Chico, CA: Scholars, 1981.

———. "'Peace I Leave with You; My Peace I Give to You': Discipleship in the Fourth Gospel." In *Discipleship in the New Testament*, edited by F. F. Segovia, 76–102. Philadelphia: Fortress, 1985.

———. "The Structure, *Tendenz*, and *Sitz im Leben* of John 13:31—14:31." *Journal of Biblical Literature* 104 (1985) 471–93.

———. "The Tradition History of the Fourth Gospel." In *Exploring the Gospel of John: In Honor of D. Moody Smith*, edited by R. Alan Culpepper and C. Clifton Black, 179–89. Louisville: Westminster John Knox, 1996.

Shaw, Alan. "Image and Symbol in John 21." *Expository Times* 86 (1975) 311.

Shiner, Whitney T. *Follow Me! Disciples in Markan Rhetoric*. Society of Biblical Literature Dissertation Series 145. Atlanta: Scholars, 1995.

Sheehan, John F. X. "Feed My Lambs." *Scripture* 16 (1964) 21–27.

Sheldrake, Philip., ed. *The New Westminster Dictionary of Christian Spirituality*. Louisville: Westminster John Knox, 2005.

———. "The Study of Spirituality." *The Way: A Review of Christian spirituality* 39, no. 2 (1999) 162–72.

———. "What is Spirituality?" In *Exploring Christian Spirituality*, edited by Kenneth J. Collins, 21–42. Grand Rapids: Baker, 2000.

Shepherd, David. "'Do You Love Me?' A Narrative-Critical Reappraisal of ἀγαπάω and φιλέω in John 21:15–17." *Journal of Biblical Literature* 129 (2010) 777–92.

Shepherd of Hermas. *Similitude*. BibleWorks 9.0. Norfolk: BibleWorks, 2011.

Sidebottom, Ernest M. "The Descent and Ascent of the Son of Man in the Gospel of St. John." *Australasian Theological Review* 39, no. 2 (1957) 115–22.

Simoens, Yves. *La Gloire d'aimer: Structures Stylistiques et Interpretatives dans le Discours de la Cene (Jn 13–17)*. Analecta Biblica 90. Rome: Biblical Institute, 1981.

Siker-Gieseler, Jeffrey S. "Disciples and Discipleship in the Fourth Gospel: A Canonical Approach." *Studia Biblica et Theologica* 10 (1980) 199–227.

Skinner, Matthew L. "Denying Self, Bearing a Cross, and Following Jesus: Unpacking the Imperatives of Mark 8:34." *Word & World* 23 (2003) 321–31.

Smalley, Stephen S. "Johannine Spirituality." In *The Westminster Dictionary of Christian Spirituality*, edited by Gordon S. Wakefield, 230–32. Philadelphia: Westminster, 1983.

———. "The Sign in John XXI." *New Testament Studies* 20 (1974) 275–88.

Smith, Dwight M. *The Composition and Order of the Fourth Gospel*. New Haven: Yale University Press, 1965.

———. "The Contribution of J. Louis Martyn to the Understanding of the Gospel of John." In *History and Theology in the Fourth Gospel*, 1–23. 3rd ed. Louisville: Westminster John Knox, 2003.

———. *The Fourth Gospel in Four Dimensions: Judaism and Jesus, the Gospels and Scripture*. Columbia: University of South Carolina Press, 2008.

———. *Johannine Christianity: Essays on its Setting, Sources, and Theology*. Columbia, South Carolina: University of South Carolina Press, 1984.

———. "Johannine Christianity: Some Reflections on Its Character and Delineation." *New Testament Studies* 21 (1975) 222–48.

———. "Johannine Studies since Bultmann." *Word & World* 21 (2001) 344–51.

———. *John*. ANTC. Nashville: Abingdon, 1999.

———. *The Theology of the Gospel of John*. Cambridge: Cambridge University Press, 1995.

Soulen, Richard N., and R. Kendall Soulen. *Handbook of Biblical Criticism*. 3rd ed. Louisville: Westminster John Knox, 2001.

Spencer, F. Scott. "'Follow Me': The Imperious Call of Jesus in the Synoptic Gospels." *Interpretation* (2005) 142–53.

Spencer, Patrick E. "Narrative Echoes in John 21: Intertextual Interpretation and Intratextual Connection." *Journal for the Study of the New Testament* 75 (1999) 49–68.

Spicq, Ceslas. *Agape in the New Testament*. 3 vols. Translated by Sister Marie Aquinas McNamara and Sister Mary Honoria Richter. London: Herder, 1963–1966.

Staley, Jeffrey L. *The Print's First Kiss: A Rhetorical Investigation of the Implied Reader in the Fourth Gospel*. Society of Biblical Literature Dissertation Series 82. Atlanta: Scholars, 1988.

Stauffer, Ethelbert. *Jesus and His Story*. Translated by Richard and Clara Winston. New York: Knopf, 1960.

Stein, Robert H. *Mark*. Baker Exegetical Commentary on the New Testament. Grand Rapids: Baker, 2008.

Stibbe, Mark W. G. *The Gospel of John as Literature: An Anthology of Twentieth Century Perspectives*. Selected and introduced by Mark W. G. Stibbe. Leiden: Brill, 1993.

———. *John*. Sheffield: Sheffield Academic, 1993.

———. *John as Storyteller: Narrative Criticism and the Fourth Gospel*. Society for New Testament Studies Monograph Series 73. Cambridge: Cambridge University Press, 1992.

Stock, Augustine. *Call to Discipleship: A Literary Study of Mark's Gospel*. Good News Studies 1. Wilmington, DE: Glazier, 1982.

Stringfellow, William. *The Politics of Spirituality*. Philadelphia: Westminster, 1984.

Stuart, Douglas. *Old Testament Exegesis*. 3rd ed. Louisville: Westminster John Knox, 2001.

Sweetland, Dennis M. *Our Journey with Jesus: Discipleship according to Mark*. Wilmington, DE: Glazier, 1987.

Swete, Henry B. *The Apocalypse of St. John*. London: Macmillan, 1906.

Talbert, Charles H. "The Myth of a Descending-Ascending Redeemer in Mediterranean Antiquity." *New Testament Studies* 22 (1976) 418–40.

———. *Reading John: A Literary and Theological Commentary on the Fourth Gospel and the Johannine Epistles*. London: SPCK, 1992.

Talmon, Shemaryahu. "The Community of the Renewed Covenant: Between Judaism and Christianity." In *The Community of the Renewed Covenant: The Notre Dame Symposium on the Dead Sea Scrolls*, edited by Eugene Ulrich and James VanderKam, 3–24. Notre Dame: University of Notre Dame Press, 1993.

Tannehill, Robert C. "The Disciples in Mark: The Function of a Narrative Role." In *The Interpretation of Mark*, edited by William Telford, 134–57. Philadelphia: Fortress; London: SPCK, 1985.

Taylor, Barbara Brown. "Following Jesus through Mark." *Quarterly Review* 11 (1991) 87–106.

Thatcher, Tom, and Stephen D. Moore, eds. *Anatomies of Narrative Criticism: The Past, Present, and Futures of the Fourth Gospel as Literature*. Atlanta: Society of Biblical Literature, 2008.

Thayer, Joseph H. *A Greek-English Lexicon of the New Testament*. Peabody, MA: Hendrickson, 2000.

Theophrastus. *Characters*. Accessed 2 July 2012. http://perseus.uchicago.edu/perseus-cgi/citequery3.pl?dbname=GreekTexts&getid=0&query=Theophr.%20Char.%20188.

Thomas, W. H. Griffith. "The Purpose of the Fourth Gospel: John 21." *Bibliotheca sacra* 125 (1968) 254–62.

Thompson, Marianne Meye. *The God of the Gospel of John*. Grand Rapids: Eerdmans, 2001.

———. *The Humanity of Jesus in the Fourth Gospel*. Philadelphia: Fortress, 1988.

———. "What is the Gospel of John?" *Word & World* 21 (2001) 333–42.

Thucydides. *The Peloponnesian War*. Accessed 5 June 2012. http://www.perseus.tufts.edu/hopper/text?doc=Perseus%3Atext%3A1999.01.0199%3Abook%3D7%3Achapter%3D57%3Asection%3D9.

Tiedtke, E., and C. Brown. "ἁρπάζω." *NIDNTT* 3:601–5.

Tolmie, D. Francois. *Jesus' Farewell to the Disciples: John 13:1—17:26 in Narratological Perspective*. Biblical Interpretation Series 12. Leiden: Brill, 1995.

———. "The (Not So) Good Shepherd: The Use of Shepherd Imagery in the Characterization of Peter in the Fourth Gospel." In *Imagery in the Gospel of John: Terms, Forms, Themes and Theology of Johannine Figurative Language*, edited by Jorg Frey, Jan G. van der Watt, and Reuben Zimmermann, in collaboration with Gabi Kern, 353–67. Wissenschaftliche Untersuchungen zum Neuen Testament 200. Tubingen: Mohr/Siebeck, 2006.

Torrance, James B., and Roland C. Walls. *John Duns Scotus in a Nutshell*. Edinburgh: Handsel. 1992.

Torrance, Thomas F. *The Christian Doctrine of God: One Being Three Persons*. London: T. & T. Clark, 2006.

Trakatellis, Demetrios. "Ακολούθει μοι/Follow me" (Mark 2:14) Discipleship and Priesthood." *Greek Orthodox Theological Review* 30, no. 3 (1985) 271–85.

Trible, Phyllis. *Rhetorical Criticism: Context, Method, and the Book of Jonah*. Minneapolis: Fortress, 1994.

Turretin, Francis. *Institutes of Elenctic Theology*. 3 vols. Edited by James T. Dennison Jr. Translated by George M. Giger. Phillipsburg, NJ: P&R, 1994.

Ursinus, Zacharias. *Commentary on the Heidelberg Catechism*. Translated by George W. Williard. 1852. Repr., Phillipsburg, NJ: P&R, 1992.

Van der Merwe, D. G. "The Character of Unity Expected among the Disciples of Jesus, according to John 17:20–23." *Acta patristica et byzantina* 13 (2002) 224–54.

———. "Discipleship in the Fourth Gospel." DD thesis, University of Pretoria, 1996.

———. "Early Christian Spirituality according to the First Epistle of John: The Identification of Different 'Lived Experiences.'" *HTS Teologiese Studies/Theological Studies* 69, no. 1 (2013). Art. #1286, 9 pages. http://dx.doi.org/10.4102/ hts.v69i1.1286.

———. "A Historical Survey and Critical Evaluation concerning Discipleship in the Fourth Gospel." *Skrif en kerk* 17, no. 2 (1996) 427–42.

———. "*Imitatio Christi* in the Fourth Gospel." *Verbum et Ecclesia* 22, no. 1 (2001) 131–48.

———. "The Interpretation of the Revelatory Events in John 17:24–26: An Exegetical Exercise." *Verbum et Ecclesia* 25, no. 1 (2004) 311–29.

———. "Jesus Appoints His Disciples as His Agents to Continue His Divine Mission according to John 17:17–19." *Acta Patristica et Byzantina* 14 (2003) 303–24.

———. "Old Testament Spirituality in the Gospel of John," *Verbum et Ecclesia* 35, no. 1 (2014). Art. #837, 9 pages. http://dx.doi. org/10.4102/ve.v35i1.837.

———. "Towards a Theological Understanding of Johannine Discipleship." *Neotestamentica* 31, no. 2 (1997) 339–59.
Van der Watt, J. G. "I am the Bread of Life. Imagery in John 6:32–51." *Acta Theologica* (2007) 187–204.
———. *An Introduction to the Johannine Gospel and Letters*. New York: T. & T. Clark, 2007.
———. "Johannine Style: Some Initial Remarks on the Functional Use of Repetition in the Gospel according to John." *In die Skriflig* 42, no. 11 (2008) 75–99.
Van Ness, Peter H. "Introduction: Spirituality and the Secular Quest." In *Spirituality and the Secular Quest*, edited by Peter H. Van Ness, 1–17. New York: Crossroad, 1996.
Van Tilborg, Sjef. *Imaginative Love in John*. Biblical Interpretation Series 2. Leiden: Brill, 1993.
Vellanickal, Matthew. "Discipleship according to the Gospel of John." *Jeevadhara* 10 (1980) 131–47.
———. *The Divine Sonship of Christians in the Johannine Writings*. Rome: Biblical Institute, 1977.
———. "Evangelization in the Johannine Writings." In *Good News and Witness*, edited by Lucien Legrand, Joseph Pathrapankal, and Matthew Vellanickal, 121–68. Bangalore: Theological Publications in India, 1973.
Von Wahlde, Urban C. *The Earliest Version of John's Gospel: Recovering the Gospel of Signs*. Wilmington, DE: Glazier, 1989.
———. *The Gospel and Letters of John*. Eerdmans Critical Commentary. Grand Rapids: Eerdmans, 2010.
———. "'The Jews' in the Gospel of John: Fifteen Years of Research (1983–1998)." *Ephemerides Theologicae Lovanienses* 76 (2000) 30–55.
———. "The Johannine 'Jews': A Critical Survey," *New Testament Studies* 28 (1982) 33–60.
Vorster, Willem S. "The Growth and Making of John 21." In *Speaking of Jesus: Essays on Biblical Language, Gospel Narrative & the Historical Jesus*, edited by J. Eugene Botha, 199–215. Leiden: Brill, 1998.
Waaijman, Kees. *Spirituality: Forms, Foundations, Method*. Dudley, MA: Peeters, 2002.
Waetjen, Herman C. *The Gospel of the Beloved Disciple: A Work in Two Editions*. New York: T. & T. Clark, 2005.
Wakefield, Gordon S., ed. *The Westminster Dictionary of Christian Spirituality*. Philadelphia: Westminster, 1983
Ware, Timothy. *The Orthodox Church*. New ed. London: Penguin, 1997.
Watts, Rikki E. *Isaiah's New Exodus in Mark*. Wissenschaftliche Untersuchungen zum Neuen Testament 2/88. 1997. Biblical Studies Library. Repr., Grand Rapids: Baker Academic, 2000.
Wead, David W. *The Literary Devices in John's Gospel*. Theologische Dissertationen 4. Basel: Friedrich Reinhardt Kommissionsverlag, 1970.
Webster, Jane S. *Ingesting Jesus: Eating and Drinking in the Gospel of John*. Atlanta: Society of Biblical Literature, 2003.
Wegener, Mark I. *Cruciformed: The Literary Impact of Mark's Story of Jesus and His Disciples*. New York: University Press of America, 1995.

Weima, Jeffrey A. D. "Literary Criticism." In *Interpreting the New Testament: Essays on Methods and Issues*, edited by David Alan Black and David S. Dockery, 150–69. Nashville: Broadman & Holman, 2001.

Westcott, Brooke F. *The Gospel According to St. John*. London: Murray, 1908.

Whitacre, Rodney A. *John*. IVP New Testament Commentary. Downers Grove, IL: InterVarsity, 1999.

Whitters, Mark F. "Discipleship in John: Four Profiles." *Word & World* 18 (1998) 422–27.

Wiarda, Timothy. "John 21.1–23: Narrative Unity and its Implications." *Journal for the Study of the New Testament* 46 (1992) 53–71.

Winbery, Carlton L. "Abiding in Christ: The Concept of Discipleship in John." *The Theological Educator* 38 (1988) 104–20.

Winn, Albert C. *A Sense of Mission: Guidance from the Gospel of John*. Philadelphia: Westminster, 1981.

Witherington, Ben III. *John's Wisdom: A Commentary on the Fourth Gospel*. Louisville: Westminster John Knox, 1995.

Witsius, Hermann. *The Economy of the Covenants between God and Man*. 2 vols. London, 1822. Reprint, Kingsburg: den Dulk Christian Foundation, 1990.

Woll, D. Bruce. "The Departure of 'The Way': The First Farewell Discourse in the Gospel of John." *Journal of Biblical Literature* 99 (1980) 225–39.

Woods, Richard. *Christian Spirituality: God's Presence through the Ages*. Allen: Christian Classics, 1996.

Xenophon. *Hellenica*. Accessed 5 June 2012. http://perseus.uchicago.edu/perseus-cgi/citequery3.pl?dbname=GreekTexts&query=Xen.Hell. 5.2.26&getid=0.

Zimmermann, Ruben. "Imagery in John: Opening up paths into the tangled thicket of John's figurative world." In *Imagery in the Gospel of John: Terms, Forms, Themes and Theology of Johannine Figurative Language*, edited by Jorg Frey, Jan G. van der Watt, and Reuben Zimmermann, in Collaboration with Gabi Kern, 1–43. Wissenschaftliche Untersuchungen zum Neuen Testament 200. Tubingen: Mohr Siebeck, 2006.

Zumstein, Jean. "Intratextuality and Intertextuality in the Gospel of John." In *Anatomies of Narrative Criticism: The Past, Present, and Futures of the Fourth Gospel as Literature*, edited by Tom Thatcher and Stephen D. Moore, 121–35. Atlanta: Society of Biblical Literature, 2008.

Scripture Index

Old Testament

Genesis

1:2	31
1:2–3	125n37
1:3	118, 128
1:26	31
3	57
4	57
3:15	51
6:5	187n30
15:17	118
22:8	97
22:10–13	97
28:12	97, 112n54, 113
29:7	216n61
29:9	216n61
32:11	149n44
37:3	209n35
37:4	209n35
37:12	216n61
37:16	216n61
37:33	148n43
40:13	160
40:19–22	160

Exodus

3:6	53n43
12:46	157
13:21	65, 119, 146n30, 237
13:21–22	132, 235
13:22	65, 237
15:13	146n30
17:12	219
20:6	211
29:38–46	97
33:11	162
33:18	109n48
40:36–37	146n31

Leviticus

6:4	148n43
14:12–13	97, 234
14:21–25	97, 234
16	97
19:13	148n43

Numbers

5:22	111n51
9:12	157
9:15–23	146n31
21:8	160
21:9	160
22:20	65
24:23	80n73
27:17	146n28

Deuteronomy

1:33	237
4:3	64
4:24	65
4:37	212
6:5	211
6:14	64
7:8	212
7:9	211
8:2	146n30
10:12	64, 211
10:15	212
11:1	211
11:13	211
11:22	211
13:3	211
13:5	64
23:5	212
26:17	64
28:9	64
29:18–19	178n8
30:6	211
30:15–20	120

Joshua

1:7	162
22:5	64, 211
23:11	211
24	12
24:30	162

Judges

2:12	64
2:14	149n44
3:10	32
6:34	32
14:6	32
14:9	32
15:4	32
21:23	148n43

Ruth

1:15	65, 66
4:13–22	66

1 Samuel

17:34–35	147

2 Samuel

5:2	146n28
9:7	74n51
9:11	74n51
9:13	74n51

1 Kings

8:58	64
19:5–8	207, 239
19:15–16	207
19:16–17	67
19:19–21	67
19:20	67
21:26	64
22:17	146n29

2 Kings

2:8	67
2:13–14	67

1 Chronicles

11:2	146n28

2 Chronicles

20:6	149n44

Ezra

7:6	149n44

Nehemiah

1:5	211
8:6	111n51
9:12	146n30

Job

5:18	149n44

Psalms

8:6	166n36
14:1–3	187n30
14:2	239
18:1	162, 212
23:1	216, 231
23:5	159
27:1	118, 128
27:10	53
28:9	216
31:23	211
35:19	57
36:1	162
41:9	179
41:44	111n51
48:14	216
50:22	148n43
51:8-12	31
53:1–3	187n30
69:4	57
72:19	111n51
77:19	65
77:20	146n27, 216n63
78:14	146n30, 237
78:52	146n27, 146n30, 216n63, 237
78:70–72	146n28
79:13	216n63
80:1	146n27, 146n30, 216, 216n63, 237
89:21	149n44
100:3	216n63
104:30	31
106:9	146n30
109:3	57
119:105	118
136:16	146n30
139:1–6	211
145:16	149n44

Proverbs

6:23	118
8:22	118
8:23	233
8:30	233
8:35	120

Ecclesiastes

11:5	31

Isaiah

2:3	64
8	121
8:1–22	121
8:22	121
8:22—9:1	125n37
9	121
9:1	119, 121, 128
9:1–2	120, 121
9:1–7	121
9:2	125n37
10:2	148n43
11:2	32
25:8	222
40:11	146n30, 216, 216n63, 231, 237
42:1	162, 233
42:19	162
43:1	140

Isaiah (continued)

45:14	65
48:21	146n30
49:3	162
49:6	119, 159n11
49:16	149n44
51:16	149n44
53	97
53:6–7	97, 234
53:7	99n16
56:10–12	147n33
58:6–7	75
63:11	146n27, 216n63
63:14	146n30, 237
64:1	112n57
65:2	219

Jeremiah

2:2	64
2:6	146n30
3:2	85n87
3:15	146n29, 216
11:10	64
11:19	97
13:27	85
17:9	187n30
23:4	216
27:6–7	149n44
31:10	216

Ezekiel

16:15–58	85n87
23:1–49	85n87
29:16	67
34	138, 216
34:2	216
34:2–4	147n33
34:3	216
34:8	216
34:10	216
34:11–16	231
34:13	216
34:14	216
34:15	216
34:16	216
34:23	146n28, 216
36–37	15
37:2–10	32
37:24	146n28
43:7	85n87
47:10	205n24

Daniel

7:13–14	179n14

Hosea

1:2	64
2:5 (7)	64, 66
2:13	64
5:4	85n87
5:14	148n43
6:1	148n43
6:10	85n87
11:3–4	146n30
13:5	216
13:14	222

Amos

2:10	146n30
3:4	148n43

Micah

3:2	148n43
4:2	64
5:3	216
7:14	216

Zechariah

14:7	118

Apocrypha

Baruch

4:2	120

Judith

2:4	66
5:6–8	66
12:2	67
15:13	65

2 Maccabees

8:36	67

Sirach/Ecclesiasticus

15:11–20	220
15:16	220, 221
17:11	120
24:27	120

Wisdom of Solomon

7:26	118, 119
18:3–4	119
18:4	120

Pseudepigrapha

1 Enoch

89:46	98n15

Testament of Joseph

19:8	98n15

Testament of Levi

14:4	118

New Testament

Matthew

1:5	66
1:20–24	192
3:17	233
4:14–16	120
4:16	119, 125
4:17	71, 71n43
4:18–22	72n44
4:19	71
4:20	69, 70, 71, 75, 228n1
4:20–22	102
4:22	69, 70, 71, 75, 228n1
4:23	71, 72n44
4:25	69, 82
5:3	192
5:10–12	53n45
5:14	119
8:1	69

Matthew (continued)

Reference	Pages
8:10	69
8:11	159n11
8:12	179n12
8:14–17	72
8:18	73n48
8:18–22	72
8:19	69, 70, 72, 228n1
8:19–20	72, 86
8:19–22	67
8:20	72, 73n45, 73n48
8:21	72, 73
8:21–22	73
8:22	9, 69, 70, 72, 73n48, 75, 228n1
8:23	69
8:23–24	73n48
8:23–27	72
8:30	216n62
8:33	216n62
9:2	74n51
9:2–8	74
9:5	74n51
9:6	74n51
9:9	69, 70, 74, 228n1
9:10	74, 74n51
9:11	74
9:13	74
9:14–17	
9:19	69
9:27	69
10:3	106
10:7	105
10:14	73n47
10:16–20	73n47
10:16–42	53n45
10:21–22	73n47
10:22	159
10:23	73n47
10:37	75
10:38	69, 70, 75, 77, 77n65, 228n1
10:39	75, 76
11:7–11	98
11:29	75n56
12:1–14	49
12:15	69
12:28	20
12:29	148n43
13:13–14	239
14:5	48n29
14:13–14	69
16:16	111
16:17	111
16:21–23	76
16:24	69, 70, 76, 77, 77n61, 228n1
16:24–28	154
16:25	76
16:27	81
16:27–28	76
16:27—17:8	77
17:1–8	76
17:5	233
19:2	69
19:13–15	78
19:16	78, 79, 81
19:20	79
19:21	69, 70, 78, 81, 228n1
19:22	81
19:23–26	78
19:24	80
19:26	80, 81, 187
19:27	78, 81
19:27–28	69, 70, 78, 81, 228n1
19:28	78, 81
19:29	78, 81
20:1–16	78
20:17–19	78
20:23–23	78
20:29	69, 82
20:34	69, 82
21:9	69

22:13	179n12	3:7	70
		3:14	102
23:37	48n29	3:14–15	102
		3:18	106
24:9	58n29, 159	3:38—9:8	77
24:9–14	53n45		
24:39–40	191	4:22	203n14
		4:21–25	118
25:30	179n12		
		5:11	216n62
26:29	74n51	5:12	105
26:31	54n48, 174	5:14	216n62
26:31–35	174	5:24	70
26:32	174, 175	5:37	69n36
26:33	174, 175, 194		
26:34	77, 174, 175	6:1	70
26:35	77, 174, 175, 186, 194	6:7–13	105
		6:19	48n29
26:38–39	154	6:52	82
26:58	69		
26:75	77, 210	7:24–30	109
27:3–5	194	8:17–18	82
27:55	69	8:21	82
		8:27	83
28:18	151, 180	8:31	48n29
		8:31–33	76
		8:34	70, 76, 77, 77n61, 228n1
## Mark		8:34–38	154
		8:35	76
1:10	112n57	8:38—9:1	76
1:14	71		
1:15	71, 105	9:2–8	76
1:16–18	67, 197	9:31	48n29
1:17	71	9:33–34	83
1:17–18	102	9:38	70, 70n41
1:18	70, 71, 75, 228n1		
1:20	71, 75	10:13–16	78
1:38	105	10:17	78, 79, 83
		10:18	80
2:1–12	74	10:21	70, 78, 79n73, 81, 228n1
2:14	70, 71, 74, 228n1		
2:15	70, 71, 74	10:23–27	78
2:17	74	10:25	80
2:18–22	74	10:27	80, 81, 187
2:23–28	49		

Mark (continued)

10:28	70, 78, 81, 228n1
10:29	78
10:30	78, 81
10:32	70, 83
10:32–34	
10:34	48n29
10:35–40	78, 83
10:35–45	82, 82n78
10:45	162
10:46–52	82, 82n78
10:47–48	82
10:52	70, 82, 83, 228n1
11:1–11	82, 82n78
11:9	70
12:5ff	48n29
12:35	83n81
13:9–13	53n45
13:11	20
14:13	70
14:27	174, 186, 207
14:27–31	174
14:28	174, 175
14:29	174, 175
14:30	77, 174, 175
14:31	77, 174, 175
14:32–36	154
14:51	69n36
14:54	70
14:72	77, 209
15:41	70
16:12	203n14
16:14	203n14
16:17	69n36
16:20	69n36

Luke

1:3	69n36
1:16–17	98
1:66	149n44
1:74	204n16
1:79	125
2:29–32	119
3:16	189n43
3:21	112n57
4:1	20
4:14	20
4:18	20
4:43	71
4:44	71
5:1–11	198n5
5:1—6:16	75n53
5:6	71
5:10	71
5:10–11	102
5:11	70, 71, 75, 228n1
5:17–26	74
5:27	74
5:27–28	70, 74, 228n1
5:27–32	65n56
5:28	74
5:29	74
5:32	74
5:33–39	74
5:43	71
5:44	71
6:1–5	49
6:14	106
6:22–23	53n45
6:26	53n45
7:1–10	109
7:9	70
7:46	159
8:32	216n62
8:34	216n62
9:11	70
9:21–22	76

9:23	70, 76, 77n59, 77n61, 228n1	22:39	70
		22:39–44	154
9:23–27	154	22:53	179n12, 190
9:24	76	22:54	70
9:26–27	76	22:57	77
9:28–36	76, 77		
9:49	70, 70n41	23:27	70
9:51–56	72	23:46	149n44
9:57	70, 72, 228n1	23:49	69n36
9:57–58	72, 75, 86		
9:57–62	67, 72	24:13–16	204
9:58	72, 73n45	24:32	204
9:59	70, 72, 73, 228n1		
9:59–60	73		
9:59–62	75	## John	
9:60	9, 72, 73		
9:61	70, 72, 73, 228n1	1	91n2
9:62	72	1–12	154, 183
		1–20	196n1
10:1–12	72	1:1	133, 232, 232n4, 232n5, 232n6, 233, 234
14:27	75, 76		
		1:2	133, 232, 232n5, 233, 234
15:15	216n62		
		1:1–2	90, 109
		1:3	129n48, 235
18:15–17	78	1:3–4	132
18:18	78	1:4	129n48, 130, 130n51
18:22	70, 78, 81, 228n1		
18:24–27	78	1:5	47, 125n37, 128
18:27	81	1:6	98
18:28	70, 78, 81, 228n1	1:6–9	95
18:29	78	1:9	128, 130, 130n51
18:31–33	78	1:10	95, 129n48
18:31–34	82	1:10–11	47
18:34	78	1:11	140, 140n8, 169
18:38–39	82	1:13	56n58, 80, 129, 187
18:43	70, 82, 228n1		
		1:14	4n6, 103, 112n53
19:28–40	82	1:16	21n74
		1:18	5, 47, 90, 109, 133, 232, 234, 241
21:12–19	53n45		
		1:19	21n74
22:10	70	1:19–28	95
22:31	174	1:22	21n75
22:31–34	174	1:24	21n74
22:32	174, 175, 192n49		
22:33	174, 175, 194		
22:34	174, 175		

John (continued)

1:29	86n90, 91, 93, 94, 95, 96, 99, 148, 154n2, 157, 188, 229, 234, 236
1:31	203
1:32	20
1:33	21n75, 95, 189n43
1:34	95
1:35	95
1:35–37	148, 229
1:35–42	95
1:35–51	3, 12, 19n69, 90, 91, 93, 94, 105n37, 106, 111, 113, 135, 146n26, 154n2, 181, 214, 229, 234, 236
1:36	86n90, 91, 93, 94, 95, 96, 99, 113, 114, 154n2, 157, 188, 234, 236
1:37	6, 18, 91, 93, 94, 95, 96, 101, 181, 219, 234
1:38	6, 18, 89, 91, 94, 96, 101, 102n31, 181, 219, 229
1:38b	94
1:39	89, 91, 93, 94, 101, 102, 103, 105, 111, 181, 219, 229, 236, 238
1:39a	102n31
1:39b	102n31
1:39c	102n31
1:40	6, 18, 91, 94, 96, 101, 104, 111, 181, 219
1:40–42	93, 173n4
1:41	96, 104, 196
1:41–42	150, 215, 236
1:42	196, 234
1:43	6, 13, 18, 91, 93, 94, 104, 106, 114, 193, 194, 219, 229, 234
1:43–46	106, 107
1:44	106
1:45	97, 104, 106, 107, 110
1:45–46	93, 150, 215, 236
1:46	105, 106, 107, 234
1:47	97
1:48	91, 106, 143
1:49	97, 107, 111
1:50	94, 111
1:51	93, 94, 97, 111, 112, 113, 114, 135, 148, 152, 181, 222, 229, 235, 238
2	162
2:1–11	108, 206n22
2:4	160
2:4–7	50n34
2:5	161, 162, 237n21
2:7	162
2:8	162
2:9	91, 161, 162, 237n21
2:11	162, 203
2:13	108
2:16	17, 49n31
2:18–19	47
2:19	91
2:22	91
2:23–25	214
3:3	130, 187, 239
3:3–8	187
3:5	130, 187, 239
3:6	21
3:8	21, 56n58, 91
3:13	90, 113
3:14	91, 160, 161, 240n32
3:14–15	148n39
3:14a	160
3:14b	160
3:16	212
3:17	21n74
3:19	190
3:19–21	120
3:20	50
3:21	203

SCRIPTURE INDEX

3:28	21n74	5:38	21n74
3:31	90	5:41	166, 167, 169
3:32	169	5:43	49n31, 169
3:34	20, 21n74, 189n43	5:44	166, 167, 169
3:35	133, 149n44, 151, 212, 233	6	91n2, 92, 106
		6:1	108
4:1–3	47	6:2	18, 92
4:10	131	6:3	108
4:11	91	6:4	108
4:14	131	6:5	92, 106, 108
4:20	91	6:5–7	107, 229
4:21	160	6:6	108n44
4:23	160	6:6–7	109, 239
4:24	21	6:7	106, 108
4:28–29	236n18	6:11	206
4:28–30	105, 150	6:15	148n43
4:29	105	6:23	92
4:34	21n75, 163	6:29	21n74
4:34–38	218n72	6:32	49n31, 133
4:38	21n74	6:35	131
4:39	236n18	6:37	141, 233, 234
4:40	105, 105n37	6:38	21n75
4:44	166	6:39	21n75, 141, 233, 234
4:46	91	6:40	49n31, 133
4:48–50	50n34	6:44	21n75, 132, 141, 193, 239
4:50	147n32	6:46	109, 133
5:15–18	44, 47, 48, 228	6:51	131, 147n37
5:16	46, 47, 48, 48n30, 49, 55	6:57	21, 21n74, 132, 218n73
5:17	49, 49n31, 133	6:61	54n48
5:18	46, 48, 48n30, 55n53, 91, 158	6:62	90, 92, 113
5:19	163, 205	6:63	21
5:19–20	133	6:65	141
5:20	208n32, 212, 233	6:68	173n4
5:23	21, 21n75, 167, 169, 218n73	6:68–69	196, 231
		6:70	56
5:24	21n75, 204n16		
5:25	160	7	92, 115, 116, 117, 120, 121, 122, 122n35, 123n36, 125, 125n39, 126, 132, 134
5:28	160		
5:30	21, 21n75, 162, 163, 205, 218n73		
5:33	21n74		
5:36	21n74, 132, 162, 237	7:1	44, 46, 48, 48n29, 50, 55n53, 92, 122, 124, 125n38, 158, 228
5:36–37	133		
5:37	21n75, 132, 133		

John (continued)

7:1–13	116n6
7:4	203
7:7	44, 46, 50, 54, 56, 123, 228
7:8	50n34
7:10	50
7:11	92, 125n38
7:12	123, 125n38
7:13	45n22, 51, 125n38
7:14	50, 127
7:14–31	128
7:14–36	116n6
7:15	125n38
7:16	21n75, 123, 127, 128n47, 130n51, 132
7:17	123, 128
7:18	21n75, 123, 166
7:19ff	48n29
7:19	44, 46, 48, 50, 55n53, 92, 122, 124, 158, 228
7:20	50, 92, 122, 124, 125n38, 158
7:21–24	50
7:23	123
7:24	50
7:25	44, 46, 48, 50, 55n53, 92, 122, 124, 125n38, 158, 228
7:27	92, 123, 124, 126, 127, 128
7:27–28	126
7:28	21n75, 89, 92, 123, 124, 126, 128, 129, 229
7:28–29	130n51
7:29	21n74, 56n59, 123, 124, 128n47, 133, 229
7:30	50n38, 92, 122, 154n2, 160
7:31	125n38
7:32	21n74, 50n38, 122, 125n38, 125n38
7:32–36	128
7:33	21n75, 123, 124, 126, 128n47, 128, 132, 154n2, 165, 182n21, 229, 235
7:33–34	130n51
7:33–36	123
7:34	89, 92, 124, 126, 129, 164, 165, 186, 187, 219, 229, 239
7:35	92, 125n38, 128, 147n32, 219
7:36	89, 92, 124, 126, 129, 164, 165, 219, 229
7:37–39	123
7:37–52	116n6
7:39	21, 92, 179n13
7:40	125n38
7:40–43	123
7:40–52	128
7:41	120, 127
7:41–42	128
7:42	92, 219
7:43	125n38
7:44	50n38, 122
7:45	122, 125n38
7:47	125n38
7:48	125n38
7:49	123, 125n38
7:49–52	128
7:52	120, 121, 127, 128
7:53	147n32
7:53—8:11	116
8	91n2, 92, 115, 116, 117, 120, 122, 122n35, 125, 126, 132, 134
8:1–11	147n32
8:10	92
8:12ff	117
8:12	3, 6, 7, 9, 18, 90, 91, 92, 115, 116,

SCRIPTURE INDEX

	117, 119, 120, 121, 122, 122n35, 123n36, 124, 125, 125n39, 126, 127, 128, 130, 131, 132, 133, 134, 181, 214, 219, 229, 235, 236, 238	8:37	46, 48, 50, 51, 55n53, 92, 122, 124, 158
		8:37–47	44, 50, 228
		8:38	51, 133
		8:39	51
		8:39–47	129
		8:40	46, 47, 48, 50, 51, 55n53, 92, 123, 124, 158
8:12–20	116n6, 117		
8:12–29	146n26, 154n2, 181, 235	8:41	41
		8:42	21n74, 51, 123, 130n51, 132, 235
8:12–59	116		
8:13	125n38, 128	8:43	51, 123
8:14	89, 90, 92, 127, 128, 130n51, 154n2, 181, 219, 229	8:44	51, 129
		8:45–46	51
		8:47	51, 56n58, 129, 140, 140n9
8:14a	124		
8:14b	124	8:48	125n38
8:16	21n75, 123, 132	8:48–49	123
8:18	21n75, 123, 132	8:49	49n31, 123, 133, 167, 169
8:19	49n31, 56n59, 92, 123, 124, 129, 133, 229		
		8:49–50	168
		8:50	166, 167, 169, 180
8:20	92, 123, 154n2, 160	8:52	123, 125n38
		8:54	49n31, 123, 133, 166, 167, 168, 169, 179n13, 180
8:21	90, 92, 124, 125, 127, 129, 130n51, 154n2, 165, 181, 186, 187, 219, 229, 239		
		8:55	56n59, 123, 129, 133
		8:57	125n38
8:21–30	116n6	8:59	122, 123
8:22	90, 92, 124, 125n38, 127, 129, 158, 219, 229		
		9	92, 138
		9:3	203
8:23	130, 130n51	9:4	21n75
8:24	125	9:7	21n74
8:26	21n75	9:11	53
8:27	123, 154n2	9:12	21n75, 92
8:28	21, 92, 123, 124, 133, 160, 218n73, 240n32	9:17	53
		9:20–23	53
		9:21–22a	52
8:29	12n49, 21n75, 123, 130n51, 133	9:22	44, 47, 51, 52, 55n54, 138, 144, 153, 228
8:31	21, 125n38		
8:31–59	116n6	9:22b	52
8:34	125	9:28	52
		9:29	89, 92

John (continued)

Reference	Pages
9:30	89, 92
9:32	203
9:34	44, 47, 51, 52, 53, 55n54, 138, 144, 228
9:35	53, 138
9:35–37	53, 138
9:35–38	203
9:38	138
9:38a	53
9:40–41	138
9:41	231
9:44	21n75
9:45	21n75
9:49	21n75
10	91n2, 92, 122n35, 139, 145, 148n43, 149, 151, 151n54, 152, 215, 217
10:1	138n4, 217
10:1–16	139n7
10:1–18	140n8, 217
10:1–21	139
10:1–39	223
10:1–42	3, 90, 91, 136, 137, 138, 139, 139n7, 140, 143, 144, 145, 146n26, 154n2, 181n15, 214, 230
10:2	150, 217
10:3	137, 139, 140, 142, 143, 144, 145, 146, 150, 217, 230
10:4	6, 7, 9, 18, 92, 137, 138, 139, 140, 142, 143, 144, 145, 146, 146n26, 147n32, 150, 193, 194, 217, 230, 233, 237
10:5	6, 18, 92, 142
10:7	139, 154n2, 217
10:7–10	147n38
10:7–15	147
10:7–18	147n38
10:8	217
10:9	139, 217
10:10	139, 147, 150, 205, 217
10:10–11	148
10:11	92, 137, 138, 139, 145, 146, 147, 147n37, 150, 154n2, 193, 194, 217, 230, 231, 238, 239
10:11–13	147n38
10:12	137, 140, 140n8, 148n43, 148, 151, 217
10:13	217
10:14	137, 139, 140, 142, 143, 147, 152n52, 193, 217, 230, 231, 233, 238
10:14–15	139
10:14–16	147n38
10:15	21, 56n59, 92, 133, 137, 138, 139, 142, 143, 145, 146, 147, 147n37, 148, 150, 154n2, 193, 194, 217, 218n73, 230, 238, 239
10:16	109, 150, 159n11, 217, 218, 237
10:17	92, 137, 147, 150, 209n35, 217, 239
10:17–18	133, 147n38
10:18	12n49, 49n31, 137, 150, 151, 163, 217, 230, 233, 237
10:22	139n7
10:22–42	139
10:25	49n31, 137, 150, 151
10:26	137, 140, 217
10:26–27	139n7
10:26–30	217

10:27	6, 7, 9, 18, 92, 137, 139, 140, 142, 144, 145, 148, 193, 217, 230, 233	11:51	156, 157, 158, 182, 230n2, 235n13
		11:52	159n11
10:28	137, 139, 145, 146, 148, 148n42, 148n43, 149n44, 150, 151, 192, 193, 194, 217, 230	11:53	46, 48, 48n29, 55n53, 92, 156, 157, 158, 158n7, 182, 230n2, 235n13
10:28–29	145, 149n47, 239	11:55	156, 157, 182, 230n2, 235n13
10:29	49n31, 133, 137, 139, 140, 145, 146, 148n42, 148n43, 149n44, 150, 151, 192, 193, 194, 217, 230, 233, 234	11:57	50n38, 92
		12	91n2, 92, 106, 122n35
		12:1	92, 156, 157, 182, 230n2, 235n13
10:30	137, 139, 151, 151n49	12:2	161, 237n20
		12:7	156, 157, 159, 182, 230n2, 235n13
10:31	139		
10:32	137, 150, 151		
10:34	4n6	12:10	46, 55n53, 156, 157, 158, 158n7, 182, 230n2, 235n13
10:36	21n74, 137, 151		
10:37	49n31, 133, 137, 139, 150, 151, 175		
10:38	133, 137, 142, 144, 151	12:11	43
		12:12–20	108
10:39	50n38, 139	12:13–15	159
10:40	92	12:16	179n13
		12:20	157, 159
11	91n2, 92	12:20–22	107, 109, 229, 239
11:1–44	43	12:20–26	90
11:3	21n74, 209n35	12:20–36	91, 146n26, 154, 154n2, 155, 181
11:5	209n35		
11:11	147n32	12:21	106
11:30	92	12:21a	108
11:31	18, 92	12:22	106, 108
11:32	92	12:23	156, 157, 159, 160, 179n13, 182, 230, 230n2, 235n13
11:34	92		
11:42	21n74		
11:50	156, 157, 158, 182, 230n2, 235n13	12:23–24	92, 148n39
		12:23–33	159
11:50–51	92	12:24	156, 157, 158, 160, 182, 230n2, 235n13
11:50–53	147n37		
		12:24–26	154

John (continued)

12:25	55n52, 76n58, 158	13–20	154
12:26	3, 6, 7, 8, 9, 18, 89, 91, 92, 103, 154, 154n2, 155, 156, 157, 158, 159, 160, 161, 162, 163, 164, 165, 166, 168, 169, 170, 181, 182n18, 193n51, 214, 219, 222, 230, 235, 237, 237n20, 237n21, 238	13:1	92, 140, 140n8, 156, 157, 159, 160, 182, 182n21, 212, 214, 230n2, 231, 235, 235n13
		13:2	179
		13:3	90, 149n44, 182n21
		13:6–9	173n4
		13:14–15	237n22
		13:15	20, 21, 213n53, 218n73, 228, 237n22
12:27	92, 133, 154, 156, 157, 159, 160, 182, 230n2, 235n13	13:16	21n75, 55
		13:18	56, 179
		13:20	21n75
		13:21	173, 176, 177, 178, 179, 183n22, 184, 185, 190, 191, 194, 239
12:27–28	159		
12:28	179n13		
12:31	159	13:21–22	183n22
12:32	148, 150, 156, 157, 159, 160, 182, 230n2, 235n13, 239	13:21–38	91n3, 175n6, 183, 184
		13:21—14:3	3, 91, 110, 172, 173, 175, 176, 177, 178, 180, 188, 189, 193, 194, 195, 202, 214
12:32–33	161		
12:32–34	92, 240n32		
12:33	156, 157, 158, 160, 161, 182, 220, 230n2, 235n13, 238		
		13:22	183n22
		13:26	176, 177, 178
		13:26–30	178
12:34	156, 157, 160, 161, 182, 230n2, 235n13	13:27	176, 177, 178, 179, 183n22, 190, 191, 194, 239
12:35	92, 126, 131, 181, 219, 229, 235	13:27–28	183n22
		13:28	183n22
12:37–50	154	13:30	173, 176, 177, 178, 179, 190, 191, 194, 239
12:42	47, 52, 138		
12:43	167, 169		
12:46	119	13:30–31	179
12:49	12n49, 132, 163, 230	13:31	92, 173, 176, 177, 179, 179n13
12:50	21, 163	13:31–32	179, 179n14, 238
		13:31–38	187
13	91n2, 92, 106, 122n35, 209	13:31—14:3	146n26, 182, 183, 235, 237n22
13–17	12, 53n46, 175		

13:32	166, 168, 169, 176, 177, 179, 179n13		202, 207, 210, 230, 231
13:33	90, 92, 176, 177, 180, 182, 182n19, 183, 185, 186, 187, 188, 190, 191, 196, 219, 237n22, 239, 240	14	92, 106
		14–20	188, 195, 230
		14:1	165, 176, 177, 178, 180, 188, 189, 190, 191, 192, 195, 231
13:33–38	176n6	14:1–3	91n3, 175n6, 182, 188, 189
13:33—14:3	181		
13:34	21, 207, 218, 218n73, 237n22	14:1–4	172n1, 176n6, 186n26
13:34–35	237n22	14:1–7	165
13:35	218	14:1–24	110
13:36ff	8	14:2	17, 49n31, 147n32, 176, 177, 180, 182, 235
13:36	6, 9, 18, 20, 90, 92, 172n1, 173, 174, 176, 177, 180, 182, 182n19, 183, 184, 185, 186, 186n26, 188, 190, 191, 219, 230, 237n22	14:2–3	238
		14:3	8, 89, 92, 113, 133, 147n32, 164, 165, 169, 176, 177, 180, 182, 189, 190, 191, 193, 193n53, 194, 195, 231, 235
13:36–37	183, 188, 239		
13:36–38	172, 172n1, 173, 173n4, 174, 175, 176n6, 187, 194, 230, 230n3, 239, 240	14:3–5	103
		14:4	90, 92, 165, 182n19
		14:5	90, 92, 182, 182n19
13:36—14:3	90, 231	14:6	112, 165, 182, 236
13:36—14:4	6	14:7	49n31, 109, 133
13:37	6, 9, 18, 20, 92, 147, 147n37, 173, 174, 176, 177, 180, 183, 184, 185, 190, 194, 196, 210, 211, 214, 219, 230, 237n22	14:7–10	107, 229
		14:8	106, 109, 236, 240
		14:8–10	109
		14:8–11	239
		14:9f	112n53
		14:9	106, 109, 114, 133, 143, 240
		14:10	4n4, 133, 144
13:37–38	92	14:10–11	152
13:38	58, 147n37, 173, 174, 175, 176, 177, 178, 184, 185, 186, 190, 191, 193, 194,	14:11	4n4, 144
		14:12	147n32, 182n21, 218n72, 235
		14:13	168, 179n13
		14:16	194, 240
		14:16–18	188

John (continued)

14:17	21, 56n59, 240
14:18	110, 191, 193
14:18–20	15
14:20	110, 133, 143, 144
14:20–21	49n31
14:21	166, 212
14:23	49n31, 133, 166, 212
14:24	21n75, 132
14:26	20, 21, 21n75, 188, 240
14:27	53
14:28	147n32, 151, 182n21, 235
14:31	21, 162, 163, 212, 218n73, 230, 237
14–17	4n6
15	57, 92
15–16	54n47
15:1	49n31, 133
15:1–8	202
15:1–11	54n46
15:5	205
15:8	21, 49n31, 133, 167, 169, 179n13
15:9	21, 213n53, 218n73, 233
15:10	12n49, 21, 49n31, 162, 163, 218n73, 230, 237
15:11	205
15:12	21, 207, 218n73
15:12–17	54n46
15:13	147, 147n37
15:13–14	212
15:15	49n31, 133, 143, 162, 239
15:16	56, 58, 205, 238
15:18	46, 47, 54, 55n52, 56
15:18–20	153
15:18–21	45, 54n47, 159
15:18–25	54n47, 138
15:18—16:3	53n46
15:18—16:4	53, 123n36, 228
15:18—16:4a	44, 50n33, 54n47
15:19	47, 55n52, 56
15:20	46, 48, 54, 55, 56
15:20–21	123
15:21	21n75, 56
15:21–25	54n47
15:22	56
15:22–25	54n47
15:23	55n52, 56
15:23–24	49n31, 133
15:23–25	46
15:24	55n52, 56
15:25	55n52, 57
15:26	21, 21n75, 57, 58, 194, 240
15:26–27	54n47, 188
15:26—16:4a	54n47
15:27	57
16	92
16:1	54n48
16:1–4	53
16:1–4a	54n47
16:2	43n11, 46, 47, 52, 55n53, 92, 138, 153, 158
16:2a	55
16:2b	55
16:2–3	123
16:3	56
16:4	54
16:5	21n75, 90, 92, 132, 182n21
16:5–15	188
16:7	21n75, 58, 147n32
16:8–11	58
16:10	182n21, 235
16:13	20, 21, 110, 194, 240
16:14	179n13
16:15	233
16:17	182n21, 235
16:24	205
16:27	166, 212
16:28	90, 133, 147n32, 182n21, 234, 235

16:32	58, 186, 203n13, 207		165, 168, 169, 192, 192n49, 193, 212, 230, 232, 233, 234, 238, 241
16:33	45n22, 53, 153, 159		
		17:24–26	110, 166
17	4n6, 92, 141, 193	17:25	21n74, 56n59, 132
17:1	92, 168, 169, 179n13, 180	17:26	152n52, 213, 239
17:2	151, 169, 234	18	92
17:3	21n74, 56	18–20	175, 188
17:4	12n49, 162, 163, 168, 169, 179n13, 230, 233, 237	18:1	92
		18:2–3	239
		18:3–5	194
17:5	12n49, 133, 168, 169, 179n13, 180, 233	18:9	141n14, 233
		18:10–11	173n4
		18:14	92, 147n37, 158
17:6	12n49, 141n14, 143, 169, 203, 212, 230, 233, 234, 239	18:15	18, 92, 197
		18:15–18	194
		18:15–27	173n4
		18:16–18	197
17:8	21n74	18:17	58, 202, 210, 231
17:9	141, 141n14, 230, 233, 234	18:18	198n5
		18:20	92
17:10	141, 152n52, 167, 169, 179n13, 230, 233, 234	18:24	21n74
		18:25	202, 210, 231
		18:25–27	58, 194, 197
17:11	21, 148n42, 151, 182n21, 218n73, 235, 239	18:27	180, 202, 207, 210, 231
		18:31	158
17:12	148n42, 151	18:32	92, 158, 220, 238
17:13	182n21, 235	18:36	55n51
17:14	21, 47, 53, 56, 153, 218n73	18:37	140n9
17:15	148n42, 151, 239	19	92
17:16	21, 218n73	19:6	92
17:18	21, 21n74, 104n36, 218n73	19:6–7	55n55
		19:7	92
17:19	147n37	19:9	92
17:20	218n72	19:13–16	55n55
17:20–23	240	19:15–42	92
17:21	21, 132, 144, 152, 218n73, 232	19:18	92
		19:20	92
17:21–23	152n52	19:30	163
17:22	21, 218n73	19:36	157
17:23	21, 21n74, 144, 212, 218n73	19:38	45n22
		19:41	92
17:24	89, 92, 103, 113, 133, 141n14, 164,	20	15, 91n2, 92

John (continued)

20–21	12	21:5–6	217
20:1–10	173n4	21:6	199, 200, 201, 202, 205, 205n20, 237
20:2	92, 209n35	21:7	198n5, 199, 200, 202, 209, 209n35, 210
20:6	18, 92		
20:12	92		
20:13	92	21:8	199, 200, 201, 205, 205n20
20:15	92		
20:16	83n79	21:9	198n5, 199, 200, 201, 206, 208
20:17	49n31, 90, 133, 147n32, 182n21, 234, 235	21:9–13	217
		21:9–14	198
20:19	15, 45n22, 58, 92, 204	21:11	173n4, 198n5, 199, 200, 202, 203n15, 205, 208, 237
20:21	21, 21n74, 21n75, 104n36, 132, 218n73		
		21:11a	201, 205, 205n20
20:21–23	218n72	21:11b	201, 205, 205n20
20:22	20, 21	21:12	198, 199, 200, 201, 203, 206, 209
20:26			
20:27	58	21:12–13	208
20:30–31	121	21:13	199, 200, 201, 202, 206, 206n24, 207, 209
21	92, 106, 122n35, 175, 196n1, 209, 217	21:14	199, 200, 203, 203n15, 208
21:1	199, 200, 203, 203n15, 206, 208	21:15	86n90, 198, 199, 200, 201, 208n32, 209n33, 209n34, 215, 216
21:1–14	58, 198, 198n5, 198n6, 198n7, 201, 203, 206, 210, 213, 215, 217, 222, 223, 231, 238	21:15–17	198, 201, 203, 208, 208n32, 211, 211n47, 212, 213, 214, 215, 216n60, 217, 231, 237, 238
21:1–17	239	21:15–18	214
21:1–19	3, 91, 110, 146n26, 193n51, 196, 197, 198, 198n5, 199, 200, 202, 222, 223, 239	21:15–19	90, 153, 173n4, 197, 198, 198n5, 198n6, 198n7, 202, 214, 215, 217, 218, 218n72, 222, 223, 231, 237
21:3	198n5, 199, 200, 201, 203n13, 204, 205n20, 231	21:15–22	173n4
21:4	199, 200, 201, 203, 217	21:16	199, 200, 208n32, 209n33, 209n34, 215, 217
21:4–8	208	21:17	143, 193, 199, 200, 208n32,
21:5	199, 200, 201, 204, 205n20		

SCRIPTURE INDEX

		209n33, 209n34, 210, 215, 216, 217	22:4	83
21:18f	8	23:10	148n43
21:18	92, 197, 199, 200, 201, 214, 219, 220, 221, 222, 223, 238	23:12–14	48n29
		24:14	83
		24:22	83
		26:18	179n12
21:18–19	55n53, 219, 222, 231, 238, 239		
21:19	6, 7, 8, 9, 13, 18, 92, 168, 169, 179n13, 188, 194, 196, 197, 198n5, 199, 200, 201, 207, 208, 213, 215, 219, 220, 221, 222, 223, 231		

Romans

1:4	
1:6	140
3:9	187
3:10–12	187
3:11	109n49, 239
3:23	187
5:12	125
5:19	163, 230
5:21	125
6:16	125
6:23	125
7:14	26
8:2	125
8:2–4	80
8:17	169
8:21–27	32
11:32	187
15:8	162
15:27	26

21:19–23	19n69
21:20	6, 18, 92, 203
21:22	6, 7, 9, 13, 18, 92, 198n5

Acts

1:5	189n43
1:8	189n43
1:24	211n46
2:23	55n53
3:15	55n53
7:57—8:3	55n55
8:1–2	55n55
8:32	99n16
9:2	83
9:4	56n56
9:5	56n56
12:2	55n53
12:8	84n82
12:9	84n82
13:43	84n82
13:47	119
16:17	83
18:25–26	83
19:9	83
19:23	84
20:28	215, 231
20:30	186
21:31	48n29
21:36	84n82

1 Corinthians

1:18–25	83
1:24	165
2:10f	29
2:13	26
2:14–15	26
2:15	26
6:17	29
6:19	77
9:11	26
10:4	69, 84n82
12:1	26
15:54–57	222
15:56	125

2 Corinthians

3:6	162
5:14	214
11:2	85n87
11:13	186

Galatians

2:20	212
4:19	32n58
5:15–26	32
5:19	32
5:22	32
6:3	32

Ephesians

1:3	26
1:4	141n14, 233
1:4–5	212
1:5	141n14
1:20	81
1:20–22	180
2:1	187
2:4	212
2:5	81
2:6	81
2:13	160n12
3:7	162
3:18–19	213
4:11	215, 231
5:2	212
5:8	119
5:19	26

Philippians

2:6–11	180
2:7–8	163, 230
2:15	119

Colossians

1:9	26
1:12	119
1:13	119, 204n16
2:13	187
3:4	204n16

1 Thessalonians

2:15	48n29, 55n53

1 Timothy

1:19–20	186
4:6	69n36, 162
5:10	69n36
5:24	69n36
6:16	133

2 Timothy

2:19	233
3:10	69n36

Hebrews

2:7	166n34
2:9	166n34
2:14–15	222
5:8	163, 230
6:4–6	186

1 Peter

1:18–20	233
1:19	86n90, 99n16
1:20	233
2:9	119
5:1ff	215
5:1–4	231
5:6	211

2 Peter

1:4	4n6
1:16	69n36
2:2	69n36
2:15	69n36
2:21	69n36

1 John

1:1–3	207
1:5	119, 130n51
1:5–7	125
2:2	160n12, 188
2:8–9	125
2:11	125
2:10	54n48
2:19	186
3:1	212
3:2	169, 204n16
3:5	188, 204n16
3:8	204n16
3:16	147, 212
4:8	233
4:9	212
4:12	133
4:16	233
5:20	239

Jude

23	148n43

Revelation

1:5	188, 212
2:10	86
2:13	86
3:29	74n51
5:6	86
5:8	86
5:12	86
5:13	86
6:8	84n82
6:16	86
7:14	86
7:17	86n98, 97
12:11	86
13:1–18	84
13:2–4	86
13:3	84, 86
13:4	84, 86
13:8	84, 86
13:11–18	85n87
13:12	84
13:15	86
13:16–17	84
14:1	84, 86
14:1–5	84, 85m92, 86, 87, 97, 228n1
14:2	84
14:3	84
14:3b	85
14:4	84, 84n82, 85, 86
14:4a	85
14:4b	84, 85
14:4c	84, 85
14:4d	84
14:5	84, 85
14:6–7	84
14:8	84n82
14:9	84, 84n82
14:10	86
14:11	84
14:13	84n82
15:3	86
17:10	86
17:14	86, 97
18:24	86
19:14	84n82
19:16	86
20:4	86
21:4	222
22:1	86
22:3	86

www.ingramcontent.com/pod-product-compliance
Lightning Source LLC
Chambersburg PA
CBHW071236230426
43668CB00011B/1462